# Recovering Political Philosophy

Postmodernism's challenge to the possibility of a rational foundation for and guidance of our political lives has provoked a searching re-examination of the works of past political philosophers. The re-examination seeks to recover the ancient or classical grounding for civic reason and to clarify the strengths and weaknesses of modern philosophic rationalism. This series responds to this ferment by making available outstanding new scholarship in the history of political philosophy, scholarship that is inspired by the rediscovery of the diverse rhetorical strategies employed by political philosophers. The series features interpretive studies attentive to historical context and language, and to the ways in which censorship and didactic concern impelled prudent thinkers, in widely diverse cultural conditions, to employ manifold strategies of writing strategies that allowed them to aim at different audiences with various degrees of openness to unconventional thinking. Recovering Political Philosophy emphasizes the close reading of ancient, medieval, early modern and late modern works that illuminate the human condition by attempting to answer its deepest, enduring questions, and that have (in the modern periods) laid the foundations for contemporary political, social, and economic life. The editors encourage manuscripts from both established and emerging scholars who focus on the careful study of texts, either through analysis of a single work or through thematic study of a problem or question in a number of works.

More information about this series at
http://www.springer.com/series/14517

Nelson Lund

# Rousseau's Rejuvenation of Political Philosophy

## A New Introduction

palgrave
macmillan

Nelson Lund
Antonin Scalia Law School
George Mason University
Arlington, Virginia, USA

Recovering Political Philosophy
ISBN 978-3-319-82342-3 ISBN 978-3-319-41390-7 (eBook)
DOI 10.1007/978-3-319-41390-7



Printed on acid-free paper

This Palgrave Macmillan imprint is published by Springer Nature
The registered company is Springer International Publishing AG Switzerland

*For Mara and Jack, my rejuvenators*

# Texts and Translations

I have relied on the Pléiade edition of Rousseau's works (cited as *O.C.*) and on R.A. Leigh's edition of his correspondence (cited as *Corr. Comp.*). The translations are my own, though I have consulted and borrowed freely from a variety of English editions.

English translations of Rousseau's works, keyed to the Pléiade pagination, can be found in Masters and Kelly's *The Collected Writings of Rousseau*, and in Victor Gourevitch's editions of Rousseau's political writings. For the convenience of the reader, I have included parallel citations to Allan Bloom's popular English translations of the *Letter to d'Alembert* and the *Emile*.

For Greek sources, I have relied on the Oxford Classical Texts. The translations are my own, but I have consulted and borrowed freely from several English editions, especially Thomas L. Pangle's translation of the *Laws*.

# Acknowledgments

Mara Lund and Jack Lund have supported me in ways that are far too diverse, profound, and immeasurable to recount. My gratitude to them could never measure up to what they have given me.

Farther back in time, three academic advisors indulgently reviewed my first attempts to write something about Rousseau: the late Thomas McDonald, the late Richard Kennington, and Harvey C. Mansfield. Decades later, Leon Kass encouraged me to renew my efforts, and I might not have done so without his influence. For helpful comments on drafts of one or more chapters, I owe special thanks to Daniel Doneson, Robert A. Goldberg, David Leibowitz, Brenda Leong, Craig S. Lerner, Jack Lund, John O. McGinnis, and an anonymous reviewer. With incomparable generosity, Mara Lund and Stephen G. Gilles read multiple drafts of every chapter, saved me from an infinity of errors, and set standards that I could only hope to satisfy.

This project was facilitated by the liberality of my former Dean, Daniel D. Polsby, who judged that it was an appropriate way for a law professor to spend part of his time. Melanie Knapp was enthusiastically relentless in providing all the research assistance I could have hoped for, and Jane Barton provided excellent administrative assistance. Timothy W. Burns has been unfailingly generous and helpful throughout the publication process.

The book incorporates revised versions of four previously published essays: "Philosophic Anthropology in Rousseau and Elizabeth Marshall Thomas," in *Apples of Gold in Pictures of Silver: Honoring the Work of Leon R. Kass*, ed. Yuval Levin, Thomas W. Merrill, and Adam Schulman (Lanham, MD: Lexington Books, 2010); "Greatness of Soul and the

Souls of Women: Plato's *Laws* as an Introduction to Rousseau's *Letter to D'Alembert*," *American Dialectic* 2, no. 3 (2012): 216–49; "Greatness of Soul and the Souls of Women: Rousseau's Use of Plato's *Laws* in the *Letter to d'Alembert*," *American Dialectic* 3, no. 1 (2013): 1–43 (2013); "Rousseau and Direct Democracy (with a Note on the Supreme Court's *Term Limits* Decision)," Copyright 2004 *The Journal of Contemporary Legal Issues*. Reprinted with the permission of The Journal of Contemporary Legal Issues.

# Contents


| | | |
|---|---|---|
| 1 | **Introduction** | 1 |
| 2 | **Philosophic Anthropology in the *Discourse on Inequality*** | 9 |
| | *The State of Nature* | 10 |
| | *"The Happiest Epoch, and the Most Durable"* | 13 |
| | *Elizabeth Marshall Thomas and the Bushmen* | 16 |
| | *Equality and Freedom Among the Bushmen* | 19 |
| | *Social Discipline Among the Bushmen* | 22 |
| | *Jealousy and Lions* | 28 |
| | *Pre-Human Happiness* | 31 |
| | *Proto-Politics* | 33 |
| | *Conclusion* | 37 |
| 3 | **The Evolution of Humanity in Language: *Discourse on Inequality* and *Essay on the Origin of Languages*** | 39 |
| | *Greek Philosophers and the Problem of Language* | 39 |
| | *Man Alone among the Animals Has Speech* | 46 |
| | *Modern Science and Natural Sociality* | 52 |
| | *The Structure of the* Essay on the Origin of Languages | 60 |
| | *Primitive Language and Plato's* Cratylus | 63 |
| | *The Evolution of Languages* | 73 |
| | *Language, Music, and Modern Science* | 79 |
| | *Conclusion* | 88 |

4 **Greatness of Soul and the Souls of Women: Rousseau's Use of Plato's *Laws* in the *Letter to d'Alembert*** 91
*Economic Equality and the Education of Women in the* Laws 92
*Economics and Women* 99
*The Education of Women* 104
*Alternatives to the Equality of Women* 114
*Preserving Women from Miseducation: The* Letter to d'Alembert 115
*Happy Families* 125
*Unhappy Lovers* 128
*Men Unmanned* 138
*Republican Entertainments* 140
*Conclusion* 143

5 **Nature and Marriage: *Emile or On Education*** 149
*Early Education in* Some Thoughts Concerning Education 152
*Rousseau's Alternative to Locke's Early Education* 155
*Plato's* Republic *and the Transition to Adulthood* 163
*Defoe's* Robinson Crusoe 170
*Rousseau and the Savoyard Vicar* 172
*Emile and Religion* 177
*Religion and Happiness* 183
Letter to Beaumont 184
Moral Letters 186
Letter to Franquières 189
*Love, Politics, and Fénelon's* Telemachus 192
*Eros, Adversity, and Plato's* Symposium 199
*Adversity Without Eros:* The Solitaries 207
*A Quasi-Epicurean Approach to Happiness* 210

6 **Political Legitimacy, Direct Democracy, and American Politics** 213
*Political Legitimacy* 215
*Natural Rights* 216
*Hobbes* 218
*Locke* 223
*Rousseau on Direct Democracy and Political Legitimacy* 225
Discourse on Inequality 225

Social Contract 231
*Rousseau's Pessimism about Liberalism* 237
*Rousseau's Alternative to Liberalism* 242
Considerations on the Government of Poland 253
*Rousseau and the Supreme Court's* Term Limits *Decision* 258
*Conclusion* 264

**7 Conclusion** 267

**Bibliography** 271

**Index** 279

# Abbreviations

| | |
|---|---|
| *d'Alembert* | *Letter to M. d'Alembert on the Theater* |
| *Dialogues* | *Rousseau Judge of Jean-Jacques: Dialogues* |
| *Economy* | *Discourse on Political Economy* |
| *Emile* | *Emile or On Education* |
| *Essay* | *Essay on the Origin of Languages, in which something is said about melody and about musical imitation* |
| *Inequality* | *Discourse on the Origin and the Foundations of Inequality among Men* |
| *Mountain* | *Letters Written from the Mountain* |
| *N.H.* | *Julie, or The New Heloise* |
| *Poland* | *Considerations on the Government of Poland and its Projected Reformation* |
| *Reveries* | *The Reveries of the Solitary Walker* |
| *S.C.* | *On the Social Contract or, Principles of Political Right* |
| *Solitaries* | *Emile and Sophie, or The Solitaries* |

CHAPTER 1

# Introduction

*In Plato's* Banquet, *Alcibiades—that outspoken son of outspoken Athens—compares Socrates and his speeches to certain sculptures which are very ugly from the outside, but within have the most beautiful images of things divine. The works of the great writers of the past are very beautiful even from without. And yet their visible beauty is sheer ugliness, compared with the beauty of those hidden treasures which disclose themselves only after very long, never easy, but always pleasant work. This always difficult but always pleasant work is, I believe, what the philosophers had in mind when they recommended education. Education, they felt, is the only answer to the always pressing question, to the political question par excellence, of how to reconcile order which is not oppression with freedom which is not license.*

*Leo Strauss*, Persecution and the Art of Writing

*There is no occasion ... to oppose the ancients and the moderns to one another, or to be squeamish on either side. He that wisely conducts his mind in the pursuit of knowledge will gather what lights, and get what helps he can, from either of them, from whom they are best to be had, without adoring the errors or rejecting the truths which he may find mingled in them.*

*John Locke*, Of the Conduct of the Understanding



N. Lund, *Rousseau's Rejuvenation of Political Philosophy*,
DOI 10.1007/978-3-319-41390-7_1

Rousseau has been among the most influential modern philosophers, and among the most misunderstood. In the United States, his political thought was poorly received, in part because Edmund Burke blamed him for much of what was worst in the French Revolution. Today, political conservatives continue to shun him, seeing his work as a contributor to various pernicious alternatives to the healthy teachings of John Locke and the American founders. Although Rousseau has admirers, especially perhaps among those repulsed by our commercial society, his writings are seldom taken seriously as a source of enduring political wisdom. Alexis de Tocqueville, however, who is widely regarded as one of the greatest analysts of American institutions, reported that Rousseau was one of three men with whom he lived a little every day.[1]

This book seeks to reintroduce Rousseau to an American audience. His understanding of politics rests on deep and frequently prescient reflections on the nature of the human soul and the relationship between our animal origins and the achievements of civilization. The implications that Rousseau drew from those reflections continue to deserve serious attention today. With his assistance, we can deepen our own understanding of many political issues that remain alive, including feminism and the family, the role of religion in a secular society, and the proper conduct of constitutional government.

This book sprang from my effort to read Rousseau as Rousseau read Plato, an approach that does not involve novelty for novelty's sake. Two conclusions, frequently found in the existing literature, leap out from the surface of Rousseau's writings. First, he had a special attraction to Plato. Second, he sought to deploy ancient political thought against what we call the Enlightenment. The precise way in which Rousseau drew on Plato has proved to be a more difficult question, and one that has provoked significant controversy.

Leo Strauss, one of the most influential political philosophers of our own time, maintains that Rousseau did not seek to recover political philosophy as Plato practiced it: "[Rousseau's] return to antiquity was, at the same time, an advance of modernity. While appealing from Hobbes, Locke, or the Encyclopedists to Plato, Aristotle, or Plutarch, he jettisoned important elements of classical thought which his modern predecessors had still preserved" (*Natural Right and History*, 252). Similarly, Allan

[1] Tocqueville to Louis de Kergorlay (12 Nov. 1836), *Œuvres, Papiers et Correspondances*, 13:418. The others were Pascal and Montesquieu.

Bloom contends that Rousseau's greatest work, the *Emile*, is meant "to rival or supersede" Plato's *Republic* by seriously undertaking a project outlined only ironically in the *Republic* (translator's Introduction to *Emile or On Education*, 3–4).

It is true that Rousseau can *appear*, especially in retrospect, to have broken with both classical and Enlightenment thought, thus ushering in "[t]he first crisis of modernity" (Strauss, *Natural Right and History*, 252). It is also true that the *Emile* is meant to rival the *Republic* in the scope of its ambition. But in claiming that Rousseau's own political philosophy broke radically with Plato's, or that he sought to "supersede" Plato, these commentators lead the reader astray. At the very least, Rousseau was far more indebted and sympathetic to Plato than they acknowledge. If there are fundamental substantive disagreements between Rousseau and Plato, they are much more difficult to identify than Strauss and Bloom would have us believe.

At the opposite pole, David Lay Williams maintains in *Rousseau's Platonic Enlightenment* that Rousseau was a Platonist. In order to make this case, Williams begins with a very brief summary of Plato's putative positions on several difficult issues, ranging from metaphysics to epistemology to politics.[2] He then finds numerous statements in Rousseau that appear to agree with the doctrines that he attributes to Plato. In my view, this approach is seriously misguided because it assumes away abundant evidence of irony and indirection in both Plato and Rousseau. Just to take two of the most obvious examples, Plato never purports to present his own views in any of the dialogues, and Rousseau frequently puts important arguments in the mouths of fictional characters. Williams makes dogmatists of them both, which distorts their philosophy and their way of writing.

[2] Williams' understanding of Plato and Platonism is presented in a few brief pages, which can be summarized as follows. Plato believed in metaphysical dualism, that is, a sharp distinction between body or material, on the one hand, and the immortal soul and immaterial ideas perceptible only through the intellect, on the other. Immaterial substances are beyond artifice and contingency. Although indeterminate, they are knowable under certain circumstances. The immaterial ideas should guide us in the conduct of our lives, and they lead to specific recommendations about political institutions and laws. *Rousseau's Platonic Enlightenment*, xix–xxiv. Although Williams sometimes distinguishes Plato from Platonists, for example, ibid., xxiii (faith in God), he asserts that they and Rousseau agreed about one central point: "*the commitment to transcendent ideas as the ultimate authority for moral and political arguments*" (ibid., xxvii) (italics in original).

In the following chapters, I offer readings of Rousseau's texts that refrain from presupposing the conclusions reached either by Strauss and Bloom or by Williams. Rousseau had little formal education, but he became impressively erudite through a self-guided program of study. In the course of this self-education he invented his own method of reading, which he describes in the *Confessions.* First, "I made myself a law: to adopt and follow all [the author's] ideas without dragging in my own or those of another, and without ever disputing with him" (bk. 6, *O.C.*, 1:237). After several years of following this discipline with many writers, Rousseau acquired a stock of ideas that he only then began to scrutinize by "reviewing and comparing what I had read, by weighing each thing on the balance of reason, and sometimes by judging my masters" (ibid., 237–38). This two-step process is not a recipe or formula, and it is far easier to describe than to follow. I have no doubt that this is how Rousseau read Plato, and I am confident that he hoped his own works would be treated in the same spirit.

Plato's decision to refrain from speaking in his own voice served his two principal goals as a writer. First, he seeks to provoke potential philosophers to engage in philosophy. Because they are dominated by an ironic and frequently paradoxical Socrates, the dialogues discourage attentive readers from hastily attributing substantive conclusions to Plato that the reader can then hastily accept or reject. Philosophy not only requires that one think for oneself, but it means thinking completely for oneself. Through their form as much as through their content, the dialogues constantly remind the reader that he can never be altogether certain what Plato or his Socrates finally concluded, and that a serious student should care more about finding the truth than about what anyone else believes.

Second, Plato's total silence about his own views contributed to the political goal of cautioning philosophers against threatening the existing political order, and thereby inviting the persecution of philosophy. When Socrates went beyond the study of nature by subjecting ethics and politics to philosophic analysis, philosophy's uncompromising pursuit of the truth became a more vivid threat to the shared opinions on which political stability depends. By presenting a certain kind of fictional Socrates as the model philosopher, Plato's dialogues encourage the friends of political stability, or of established political opinions, to see the suppression of philosophy as a mistake. Plato's Socrates stayed resolutely out of politics, and was condemned to death by excited people who could not understand what they were doing or why they could not accomplish what they thought they were doing. Whatever Plato's political opinions may have been, the manner in which the dialogues present philosophy has made it virtually impossible for anyone to enlist Plato as an advocate for a destructive political agenda.

Rousseau's goals as a writer are in certain fundamental respects the same as Plato's. Although he usually speaks in his own name, Rousseau's presentation of his thought is deliberately paradoxical, frequently outlandish on its face, and packed with subtleties that invite careful thought. In these respects, the writings of Rousseau resemble the speech of Plato's Socrates. Like Plato, Rousseau seeks to promote philosophy by discouraging serious readers from substituting the discovery of the author's doctrines for the uncompromising pursuit of the truth.

The political situation in which Rousseau found himself, however, was far different from Plato's. Modern writers had gone far toward the goal of making philosophy and philosophers politically respectable and politically powerful. In Rousseau's view, this development was a threat to healthy political life. Natural philosophy had made genuine progress, but it now threatened human welfare in a way that pre-Socratic philosophy had never done. The problem arose from a perversion of political philosophy. The Enlightenment diminished and popularized philosophy by promoting dogmatic atheism, materialism, and consumerism. These doctrines, along with an abundance of material benefits made possible by the progress in natural philosophy, corrupt men's souls by fostering a narrow egoism and the frantic pursuit of luxuries that cannot bring happiness. The Enlightenment pointed the way to the soft despotism that Tocqueville later diagnosed, and ultimately to the "last men" described by Nietzsche.

Rousseau sought to rejuvenate political philosophy by pursuing the same goals at which Plato aimed. In the new circumstances created by the Enlightenment, this required a public stance or philosophic rhetoric that was very different from Plato's. At a time when natural philosophy was politically suspect, Plato went out of his way to avoid endorsing studies that were thought to promote atheism. At a time when philosophic materialism was becoming popular and respectable, Rousseau presented himself as a skeptic about the value of philosophy and a defender of humanity against its corrupting influence. For all their apparent differences, Plato and Rousseau both treat political philosophy as a means of protecting political life and the life of philosophy from threats that each poses to the other.

Because this book is an introduction to Rousseau's thought, not a synopsis, it does not address all of his major works or his claim that they reflect a unified and coherent system. His later autobiographical writings in particular look to me like the final steps in an educational journey that he invites us to take with him. My own book will at most suggest reasons to prepare for taking those steps. Even with respect to the works I discuss, I have chosen to focus on a few of their themes, chosen as entryways to further reflection.

Because this book is not meant to address Rousseau's place in the history of political philosophy, I will say almost nothing about the major thinkers who were influenced by him. In my view, a great deal of misunderstanding arises from the practice of looking at Rousseau through handy lenses provided by his many influential successors.

Finally, the book is designed to be useful both to experts in the field and to non-specialists. It presents a coherent and unified exposition, and the chapters are best read in the order I have presented them. I have, however, made each chapter independently intelligible, and readers who are particularly interested in certain topics can begin with the relevant chapters. In order to avoid unhelpful distractions, I have referred very sparingly to the immense secondary literature on Rousseau. Interpretations that differ from mine, and from one another, will be easy for anyone to find.

---

Chapters 2 and 3 deal with Rousseau's account of the evolution of humanity, which is central to his thinking about politics. Since his time, scientists have made fascinating new discoveries—about primitive peoples, physical evolution, and the behavior of our fellow primates—that support the principal elements of his account. This is important for at least two reasons. First, if Rousseau were refuted by newly discovered evidence, it would raise serious questions about the validity of the implications that he drew from his scientific inquiries, including the political analysis that rests on those implications. Second, Rousseau's treatment of human origins illustrates his approach to science or natural philosophy itself, an endeavor to which he gave considerable attention. His prescience suggests that he had a deeper understanding of the possibilities and limitations of modern science than many of us have today.

Chapters 4 and 5 consider some of Rousseau's efforts to bring his philosophic insight to bear on problems presented in the modern world. These include the place of women in society, the viability of traditional family structures, and the role of religion and religious freedom in nations that are becoming ever more secular. In considering these issues, I give special attention to examples that illustrate how Rousseau used what he found in Plato. Seeing how he used Plato can help us see how we, in turn, might use Rousseau.

Chapter 6 complements the treatment of natural science in Chapters 2 and 3. The American Constitution is the most successful application of the Enlightenment's new *political* science, and Rousseau was deeply skeptical about the promises made by that science. Nevertheless, when read in the manner suggested by the previous chapters of this book, the *Social Contract* and *Considerations on the Government of Poland* offer considerable support for important features of America's constitutional arrangements. At the same time, Rousseau's analysis points to the merits of certain dissident or subdominant strains in American political thought. That in turn suggests that American students of politics should reconsider the widely held view that Rousseau is a useless or dangerous guide for us. Like Plato, Rousseau illuminates the obstacles facing those who aspire to replace political philosophy with political science.

CHAPTER 2

# Philosophic Anthropology in the *Discourse on Inequality*

The nature of the soul is a matter of such manifest philosophic interest that Aristotle's *De Anima* opens with a very brief explanation of its importance. Aristotle then offers a pointed warning: "In every way, however, reaching any assured conviction about the soul is one of the most difficult undertakings" (402a10–11). This is followed by a lengthy and intimidating discussion of the methodological difficulties posed by the inquiry (402a11–403b19). I will mention only two. It is not immediately apparent whether the soul is divisible or indivisible; nor is it immediately clear how, if at all, the soul is separate from the body. In the course of the methodological discussion, Aristotle also warns against focusing exclusively on the human soul.

In his own way, Rousseau seeks to begin working through such difficulties in the *Discourse on Inequality*. The epigraph to this book is a quotation in Latin from Aristotle's *Politics*: "What is natural must be examined not in things that are corrupted but in those things that are well ordered according to nature." The quotation, which is taken from a discussion of natural and conventional slavery, is immediately preceded in the text of the *Politics* by the assertion that the soul rules the body by nature in living things generally. The quotation is immediately followed by Aristotle's assertion that one should study the human being whose body and soul are in the best condition (1254a34–1254b2).



N. Lund, *Rousseau's Rejuvenation of Political Philosophy*,
DOI 10.1007/978-3-319-41390-7_2

Rousseau's *Discourse* investigates this linkage or analogy between the rulership of human masters and what we might call self-rulership or the soul-body relationship. His method is to trace the coming into being of man and his political relations from their pre-political and even pre-human origins up to modern times. The practical importance of this undertaking, according to some of his statements, arises from its political implications. For example: "[S]o long as we do not know natural man, we will wish in vain to determine the Law which he has received or that which best fits his constitution" (*Inequality*, *O.C.*, 3:125). Those implications are potentially so radical that the truth or falsity of the underlying analysis becomes a matter of significant political importance.[1] But even apart from politics, there could hardly be many propositions whose truth or falsity matter more than Rousseau's claim that "Society no longer offers to the eyes of the wise man anything but an assemblage of artificial men and factitious passions which are the product of all these new [social] relationships, and have no true foundation in Nature" (ibid., 192).[2]

The presentation of Rousseau's thought in this book and elsewhere is simultaneously daring and cagey.[3] This chapter begins the process of untangling and clarifying his views.

## The State of Nature

As the full title of the *Discourse* suggests, and as the context of the epigraph from Aristotle's *Politics* confirms, Rousseau's focus is on the relation between natural and conventional inequality. Almost at the outset,

[1] See, for example, *Inequality*, *O.C.*, 3:180: "[T]he thing to do would have been to begin by clearing the ground and setting aside all the old materials, as Lycurgus did in Sparta, in order afterwards to erect a good Building."

[2] Observations of great apes that have been raised as pets, or like adopted human children, may give us a glimpse of what Rousseau believed he saw in human society. See, for example, Anne E. Russon, *Orangutans: Wizards of the Rainforest*, 104–12; Jane Goodall, *Through a Window: My Thirty Years with the Chimpanzees of Gombe*, 13.

[3] In the *Confessions*, Rousseau characterizes the *Discourse on Inequality* as the place where he revealed his principles "with the greatest daring, not to say audacity" (bk. 9, *O.C.*, 1:407). In an unfinished draft of a response to criticism of the *Discourse on the Sciences and the Arts*, written before he began work on the *Discourse on Inequality*, Rousseau said that he believed he had discovered great things and set them forth with a "somewhat dangerous frankness," but that he had also often "been at great pains to try to condense into a Sentence, into a line, into one word tossed off as if by chance, the result of a long series of reflections" (*Preface to a Second Letter to Bordes*, *O.C.*, 3:103, 106).

he defines the former as that which "is established by Nature, and which consists in the differences in age, health, strength of Bodies, and qualities of Mind, or of Soul" (ibid., 131). This he distinguishes from moral or political inequality, which depends on the consent of men and consists of different privileges that some enjoy, including even the privilege of making themselves obeyed. Rousseau dismisses the possibility of a correspondence between natural inequalities and disparities of political power or wealth (ibid., 131–32). Later, however, he asserts that "personal merit" or "personal qualities" are the origin of *all* the political and moral forms of inequality (ibid., 189).

The statements are not logically inconsistent, and their relationship is illuminated by Rousseau's account of the state of nature. He emphatically denies that the state of nature should be pictured as a set of circumstances in which people essentially like ourselves once existed without governments. Rather, the state of nature was an articulated period of time during which our ancestors made a gradual transition from life as independent, speechless animals to socialized beings with stable governments and laws. Natural or physical inequalities among individuals would have had little effect when individuals had little to do with one another. "[T]here was neither education nor progress, generations multiplied uselessly; and as everyone always started at the same point, Centuries passed in all the crudeness of the first ages, the species had already grown old, and man remained ever a child" (ibid., 160).[4] This original condition is sometimes described in rather disparaging terms, as in this quotation, and sometimes more appealingly. Its crucial feature, however, is that it must have ended through "the fortuitous intervention of a number of foreign causes" (ibid., 162). By this Rousseau means that changes in the natural environment or migration into new environments led individuals to begin cooperating with one another, perhaps at first in such activities as hunting for food (ibid., 166–67).

Rousseau acknowledges, as anyone must, that such acts of cooperation—and all of the much more elaborate forms and achievements of civilization—are natural in the sense that nature provided our ancestors with the capacity to bring them about. What he denies—and this seems to be

[4] Recently discovered evidence indicates that small human populations can regress toward the "crudeness of the first ages" when they become isolated from contact with their neighbors. See, for example, Joseph Henrich, "Demography and Cultural Evolution: How Adaptive Cultural Processes Can Produce Maladaptive Losses—The Tasmanian Case."

his central contention—is that *any* specific way of life is natural to man in the sense that it corresponds to our natural range of inclinations and powers.

Speaking of the city, Aristotle says: "If one were to look at how the things that concern us (*ta pragmata*) develop from the beginning, one would in this as in other cases investigate them in the finest way ... [E]very city exists by nature, if indeed the first communities really also do" (*Politics*, 1252a24–26, 1252b30–31). Rousseau denies that either cities or the first communities (other than mother-child pairs) exist by nature, at least in the sense that Aristotle is frequently thought to have said they do. Whatever disagreements he may have with Aristotle on this topic, which may be fewer and less significant than is commonly supposed,[5] Rousseau does set out to explain how human society must have "developed from the beginning."

What distinguishes man from all other animals is "the faculty of perfecting oneself; a faculty which, with the aid of circumstances, successively develops all the others, and resides among us as much in the species as in the individual" (*Inequality*, *O.C.*, 3:142). As Rousseau makes clear, however, "perfecting oneself" involves the acquisition of qualities that *conflict* with our underlying natures. We are not like bees or herd animals (cf. *Politics* 1253a7–8), where the individual is necessarily "at the end of a few months what it will be for all its life; and its species is after a thousand years what it was in the first year of that thousand" (*Inequality*, *O.C.*, 3:142). Rather, man is "compensated for the instinct he perhaps lacks by faculties capable of taking its place at first, and of raising him afterwards far above nature" (ibid., 142–43). Sadly, we might be forced to conclude that these faculties "render [man] at length the tyrant of himself and of Nature" (ibid., 142).

This very simplified summary omits Rousseau's supporting arguments and evidence, some of which will be discussed in more detail in the next chapter. It also leaves unexplored Rousseau's complex interweaving of emotional and judgmental rhetoric with dispassionate and even brutally uncompromising reasoning. But it does at least raise a question that invites immediate attention. Even if no one way of life is natural for man in the way that the lives of bees and herd animals are natural for them, is there a way of life that is naturally best for man?

[5] See Chapter 3.

## "The Happiest Epoch, and the Most Durable"

Rousseau addresses this question directly. In the course of his description of human pre-history, he identifies the last stage of the state of nature, or "nascent society," as the best for man. Before drawing this conclusion, however, he describes a transition from the first societies, which resulted from "a first revolution" that united parents and children in a common dwelling (ibid., 167–68). When these families began gradually to unite in larger bands, people began to "acquire ideas of merit and of beauty which produce sentiments of preference" (ibid., 169). This would have produced sexual jealousy, and thus bloody conflict. More generally, people would have noticed natural differences in beauty, strength, grace, and eloquence. Soon, with everyone wanting to be recognized and respected, vanity and contempt would produce shame and envy, and thus vengeance.

Notwithstanding the new motives for conflict and violence, Rousseau concludes that fully human beings were at home in this condition, prior to agriculture and metallurgy, property and laws.

> [T]his period of the development of human faculties, maintaining a fair mean between the indolence of the primitive state and the petulant activity of our amour-propre, must have been the happiest epoch, and the most durable. The more one reflects on it, the more one finds that this state was the least subject to revolutions, the best for man, (XVI.*) and that he must have come out of it only by some fatal accident, which for the common good ought never to have happened. The example of the Savages, who have almost all been found at this point, seems to confirm that Mankind was made to remain in it always; that this state is the World in the prime of its youth; and that all subsequent progress has been in appearance so many steps toward the perfection of the individual, and in fact toward the decrepitude of the species.
>
> As long as men were content with their rustic huts, as long as they confined themselves to sewing their clothing of skins with thorns or fish bones, to adorning themselves with feathers and shells, to painting their bodies with various colors, perfecting or embellishing their bows and arrows, to carving with sharp stones a few fishing Canoes or a few crude Musical instruments; in a word, as long as they applied themselves only to tasks that one could perform alone and to arts that did not require the cooperation of several hands, they lived free, healthy, good, and happy lives as far as they could by their Nature, and continued to enjoy the gentle pleasures of independent dealings among themselves. (ibid., 171)

Note XVI, which Rousseau refers to in this quotation, supports these claims with evidence of the extreme reluctance that savages often exhibit when offered opportunities to adopt civilized ways of life. The most striking anecdote involves a Hottentot from southern Africa who was raised from infancy as a European, and found to be so intelligent that he was successfully employed in the Indies by a trading company. According to a report from which Rousseau quotes at length, the young man returned to Africa after the death of his employer, and went to visit his Hottentot relatives.[6] After this visit, he informed the man responsible for his European education that he had decided to renounce the civilized life and live in the way of his ancestors. He then ran off and was never seen again. Rousseau puts so much importance on this anecdote that he depicts the Hottentot's renunciation of civilization in the frontispiece of the book and includes cross-references below the picture and in Note XVI. Rousseau also notes that Europeans have frequently chosen to join savage communities permanently, and others have experienced nostalgia after leaving such lives behind.

One should not assume that Rousseau is a credulous retailer of romantic fables. In a letter written two years before the *Discourse on Inequality* was published, the hard-headed and clear-eyed Benjamin Franklin made the same observation in comparably striking terms. After noting that the American Indians had become quite familiar with the advantages of European society, and that they "are not deficient in natural understanding," Franklin says:

> When an Indian child has been brought up among us, taught our language, and habituated to our customs, yet, if he goes to see his relatives, and makes one Indian ramble with them, there is no persuading him ever to return. And that this is not natural to them merely as Indians, but as men, is plain from this, that when white persons, of either sex, have been taken prisoners by the Indians, and lived awhile with them, though ransomed by their friends, and treated with all imaginable tenderness to prevail with them to stay among the English, yet in a short time they become disgusted with our manner of life, and the care and pains that are necessary to support it, and

[6] Rousseau's source is an abridged version of Peter Kolb's study of the native peoples of southern Africa, which is considered one of the greatest ethnographies of the eighteenth century. Kolb used the term "Hottentot" for all these peoples, which would have included groups closely related to the Bushmen discussed later in this chapter.

take the first opportunity of escaping again into the woods, from whence there is no redeeming them.[7]

Rousseau, who has been called the founder of modern anthropology,[8] offers a frankly conjectural description of the human journey through the state of nature to historical times. He consulted the science of his time, especially Buffon, but he bemoans the unreliability of travelers' reports, and holds out hope that a more complete understanding of primitive people—perhaps including some far more primitive than those who had been reliably observed—might eventually be developed. The conjectural nature of Rousseau's account of human development, however, should not be overstated. The details of the human journey are conjectural, but Rousseau believes that the starting point is not, or at least not in the same way. He is quite confident of at least this much: that our ancestors did not always have conventional languages or the distinctively human social relations that are inseparable from such languages.[9] This may have been a "conjecture," but it is one that has now been confirmed by overwhelming evidence.[10]

Still, Rousseau's analysis of the way of life best for man, and most durable, is in principle subject to enrichment and possible revision on the basis

[7] Franklin to Richard Jackson (5 May 1753), *Writings of Benjamin Franklin*, 3:136–37. James Madison and Alexis de Tocqueville reported similar phenomena. See "Address to the Agricultural Society of Albemarle" (12 May 1818), *Papers of James Madison* (Retirement Series), 1:260–85, 261; Tocqueville, *Democracy in America*, vol. 1, pt. 2, chap. 10, note 18.

[8] Claude Lévi-Strauss, "Jean-Jacques Rousseau, Fondateur des Sciences de l'Homme," 239–48.

[9] Victor Gourevitch argues that the known starting point is not the "pure state of nature" (speechless animals living largely solitary lives), but the stage at which primitive peoples encountered by traveling Europeans had arrived. The pure state of nature, he thinks, is a "statement of [Rousseau's] principles conjectured into existence, bodied forth, and given a local habitation and a name" ("Rousseau's Pure State of Nature," 59). Richard L. Velkley similarly contends that the limiting case described by Rousseau represents an impossibility (*Being after Rousseau*, 162n14). I believe, on the contrary, that Rousseau regarded the known starting point as a prelinguistic condition, and did not believe that it is impossible for our distant ancestors to have lived very isolated lives before stable families existed.

[10] A detailed discussion of Rousseau's thoughts on human evolution and the origin of languages is presented in Chapter 3.

of new evidence.[11] Such evidence exists, and some of it is presented by Elizabeth Marshall Thomas in *The Old Way: A Story of the First People.*

## Elizabeth Marshall Thomas and the Bushmen

Thomas' life has some curious parallels with Rousseau's career as a gifted intellectual outsider, non-specialist, and autodidact. Beginning at the age of nineteen in the early 1950s, she accompanied her parents and younger brother on an extraordinary series of expeditions into the Kalahari Desert. These trips were organized by her father, Laurence Marshall, a retired businessman who took his family and several other adults on a dangerous search for people who were thought to be living in a primitive fashion in the interior of the desert. The mission was successful, and the group spent considerable time over several years living among various groups of Bushmen, including especially one that calls itself the Ju/wasi (singular: Ju/wa).[12] Thomas' mother, Lorna Marshall, was a former English teacher who went on to produce careful ethnographic studies of the people. Thomas' brother, John Marshall, produced films of the Ju/wasi, married a Ju/wa woman, and remained involved in their affairs until his death. Thomas herself wrote a travelogue shortly after the expeditions, and has pursued a variety of literary projects in subsequent years. Her many books include an account of a warlike people among whom she lived for a time in northern Uganda, two novels set in the Stone Age, a book about cats, a book about the social life of deer, and two books about dogs. Her study of dogs included a period of time camped out, alone, near a den of wild

[11] Rousseau is often highly critical of extravagant claims made on behalf of modern science by some scientists, but I do not believe he ever denies that it has been the source of genuine enlightenment. In his first and quite vociferous critique of science, for example, he says that Francis Bacon is "perhaps the greatest of philosophers," and he refers to "the Bacons, the Descartes [plural] and the Newtons" as preceptors of the human race (*Discourse on the Sciences and the Arts*, *O.C.*, 3:29). Similarly, the *Emile* contends that there is no true progress of reason in the human species because the acquisition of enlightenment is accompanied by a diminution of vigor of mind (*O.C.*, 4:676, Bloom, 343). For an enlightening study of Rousseau's serious engagement with the physical science of his time, see Christopher Kelly, "Rousseau's Chemical Apprenticeship."

[12] Various terms have been used to refer to the ethnic or linguistic group often called "Bushmen," most or all of which have been regarded as derogatory at one time or another. There are controversies over the most respectful terminology, and there are different ways to represent the sounds used in their languages. I follow Thomas' usage.

wolves on Baffin Island in northern Canada. Thomas tells us that all her studies were decisively influenced by her youthful trips to the Kalahari.

*The Old Way*, written more than half a century after her first encounter with the Bushmen, supplements her youthful first-hand experiences with further reflection and research. The book has some obvious resemblances to the *Discourse on Inequality* in its general approach or method. Thomas accepts scientific findings where they are well established, but she is willing to make conjectures when facts are uncertain, and to make moral judgments on matters about which modern science is necessarily silent. She is also unwilling to be confined by all of the conventions or prejudices of modern scientists. She notes, for example, that the roots of certain plants stop feeding the vine and leaves at certain times, causing them to drop off and blow away, thus leaving the root hidden from herbivores, and concludes by saying, "This was what the root intended" (*Old Way*, 11).[13]

*The Old Way* is specifically related to Rousseau's claim that savage society was the most durable because it provided for the optimal, though not ultimate, development of human faculties. Thomas accepts the standard account of human origins offered by modern science, which traces our lineage to arboreal primates living in African rain forests. Climatic changes—an important element in Rousseau's discussion of the "fortuitous intervention of a number of foreign causes"—stimulated adaptations to what became a substantially colder and dryer environment. Our ancestors eventually evolved as terrestrial hunter-gatherers, probably on the relatively open grasslands in eastern or southern Africa that resulted from these climatic changes.[14] Modern human beings eventually covered the globe, and have undergone spectacular cultural evolution. Thomas believes that the people she observed, who lived in the same general area as the first modern humans, are descended from very early people who never left this area, and had by the 1950s undergone less cultural evolution than any other living people.

[13]Those inclined to regard the quoted sentence as a patent stupidity should consult Aristotle, *De Anima* 415a22–415b7; Charles Darwin, *The Power of Movement in Plants*, 571–73; Richard Mabey, *The Cabaret of Plants*, 328–38.

[14]For an overview, see Richard G. Klein, *The Human Career: Human Biological and Cultural Origins*. Thomas is not especially concerned with the precise details of biological evolution. She makes at least one technical error, when she assumes that human beings are descended from chimpanzees. Chimpanzees do appear to be our closest living relatives, but we are not descended from them (ibid., 94–96, 728). The closest common ancestor of chimpanzees and humans may have been physically similar to modern chimpanzees (though no fossils have been found), but nothing is known about the social life of this extinct species.

Recent work in genetic mapping supports this view. So far as modern science has been able to determine, the Bushmen with whom Thomas lived in her youth more closely resembled "the first people" than any we will ever know.[15] This means that the Ju/wa way of life may well have been, as Rousseau says, "the least subject to revolutions" and the "best for man."[16] It is important to stress that there are cultural variations among Bushmen groups, and among hunter-gatherers in various parts of the world. In many important respects, however, the Ju/wasi are fairly typical,[17] and it is at least possible that essential elements of their culture may have been the most durable of any that has ever existed.[18] That makes their way of life a plausible candidate for the state that Rousseau believed was the best for man.

Thomas' account focuses on a group of about 550 Bushmen, particularly those who were still living as hunter-gatherers in the Nyae Nyae area of the Kalahari. These people were almost untouched by other cultures. Almost, but not quite. Although some were so isolated that it took several months just to find them, they were aware of the outside world. Not so long ago, the Bushman range had been larger, and it may have extended throughout eastern and southern Africa for a considerable time after the origin of our species.[19]

By the time of the Marshall family's expeditions, the Ju/wasi lived in a relatively small area surrounded by Bantu pastoralists and European farmers and ranchers. Some of the Bushmen had been enslaved or employed

[15] See, for example, Spencer Wells, *The Journey of Man: A Genetic Odyssey*, 56–57.

[16] Rousseau anticipated that science might eventually enable us to trace our lineage back to other species, or at least to animals with radically different physical structures. He was apparently the first to suggest that humans may have developed from ape origins. See Robert Wokler, "Perfectible Apes in Decadent Cultures: Rousseau's Anthropology Revisited."

[17] Most known hunter-gatherer societies feature relative egalitarianism, land tenure based on common property, a mobile way of life, and a practice of small groups dispersing at certain seasons and coming together in larger groups at other times (*Cambridge Encyclopedia of Hunters and Gatherers*, 4).

[18] This is not to say that their culture did not change in significant ways over time, even before this people encountered invaders such as Bantus and Europeans. Such change must have occurred, and it is unlikely that science will ever be able to establish the exact extent to which the Ju/wasi or any other group of Bushmen who survived into historical times are "living fossils."

[19] The Bushmen speak one of several extremely unusual click languages. Outside the area where the Bushmen are found, the only other place where this type of language has been found is in east Africa, and skeletal material consistent with Bushman-like people has been found in paleolithic sites in Somalia and Ethiopia (Wells, *Journey of Man*, 56–57).

as servants, or had at least traded with their neighbors. All of them knew about such contacts (some had escaped from servitude and they all knew of others who never came back), and they had some foreign commodities and artifacts. The Marshall family, however, met and lived with individuals who had never seen a vehicle, a white person, or a graphic representation of any kind. Those living in the interior of the desert had a few tools made of metal obtained in trade from Bantus or Europeans, but the people were not dependent on these items, and they continued to use stone, wood, and bone versions as well.

The Bushmen have by now been intensively studied by professional anthropologists, but the early Marshall expeditions seem to have been unique. Only the Marshalls appear to have undertaken an extended and deliberate study of isolated groups that had had only minimal contact with the outside world. Though the life Thomas describes is now gone, due to invasions from our world, I will generally discuss it in the present tense. Her account of the Ju/wasi is too rich to summarize adequately, and I will focus on a few points that are particularly relevant to Rousseau's discussion of "nascent society."

## Equality and Freedom Among the Bushmen

There is no rulership here, not even that of men over women. Decisions are reached by group consensus after discussion, or by individuals making their own choices. The semi-nomadic bands in which the people live, moreover, are somewhat fluid. Bands sometimes come together for a variety of reasons, and smaller groups may pay extended visits to other bands. The bands average about twenty-five members, but some are much smaller, and people gather in larger groups at times. Although government and law in our sense do not exist, the Ju/wasi have an elaborate customary social system. This system can be illustrated with two related examples, involving the ownership of land and marriage.

At the most simple level, every person begins with the customary right to live in the place where he was born, unless his mother was only passing through at the time. The people with this right are the customary owners, but their ownership claim weakens if they leave or their close relatives are no longer there, and may fade away entirely. One may not live in a place without permission from the owners, and this principle is scrupulously observed.

Many people, however, do not live where they were born, mostly because of marriage. With some important exceptions, any man and woman may marry if they so choose, and either can divorce the other simply by announcing it (though this is not done lightly or often). Polygamy (including polyandry) is permitted, and practiced to a limited extent, while care is taken to avoid marriages between close relatives.[20] Virtually everyone marries, and people who are divorced or widowed before they are old usually remarry. In such a small population, the number of possible mates is limited, and many marriages are arranged during childhood. Such arrangements, however, do not bind the individuals when they reach marriageable age, which for girls may be as young as eight or so (though husbands do not have intercourse with their wives prior to the menarche). Through hunting, a new husband must contribute to the support of his wife's family until their third child can walk, which is seldom less than fourteen or fifteen years, and he may remain with that family for the rest of his life. Thomas found that about half the people were living where the wife was an owner and about half where the husband was an owner.

While these customs may sound to us like the fundamental elements of social organization, it is better to think of them as particular consequences of a more general and important organizing norm: sharing. Food and even water are frequently quite scarce. As we might expect from our own experience, close relatives share with each other, and the more closely they are related, the more they share. But the customs of the Ju/wasi take them far beyond this unsurprising practice.

Food is of two general kinds. Plants and small (or slow) animals like tortoises, rabbits, and snakes—which are gathered primarily but not exclusively by women—belong to the individual who gathers them. Gatherers are generally free to eat whatever they find, or to share it with anyone they choose, which they frequently do. These foods are the staples of the Ju/wa diet, and they appear to be sufficient for sustaining life and health. The other category of food consists of large ungulates, such as wildebeest and giraffe, which are hunted. This meat is intensely craved by the Ju/wasi, and it is more scarce and hard to get than gathered foods (some of which can be obtained only by exercising considerable skill and effort). Hunting

[20] Thomas observed polygyny, which was considered unremarkable though relatively uncommon. She was told that polyandry was permitted though rarely practiced, but she never observed it directly. She was also told that polygyny seems to work best when the wives are sisters (*Old Way*, 179–80).

is carried out exclusively by men, who pursue it very avidly and talk a great deal about it. Its extreme importance is illustrated by the fact that men may not marry until they have hunted successfully.

The distribution of hunted food is governed by an elaborate set of rules and rituals, which ensure that every member of the community gets a share of the kill and that the shares work out pretty evenly over time. Unlike the simple and intuitive "finders keepers" rule for gathered food, these rules are highly conventional. The right to make the initial distribution of hunted meat, for example, belongs to the person who fashioned the arrow that brought the animal down, who is often not the shooter and may even be a woman or child.

The central importance of sharing is reflected in the fact that the Ju/wasi never trade with each other, though they do with outsiders. Instead, they have a custom of bilateral friendships, called *xaro*, that begin when one person gives another a small gift, usually a luxury item such as a metal knife or ostrich-shell necklace. After a time, the recipient reciprocates, and this practice continues as long as the two people continue to find pleasure in the exchanges. Most people have about fifteen such friendships, which may involve individuals whose homes are a hundred miles distant. These special relationships, which the Ju/wasi never have with outsiders (even when they receive gifts from them), are extremely important, and people often spend three or four months of the year visiting other bands for the purpose of seeing *xaro* friends.

Like almost everything the Ju/wasi do, these friendships promote survival in the Kalahari's hostile environment. For example, the practice of visiting friends effectively widens people's access to food, promotes communication among isolated bands, and provides relief from the stresses that occur when small groups spend extended periods living together in isolation. But there are some subtler effects that are especially relevant to Rousseau's analysis.

One striking feature of Rousseau's discussion of nascent society is how little he has to say about the good and how much about the bad in the social relations of the state he calls "the best for man." Apart from a brief discussion of the awakening of sexual love that includes an emotional component that goes beyond an instinctive desire for intercourse, the only new pleasures he mentions are communal song and dance. His discussion thus leaves us to wonder what it is in this savage state that more than compensates for the ills produced by the vanity and jealousy to which he gives more attention.

In Thomas' account of the Ju/wasi, the pleasures associated with food, especially meat, figure prominently, as one might expect among people who are frequently at the edge of starvation. In addition to sexual and family loves, the social pleasures appear mostly to be of a spontaneous kind. Children's games. Music and dance, involving both children and adults, much of which is not organized, planned, or ritualized.[21] Joking and gossiping, also not organized (and also not without a dark undercurrent).

In the constellation of pleasures, *xaro* friendships are unusual. These relationships have a certain obligatory element, for one may not refuse a gift, and one is expected to reciprocate. But one does not reciprocate immediately because that would look too much like trading. More significantly, people take pleasure in preparing gifts for their *xaro* friends, anticipating the good feelings that will result on both sides. This appears to be a custom that promotes social cohesion by cultivating friendships that provide an especially pure form of social pleasure. Unlike the kin relationships that dominate the social life of the Ju/wasi, these friendships are not imbued with necessity, or not to nearly the same extent. People enter these relationships for the sake of pleasing each other, which is why it seems significant that the gifts are luxury items among people who have few luxuries and often lack necessities.

Somewhat counterintuitively, and without elaboration, Thomas says that the *xaro* bonds are "perhaps the strongest fibers in the social fabric" (*Old Way*, 223). If she is right, I think the importance of the bonds must arise from the extent to which these relationships are experienced as existing solely for the pleasure they bring. People have deeper ties to their kin, but also more burdensome and inescapable obligations. *Xaro* friendships seem to exemplify what Rousseau calls "the gentle pleasures of independent dealings among themselves," the pleasures that seem to be the distinctive social good of nascent society, the state that was "best for man."

## Social Discipline Among the Bushmen

In sharp contrast to Rousseau's brief description of nascent society, *The Old Way* offers a detailed description of the difficulties and high personal costs that the Ju/wasi experience in maintaining their social life. The prin-

[21] Music and dance—the only communal pleasures that Rousseau mentions in his description of the happiest epoch—are an extremely significant element in the lives of the Ju/wasi. See Lorna Marshall, *The !Kung of Nyae Nyae*, 363–81; Lorna J. Marshall, *Nyae Nyae !Kung: Beliefs and Rites*, 63–90, 195–200.

cipal problem she identifies, however, is exactly the one on which Rousseau puts overwhelming emphasis: jealousy. Thomas' account of the Ju/wa way of life throws new light on Rousseau's cryptic description of "nascent society" by showing how these people have addressed that problem.

The Ju/wasi usually have enough food and water to survive, but they never have much more than that, and sometimes they die of starvation or dehydration. They are seldom killed by predators, but if left alone they are likely to be taken by leopards or hyenas before long. The overwhelming importance of group membership is poignantly captured in the words of a woman who said: "It is bad to die, because when you die you are alone" (ibid., 213). And the importance of group solidarity is reflected in virtually every aspect of their relations, especially the tremendous emphasis on sharing.

Such solidarity does not occur without strong social discipline. Anything that even resembles stealing is virtually unknown, and the language has no specific word for theft.[22] Children are trained to avoid physical violence, and the Ju/wasi do not have weapons suited for combat. Their famous poisoned hunting arrows, for example, produce wounds that are invariably fatal, but the poison has a delayed and very slow effect; the Ju/wasi, moreover, do not have shields of any kind. Considering the stresses under which these people live, violence is remarkably rare. The few homicides that Thomas knew of suggest how, and with what success, the Ju/wasi have interrupted man's progress toward the Hobbesian state of war that Rousseau saw as the final departure from the state of nature (*Inequality*, *O.C.*, 3:176).

In one case, a man suddenly and without explanation shot his wife with a poisoned arrow, then returned a few minutes later and shot two other men who were sitting nearby. The next day, the attacker was hunted down and put to death. In another case, a group reluctantly decided to kill a man who had begun to exhibit signs of mental illness. Thomas reports that none of these five homicides was regarded as a crime or as a punishment. Instead, they were all considered tragedies, in much the same way that the Ju/wasi viewed a homicide in which a very young child shot a poisoned arrow at a man who was arguing with the child's father. Similarly,

[22] The one case of stealing reported by Thomas involved a man who took honey from a beehive that another man had found. This was such an extraordinary event that the original discoverer of the hive killed the thief. This is the only act of vengeance that Thomas reports, and it may not have been understood in quite that way by the killer.

Ju/wa mothers are sometimes required by necessity to put a newborn to death, because of deformities or because it would be impossible to support the child along with its older siblings. Such necessary acts of infanticide, rare because the Ju/wasi carefully space the births of their children, are regarded with extreme sadness.

Correlatively, ridicule and social snubbing—especially in the form of refusals to share—are powerful and common sanctions used against those who deviate from social norms. The challenge faced by the Ju/wasi in managing natural selfishness, natural assertiveness, and natural inequality can be illustrated with an anecdote.

A man named Short /Kwi, one of his band's most successful and respected hunters, was bitten by a poisonous snake. Gangrene set in, the lower part of his leg fell off, and Short /Kwi appeared to be doomed. Thomas' father decided to use his vehicle to take the man and his wife on the long trip to a hospital, where the couple would have to appear in clothing, which they did not have. The Marshall family dressed them in some of their own clothes as they prepared to depart. Thomas was understandably shocked by what happened next.

> We then heard raised voices at Short /Kwi's camp. The other people were erupting. The grief that all had felt turned to jealousy and anger when we gave so much to these people and nothing to anyone else. We went there and found all the people sitting together in a thick circle, recounting in impassioned voices all the slights and stinginess that anyone had ever shown to them or anyone else. *He was supposed to give me a knife. She was going to give the knife to Gao. Where is the blanket you promised my brother? When I gave her a necklace, she should give a gift in return. She never did. The necklace went to her sister. That was wrong. I have nothing. I am empty-handed. They should have controlled that necklace. Others have it now. Those people are selfish. They don't want to give. They won't give the necklace. People don't think of what they should be doing. They are stingy. All this is wrong.*
>
> Surely some of these grievances had been festering for years. In the middle of the circle was Short /Kwi in his starchy khaki shirt and trousers. Not only was he badly damaged by the loss of his leg and therefore in serious need of his people's goodwill for the future, but we were heaping him with gifts that would cause others to envy him for years to come. Already he was trying to give the clothes to other people. (*Old Way*, 241–42)

A complementary passage illustrates how natural inequality can be successfully managed:

> [Gao Feet] was unfailingly calm and gracious and had the rather rare distinction of being an excellent hunter and also an important healer. Most men were one or the other, seldom both, because no Ju/wa person wants to stand out above the rest or have more of anything than anyone else, including ability. Thus a man such as Gao Feet was in a difficult position. His people needed both his talents. Any group would. Hence to forsake one talent for the other would have been selfish, depriving his people of a service in order not to arouse jealousy. Yet Gao Feet had such a low-key manner and was so modest and unassuming that people did not hold his talents against him. That was how he managed his excellence. (ibid., 181)

Thomas reaches the same unequivocal conclusion about the way of life she observed that Rousseau reached about nascent society: "We have certainly gone downhill from the social excellence of the Ju/wasi" (ibid., 224). The most striking difference between her account of the Bushmen and Rousseau's discussion of nascent society is her emphasis on the elaborate and repressive nature of the socialization that the Ju/wasi use to control the violent and vengeful impulses that Rousseau emphasized.

This may not be a decisive correction of Rousseau's analysis. It is possible that Rousseau's picture of nascent society more accurately corresponds with an early stage of Ju/wa life, while the social system that Thomas observed came later. Among the Ju/wasi Thomas knew, for example, the oldest male owner of a territory had a special title, which came with somewhat greater obligations to be generous but no additional rights. Thomas speculates that the title may be a residuum from a time when the roles of men and women were more sharply differentiated than they are now (ibid., 78–79).

The *Discourse on Inequality* is quite cryptic in discussing the transitions to and then from the patriarchal family that resulted from the "first revolution." Indeed, one form of natural inequality about which Rousseau says almost nothing in the *Discourse* is that between men and women, whom he generally treats as equals in the sense that they are equally independent in the state of nature. But this is misleading in at least two ways. First, women could never have been as independent as men, for women have a natural social relationship with their children that men do not have.[23] Second, women have extra burdens imposed on them by our mammalian

[23] See, for example, *O.C.*, 3:147 (noting the social consequences of the mother's physical need to nurse).

nature, and thus extra incentives to enter into cooperative arrangements with other people.

In order for men to become fathers in more than a biological sense, they must overcome their natural selfishness at least to the extent that they become willing to share their food (a naturally private good) with another human being. A likely explanation for *sustained* self-overcoming of this kind is the presence of children who are seen by their parents as a shared responsibility. In the family, men and women become equal in a sense that is both natural and unnatural. It is natural because they are equally parents by nature. But it is unnatural because this formal equality of parenthood is naturally hidden by the temporal lapse between insemination and birth, and because of the greater investment that women are forced by nature to make in their children.

Similarly, the family is naturally asymmetric because the father is by nature free of the burdens imposed by motherhood. It is not hard to imagine that the earliest families were constituted through a tacit exchange in which men assumed rulership over women in exchange for food and protection, an exchange that would have been facilitated by a modification of women's natural subservience toward their children.[24] But it is hard to see why men would want this rulership, at least for extended periods of time, unless they acquired a kind of subservience toward their children that they do not have by nature.

There obviously have been many societies, both savage and political, in which a patriarchal family structure has been preserved or instituted. If the Ju/wasi did move from such a structure to the highly egalitarian marriages observed by Thomas, it could have been a consequence of the egalitarian social norms they adopted in their other relations with one another. This, in turn, might suggest that the family structure best for man is, like nascent society itself, not necessarily the one that is most natural.

Nevertheless, it must be stressed that the roles of men and women among the Ju/wasi are not completely undifferentiated. Women do not hunt, and hunting is the most important pursuit in which a Ju/wa individual performs something like what we would call public service. Ju/wa men are certainly never rulers, of their wives or other adults, but they do have a more prominently public role. The importance of that role is indi-

[24] As Susan Meld Shell points out, it is difficult to imagine how the sharing of huts that constituted the "first revolution" could have occurred except through the agency of women ("*Émile*: Nature and the Education of Sophie," 280).

cated by the fact that men may not marry before they have hunted successfully. The Ju/wasi strongly repress the amour-propre that seeks honor and glory, but they do incentivize the most important form of public service. If you don't hunt, you won't get sex (at least not very often), and you won't get the children whose support you will very likely need in your old age.

There are other primitive peoples (some of which Rousseau knew something about) that are much more violent and much less egalitarian than the Ju/wasi. The Yanomami of the Amazon rainforest offer an informative comparison with the Bushmen described by Thomas. The Yanomami, who had only minimal and sporadic contact with Westerners before the mid-twentieth century, resemble the Bushmen in their semi-nomadic and highly communal way of life. Like the Bushmen, they do not have governments or laws in our sense. The Yanomami, however, do not control violence, jealousy, and selfishness to nearly the same extent as the Bushmen, and thus their culture more closely resembles nascent society as Rousseau imagined it.[25] Remarkably, an incident much like the Hottentot anecdote related by Rousseau in Note XVI was documented just a few years ago. An American anthropologist went to study the Yanomami in 1975, became integrated into one of the communities, and took a very young bride there. After several years, external pressures required the man to return to the United States, where the couple lived in New Jersey for several years and had three children. After a trip back to visit her relatives in the rainforest, the Yanomami woman ran away at the airstrip as her husband and infant child were leaving for the return trip. And there she stayed, where she was later found living with her native people.[26]

The differences between the Ju/Wasi and other primitive peoples could be due to variations among physical environments and to the accidents that always affect cultural evolution. What may be more significant is that the central social problem faced by the Ju/wasi is exactly the one, namely pride and jealousy, that Rousseau identifies as the basis of all social ills. Thomas' account shows that the most durable solution to that problem may, in fact, have been devised without the rulership and subordination

[25] For an introduction to a large and controversial anthropological literature, see John F. Peters, *Life Among the Yanomami*.

[26] See Kenneth Good, *Into the Heart: One Man's Pursuit of Love and Knowledge among the Yanomami*; "American plans jungle trip to win back wife," *Sunday Times Plus*, 30 March 1997, http://sundaytimes.lk/970330/plus8.html; Patrick Tierney, *Darkness in El Dorado*, 250–56.

entailed in all forms of political organization.[27] It is true that this solution requires a much more intense regime of socialization than Rousseau attributed to nascent society. Still, the *best* features of that last epoch of the state of nature have largely been preserved or recovered by the Ju/Wasi. The evidence Thomas presents thus serves more to enrich Rousseau's analysis than to correct it.

## Jealousy and Lions

In the spirit of Rousseau, Thomas looks for the roots of Ju/wa practices, and some of ours, in earlier times. For example, she conjectures that the dwellings of the Ju/wasi—grass huts that take only a few minutes to construct and are abandoned when the inhabitants move—are slightly modified versions of the nests that other large primates make for themselves (*Old Way*, 8–10). Unlike Rousseau, who focuses almost entirely on the human (and proto-human) soul, Thomas is also intensely interested in understanding intelligent animals other than primates.

Rousseau understands, of course, that we are animals, and even says that our ability to think differs from that of beasts only in degree (*Inequality*, *O.C.*, 3:142). In a tantalizing passage, he begins by claiming that he "sees" in animals only ingenious machines, programmed by nature to operate in certain ways, whereas men also have the quality of a "free agent" that often deviates from nature's commands, sometimes to our advantage and sometimes to our detriment (ibid., 141). But Rousseau quickly drops the claim that human freedom operates through "purely spiritual acts about which one explains nothing through the Laws of Mechanics" (ibid., 142). In place of this claim, which he pointedly calls disputable, he identifies a natural faculty of acquiring culture (or "perfectibility") as the distinctive human quality.[28] Given what everyone knows about the progress of human history, this is more descriptive than explanatory, and it leaves us to won-

[27] Cf. *Inequality*, *O.C.*, 3:187–88, where Rousseau contends that government and laws are always an inadequate substitute for sound *mœurs* (i.e., customs or habits that have some kind of ethical or moral quality or effects).

[28] Leo Strauss interprets "perfectibility" to mean an almost infinite malleability that is without a natural limit on our power to make what we wish of the human race (*Natural Right and History*, 271). What Rousseau wrote may have contributed to such an understanding of human nature among later thinkers. I believe, however, that Strauss seriously misinterpreted Rousseau on this point. For a careful critique of Strauss' claim, see Victor Gourevitch, "On Strauss on Rousseau," 147–67.

der whether animals should also be understood as free agents, or whether men can be seen as ingenious machines.[29]

Thomas does not pursue this question directly, but she does give considerable thought to the ways in which certain other animals experience their lives, and to the relation between their experience and ours. A striking example involves the lions of the Nyae Nyae area.

Leopards and hyenas hunt the Ju/wasi, but neither presents a serious threat to the survival of the people. Leopards, which hunt alone and by stealth, are afraid of humans and easily discouraged, though they occasionally do succeed in taking a Ju/wa victim. Hyenas are more formidable, but they opportunistically focus their attention on stragglers, especially those in a weakened condition. The Ju/wasi try hard not to provide them with tempting targets.

Lions are a different story. These powerful predators routinely take animals that are much larger, tougher, and faster than human beings. They live near the same water holes on which the Ju/wasi depend. They hunt cooperatively, and they can do so day or night as they please. Their usual prey, moreover, are the same large ungulates prized by the Ju/wasi, and their hunting methods are similar, so the two are competitors for this food. The lions are fully aware of the Ju/wasi, whose camps they frequently approach at night, usually discreetly and apparently out of curiosity. Lions are known to hunt people in other places, but they do not prey on the Ju/wasi. Why not?

Thomas says that only the lions know the answer, but she suggests that the Ju/wasi and the lions of the Nyae Nyae area may have come to a tacit coexistence agreement sometime in the very distant past. The lions in this area hunt at night, and the Ju/wasi pursue the same prey during the day. The Ju/wasi also do most of their gathering during the hottest part of the day, when the lions are least active, even though this imposes extra physical stresses on the gatherers.

[29] Elsewhere, Rousseau criticizes mechanical explanations of the behavior of animals (*Essay*, chap. 15, *O.C.*, 5:417). He also suggests how and why we might sometimes view other people as mechanical beings (*Reveries*, eighth walk, *O.C.*, 1:1077). Perhaps we have the ability to "see" animals, and even other people, as nothing but ingenious machines, whereas we cannot see ourselves that way. Our own lack of freedom to see ourselves as nothing but ingenious machines cannot by itself establish that we are not just ingenious machines. Similarly, our ability or freedom to view animals or other people as nothing but ingenious machines cannot by itself establish that they are not "free agents." Cf. *Emile*, *O.C.*, 4:553, Bloom, 256 (referring to "the incomprehensible idea of the action of our soul on our body").

When the Ju/wasi do encounter a lion in the bush, they ordinarily observe a protocol that involves an affected nonchalance, neither aggressive nor fearful, and a casual departure at an oblique angle. If lions show themselves in camp, men discourage them with fire and with calm but stern commands to leave. Occasionally the Ju/wasi actually face lions down, as one group did when it came upon a pride that was trying to appropriate a wounded wildebeest that the human hunters were tracking after shooting it with a poisoned arrow (cf. *Inequality*, *O.C.*, 3:136–37). Thomas herself once encountered a lion in the bush and was so awestruck that she simply stared at the animal in spellbound fascination. The lion finally followed the usual protocol, walking calmly off at an oblique angle.

The lions are respected by the Ju/wasi beyond all other animals, but they are not loved. When confronting a lion, they address it with the same term of respect used when speaking of the gods (*Old Way*, 168). But when speaking *about* lions, the people use avoidance terms, one of which is "jealousy." Why would this be? Thomas cannot say for sure, but she offers a suggestion. The Ju/wasi sometimes attribute mysterious deaths to the existence of people who seem normal but harbor a nasty combination of jealous secrets and supernatural powers.[30] This could be a metaphor for lions, "out there in the dark not far away from you, able to kill you whenever they felt like it, refraining from killing you for reasons you were not equipped to determine. You hoped that they wouldn't kill you, but you could never be sure" (ibid., 170–71). If lions are the greatest living threat in the physical environment, jealous people are like lions in society.

There is obviously a risk of pushing metaphors and speculation too far, but perhaps this connection between jealousy and lions reflects a Ju/wa insight that the most powerfully dangerous elements in their own souls can only be managed, not really subdued. When Thomas asked the Ju/wasi what they would do if lions were to prey on them, they responded that they would not live in such a place. Many years later, when Thomas studied how the Ju/wasi had changed after their lands were invaded and they were forced to alter their way of life, she found that they did not see themselves as a people of the desert, or one defined by their way of life

[30] Caution must be exercised in interpreting explanations given by the Ju/wasi. Asked where the stars went in the daytime, one man said, "They stay where they are. We just can't see them in the daytime because the sun is too bright." The same man later said that stars were ant-lions who in the evening went up to the sky and returned to their sandy traps at dawn (*Old Way*, 245). If one heard only the second story, it would be easy to get a distorted impression of the speaker's understanding of the world.

there. Instead, they saw their community with one another as the central and enduring element of their lives.

As Rousseau would no doubt have expected, many Ju/wa individuals easily succumbed to the allures and some of the worst vices of civilization, and it is unclear today how much of their ancient social fabric can survive the disappearance of the conditions in which it developed. He would also be confident, as Thomas is, that their lives have gone downhill in becoming more like ours.

## Pre-Human Happiness

Rousseau's most succinct description of the distinctive good that people found in nascent society refers to "the gentle pleasures of independent dealings among themselves." The parallel good for "nascent man"[31] in the pure state of nature is described this way: "His soul, which nothing agitates, gives itself over to the sole sentiment of its present existence, without any idea of the future, however near it may be" (*Inequality*, *O.C.*, 3:144). This proposition must be among the most arresting in the *Discourse on Inequality*, and perhaps the most baffling. How could Rousseau believe that he had access to the inner experiences of beings so different from ourselves that they did not even have speech?[32] And what implications could he think we should draw from this description of self-contemplation, so oddly reminiscent of Aristotle's description of the unmoved mover (*Metaphysics* 1072a19–1072b31), and so obviously evocative of the "Celestial and majestic simplicity" that Rousseau promised would be found beneath the outer surface of the statue of Glaucus (*Inequality*, *O.C.*, 3:122)?

Thomas may offer a suggestion. In *The Hidden Life of Dogs*, she recounts her efforts to understand what she calls dog consciousness, primarily through the careful observation of several pet animals with whom she and her family lived. At one point, the family moved to a new home, where they built a large pen for the dogs. Although the pen included a variety of shelters constructed for the animals' comfort, the dogs built their own den in the side of a hill. No ordinary hole in the dirt, the den

[31] *Inequality*, *O.C.*, 3:164. As Rousseau's use of this term suggests, man in the pure state of nature was not yet truly human.

[32] Late in life, Rousseau suggested that his peculiar nature made him uniquely capable of this discovery (*Dialogues*, third dialogue, *O.C.*, 1:936, "the Frenchman" is speaking).

was fifteen feet deep, ending in a three feet by three feet chamber that was two feet high. The entrance was hidden in a woodpile. Most remarkably, the dogs' project was carried out in perfect secrecy. Although Thomas spent a great deal of time in the pen and frequently checked for problems and evidence of escape attempts, she never noticed any sign of the large quantity of soil the dogs had excavated.

By chance, Thomas discovered what had happened when she suddenly arrived just as one of the dogs was entering the den through the woodpile. Once their project had been discovered, the dogs used the den openly, and it became the focus of their lives. Thomas could no longer detect whatever interactions were occurring among the dogs, which suggested that they had achieved a high degree of harmony in their social relationships. The dogs also seemed to lose interest in the human members of the family, and would not even respond to Thomas beyond a bland acknowledgment of her presence. The dogs' souls had, so to speak, disappeared from her view.

In response to these developments, Thomas started joining the dogs each afternoon to do just what they were doing. Nothing. Here is how she describes the experience:

> To sit idly, not doing, merely experiencing, comes hard to a primate, yet for once I wasn't among primates. At last, as dogs learn to live among our kind, it came to me to live among theirs. In the late afternoon sun we sat in the dust, or lay on our chests resting on our elbows, evenly spaced on the hilltop, all looking calmly down among the trees to see what moved there. No birds sang, just insects. Off in the silent, drying woods a tree would now and then drop something—a pod, perhaps, or a leaf—and we would listen to it scratching down. While the shadows grew long we lay calmly, feeling the moment, the calmness, the warm light of the red sun—each of us happy enough with the others, unworried, each of us quiet and serene. I've been to many places on the earth, to the Arctic, to the African savannah, yet wherever I went, I always traveled in my own bubble of primate energy, primate experience, and so never before or since have I felt as far removed from what seemed familiar as I felt with these dogs, by their den. Primates feel pure, flat immobility as boredom, but dogs feel it as peace. (ibid., 121)

Dogs and wolves, of course, are highly social animals, and they organize themselves hierarchically. In that respect they are very different from the solitary pre-humans in Rousseau's pure state of nature. Thomas' experience on the hilltop, moreover was not a solitary experience, either for her or for the dogs. Still, even if it is someday proved that Rousseau wrongly conjectured that our direct ancestors lived in nearly total isolation, he might have been right to suggest that our soul has a craving to be agitated by nothing, to be given over to something like the sole sentiment of its present existence, without any idea of the future, however near it may be. That is not to say that such peacefulness is *the* good for dogs or for humans, for both display another strong craving for activity, for exploration and interaction, as Rousseau well knew.[33] But it might still be *an* experience for which we have not lost the desire. And it might be an experience that social life should at least not make impossible.[34]

## Proto-Politics

The pre-human condition is obviously irrecoverable, and Rousseau does not pretend that there is any going back to the state of nascent society that he calls the best for man (e.g., *Inequality*, *O.C.*, 3:133, Note IX, 207). That does not prevent him from concluding that there are better and worse possibilities among the various forms of political organization that have been devised in historical times. The *Discourse on Inequality* is more suggestive than definitive about the contribution that its analysis can make to identifying and fostering the better possibilities, though Rousseau does coyly say that "every attentive Reader ... will find the solution to an infinity of problems in morals and Politics that the Philosophers cannot resolve" (ibid., 192).

Thomas evinces little interest in such questions, but her interest in the souls of animals provokes a number of suggestions that recall Aristotle's assertion that "man is a political animal *more* than any bee or any herd animal" (*Politics* 1253a7–8, emphasis added). Thomas, who sometimes characterizes our pets as slaves (who are suited by their nature to be our slaves in a way that our fellow humans are not), also believes that we

[33] In the *Essay on the Origin of Languages*, Rousseau says that only the passion for self-preservation is stronger and more primary than the passion for doing nothing, but he also refers to "natural restlessness" and he says that primitive people are subject to boredom (*O.C.*, 5:376, 401n, 402, 406). Similarly, in the *Emile*, he says: "To live is not to breathe, it is to act; it is to make use of our organs, of our senses, of our faculties, of all the parts of ourselves that give us the sentiment of our existence" (*O.C.*, 4:253, Bloom, 42; see also ibid., 429, Bloom, 167).

[34] Rousseau reports having had experiences somewhat similar to Thomas'. In one account, he finds himself briefly feeling that "[m]y dog himself was my friend, not my slave, we always had the same will but he never obeyed me" (*Letters to Malesherbes*, lett. 3, *O.C.*, 1:1141).

can have political relationships with them. She argues, for example, that wolves decided to form partnerships with our kind, contrary to the common assumption that we have dogs because our ancestors decided to domesticate wolves.[35]

Another kind of political analysis is offered in one of her stories. Dogs typically use seniority as a default rule in determining social dominance, but they also engage in struggles for status. One such struggle took place when Thomas introduced a new dog into her household's complex multispecies society. About a month before this happened, the dominant dog had died after a long and debilitating illness. The second-ranking dog had previously struggled hard to obtain her current rank, but had never become completely secure there. Apparently, both she and the third ranking dog recognized that she was unsuited for the dominant position. Accordingly, the third ranking dog, named Pearl, unobtrusively took over as leader during the illness of the dominant dog: "Pearl had occupied Place One in much the same way that a teacher takes charge of a classroom. The teacher doesn't want to suppress and dominate the students—she wants to help them. She takes the leadership because she has more knowledge and experience than they do" (*Social Life of Dogs*, 204).

Thomas first noticed Pearl's new status when she brought the new dog, named Sheila, into the house. Sheila was extremely apprehensive, and apparently ready to defend herself from aggression, but Pearl stepped forward to welcome her. A young stray who had been living on the streets, Sheila started at the bottom of the hierarchy, but soon proved politically ambitious. Using threats and physical aggression, she quickly subordinated the two lowest-ranking dogs, and then the insecure second-ranking dog. Still not satisfied, Sheila began trying to intimidate Pearl. Thomas reports:

> Pearl was like a dedicated teacher who has been insulted by a student for whom the teacher had always done her utmost and with the best of intentions. The student might want to chase away the teacher, but would lack the knowledge or ability to teach the class .... Short of getting rid of Sheila, I didn't really know how to help Pearl. The dog politics of the household would boil around me with an energy of their own no matter how much I tried to suppress them. I felt at a loss, unable to solve the problem. (ibid., 212)

During this period of conflict, Pearl began having troubled dreams—growling, snarling, and crying out in her sleep. Suddenly this stopped, and

[35] *The Social Life of Dogs*, 123–28.

so did the aggression between Pearl and Sheila. The political problem had apparently been solved, but how? Thomas noticed that Pearl had begun treating Sheila the way female dogs typically treat their daughters, and she believes that Pearl had in effect adopted the other dog.

> Among dogs and wolves and many other kinds of animals including people, the children of high-ranking parents have high rank too. Thus Pearl was solving the problem of Sheila. Sheila was a high-powered dog who wanted significant status, and her adoption by Pearl raised her status. She would have fought for status if she had to, but she didn't have to. Pearl gave it to her, and meanwhile kept her own. (ibid., 212–13)

Thomas emphasizes her belief that other dogs—especially males but also other females with a different temperament and less intelligence—would have handled this situation differently, and not nearly as well. I would add the additional observation that these events occurred in a highly artificial environment composed of masters (however benevolent) and slaves, of different species. Dogs are descended from wolves, and show it in many ways, but they are not simply slaves of lupine instinct any more than they are simply the compliant slaves of their human masters.

It would be easy to ridicule the kind of analysis that Thomas offers here, and in many other discussions of her pets. But if this is not all just a lot of anthropomorphic nonsense, perhaps it suggests that more attention should be paid to a point made subtly, almost invisibly, in the *Discourse on Inequality*.

Rousseau finds the natural source of our social virtues in a primitive sentiment that he calls pity or commiseration, which softens the stronger natural desire for self-preservation, and which is "so Natural that the Beasts themselves sometimes give perceptible signs of it" (*Inequality*, *O.C.*, 3:154).[36] In support of his claim, he offers several pieces of evidence, beginning with maternal tenderness and the bravery mothers display in

[36] Modern scientists have found, through observation and experiments, evidence of empathy in a wide range of mammals. Not just primates, elephants, canines, and cetaceans, but even such ancient and lowly animals as mice and rats. See, for example, Marc Bekoff and Jessica Pierce, *Wild Justice: The Moral Lives of Animals*, 101–105; D.J. Langford, et al., "Social Modulation of Pain as Evidence for Empathy in Mice"; Inbal Ben-Ami Bartal, et al., "Empathy and Pro-Social Behavior in Rats"; Nobuya Sato, et al., "Rats Demonstrate Helping Behavior Toward a Soaked Conspecific." For some very striking examples among a species of great ape, see Frans de Waal and Frans Lanting, *Bonobo: The Forgotten Ape*, 156–59.

guarding their young, which are conspicuous manifestations of our mammalian nature. The second example is an image of an imprisoned man forced to watch helplessly as a wild beast tears a child from its mother's breast. The next example is an ancient tyrant who dared not attend a tragedy lest others see him sympathizing with the wife and father of the fallen Hector. The last piece of evidence contains the one vivid reference to civilized women in the body of the *Discourse on Inequality*: "In Riots, in Street fights, the populace assembles, the prudent man moves away; it is the rabble, it is the Market women, who separate the combatants and prevent basically decent people (*honnêtes gens*) from cutting each other's throats" (ibid.,156).[37]

This thread of examples begins with maternal love, which appears to be extended by analogy or imagination to other social contexts.[38] In a Note appended to his discussion of natural pity, Rousseau says that "Love of oneself is a natural sentiment which inclines every animal to watch out for its own preservation, and which, directed in man by reason and modified by pity, produces humanity and virtue" (ibid., Note XV, 219).[39] The story of Pearl and Sheila suggests one way in which something like this might happen even without the guidance of human reason. Perhaps it would not be completely fanciful to think that Pearl's political acumen may have human analogues, not just in family life but also in the work of exceptionally skillful managers of small human groups within modern societies. And it may not be altogether coincidental that Pearl's behavior resembles the justice that Socrates is said by Xenophon to have practiced (*Memorabilia* 4.8.11).

[37] A blandly disapproving reference to the use of feminine wiles by civilized women occurs shortly thereafter in the text (*O.C.*, 3:158). Outside the body of the *Discourse*, we find a condemnation of abortion and infanticide by civilized women in Note IX, and a vivid statement about the virtue of Spartan women in the Epistle Dedicatory (ibid., 119, 204).

[38] The importance of this extension is suggested by Rousseau's comment elsewhere that natural pity would remain eternally inactive without imagination to set it in motion (*Essay*, chap. 9, *O.C.*, 5:395). It may also be significant that Rousseau characterizes conjugal and paternal love, but not maternal love, as the sweetest sentiments that we know (*Inequality*, *O.C.*, 3:168). Compare the discussion of *xaro* friendships above.

[39] Charles Darwin suggests a similar account of human sociality, while allowing for the possibility that natural selection may have produced more refined social instincts than the primitive form of pity described by Rousseau (*Descent of Man*, 1:71–83, 95–96).

## Conclusion

The rhetoric of the *Discourse on Inequality* is overwhelmingly aimed at puncturing unexamined assumptions about the superiority of civilized life and civilized people. Thomas, who does not begin with the usual prejudices, is nonetheless herself quite different from the Ju/wasi for whom she has so much admiration.

Thomas, for example, differs from the Ju/wasi in her disposition toward non-human animals. The Ju/wasi, who have tremendous practical knowledge about the living things in their environment, are completely indifferent to the suffering of animals, both the large animals they hunt and the smaller animals that they gather.[40] Unlike the Ju/wasi, who have no pets, Thomas keeps animals for the pleasure of their company, powerfully commiserates with them, and feels a strong moral responsibility toward them.

Thomas never assumes an attitude of moral superiority toward the Ju/wasi. She would no doubt observe that there is a crucial difference between killing animals for food, even without a concern to minimize their suffering, and benevolently enslaving animals as pets. And she might therefore conclude that both she and the Ju/wasi implicitly, though for different reasons, respect Rousseau's suggestion that as beasts "share something of our nature through the sensitivity with which they are endowed, one will judge that they should also participate in natural right, and that man is subject to some sort of duties toward them. ... [so that perhaps this shared sensitivity] should at least give the one the right not to be *uselessly* mistreated by the other" (*Inequality*, *O.C.*, 3:126, emphasis added).[41]

Apart from questions of natural justice, Thomas' feelings about her pets seem to be inseparable from her efforts to understand them.[42] The same kind of sympathy informs her efforts to understand the Ju/wasi. Although Rousseau declares that we owe what is best as well as worst in civilized life to a "furor to distinguish oneself" (ibid., 189), he also says that "natural

[40] See, for example, Elizabeth Marshall Thomas, *The Harmless People*, 52.

[41] The Ju/wasi exhibit the same acceptance of their own physical suffering that they display toward that of other animals. For a striking example involving a young girl who stoically endured several painful and dangerous hours caught in a metal trap that a member of the Marshall party had set in the desert, see *Old Way*, 216–17.

[42] A related phenomenon can be found among scientists who have done field work with great apes. Not infrequently they find that they cannot separate their desire to understand the animals from a desire to protect those they have come to know. Prominent examples include Jane Goodall, Dian Fossey, and Biruté Galdikas, and it is probably no mere accident that this group consists entirely of females.

commiseration … no longer resides in any but a few great Cosmopolitan Souls, who leap over the imaginary barriers that separate peoples and who, after the example of the sovereign being that created them, embrace the whole Human Race in their benevolence" (ibid., 178). In her efforts to promote appreciation of a human way of life that may have been the most durable of all conventional social arrangements, Thomas has certainly distinguished herself as a cosmopolitan—not just from a "furor" for distinction but not without some displays of *thumos* either.[43] And in her sympathetic observations about other animals, she has provided a vivid reminder of the difficulty—stressed by Rousseau and Aristotle alike—of determining with precision what the soul is and what it seeks.[44]

[43] See, for example, Elizabeth Marshall Thomas, "Reply to Melvin Konner."

[44] See, for example, Aristotle, *De Anima* 402a11–403b19, 432a22–432b3; *Inequality*, *O.C.*, 3:122–24, 141–42.

CHAPTER 3

# The Evolution of Humanity in Language: *Discourse on Inequality* and *Essay on the Origin of Languages*

The previous chapter focused on Rousseau's claims about the social arrangements most conducive to human happiness, and on some of the evidence from modern science supporting those claims. Rousseau's position stands in stark opposition to the great tradition of Western political philosophy, which finds the best way of life within civilization. He does, however, agree with both the classical and modern strands of that tradition in seeking to take nature as a guide in evaluating social arrangements and promoting human happiness. This invites us to ask exactly why or to what extent he arrives at such a radically different conclusion. This chapter will begin to address that question by considering some of Rousseau's arguments and some of the relevant evidence discovered by modern science.

## Greek Philosophers and the Problem of Language

When Rousseau sets out in search of man "as Nature formed him," he begins with a remarkable mistake: "I will not examine whether, as Aristotle thinks, his elongated nails were not at first hooked claws; whether he was not hairy like a bear, and whether walking on four feet, (III.*) his gaze directed toward the Earth, and limited to a horizon of a few steps, did not mark at the same time the character and the limits of his ideas" (*Inequality*, *O.C.*, 3:122, 134). The reason he gives for setting these hypotheses aside is both cautious and prescient: comparative anatomy and the observations



N. Lund, *Rousseau's Rejuvenation of Political Philosophy*,
DOI 10.1007/978-3-319-41390-7_3

of naturalists had not *yet* made enough progress to provide a foundation for solid reasoning (ibid., 134). The importance of Rousseau's suggestion that we may be the descendants of physically dissimilar animals can hardly be overstated. First, his general account of human cultural evolution as a response to environmental changes, including migration into new environments, parallels what is now the standard scientific account of our biological evolution. Second, Rousseau suspected that human beings far more primitive or natural than those known to the science of his time might someday be found (ibid., Note X, 208–14). This suspicion has now effectively been confirmed by fossil evidence demonstrating that many populations of animals that are very closely related to us once lived in various places in Africa, Europe, and Asia. Some scientists even contend that some of these extinct animals should be classified as a subspecies of *Homo sapiens.*[1]

Where Rousseau is able to engage in solid reasoning, he does so. Note III, for example, provides a well-reasoned argument for the conclusion that man is probably by nature a biped.[2] But the allusion to Aristotle is a plain error, for no one has identified any such assertion anywhere in Aristotle's works.[3]

Perhaps it is just a mistake, of the kind that anyone can make. But this seems unlikely for two reasons. First, the allusion to Aristotle appears to be wholly gratuitous. Second, the error is quite egregious. Aristotle never propounded what we would call a theory of evolution. Nor, so far as I am aware, did he ever propose that the descendants of some living things have radically different physical characteristics than their ancestors. Some of Rousseau's readers probably would have assumed, as many modern commentators do, that Aristotle believed that biological species are dis-

[1] See, for example, Clive Finlayson, *The Improbable Primate*, vii–xii.

[2] Modern scientists have treated upright posture or bipedalism as the defining characteristic of humans in the broadest sense of the term, although this has now been brought into question. See, for example, Klein, *Human Career*, 130, 729.

[3] In the *Parts of Animals*, Aristotle notes that human hands are a more versatile tool than the horns, talons, or claws of other animals (687a31–b5). He also characterizes our nails as protectors for the tips of the toes and fingers (687b22–25). But he does not even analogize nails to claws, let alone suggest that one developed from the other. In the *Discourse*, Rousseau signals his familiarity with Aristotle's biological works by posing a problem worthy of "the Aristotles and Plinys of our century" (*O.C.*, 3:123). See also *Emile*, *O.C.*, 4:455, Bloom, 184 (mentioning Aristotle along with Pliny and Buffon).

crete and immutable, which is almost the opposite of what Rousseau attributes to him. That assumption would be consistent with a Christianized interpretation of Aristotle that was widely accepted at the time. Thus, Rousseau's mistake might have made him look like an ignoramus, which he certainly was not. His mistaken allusion to Aristotle thus seems worthy of closer attention.

All of us employ the concept of biological species on a regular basis, for the simple reason that living things manifestly tend to generate offspring that resemble themselves. It is not clear, however, to what extent nature itself provides a rule or definition that we can rely on to distinguish one species from another. Different lines of demarcation—such as the degree of anatomical similarity, or the ability to produce fertile offspring, or the fact that a breeding population of the organisms exists in nature—may be useful for different purposes. But these lines do not always coincide, and the modern theory of evolution suggests that we should not expect them to be perfectly coincident.

Aristotle maintained that natural philosophers should begin with the common sense classifications that arise from our ordinary observations of the world (e.g., *Parts of Animals* 643b10–12). Such observations obviously suggest that species are discrete, but Aristotle emphasizes how difficult it can sometimes be to discern whatever natural demarcations there are (e.g., ibid., 681a9–15; *History of Animals* 588b4–12). Both of these points are consistent with the modern theory of evolution.[4] Some commentators have claimed that Aristotle had a theoretical commitment to the fixity of species,[5] and such an interpretation has been attributed to

[4] Darwin himself concluded that "we shall have to treat species in the same manner as those naturalists treat genera, who admit that genera are merely artificial combinations made for convenience. This may not be a cheering prospect; but we shall at least be freed from the vain search for the undiscovered and undiscoverable essence of the term species" (*Origin of Species*, chap. 14, 456). Similarly, a modern scientist maintains that "we have to recognize that species concepts are humanly produced categories which may or may not always work when compared with the reality of nature" (Chris Stringer, *Lone Survivors: How We Came to Be the Only Humans on Earth*, 54). Evolutionary biologists often define a species with notable imprecision, as in this formulation: "a group (or population) of organisms that look more or less alike and that interbreed to produce fertile offspring" (Klein, *Human Career*, 1).

[5] See, for example, Daniel Dennett, *Darwin's Dangerous Idea*, 36; Ernst Mayr, *The Growth of Biological Thought*, 305–07; G.E.R. Lloyd, *Aristotle: The Growth and Structure of His Thought*, 86–90; Marjorie Grene, *A Portrait of Aristotle*, 136–37.

medieval Aristotelianism.[6] The evidence for such a reading of Aristotle, however, is lacking.[7]

I know of only one sentence in the biological works that might be thought to support the fixity-of-species thesis: "So there is always (*aei*) a kind (*genos*) of human beings and animals and of plants" (*Generation of Animals* 731b35–732a1). In the preceding passage, Aristotle had said that animals cannot be eternal (*aidios*) as individuals, but can be eternal only in the way possible for them. The exact way in which it is possible for them to be eternal is not clearly or precisely spelled out. Aristotle *could* mean to suggest that individual living things participate in something eternal, namely the kind or species to which they belong, by being mortal examples of that kind. But that is not what the sentence quoted above actually says. The sentence occurs, moreover, in a passage that seeks to explain why living things produce offspring, and how the male and female each contributes to reproduction. In that context, Aristotle implies little beyond the conclusion that living things have an internal drive that causes them to generate other individuals resembling themselves, a drive that results in the persistence of biological kinds. It is a fact that there is "always a kind of human beings and animals and of plants," in the sense that we observe such kinds and can reasonably expect that they are likely to persist. Thus, anyone could reasonably say that individual organisms are eternal in the limited way that is possible for them, namely by resembling their ancestors and descendants. This does not imply that individuals of the kind to which they belong literally always existed or always will exist. Nor does it imply that all of the distant ancestors and descendants of an organism necessarily

[6]Arthur O. Lovejoy contends that the early modern focus on classifying biological species was heavily influenced by presuppositions about the *scala naturae* that can be traced back to one of two "modes of thought" found in Aristotle and in late medieval philosophy (*The Great Chain of Being*, 227–28). More dramatically, James Franklin suggests that Linnaeus' system of static and discrete species was simply the result of filling in the abstract [Porphyry's] Tree with the names of actual species ("Aristotle on Species Variation," 251–52).

[7]Modern commentators who attribute to Aristotle the view that biological species are discrete and immutable sometimes refer to passages in the *Organon* and *Metaphysics* that do not in fact imply this conclusion. See, for example, Richard Sorabji, *Necessity, Cause, and Blame: Perspectives on Aristotle's Theory*, 145–46. For refutations of the discrete-and-immutable interpretation, see, for example, Richard A. Richards, *The Species Problem: A Philosophical Analysis*, 17–48; James G. Lennox, *Aristotle's Philosophy of Biology*, 131–81; John S. Wilkins, *Species: A History of the Idea*, 15–21.

vary in their characteristics only within the range that we observe within the classes that we call "human beings" or "animals" or "plants."

However common it may have been at various times to attribute the fixity-of-species thesis to Aristotle, the long entry on Aristotelianism in the *Encyclopedia* does not do so. This entry in the ambitious Enlightenment project of d'Alembert and Diderot includes the usual strong criticism of the use of Aristotelian logic and metaphysics by the Scholastics, while noting that Aristotle's biological works focus carefully on the natural world as it is actually observed. Rousseau and his most knowledgeable readers could therefore easily have believed that Aristotle's position on the fixity of species was identical with Rousseau's own position, namely that the extant studies of comparative anatomy and observations of naturalists could not yet justify a confident conclusion one way or the other about biological evolution.

Those who recognized Rousseau's mistake might have seen it as a signal that he did not accept a Christianized interpretation of Aristotle. The possibility of such a signal is strengthened a few lines later in the text of the *Discourse*, where Rousseau says that he will assume that man is by nature bipedal "without having recourse to the supernatural *knowledge* that we have on this point, and without considering the changes that *must have* occurred in the conformation of man, internal as much as external, to the extent that he put his limbs to new uses and nourished himself with new foods" (*O.C.*, 3:134, emphasis added). This is a very odd juxtaposition—apparent deference to the religious doctrine that man as we see him today was the special creation of God, along with another hint at biological evolution.[8] In light of this oddity, Rousseau's mistaken allusion to Aristotle might be a way of indicating that he agrees with Hobbes, who referred to "the Errors, which are brought into the Church, from the *Entities*, and *Essences* of Aristotle: which it may be he knew to be false Philosophy; but writ it as a thing consonant to, and corroborative of their Religion; and fearing the fate of Socrates" (*Leviathan*, chap. 46, 527).

Rousseau was well aware of the prudent caution that philosophers have felt compelled to exercise when conveying views at odds with the dominant political and religious opinions of the societies in which they lived. Whether from fear of persecution, or of corrupting the unphilosophic multitude, or both, this caution was once almost standard operat-

[8] It is only a hint because Rousseau does not say how much man's conformation must have changed, or how.

ing procedure.[9] The allusion to Aristotle might thus be a way of indicating that Rousseau rejected Christian doctrine. Doing so indirectly, by rejecting a Christianized interpretation of Aristotle, would be consistent with the philosophic traditions of personal prudence and paternalistic reticence.

I doubt that this commonplace form of indirection, or double teaching, is an adequate explanation for the mistaken allusion to Aristotle. There are, moreover, other statements suggesting that the *Discourse* as a whole employs a deeper and more complex rhetorical strategy. Rousseau's clearest reference to a double teaching is at the end of the First Part, where he distinguishes "ordinary Readers" from his "Judges" (*O.C.*, 3:163). Just before beginning the First Part, he had told us who his judges are:

> My subject being of interest to man in general, I will try to take a language that suits all nations; or rather, forgetting times and Places, in order to dream only of the Men to whom I speak, I will suppose that I am in the Lyceum of Athens, repeating the Lessons of my Masters, having Platos and Xenocrateses for Judges and the Human Race for an audience. (ibid., 133)

This passage, far from providing us with an easy distinction between two audiences, suggests that Rousseau is pointing to a deep perplexity. No universally shared language exists, as Rousseau acknowledges by immediately abandoning the hope of using it. But why does he raise the possibility at all? Rousseau points out that a universal language would enable one to speak to every man. Useful as this might be, perhaps more important is what such a language could tell us *about* all men. For a universal language, if we had it by nature, would mark us as a naturally social or political species, just as the natural languages of bees and many other animals do.

Since men are distinguished from the other animals by their possession of speech,[10] and since they are distinguished from one another by the

[9] A modern myth that denies the existence of this practice is thoroughly debunked in Arthur M. Melzer, *Philosophy Between the Lines: The Lost History of Esoteric Writing*. Rousseau previously referred to "the faith that every Christian Philosopher owes to the Writings of Moses," and said that "Religion *orders* us to believe that God himself [drew] Men out of the state of Nature" (*Inequality*, *O.C.*, 3:132, 133, emphasis added). In context, these statements do not imply that Rousseau himself is a Christian philosopher or one whose own thinking takes orders from religious dogma. In this passage, moreover, Rousseau says that Adam and Eve were not in the state of nature, which could help explain why he had said earlier that the state of nature may never have existed (ibid., 132, 123).

[10] I will reserve the term "speech" for compositional language, that is, the peculiarly human form of language in which a limited number of symbols, used according to grammatical rules, enable us to generate an unlimited number of expressions of unlimited complexity.

particular languages they use, human speech itself raises a real question about human nature. Its use is now a distinctive and common attribute of our species, but this fact might obscure the truth about our nature if the differences among the several particular languages are sufficiently fundamental. Our lack of a language that suits all nations is one sign that we do not begin by knowing precisely what man naturally is.

In the second clause of the statement quoted above, Rousseau proposes a way around the difficulty posed by the variety of languages. The proposal consists of a series of bizarre, mutually contradictory impossibilities. If one were truly to forget times and places, what could one say to other men, who always live and think in particular times and places? Would not such forgetfulness merely enslave one to one's own age and culture, or leave one with nothing to say to anyone? As if to acknowledge this, Rousseau puts himself in fourth-century Athens. But why there? And why in the place associated with Aristotle, who did not found his school until after Plato's death? Who are Rousseau's unnamed masters, and why should a Plato be his judge, let alone a Xenocrates? Is Rousseau imagining that he can talk with the dead and be judged by them? And how could anyone be listened to by the *human race*, which is either an abstract idea or a collection of members who cannot be gathered together even in the imagination?

This weird mélange of supposed circumstances might seem to reveal nothing so much as the comical effects that could result from trying to forget times and places, from trying to free oneself from the particular circumstances in which we all have to think and act. And yet, this strange picture of Rousseau's imaginary audience does force us to consider how radical the problem of writing may be. If Rousseau's intention demands a language that is unavailable or an audience that cannot exist, it is not likely that the paradoxes, irregularities, and disorder in the *Discourse* are merely the effects of straightforward political prudence.[11] Two aspects of the passage in question may hint at a path we are invited to follow.

First, Rousseau indicates here, and nowhere else in the *Discourse*, who his appropriate judges would be—Platos and Xenocrateses are the only ones he ever clearly distinguishes from ordinary readers.[12] But everything

[11] Leo Strauss calls attention to this passage in which Platos and Xenocrateses are mentioned, but confines himself to pointing out its anti-Biblical implications (*Natural Right and History*, 267).

[12] A few pages before, Rousseau had seemed to identify his judges with the members of the prize committee at the Academy of Dijon (*O.C.*, 3:131). But that passage is ambiguous, and almost certainly ironic.

we know about Xenocrates is second-hand. Plato's dialogues, moreover, never purport to state Plato's own views about anything, and his writings rival Rousseau's for dazzling paradoxes, charming absurdities, and fascinating inconsistencies. Significantly, however, Rousseau puts his judges' names in the grammatical plural, which suggests that he wants to be judged by readers *like* them, who may exist at other times and places than ancient Greece, or Rousseau's Europe.

Second, Rousseau suggests more generally that the proper context in which to read the *Discourse* is, in some obscure way, Greek philosophy. The book contains other suggestions to the same effect, for example in the epigraph's quotation from Aristotle's *Politics*, and again in Note X, where the names of Plato and two pre-Socratic Greek philosophers are linked with "the common science of the wise" (*O.C.*, 3:213). Why this should be so is left unclear. What is clear is that Rousseau is not appealing to the *authority* of Greek philosophy. In the next paragraph, he indicts all books, including his own:

> O Man, from whatever Country you may be, whatever your opinions may be, listen; here is your history as I believe I have read it, not in the Books of your fellows who are liars, but in Nature which never lies. Everything that will be from her, will be true: Anything false in it will be only what I will have mixed in of my own without wishing to. (ibid., 133)[13]

As we will see, reading the truth in nature is a challenge to which human language is an impediment as well as an indispensable tool. For that reason, a philosophic investigation of language is a necessary part of the philosophic anthropology that we began to examine in the previous chapter. As we will also see, Rousseau regards Greek philosophy and the Greek language as particularly useful points of entry into that investigation.

## Man Alone among the Animals Has Speech

The question that provides the theme for the *Discourse* is itself linked with the problem of language and with Greek philosophy. The *Discourse* was submitted in a 1754 essay contest for responses to this topic: "What the

[13]Years earlier, Rousseau had indicated that he had given considerable thought to the attack on writing in Plato's *Phaedrus* ("Letter to Grimm About the Refutation of [Rousseau's] Discourse [on the Sciences and the Arts] by M. Gautier" (1751), *O.C.*, 3:64). The enormous influence of this passage in the *Phaedrus* is also reflected in his later writings. See, for example, *Emile*, *O.C.*, 4:454, 643, Bloom, 184, 319.

origin of inequality among men is, and whether it is authorized by the natural Law" (ibid., 129). Just as Plato's Socrates frequently invites his interlocutors to confront a deeper question than the one with which they are at first concerned, Rousseau alters the question posed for the contest. The full title of the book substitutes the more general term "foundations" for the reference to the natural law. In the Preface, Rousseau indicates that even this question may presuppose a little too much, "for how will the source of inequality among men be known, if one does not begin by knowing men themselves?" (ibid., 122). Rousseau goes on to mock the unsubstantiated premises of the natural law tradition, and effectively replaces the question posed by the Academy of Dijon with a much more radical question that evokes the original Academy: What is man? (ibid., 124–25).[14]

The Preface dwells on the difficulty of giving a satisfactory answer to the question. Here and throughout the *Discourse*, Rousseau declines to repeat the traditional answer, most famously articulated in Aristotle's *Politics*: man alone among the animals has speech (1253a9–10). Rousseau indicates that he has not forgotten this statement, or the Aristotelian tradition, by choosing a quotation from a nearby passage in the *Politics* for the epigraph to the book. No less important, he subtly indicates that he considers Aristotle's definition correct.

We can see this by considering one of Rousseau's apparently most anti-Aristotelian remarks. In the passage where Rousseau addresses himself to the distinction between man and the other animals, he begins by reminding us of the fact that many animals give clear signs of engaging in mental operations, and concludes: "It is therefore not so much the understanding that provides the specific distinction of man among the animals as it is his quality as a free agent" (*O.C.*, 3:141). Though he says only that the understanding is somehow less significant than freedom, even this much depreciation of intellect seems incompatible with the received view of Aristotle's teaching. But rather than elaborate on the relation between freedom and understanding, Rousseau admits that the claim is open to dispute, and drops this definition in favor of one that rests on a unique human quality that he calls "the faculty of perfecting oneself," which he says is found in

[14] At the beginning of the Preface, Rousseau had called Plato and his Academy to mind by mentioning one of the inscriptions at Delphi and the statue of Glaucus. Compare *Inequality*, *O.C.*, 3:122, with *Phaedrus* 229e and *Republic* 611b–d.

both the individual and the species (ibid., 142).[15] As presented here, this new definition is singularly unilluminating, since it offers little more than an allusion to the undeniable fact that humans have undergone a continuing cultural evolution unmatched in the animal kingdom. But what is the proximate cause of this phenomenon?

A few pages later, in a different context and an almost offhand manner, Rousseau gives the answer:

> [G]eneral ideas can be introduced into the mind only with the aid of words, and the understanding grasps them only through propositions. This is one of the reasons why animals neither know how to form such ideas nor ever acquire the perfectibility that depends on them. (ibid., 149)

Thus, man is distinguished by the faculty of perfectibility, and the exercise of this faculty depends on general ideas, whose use in turn depends on words and propositions: the cause of man's distinctiveness among the animals is the acquisition of speech or compositional language. It is therefore true, as Aristotle says, that man alone among the animals has speech, and it is true, as Aristotle implies, that this is man's most important distinguishing characteristic.

Why should Rousseau obscure his agreement with Aristotle on this fundamental point? It must be that he considers the traditional definition of man misleading despite its correctness. First, it might suggest false explanations for the cause of man's possessing speech. Second, it might lead us to draw false implications from the fact that human speech everywhere exists. In addition, the traditional understanding of Aristotle's statement that "man alone among the animals has speech" (1253a9–10) may have carried too many connotations associated with reason, argument, and cal-

[15] Rousseau's use of the term "faculty" does not imply that he accepted traditional teleological assumptions about human nature. Responding to a critic of the *Discourse on Inequality*, he vividly elaborated his own view:

> [A]ccording to me society is natural to the human species as decrepitude is to the individual, and arts, Laws, Governments are necessary to Peoples as crutches are to the elderly. The whole difference is that the state of old age follows solely from the nature of man and that the state of society follows from the nature of the human race, not immediately as you say, but solely, as I have proved, with the help of certain external circumstances which could have existed or not existed, or could at least have arisen sooner or later, and consequently accelerated or retarded the progression. (*Letter to Philopolis*, *O.C.*, 3:232)

culation. When we turn to the *Essay on the Origin of Languages*, we will see why Rousseau would wish to avoid such connotations.[16]

The first of these objections would relate to issues raised in philosophic anthropology and the second to issues raised in ethics and politics. At first glance, Rousseau looks resolutely anti-Aristotelian on both questions. He says, for example, that "although the organ of speech may be natural to man, speech itself is nonetheless not natural to him" (*Inequality*, Note X, *O.C.*, 3:210). And whereas Aristotle asserts that man is by nature a political animal (1253a2–3), Rousseau emphasizes again and again "how little care Nature has taken to bring men together through mutual needs, and to facilitate their use of speech, how little she has prepared their Sociability, and how little of her own she has put into all that they have done to establish the bonds of Sociability" (*Inequality*, *O.C.*, 3:151).

The disagreement between Rousseau and Aristotle is smaller than it seems to be, if it exists at all. Near the beginning of the *Politics*, Aristotle argues that the first two communities—male and female, master and slave—came together from the biological needs for self-preservation and reproduction (1252a24–34). Households formed out of these two communities spawned villages "by nature" when the biological descendants of the original households became sufficiently numerous (1252b15–22). When enough villages, or what we might call extended families, came together to allow for self-sufficiency, there could be a city which, "though it comes into being for the sake of living, exists for the sake of living well" (1252b29–30).

[16]The word Aristotle uses here for speech, *logos*, has a broad range of possible meanings. It can refer to something as simple as a word or utterance, or to something as complex as Homer's *Iliad* or Plato's *Timaeus*. Rousseau probably read the *Politics* in Latin (which has no close equivalent to *logos*), presumably using a translation from which the epigraph to the *Discourse* was drawn. Unfortunately, I have not been able to find any edition in which that passage matches the translation in Rousseau's epigraph. Nor, I should add, does the epigraph match the translation given by Grotius in *De Jure Belli ac Pacis*. Cf. *Diskurs über die Ungleichheit/Discours sur l'inégalité*, ed. Heinrich Meier, 6n4 (noting that Grotius had quoted the same passage from Aristotle).

The first Latin translation of the *Politics*, by William of Moerbeke, renders *logos* in the statement at 1253a9–10 as *ratio*, which has the narrow focus on calculation and rationality that Rousseau would have wanted to avoid. This is the translation on which Thomas Aquinas relied, and it must have had enormous influence on the Scholastic tradition. Several later translations render *logos* in this statement as *sermo* or *oratio*, both of which refer primarily to ordinary speech. In any event, Rousseau effectively avoids associating himself with the kind of Aristotelianism that defines man as "the rational animal," while indicating that he agrees with what Aristotle actually says, namely that man alone among the animals has speech.

Aristotle famously says that this implies that "every city exists by nature" (1252b30). Less famous is the comment that immediately follows this assertion: "if indeed the first communities also do [exist by nature]."[17] Until this point in the *Politics*, the only reason we have been given for supposing that the earlier communities existed "by nature" is that they resulted from the natural drives for self-preservation and procreation. One might wonder, as Rousseau certainly does, whether slavery was indeed among the earliest results of the indisputably natural drive for self-preservation.[18] Rather than address that question, Aristotle introduces a very different notion of naturalness, saying: "For the city is the end (*telos*) of those [earlier] communities and nature is an end; what each thing's nature is when its coming into being is at its end is, we say, its nature, such as a human being, a horse, or a household" (1252b31–34).[19]

The reference to a household alerts us to what Aristotle soon makes explicit.[20] Cities are not generated by nature in the same way that a human being or a horse is. Rather, a city must be deliberately put together (1253a30–31).[21] Those who have done this *might*, at least in some cases, have been aiming at what Aristotle identifies as the benefits of a city: "law and right" as well as "prudence and virtue" (1253a31–35). But he care-

[17] *Eiper*, which I have translated as "if indeed," could also be taken to mean "if, as is the case."

[18] Aristotle's account of natural slavery at 1252a31–34 depends on the assumption that the relationship is beneficial for both parties. The only obvious and commonplace example of such a natural relationship is that of parent and child, an example that Rousseau acknowledges when he explains why the family is the only natural society (*S.C.*, bk. 1, chap. 2). Rousseau could also point out that Aristotle describes the first community arising from the natural urge to reproduce only as a "coupling" like the ones we observe in other animals, and even in plants (1252a26–30). Aristotle's account of natural slavery thus does not necessarily contradict Rousseau's claim in the *Discourse on Inequality* that the community of mother and child is the most natural society and the only one that strictly and indisputably arises by nature.

[19] The qualifier "we say" (*phamen*) in this sentence suggests that Aristotle may be articulating a widely held view that he does not himself necessarily share.

[20] The primary meaning of the word used here for "household" (*oikia*) refers to a physical dwelling. Because Aristotle had earlier used the word in a context that clearly meant "household," see 1252b10, that is presumably the way he is using it here. But the word can remind us that just as most houses are artificial, households come into being somewhat differently than human beings and horses do.

[21] Aristotle reminds us that extended families or villages can easily grow into tribes and nations bound together by kinship, without becoming cities (1252b19–22). This was obviously the most common—and most obviously natural—path of development.

fully refrains from asserting that these are the ends or purposes of the founders of cities. And he almost implies that they are not when he says that a city comes into being for the sake of living rather than for the sake of living well.

What exactly it would mean to say that law, right, prudence, and virtue are *nature's* end is left quite unclear. Aristotle never explains why one should think that a city has a natural end or *telos* in the same sense that a human being, a horse, or even a household does. The fact that nature permits us to reap benefits from living in cities does not imply that cities exist "by nature." If it did, one could almost as easily say that Sea World exists by nature if dolphins live longer and more easily when they are protected from predators and cared for by veterinarians. By blurring the distinction between nature and art or convention in this passage, Aristotle raises more questions than he answers.

It is in this context that Aristotle says: "It is clear, then, that a human being is more of a political animal than any bee or any herd animal. For nature, as we say, makes nothing in vain, and man alone among the animals has speech" (1253a7–10).[22] Aristotle is quite ambiguous as to whether speech is natural in the way that humans and horses, or even households and villages, are natural. Human beings, moreover, are said to be unique in possessing speech, though not in being political.[23] Only if speech is natural in the same way that the social behavior of other "political animals" is natural would it seem to follow that every city exists by nature in the same sense that the "first communities" can plausibly be thought to have existed by nature. But Aristotle does not establish, or even assert, this crucial and questionable premise.[24]

Aristotle could not have been unaware of this omission, which serves as a quiet invitation to consider the very claim that Rousseau articulates in

[22] Once again, the qualifier "as we say" (*hōs phamen*) suggests that Aristotle may be articulating a commonly held belief about nature rather than confidently asserting the proposition himself.

[23] In the *History of Animals*, as well, Aristotle gives several examples of political animals: human beings, bees, wasps, ants, and cranes (488a7–11).

[24] Aristotle does, of course, point out that the nature of animals allows them to express through their voices what is pleasant and painful, whereas human speech reveals what is advantageous and harmful, and that human beings therefore perceive such things as good and bad, just and unjust (1253a10–18). This passage, however, does not say that the peculiarly human phenomenon of speech, which is beyond the natural capacity of other animals, itself arises by nature.

opposition to the Aristotelian tradition: that speech is not natural in the way the organs of speech are natural, and that the political bonds that men have established among themselves have much less of nature in them than is commonly supposed. Rousseau, for his part, effectively invites us to consider whether his challenge to the great tradition associated with Aristotle is necessarily also a challenge to Aristotle's genuine teaching.

As we have seen, Aristotle and Rousseau agree that man is an animal, and that man alone among the animals possesses speech. Aristotle also endorses the central methodological premise of Rousseau's *Discourse* when he says: "If one were to look at how the things that concern us (*ta pragmata*) develop from the beginning, one would in this as in other cases investigate them in the finest way" (1252a24–26). Aristotle makes no effort to trace the origins and development of speech, but neither does he assert that our kind has always had it. Rousseau confidently argues that we have not always had it, and suggests that it is almost impossibly difficult to understand how we could have gotten it. Thus, Rousseau brings to light what Aristotle leaves us to infer: the proposition that "every city exists by nature" is based on a teleological understanding of nature for which Aristotle does not actually provide an argument. By the way he treats Aristotle in the *Discourse*, Rousseau rejects the view of human nature traditionally attributed to Aristotle while leaving us to wonder whether Aristotle himself shared that view.

## Modern Science and Natural Sociality

Rousseau's claim that human sociality is an acquired characteristic is presented most vividly in his picture of the pure state of nature populated by speechless animals roaming in the forest. It is perfectly possible for large and highly intelligent primates to lead independent and largely solitary lives in the kind of rain forests where our distant ancestors lived. Orangutans, a species about which scientists have only recently begun to acquire detailed information, offer conclusive evidence for this proposition. The following brief summary is based primarily on fieldwork reported in Biruté M.F. Galdikas, *Reflections of Eden: My Years with the Orangutans of Borneo*, and Carel van Schaik, *Among Orangutans: Red Apes and the Rise of Human Culture*.

On average, wild orangutans give birth once every eight years, and the offspring are weaned only when the mother becomes pregnant again. The mother-child relationship is extremely close and intense. Fathers have no role beyond insemination, and offspring may remain with their mothers for several years after the arrival of a sibling (with daughters remaining longer than sons). The animals go through a playful and gregarious phase during the period between infancy and adulthood.

In most environments, orangutans spend almost all of their adult lives foraging alone. Their primary interests are food and sex, and they display a high degree of intelligence, comparable to that of chimpanzees and perhaps greater. Tool use is common, and it differs from place to place, suggesting cultural transmission.[25] Adult females usually have overlapping ranges (typically near their place of birth) and long-lasting dominance relationships, and they sometimes form transitory foraging parties. Males become much larger and stronger than females, and they are substantially more nomadic.

Both sexes compete for desirable mates—males by displays of virility and sometimes by fighting, females by resisting unwanted suitors (frequently without success) and by seductions (also frequently unsuccessful) of attractive males. Orangutans ordinarily mate in a face-to-face position. Dominant males have a distinctive appearance and a distinctive call, and will not tolerate the presence of another male that has these characteristics. Some males appear to delay the development of these secondary sex characteristics (though not the ability or desire to copulate) while living near an established dominant.

Individual orangutans exhibit significant variation in natural aptitude and personality type. Where population density is high (as in especially food-rich forests), the animals have more social interaction.[26] In captivity, they readily form complex social relationships, not only with other orangutans but with humans as well. Indigenous people tell stories of male orangutans abducting human females, and there has been at least one documented case of a semi-wild orangutan forcibly copulating with a woman.[27] One female orangutan at a rehabilitation center effectively

[25] A large study of genetic, environmental, and behavioral variation among distinct populations of orangutans has provided evidence that cultural differences explain much of the behavioral variation (Michael Krützen, et al., "Culture and Geographic Variation in Orangutan Behavior").

[26] See, for example, Carel P. van Schaik, "The Costs and Benefits of Flexibility as an Expression of Behavioural Plasticity: A Primate Perspective."

[27] Similarly, a male researcher reports that a female orangutan sought to have intercourse with him. When her advances were rejected, she refused to cooperate any further in his research (Thomas Suddendorf, *The Gap: The Science of What Separates Us from Other Animals*, 25).

became bicultural, acquiring a substantial sign-language vocabulary, living for extended periods in the wild, and acting as a kind of self-appointed ambassador between humans and orangutans.

The lives of wild orangutans thus bear more than a passing resemblance to that of man in Rousseau's pure state of nature, and their nature appears to include a significant element of what Rousseau calls "perfectibility" (see *Inequality*, *O.C.*, 3:142). The line of descent leading to orangutans apparently split off from the line that led to human beings earlier than the line that led to chimpanzees and gorillas.[28] It is arresting, and perhaps significant, that the social structures of three extant great apes correspond quite closely to the three main stages of human social evolution that Rousseau attributes to the state of nature. Orangutans live much like man in Rousseau's pure state of nature; gorillas generally live in patriarchal family bands, much as Rousseau imagines man must have lived after the "first revolution"; and chimpanzees are cooperative and contentious hunter-gatherers, like the people in Rousseau's "nascent society." At the very least, this suggests that our fundamental ape nature lent itself to all these possibilities, even if it is someday established that none of our actual ancestors lived like orangutans or gorillas.[29]

Of course, just as it is possible that our pre-human ancestors once lived solitary lives, so is it possible that the ancestors of modern orangutans were more social, and that these animals later became more solitary as part of an adaptation to new or changed environments.[30] Like many human hunter-gatherers, all great apes exhibit varying degrees of "fission-fusion

[28] See Klein, *Human Career*, 94–96, and compare Rousseau's discussion of the inadequacy of the reports available to him about great apes in the *Discourse on Inequality* (Note X, *O.C.*, 3:208–14).

[29] The bonobos suggest yet another possibility. These highly social apes maintain unusually peaceful relations within groups and even between neighboring groups. This peacefulness is facilitated by frequent non-reproductive sexual contact. The variety of these contacts rivals or exceeds that in humans, involving individuals of all ages in almost every possible combination and position. The only "taboo" appears to be that mothers do not have sexual contact with their adult sons. Females develop stronger friendships with one another than males do with other males, and bonobo society appears to verge on matriarchy. See generally Takayoshi Kano, *The Last Ape: Pygmy Chimpanzee Behavior and Ecology*; Frans de Waal and Frans Lanting, *Bonobo: The Forgotten Ape*. There is no reason to think that any of our distant ancestors ever lived this way. Nor has human cultural evolution led to this way of life, at least not yet.

[30] See Robin I.M. Dunbar, "Brains on Two Legs: Group Size and the Evolution of Intelligence," 270n4.

sociality," in which groups wax and wane in size, often when resources become more scarce or abundant. Thus, based on what scientists currently know about other primates, it apparently would have been possible for human cultural evolution to proceed very much as Rousseau imagined, even if fortuitous causes in fact produced a somewhat different path of development.

But does modern science ultimately support Rousseau? Roger D. Masters advances the following criticism of Rousseau: "[H]umans are innately social animals whose psychology and politics are more clearly understood by the ancient tradition of Plato and Aristotle than by modern political philosophy."[31] The crucial thesis underlying this conclusion is that Rousseau's "explanation of amour propre has been ***demolished*** by primatological observation, neuroscientific research, and psychological experimentation" ("Rediscovery," 133, emphasis added). Masters' claim is sweeping, categorical, and final. It is also mistaken, for it is based on misunderstandings of both Rousseau and modern science.

As Masters notes, Rousseau understands amour-propre as "social comparison leading to competition for dominance" (ibid., 117). Masters is also right that Rousseau sees this passion as one that is primarily artificial. Its natural basis, according to Rousseau, is the love of oneself (*amour de soi* or *amour de soi-même*), an instinct that prompts every animal to pursue its own preservation. This genuinely innate passion prompts us to seek our own preservation and welfare, but it does not necessarily produce amour-propre. Life in society turns this natural instinct in the direction of competition for social dominance, but that modification does not take place by nature, at least not in the sense that puberty and senescence do. Masters maintains, contrary to Rousseau, that amour-propre is an "innate characteristic" of human beings (ibid.). This claim is based on a misinterpretation of the findings of modern science.

In order to see why Masters misinterprets the scientific evidence, one must first summarize Rousseau's account of amour-propre more precisely than Masters does. The transformation of *amour de soi* into amour-propre is only one effect of a more general distinguishing characteristic of human beings. That trait, which Rousseau calls "perfectibility," is indeed natural

[31] "Rousseau and the Rediscovery of Human Nature," 111. See also ibid., 135: "Ultimately, consideration of Rousseau's scientific legacy has the paradoxical effect of suggesting a return to the ancient naturalism of Plato and Aristotle in preference to modern theories of human nature."

or "innate." It is a capacity or ability to acquire certain characteristics, including amour-propre, that are not innate in the way that *amour de soi* is.

Rousseau's understanding of perfectibility can accommodate a wide range of possible courses for human evolution. He suggests in the *Discourse on Inequality* that we may have evolved from a non-human ancestral species, and the *Essay on the Origin of Languages* indicates that physical evolution must have altered even our indisputably human ancestors (*Inequality*, *O.C.*, 3:134; *Essay*, chap. 10, *O.C.*, 5:407). The pure state of nature "may never have existed," at least in quite the way it is described in the *Discourse on Inequality*,[32] and Rousseau very emphatically says that the road to our present state, from whatever our original condition precisely was, may have been different than he has imagined it (*Inequality*, O.C., 3:122, 162–63). What is crucial in Rousseau's account is that our biological nature did not determine the path that our cultural evolution took. That evolution was certainly constrained within bounds set by our physical nature, but environmental factors and other accidental influences must have determined exactly how cultural evolution proceeded.

No one could dispute the fact that we have the natural or biological capacity to live as social animals, and Rousseau affirmatively accepts that we do. "[I]f, as one cannot doubt, man is a sociable animal by his nature or at least made to become so, he can be so only through other inner sentiments [i.e., other than love of oneself, fear of pain and of death, and the desire for well-being] relative to his species."[33] Accordingly, Rousseau can even call amour-propre "the first and the most natural" of all the passions if the term is understood to mean self-love in itself and relative only to ourselves, or *amour de soi* as he usually uses that term.[34] But it does not follow that our kind, or an ancestral species from which we descended, always did live as social animals, let alone that we are "innately social animals" in a biologically necessitated sense. The important question, seldom asked let alone answered, is how we can distinguish what is strictly natural,

[32] The *Essay on the Origin of Languages* offers an account of human evolution that largely parallels the account in the *Discourse*, but it begins with isolated family groups rather than with isolated individuals. This suggests that the factual accuracy of Rousseau's depiction of nearly perfect isolation in the hypothesized pure state of nature is not crucial to his account of human nature.

[33] *Moral Letters*, lett. 5, *O.C.*, 4:1109. Rousseau later put this same statement into the mouth of the Savoyard Vicar (*Emile*, *O.C.*, 4:600, Bloom, 290).

[34] *Emile*, *O.C.*, 4:488, 322, Bloom, 208, 92.

or determined by our biological nature, from what is artificial, or the effect of social life and cultural evolution.

Stated most succinctly, Rousseau's conclusion is that we have a strong biological instinct for self-preservation and for procuring our own welfare, along with a weaker natural passion he calls pity or commiseration, which would largely have remained dormant until activated by the imagination in social interactions. Amour-propre is certainly natural in the sense that we have the biological capacity to experience it, and in the sense that it is a modification of its strictly natural root, *amour de soi*.[35] In society, it quickly and inevitably triggers cooperation and competition, and it would be foolish to think that anything else could happen.[36]

Unlike the bare instinct for self-preservation, however, amour-propre as we observe it is unnatural in the sense that it requires social relations for its development, and those relations are not biologically determined. We are not innately social for the same reason that we are not innately virtuous. Living in society is a necessary condition for the transformation of *amour de soi* into a social passion. Similarly, the social virtues cultivated in society are ultimately rooted in natural pity (*Inequality*, Note XV, *O.C.*, 3:219–20), but they are not natural in the sense that primitive or instinctual pity is.

Masters rests his claim that we are "innately social animals" on several areas of contemporary research. The research he cites does not "demolish" Rousseau's argument, and it does not prove the validity of the position that Masters attributes to Plato and Aristotle.

First, observations of orangutans support Rousseau's contention that an intelligent ape can live much as Rousseau imagined that our ancestors did in the pure state of nature. Masters dismisses this evidence on the ground that "[o]ur earliest ancestors were forced to adapt to a savanna habitat that would have precluded asocial foraging like that among the orangutans (who live in a forest environment of abundant food and few predators)" ("Rediscovery," 127). This argument arbitrarily designates our "earliest" ancestors as those who lived in environments where survival would have required social life. But such an arbitrary designation begs the

[35] See ibid., 491, Bloom, 212–13. In this passage, Rousseau implicitly acknowledges that some modifications of *amour de soi* can occur without the influence of social interactions. The two most obvious examples of such passions are natural pity (which extends to sensitive beings generally and is therefore not a social passion) and bare sexual desire.

[36] See, for example, ibid., 490–524, Bloom, 212–236.

question. Modern science has no direct evidence at all about the way of life followed by our earliest human ancestors, and the unconfirmed speculations of some modern scientists are not an adequate substitute for such evidence.[37]

Second, even if it were proved that our kind has been living for a very long time in environments where cooperation was necessary for survival, that would only confirm what nobody could possibly deny: human beings have the biological capacity to cooperate with one another. It would not imply that we are "innately social animals" in the sense that we are biologically prompted to live in societies, as some animals (such as bees and other social animals mentioned by Aristotle) seem to be.

Third, neuroscientific research and psychological experiments have certainly enriched our understanding of the ways in which our brains *enable* us to participate in very complex forms of social life.[38] But the fact that we have this natural capacity has never been denied by Rousseau or anyone else, and it is a capacity that we share even with orangutans. Some of the research on brains may undermine Rousseau's view of the relation between the body and the mind or soul as he set them out in some of his writings.[39] Or maybe not. Rousseau's understanding of the human soul is never presented in the tidy package suggested by Masters, namely as an essentially Lockean psychology that may have been modified by "personal theological beliefs [that led Rousseau] to a preference for a dualist view of

[37] Masters purports to acknowledge that this is so, but nonetheless chooses to embrace unconfirmed speculations advanced by certain modern scientists ("Rediscovery," 127–28).

[38] Masters' discussion of this body of research is quite thin. See ibid., 116–20. Leaving aside certain suggestions that Masters himself admits are speculative and controversial, his principal evidence is that "[h]appiness and reassurance are social cues that correspond to preprogrammed perceptual and motor responses in the human infant" (ibid., 120). He then leaps to the conclusion that the human central nervous system should be called a "social brain." Rousseau, however, never denied that there is a biologically determined social relationship between mothers and their offspring, which is all that this evidence about infant behavior actually establishes. Nor did Rousseau ever deny that we have innate biological characteristics, which modern science has now more precisely identified in the structure of the brain, that enable us to have more complex social relationships than mothers have with their infant offspring. Rousseau, moreover, affirmatively maintained that environmental factors have caused physical changes to take place in our species (*Essay*, chap. 10, *O.C.*, 5:407). His account of human evolution can accommodate the possibility that the human brain has been altered through natural selection in response to changes in the social environment, such as increases in the size of human social groups. That possibility, however, falls far short of showing that we are innately social in the way that many other animals are.

[39] See Masters, "Rediscovery," 115, 118 (citing *Dialogues* and *Emile*, respectively).

the mind" ("Rediscovery," 117–18). Before deciding whether Rousseau's psychology has been overthrown by modern neuroscience, one would have to establish exactly and precisely what is essential to that psychology. Masters has not done so.[40]

The principal arguments in the *Discourse* and the *Essay* do not depend on assumptions that have been falsified by modern science.[41] It is therefore not the case that provably false assumptions are the "foundation" of Rousseau's understanding of the social passions (see "Rediscovery," 118). When Masters implies that the human brain is a "social organ" in the sense that it makes us social animals in the way that some other species are (ibid., 120), he once again begs the question.

Two examples may help to clarify how Masters goes wrong. First, he says that amour-propre "is an *innate characteristic* of the monkeys and apes who provide evidence of our animal origins" (ibid., 117, emphasis added). This is a logical error. Humans, like some other primates, obviously have an innate *ability* to experience amour-propre. It does not follow that amour-propre is an innate *characteristic* of humans, unless one conflates what is natural with what is conventional or artificial. Human beings have the ability to wear clothing, and they want to do so when the climate or social custom discourages nudity, which is almost always. It does not follow that a desire to be clothed is an innate characteristic of human beings.

Second, a series of experiments indicated that young American children tend to show a preference for pictures of the African savannah over pictures of deciduous forests, coniferous forests, tropical rainforests, and deserts; the preferences of older children and adults shift toward pictures of land-

[40] Characterizing Rousseau's psychology as essentially Lockean is extremely dubious. See, for example, Terence Marshall, "Epistemology and Political Perception in the Case of Rousseau." Masters infers Rousseau's personal theological beliefs from statements attributed to a fictional Savoyard Vicar in the *Emile* ("Rediscovery," 118 & n20), which Rousseau expressly declined to endorse.

[41] Perhaps science will someday uncover evidence that would cast serious doubt on Rousseau's account. If, for example, we learned that humans are directly descended from a species that instinctively lived in political societies resembling those of the chimpanzees, one could plausibly argue that we are naturally social or political animals in a way that orangutans and gorillas are not. Such evidence might not be conclusive, given how extraordinarily adaptable human beings manifestly are, but it would at least suggest that we are instinctively political. No evidence of this kind has yet been discovered.

scapes that are more familiar to them.[42] This suggests an innate preference that we have inherited from our distant ancestors, but it does not suggest that we are innately African savannah dwellers. On the contrary, these experiments tend to confirm Rousseau's claim that innate "perfectibility," or a very high degree of adaptability, is the crucially distinguishing natural characteristic of our species.

Finally, Masters maintains that modern science suggests that we should return to the "ancient naturalism" of Plato and Aristotle (ibid., 135). Masters does not explain exactly what this "ancient naturalism" is, though the context suggests a strong form of natural teleology as an account of politics. As my discussion of Aristotle earlier in this chapter indicates, this widely held interpretation is by no means obviously correct. Masters' "innately social" interpretation of "ancient naturalism" apparently rests on the claim that Aristotle views man as "*the* political animal," and that Aristotle's biology points to an understanding of humans as "the *zoön politikon*" (ibid., 112, emphasis added, 135–36). But this is not what Aristotle said. In fact, Aristotle treats man as one of *several* political animals (*Politics* 1253a7–10; *History of Animals* 488a7–11). It is true that Aristotle says in the *Politics* (though not in the *History of Animals*) that human beings are *more* political than bees or herd animals. But it is also true that these animals are *more* obviously "innately social" than we are. Aristotle's statements thus implicitly raise, without resolving, difficult questions about the contributions that nature, convention, and art, respectively, have made to the distinction that undoubtedly exists between man and all other extant animals. The challenging questions raised by Aristotle's cryptic dicta are not adequately resolved by assuming that he (let alone Plato) believed what Masters mistakenly thinks that modern science has proved.

## The Structure of the *Essay on the Origin of Languages*

The discussion of the origin of language in the *Discourse* occurs within a larger argument aimed at showing that our ancestors once lived in a purely animal condition. The discussion can be summarized as follows: Languages would not have been invented until they became useful, and they could not have been useful before people had close social relations

[42] John D. Balling and John H. Falk, "Development of Visual Preference for Natural Environments."

with a sufficiently large number of other people. Assuming such relations, speech as we know it presupposes general ideas that could not have been grasped by beings who lacked language. Accordingly, the earliest form of communication must have been nothing more than the cry of nature, namely instinctive and inarticulate appeals for assistance at moments of danger or discomfort, which we see even in the youngest children. The first signals must have been gestures and onomatopoeic sounds, and the first nouns must have been names for specific, physical objects. More general names could not have been adopted until people developed a new ability to conceptualize things that cannot be imagined, such as "nut" or "tree." Whatever these first general names may have been, they must have been overly general because the inventors could not have understood all of the significant differences among the kinds of beings, let alone such abstract concepts as matter and motion.

In this discussion, Rousseau treats the invention of general names as the crucial and apparently unexplainable step in the invention of conventional languages. He then asks his "Judges"—that is, whatever Platos and Xenocrateses there may be in his imaginary Lyceum—to stop reading and consider how far our own languages fall short in serving their most obvious purpose, namely "to express all of men's thoughts, to take on a stable form capable of being spoken in public and of having an influence on Society" (*Inequality*, *O.C.*, 3:151). He then asks these "Judges" to reflect on how much time and knowledge would be required "to discover numbers (XIV.*), abstract words, Aorists, and all the tenses of Verbs, particles, Syntax, to connect Propositions, reasonings, and to formulate the entire Logic of Discourse" (ibid.). The aorist is a grammatical aspect that occurs in only one language that would have been familiar to educated readers in eighteenth-century Europe, namely Greek. Note XIV praises Plato for mocking those who believed that numbers were invented during the siege of Troy, but also argues that the most primitive people would not have had sufficient philosophy to count the fingers on their hands.[43]

Rousseau concludes by suggesting that it may be impossible to explain the origin of languages, and poses a question for someone else to discuss:

[43] Rousseau had seen reports of such people (*Emile*, *O.C.*, 4:572n, Bloom, 271n). There have indeed been peoples who relied on concepts like "one, two, several, many," presumably because they got along just fine without a more advanced mathematics. See, for example, Darwin, *Descent of Man*, chap. 2, 1:23; *A General Collection of Voyages and Travels*, ed. John Pinkerton, 16:35; Franz Boas, *The Mind of Primitive Man*, 197–98.

"which was more necessary, Society already bound together for the institution of Languages, or Languages already invented for the establishment of Society?" (ibid., 151).

Rousseau pursues this question at more length in his *Essay on the Origin of Languages*, where we find additional reasons for considering the central significance of names and naming, and to consider what Plato wrote about them.[44]

Rather surprisingly, the *Essay* gives a brief and straightforward answer to the question that the *Discourse* posed as a baffling puzzle: "The earth nourishes men, but when the first needs have dispersed them, other needs reunite them, and it is then that they speak and that they make themselves spoken of ... [I]n striving to make oneself understood, one learns to explain oneself" (*Essay*, chap. 9, *O.C.*, 5:401, 406).

In another striking contrast with the *Discourse*, the *Essay* opens in the most Aristotelian way possible: "Speech distinguishes man among the animals" (ibid., chap. 1, 375). The first chapter ends in an equally traditional way: Rousseau distinguishes the "natural languages" of animals from "conventional languages" that depend on a "faculty specific to man" (ibid., 379). This faculty, however, corresponds to what is called "perfectibility" in the *Discourse*, and the *Essay* proposes a novel account of the origin and evolution of speech, which parallels the evolution of other social institutions in the *Discourse*.

The first eleven chapters of the *Essay* deal with the origin and development of languages. The next eight chapters are about music and its moral power. The concluding chapter is about the relation between languages and government. The first section of the book distinguishes two general elements in human speech—a rational element originally associated with physical need, and an emotional or passionate element associated with music. Rousseau tries to show that improvement over time in the rational dimension of speech would be accompanied by a diminution of its musical qualities. The second section argues that what we call music is this moral or passionate element of speech displaced from its original context. Rousseau argues that this displacement entails some corruption of speech, while music is a kind of asylum that is threatened by rationalistic tenden-

[44] The *Essay* probably began as a projected Note for the *Discourse on Inequality*. See Draft Preface, *O.C.*, 3:373; Pierre-Maurice Masson, "Questions de Chronologie Rousseauiste," 45–49. Although Rousseau never published the essay, it is a completed work that he expected to include in a collection of his writings (*Emile*, *O.C.*, 4:672n, Bloom, 340n).

cies in certain modern theories of music.[45] The final chapter draws the conclusion that the deterioration of the passionate or moral qualities of speech leads languages to become progressively less effective in supporting political life.

Rousseau claims that he has new insights that may require a wholly new way of thinking about the origin of languages. The two key insights are a distinction between human needs and passions as contributors to the formation of language, and attention to the interaction between needs and passions on the one hand and the physical environment on the other. As in the *Discourse*, he takes into consideration the relevant scientific literature that was available to him, but always with a critical eye.

## Primitive Language and Plato's *Cratylus*

The problem that Rousseau sets out to solve is formulated in the first paragraph of the *Essay*:

> Speech distinguishes man among the animals: language distinguishes nations from each other; one knows where a man is from only after he has spoken. Usage and need make everyone learn the language of his country; but what makes this the language of his country and not of another? In order to tell, one has to go back to some reason which is in the locale and which is anterior to *mœurs* themselves: speech being the first social institution, it owes its form solely to natural causes. (*O.C.*, 5:375)[46]

The first four chapters of the *Essay* begin to address this question, but they conclude by sending us back to Plato.

Nature gives us two principal ways of communicating: gesture and voice. Of the two, gesture is the more natural way to communicate ideas. Indeed, gesture is so well suited to this task that sign languages have been devised as substitutes for spoken speech. Rousseau goes so far as to say that if we had had only physical needs, we might have "instituted laws, chosen chiefs, invented arts, established commerce and in a word done almost as

[45] The principal target of this critique was Rameau (Downing A. Thomas, *Music and the Origins of Language*, 91–97). Rousseau, who was a successful composer and sophisticated musical theorist, would undoubtedly feel more than vindicated if he could return to hear some of the intellectually sophisticated atonal music composed during our own age.

[46] The word *mœurs* refers to customs or habits that have some kind of ethical or moral quality or effects.

many things as we are doing with the assistance of speech" (ibid., 378). Or, to put it differently, if all we ever wanted was to arrange mutually beneficial transactions with other people, a conventional language consisting solely of visible signs would probably be sufficient. Today, for example, we conduct much of our business through written communications, and one can imagine a race of deaf-mutes developing a similarly serviceable language. In any case, whatever may have prompted the first communicative gestures, Rousseau is confident that the first voiced utterances were dictated by the passions, and that these utterances were the primitive basis of what became human speech.

The trigger for the origin of languages must have been "moral needs, passions" (ibid., chap. 2, 380). Everyone can silently satisfy the physical needs to eat, drink, and rest. But to persuade someone to do what you want before a conventional language has developed, "nature dictates accents [i.e., modulations of pitch or tone], cries, plaints: here are the oldest invented words, and here is why languages were lilting (*chantantes*) and passionate before being plain and methodical" (ibid., 380–81). Rousseau warns that this formulation will need to be qualified later, but he insists that the form of the most primitive languages would have reflected the effects of the passions. "[M]ost root words would be imitative sounds, either the accent of the passions, or of the effect of sensible objects [i.e., passions in a most literal sense]: onomatopoeia would be felt in them constantly" (ibid., chap. 4, 383). He concludes the discussion with the following enigmatic remark: "Extend these ideas in all their ramifications, and you will find that Plato's *Cratylus* is not as ridiculous as it appears to be" (ibid.).

Unpacking the meaning of this provocative comment turns out to be no small challenge. The *Cratylus* is among the most obviously comical of the dialogues, and we are always obliged to assume that something serious underlies the ridiculous suggestions that we encounter in Plato. In the following discussion, I will look for what Rousseau may have seen below the surface.

The dialogue begins abruptly, with Hermogenes asking Cratylus whether they should invite Socrates to join their discussion about the correctness of names.[47] Hermogenes takes the common sense position that

[47] Hermogenes frequently associated with Socrates. See Plato, *Phaedo* 59b6–10; Xenophon, *Apology of Socrates to the Jury*; Xenophon, *Symposium*; Xenophon, *Memorabilia* 2.10. Socrates does not appear to have exercised any significant influence on Cratylus.

names are assigned to things entirely by custom or convention. Cratylus maintains that each thing has a naturally correct name, and that using any other word results only in meaningless noise. Hermogenes has been frustrated by Cratylus' refusal to explain how one can distinguish a correct name from noise. At considerable length, Socrates engages Hermogenes in an effort to provide the explanation that Cratylus will not or cannot articulate. The bulk of this colloquy has Socrates proposing etymologies supposedly meant to show that many names we use are modified imitations or descriptions of the things they name.

During this portion of the dialogue, Socrates repeatedly indicates that he is well aware of the ridiculous nature of his proposals. Hermogenes, too, seems to be in on the joke, at least to some extent. And a reader of the dialogue would have to be asleep to miss it. Rather than offend my own readers by explaining jokes, I will just point out one example. Well into the discussion of etymologies, Hermogenes asks why the name for names, the very subject of their conversation, has this name. Socrates responds that "name" (*onoma*) seems to be a highly compressed derivative of a phrase saying "this is a being for which there is a search" (*tout' estin on, hou tuchanei zētēma*). That is so implausible on its face that Socrates has to claim that one can see the etymology more clearly if one thinks about *omaston* ("the thing named"), which clearly says: *on hou masma estin* ("the being for which there is a search") (421a7–b1).

By the end of the dialogue, the etymologies appear to be elements in a kind of *argumentum ad absurdum*. In a very simplified form, the argument runs as follows. If all genuine names are natural or correct, they must have been established by an authority who chose them because they correctly described or imitated the nature or being of the thing named. But we know that the same things often had different names in the past. One must, therefore, seek the hidden meaning of the names we use. Such an investigation, however, turns out to be fruitless because one can concoct different and even contradictory hypothetical etymologies. Or, to put it differently, the plausibility of the concocted etymologies depends on the assumption that the investigator knows the nature or being of the things named, and on the further assumption that the original authoritative namegivers possessed and used the same knowledge. These premises assume the conclusion. At the end of the dialogue, Cratylus is unable to deny that one must try to learn about beings in some other way than through their names.

That proposition, however, had never been denied by Cratylus. What is more, Socrates never purports to establish the truth of the position originally maintained by Hermogenes. If some names appear, as far as we can tell, to be entirely arbitrary or conventional, many others do not. Obvious examples, which Socrates hints at in a discussion of the naturally correct letters to use in constructing names (421d–427d), involve onomatopoeia.[48] Many other names, moreover, plainly were chosen to communicate something about the nature or being of the thing named. *Tyrannosaurus rex* and *Lactarious deliciosus*. Carbon dioxide. Whooping cough and pertussis. *Eudaimonia*. Such names obviously do not fully describe the things they name, but neither are they arbitrary or merely conventional. Socrates does not mention examples like these, leaving us to recognize what he has omitted. Once one does so, it does not seem completely ridiculous to suppose that the earliest names, perhaps even most of the ancestral forms of the names we use, sought to express what the namegivers believed about the nature of the things they named.

What *is* ridiculous is to think that we could use etymological research to discover the natures of things. Apart from the fact that much information about the evolution of language has been irretrievably lost, the most we could hope for would be to discover why the original names were chosen. Those choices might tell us little or nothing about the things themselves. Consider, for example, "Graves disease." Graves was a physician who identified the syndrome, but this tells us nothing about the nature of the disease.[49]

The original names, moreover, would inevitably have been at best incomplete in describing or imitating things. When we use an improper noun, we implicitly assume that all the things named by that noun are significantly alike in their nature or being, and significantly different from

[48] It is now known that primitive peoples often make extensive use of onomatopoeia in the names they use for animals. They also use what might be called "sound synathesia," which involves mapping a variable like size onto particular sounds, a practice that Socrates also suggests would have played a part in primitive name-giving. Experiments have shown that Anglophone subjects presented with a pair of words in the language of one of these peoples, along with a choice between two kinds of animal, can guess with a high degree of accuracy which name goes with which animal (Steven Mithen, *The Singing Neanderthals*, 169–72).

[49] Even someone who fails to appreciate the jokes in the *Cratylus* would presumably find it mildly amusing if someone diagnosed with Graves' disease assumed that he was headed straight for the grave or if someone avoided playing baseball for fear of contracting Lou Gehrig's disease.

the things to which we give a different name. Every language therefore teaches those who use it to classify things (including actions and attributes) according to the vocabulary of that language. One can see this taking place when parents correct certain linguistic mistakes that children often make. When a child refers to the cover on a pot as a "hat," the parent may use the occasion to teach the word "lid." Our language assumes that a hat and a lid are sufficiently different to require different names. But this assumption obscures the similarity between the two things, which we sometimes acknowledge by referring colloquially to hats as "lids." Similarly, British slang uses the word "hat" to refer to condoms, drawing on a different aspect of a hat's nature or being.

A naturally correct vocabulary would always classify things correctly, reflecting the nature or being of the things. Cratylus is right that names are in some important way better when they correctly inform us about the nature or being of the thing named, which is why we all know about the risk of being misled by euphemisms.[50] Socrates offers simple examples to illustrate the importance of the way that names classify, and can misclassify (393a–d). The nature of a living thing is generally the same as its parents', so we call the offspring of a lion a lion and of a horse a horse. But if, contrary to nature, a calf were born from a horse, the offspring should not be called a horse. And if something that is not human were born from a woman, it should not be called a human being.

So far, so good, if we can distinguish monsters from natural offspring. But how reliably can we do so? The calf example seems easy because we never see calves born from horses and would certainly expect to recognize a calf as a calf even if we saw it emerge from a mare. But what about mules, which are indeed born from mares? Socrates does not discuss this kind of example, but he tells Hermogenes to beware lest he assume that any offspring of a king should be called a king. Another easy case, it would seem, which calls attention to the distinction between nature and con-

[50] Socrates does not make this point directly, but he does point out that proper names, like "Theophilus," are often assigned to children in the hope that they will turn out to be fitting. Elizabeth Marshall Thomas, whose work is discussed in Chapter 2, offers an even more interesting and revealing example. When she first went to the Kalahari, she was given a name meaning "one who laughs" in the native language, apparently because the namegivers recognized that she laughed a lot because her heart was sad (*A Million Years with You: A Memoir of Life Observed*, 38).

vention. But it should also focus our attention on the harder case that Socrates only mentions: distinguishing a human from a non-human.[51]

Perhaps Rousseau had this passage from the *Cratylus* in mind when he wrote the following:

> A savage man upon encountering others will at first be frightened. His fright will have made him see these men as bigger and stronger than himself; he will have given them the name *Giants*. After many experiences he will have recognized that these supposed giants being neither bigger nor stronger than himself, their stature does not agree with the idea that he had at first attached to the word Giant. He will then invent another name common to them and to him, such as, for example, the name *man*, and will reserve the name *Giant* for the false object that had struck him during his illusion. This is how the figurative word is born before the proper word, when passion bewitches the eyes and the first idea that it presents to us is not that of the truth. What I have said about words and names is without difficulty with respect to turns of phrase. The illusory image presented by passion appearing first, the language that corresponded to it was also the first to be invented; it then became metaphorical when the enlightened mind, recognizing its initial error, employed its expressions only under the influence of the same passions that had produced it. (*Essay*, chap. 3, *O.C.*, 5:381–82)

Rousseau presents fear as the dominant passion in this encounter. In other passages in the *Essay*, both preceding and following this one, he indicates that other passions would also be at work in the birth of speech.[52] The giant/man story is not about the genesis of speech, but rather about the genesis of self-reflection. Fear is the natural response to encountering a strange animal in an environment where dangerous animals exist. The passion is not caused by the sense impression of the animal, but by ignorance of its powers and intentions. As Rousseau points out, and as we can confirm from our own experience, sense impressions are not received on a blank screen but are always interpreted by the animal that receives the impressions.[53] Fear is taken here as the crucial passion because it can be caused by ignorance, and the phenomenon at the basis of Rousseau's

[51] In the *Discourse on Inequality*, Rousseau alludes to an easy case like Socrates' example of kings (*O.C.*, 3:131–32), and then goes on to undertake a serious and lengthy investigation of the harder case.

[52] See, for example, chap. 2, *O.C.*, 5:376; chap. 9, 405–06; chap. 10, 407–08.

[53] In the *Emile*, Rousseau develops this point in considerable detail (*O.C.*, 4:382–97, Bloom, 134–43).

story is one familiar to us all: alone in the woods at night, one is sometimes spooked by the appearance of harmless plants that one fears might be dangerous animals.

What makes the giant story odd, and Rousseau hopes revealing, is that here a man is taken to be unfamiliar with other men. For this reason, we must not confuse the name giving described in the story with any name giving act that we might perform. When Rousseau's savage calls other men "giants," he is not necessarily assimilating a new experience into a pre-existing linguistic structure. What Rousseau presents as the act of using or coining the term "giant" might be little more than a way of remembering the experience of fearfully perceiving another animal as taller and stronger than oneself. Except for what happens later in the story, this kind of remembering would hardly be different from behavior that we frequently observe in other animals.

The crucial step in the story is the substitution of the concept "man" for the concept "giant." According to Rousseau, this substitution would occur only after repeated experiences, which implies that the comparison of experiences makes such substitution possible. Such comparison is possible only if the experiences are retained in the memory as images or ideas, which of course is something that many animals can do. The recognition of these images as images would prepare the way for human language because it would open the animal mind or soul to reflection in the most basic sense: the awareness of a discrepancy between what appears and what is.

Moving giants/men from one category to the other constitutes the correction of an error, which is recognized and remembered as such. It thereby represents progress and enlightenment. The extent of the discovered community with other men, however, remains unclear. The partial character of this community, the fact that one's fellows are both same and other, would cause our savage to come into a new kind of ignorance. This is not an ignorance for which nature specifies a response like fear and caution, but an ignorance that would ignite further errors and further corrections. To determine the extent to which one's fellows are "giants" (i.e., alien and dangerous), and the extent to which they are "men" (i.e., like oneself and therefore potentially helpful), requires a whole new succession of category shifts involving them and oneself: as soon as one had the concept "man," one would have to begin correcting or supplementing it with new categories such as friend/enemy, and eventually ruler/ruled.

Rousseau does not directly point out this last problem latent in the name "man," just as he does not tell us that the discovery of this concept marks a decisive turning point in the emergence of humanity. The reason has to do with the mythical character of the story: the genesis of language would not have proceeded in the manner described here because it is only after someone else recognizes one as a being like himself that one seeks a way to communicate (*Essay*, chap. 1, *O.C.*, 5:375).

In the *Discourse on Inequality*, Rousseau suggests a non-mythical account of the earliest efforts to communicate, in which the most primitive men begin to notice various qualities of other animals in the course of trying to survive among them. They also notice that other men largely seem to behave as they would themselves behave in similar circumstances. This in turn could lead to temporary cooperative arrangements to advance a common interest, say in hunting, as well as the use of force or cunning when people found themselves in competition for food. Such interactions would not require a more sophisticated form of language than we observe in several other species that signal each other with inarticulate noises, gestures, and imitative sounds (*Inequality*, *O.C.*, 3:165–67).

This general account has now received support from the observations of modern scientists. Elephants, for example, are remarkably adept at classifying the speech of different kinds of people according to the danger they are likely to pose.[54] Even more impressively, dolphins in several parts of the world have learned to enter into cooperative hunting arrangements with human beings, which the dolphins initiate with ritualized signals.[55] If elephants and dolphins can deal with human beings in these ways, certainly humans could once have had similar dealings with one another before compositional languages had arisen, just as Rousseau suggests.

The giant/man story is meant to help us see that the earliest names would have incorporated errors, capable of being corrected, but also reflecting the truth of experiences that are later relied on in the metaphorical use of those names. Or, to anticipate an argument that Rousseau will

[54] See, for example, Karen McComb, et al., "Elephants Can Determine Ethnicity, Gender, and Age from Acoustic Cues in Human Voices."

[55] See, for example, Paulo C. Simões-Lopes, et al., "Dolphin Interactions with the Mullet Artisanal Fishing on Southern Brazil: A Qualitative and Quantitative Approach"; Brian D. Smith, et al., "Catch Composition and Conservation Management of a Human-Dolphin Cooperative Cast-Net Fishery in the Ayeyarwady River, Myanmar"; F.G. Daura-Jorge, et al., "The Structure of a Bottlenose Dolphin Society Is Coupled to a Unique Foraging Cooperation with Artisanal Fishermen."

develop in more detail, the truth that humans seek is inseparable from the passions that provoke the search for enlightenment.

Socrates indirectly makes a similar point through a self-contradiction into which Cratylus falls. This thread of the dialogue begins when Socrates seeks to confirm that Hermogenes takes the conventionalist view only with respect to names, not to beings. Hermogenes acknowledges that he has sometimes become so perplexed as to be driven toward the view of Protagoras, according to which truth and opinion are indistinguishable: whatever anyone believes is the truth for him. But Hermogenes resists this view because one would then be unable to distinguish the wise and the good from the foolish and the bad. He also rejects the related view of Euthydemus, according to which all things simultaneously have all attributes, which would mean that nothing one said about them would be any more or less true than anything else.

Socrates begins with homely examples meant to confirm Hermogenes' resistance to Protagoras and Euthydemus. Cutting and burning simply will not work if one proceeds according to seriously mistaken assumptions or opinions about things and the tools we use to work on them (386e–387b). Although Socrates does not mention it, anyone can also see that less radically mistaken opinions may allow one to carry out these actions, though not as well as one can with more knowledge about the appropriate tool and the appropriate way to use the tool for the task at hand.[56] As Socrates suggests in this context, a name is a kind of tool (388a–c), as is speech generally (387b–c). If we think back to his earlier examples, we can recognize that names can cut (by classifying) and burn (by making truths and falsehoods alike disappear). A name can accomplish something that its user wants to accomplish, but it may fail to one degree or another unless the name is somehow made to fit the things named in accordance with their nature or being.

A larger problem, which Socrates does not mention, is that tools can often be used quite effectively even if the user is radically mistaken about their nature or the nature of the things on which they work. Suppose, for example, that someone unfamiliar with modern technology believed that an electric knife was made by a god, or that a butane lighter was itself a god. This individual might be able to cut and burn just as effectively as anyone else. Is this also true of names and speech generally?

[56] Elsewhere, Socrates indicates that he is well aware of this (*Republic* 353a).

In the long mock investigation of etymologies with Hermogenes, Socrates finds that a great many words reflect a belief, associated with Heracleitus, that all things are always in flux. At the end of the dialogue, it transpires that Cratylus believes in this teaching of Heracleitus, though it is not entirely clear when Cratylus adopted this opinion. Perhaps he did so during the course of the dialogue, as some commentators have concluded.[57] Or perhaps, as I think more likely, Socrates invented these etymologies in part because he already knew that Cratylus was a follower of Heracleitus.[58] Either way, this thesis of Heracleitus is irreconcilable with the claim—which Cratylus never disavows in the dialogue—that everything has a naturally correct name.[59] At the high point of the discussion of Heracleitus with Hermogenes, in the center of the dialogue, Socrates offers what he calls an inspired thought:

> [T]he exceedingly ancient people who laid down names were quite like many of the wise ones now, who get dizzy by constantly turning round while seeking how the beings are, and then the things themselves appear to be carried around and moving in every way. Not holding their own passion within themselves responsible for being the cause of this opinion, they instead hold the things themselves responsible for being this way in their own nature, and none of them to be stable, none of them durable, but that they are always flowing and moving and filled with every kind of motion and coming into being. (411b3–c5)

In the *Cratylus*, Socrates is noncommittal about the *extent* to which such passions cause a distortion of the truth. Toward the end of the dialogue, he denies knowing whether Heracleitus is right, and mentions a *dream* he

[57] See, for example, David Sedley, *Plato's Cratylus*, 18 & n40.

[58] Cratylus states that his agreement with Heracleitus is well considered, but does not clearly indicate when he adopted that view (440d8–e2). It seems to me unlikely that Socrates would have accidentally introduced the doctrine of Heracleitus into the discussion without knowing that it would enable him to show that Cratylus held inconsistent beliefs.

[59] There are stories, which Plato may have assumed his readers would know, according to which Cratylus eventually stopped using words entirely, thus relinquishing his claim to know a naturally correct vocabulary in favor of his Heracleitianism. See Aristotle, *Metaphysics* 1010a7–15. Aristotle also reports that Plato himself became acquainted with the doctrine of Heracleitus through Cratylus, and that Plato continued to believe that the objects of sense perception are in perpetual flux (ibid., 987a32–b7). Plato, of course, did not stop using words.

often has about unchanging objects of intellection (439b–440d).[60] Plato unmistakably invites his readers to pursue the questions that Socrates leaves hanging when he sends Cratylus and Hermogenes on their way at the end of the dialogue.

Rousseau might have seen in the *Cratylus* the root of a tension or shortcoming within human language itself, to which he so strikingly calls attention in the passages of the *Discourse on Inequality* discussed at the beginning of this chapter. In Rousseau's view, human language always incorporates questionable assumptions, including important assumptions that originate from passions that arise within human beings.[61] The relationship between these passions and intellectual enlightenment is the key investigation begun in the *Essay*, which takes as its starting point an inquiry into the distinct roles that passions and enlightenment must have played in the origin of languages.

## The Evolution of Languages

In Chapters 5–7 of the *Essay*, Rousseau stresses the ways in which the invention and spread of writing enhanced the precision of language and its capacity to convey ideas, at great cost to its emotional expressiveness.

[60] Leo Strauss deprecates Rousseau's own philosophizing and suggests that it marks a significant departure from Socrates and Plato: "One must contrast the dreamlike character of Rousseau's solitary contemplation with the wakefulness of philosophic contemplation" (*Natural Right and History*, 293). In light of this passage from the *Cratylus*, one might wonder whether the modes of contemplation in which Socrates, Plato, and Rousseau sought to engage were necessarily as different as Strauss seems to imply. In a discussion of the difference between erudition and knowledge, moreover, Rousseau implicitly likens his manner of teaching to that of Socrates: "I give my dreams as dreams, leaving the reader to discover whether they contain something useful to people who are awake" (*Emile*, *O.C.*, 4:351n, Bloom, 112n).

[61] If or to the extent that a philosopher wants to help his readers escape the grip of these assumptions, he will likely need to revise the vocabulary he has been given by his society. This is something that Rousseau frequently does, most conspicuously in the *Social Contract* but in other places as well. See, for example, *Emile*, *O.C.*, 4:299, 426, Bloom, 77, 165. In a draft preface to the *Confessions*, he said, "For what I have to say, it would be necessary to invent a language as new as my project" (*O.C.*, 1:1153). Even in his private correspondence, Rousseau insisted that his readers must learn his "dictionary" because he does not always use terms in their ordinary sense (Rousseau to Mme. d'Epinay, March 1756, *Corr. Comp.*, no. 391, 3:296). He often complicates matters, however, by shifting back and forth between different usages, sometimes even within the same book, as he acknowledges (*Emile*, *O.C.*, 4:345n, Bloom, 108n).

He then begins to supply the qualifications that he had promised earlier about his description of primitive languages: "Everything I have said up to this point applies to primitive languages in general and to the progress that results from their continuation, but it explains neither their origin nor their differences" (chap. 8, *O.C.*, 5:394).

Rousseau begins with the assumption that our species originated in a warm climate, and he mentions in passing that "the human species *like all the others* was born in the warm countries" (ibid., emphasis added). Because he obviously knew that many organisms are very ill-suited to life in warm climates, this may be an even bolder suggestion about the evolution of species than he offered in the *Discourse on Inequality*. He then argues that the search for food would have dispersed men so long as the environment remained abundant in this resource. Genuine languages could not have developed so long as human beings still lived in the kind of isolated family groups that existed after the first great step out of what the *Discourse* treats as the earliest stage of the state of nature.[62] New circumstances—such as climate change and migration into new environments—would have required new ways of providing for subsistence. The concomitant acquisition of new knowledge would have served as both a precondition and an incentive for the kinds of human interaction in which language could become useful. The economic character of this explanation deserves considerable emphasis, but it should not obscure the inadequacy of such factors in explaining the development of uniquely human compositional languages. Countless species, we now know, have gone extinct because of environmental changes, or adapted to new environments without acquiring conventional languages.

Rousseau divides early languages into two main categories: those of the South, where the climate was milder and relatively generous with

[62] In the *Essay*, Rousseau does not discuss what the *Discourse* calls the pure state of nature. Perhaps this is only because it is obvious that truly isolated individuals would not have the slightest need to develop anything like our languages. It is also possible, however, that this is an indication that his account of human evolution is not crucially dependent on the claim that humans actually lived in near-total isolation at one time. Thus, if our earliest ancestors in fact lived more like polygynous gorillas or monogamous gibbons than like orangutans, little or nothing would have to change in Rousseau's account of human nature and the development of human societies. See also *S.C.*, bk. 1, chap. 2, *O.C.*, 3:352, where Rousseau characterizes the family as the only natural society, while noting that once a child no longer depends on its father for its preservation the family maintains itself by convention rather than by nature.

the means of subsistence, and those of the North, where the climate was harsher and the land more niggardly. In the milder climates, Rousseau proposes, the most important economic innovation would have been a transition from hunting to herding, and language would have developed through contacts made at water sources in arid environments. In such circumstances, sexual passions would dominate attempts to communicate. Why? Without a scarcity of some life-sustaining resource, people would ordinarily have had little reason to congregate for long in significant numbers. And without leisure, sexual passions would have to take a back seat to mere survival. Gatherings near a water source provide the perfect picture, if not the only picture, of circumstances conducive to developing the social passion that grows out of natural sexual desire.

In the *Discourse*, Rousseau briefly mentions a variety of environmental changes—such as floods, earthquakes, and the formation of islands—that might have forced people to live in larger groups than they had before (*O.C.*, 3:168–69). The same general causes are mentioned in the *Essay* (chap. 9, *O.C.*, 5:402). The merely illustrative nature of the water source example is emphasized by the immediately preceding example, where Rousseau suggests that even in the very harsh climate of the arctic regions, people would sometimes be drawn together by boredom (*l'ennui*) (ibid., 402–03). Because he had just said that "[t]o do nothing is man's first and strongest passion after that of self preservation" (ibid., 401n), this seemingly casual comment about the moving power of boredom suggests that humans may be somewhat more naturally sociable than the main line of his argument seems to indicate.[63]

In the more compressed account of the *Discourse*, Rousseau emphasizes the quick transition from love that is more than a blind copulatory urge to the furies of jealousy. In the *Essay*, he puts more emphasis on the genesis of love itself, understood as a desire to attract a specific mate in circumstances where multiple potential mates, and potential rivals, are at hand. This desire is a precondition for jealousy, and one that arises from a different source than the incestuous matings that he argues must have allowed the species to perpetuate itself when people lived in isolated families. It is a short step from love in this sense to a desire to attract admiration and respect more generally. This desire is amour-propre as Rousseau

[63] See also *Essay*, chap. 1, *O.C.*, 5:379 ("[P]rovided only that there is some means of communication between himself and his fellows by which the one can act and the other feel, they will eventually manage to communicate to one another as many ideas as they have.").

ordinarily uses the term, and it is ultimately the passion that drives much of political life.

In what Rousseau calls the North, economic incentives would have been more immediately important than the urge to mate in driving social interactions. For that reason, the early languages here would have been marked more by clarity than by seductiveness and persuasive power. One who wants love speaks obscurely and allusively, whereas one who issues commands, threats, and other appeals to self-interest speaks as clearly as he can. Only in a farce would someone use the same terms to attempt a seduction and to negotiate a prenuptial agreement. In Rousseau's formulation, the first words in the South would have been *aimez-moi* ("love me") and in the North *aidez-moi* ("assist me") (ibid., chap. 10, 408). Both sentences may be in the imperative mood grammatically, but the human moods they reflect are very different. Note that what Rousseau calls the first "words" are in French simple sentences. An important implication of his account is that people would have been using their voices to manipulate the passions and behavior of other people before they had a system of names or words that could be combined into what we call sentences by following grammatical rules. As we will see, this claim is supported by recent studies of the natural languages used by other primates.

The languages of the South would have developed under conditions closer to those of man's original home, and Rousseau appears to give them a privileged place in his account.[64] The reason is not that they were more natural, but that he believes they were more effective agents of social bonding. Rousseau contends that modern languages still retain signs of these differences, though they have greatly diminished with the progress of civilization and with increasing interaction among different peoples.

> French, English, German are the private languages of men who assist one another, who reason with one another in cold blood, or of hot-tempered people who get angry; but the ministers of the Gods proclaiming the sacred

[64] Rousseau frequently seems to assume that various languages originated independently, but nothing crucial in his account depends on such an assumption. Northern languages almost certainly developed later than southern languages, given that the human race originated in a warm climate and that most of the world is relatively warm (ibid., chap. 8, *O.C.*, 5:394). But whether the northern languages arose independently or through a modification of a language that people brought with them from the south, Rousseau's explanation of the differences between them could still be valid.

mysteries, the wise giving laws to peoples, chiefs leading the multitude must speak Arabic or Persian. (ibid., chap. 11, *O.C.*, 5:409, footnote omitted)[65]

Both kinds of language appeal to human passions, but one lends itself more to reasoned assessments that serve the most fundamental passion of self-preservation and thus narrow self-interest more generally. The other plays more to the social passions that are ultimately rooted in the natural passion of pity or commiseration.

These are obviously differences of degree, and all human languages are capable both of intellectual clarity and of persuasive power that is independent of rational argument. But differences of degree can have profound effects. In Rousseau's view, the same kinds of forces that initially triggered the invention of languages have also caused a corruption of the languages that most fully reflected the ultimate natural source of the genuine social virtues.

Rousseau maintains that verse, songs, and speech had a common origin and were initially indistinguishable, especially if perhaps not exclusively in the South where melody was a central element of speech (ibid., chap. 12, 410–11). As language was increasingly adapted to the communication of complex ideas, a separation of music and speech gradually arose. In order to see the force of this argument, it may be useful to reflect for a moment on our own popular music. The lyrics of our songs are invariably very simple, and often not even intelligibly articulated. Nobody would take any real interest in hearing them spoken, let alone in reading them. But add an affecting melody, and even a mediocre singer can produce a significant emotional response. That response would not be enhanced, and might be reduced, if the lyrics were given more complex intellectual content. Now go one step further and consider how some singers—like Billie Holiday, Hank Williams, Patsy Cline, and Otis Redding—can greatly magnify the emotional impact of a song with subtle attention to phrasing and intonation. Or consider the recordings of "Together Again" and "Crying Time"

[65] In his *Dictionary of Music*, Rousseau says that the laws, the histories, and the praises of gods and heros were all sung among the ancients before they were written, adding on the authority of Aristotle that this explains why the Greeks used the same word for laws and songs (*O.C.*, 5:690). The apparent source for Rousseau's reference to Aristotle is *Problems* 19.28, 919b38–920a2, which says that before people knew how to write, they sang their laws in order not to forget them, and later continued to call their laws songs. Characteristically, Rousseau suggests a different explanation than Aristotle's, after having thought for himself about what Aristotle says.

by Ray Charles, which are significantly more affecting than the versions recorded by the writer of the songs, Buck Owens. Nor is increased emotional impact a function of the beauty of a singer's voice, as one can easily recognize by comparing Bob Dylan's early recordings with the covers of his songs by Joan Baez.

The intellectual and musical simplicity of so much of our popular music looks like a kind of echo of what our ancestors may have been doing early in the development of compositional languages.[66] The fact that such music is popular suggests that it gives us something we want that we are not getting from written and spoken speech. If that is so, it is not ridiculous to think that the perfection of language would occur when it became capable of conveying complex intellectual content without having lost its musicality.

Rousseau makes this point with an account of the history of ancient Greek, a southern language in his terminology. He doubts that Homer knew how to write, and he is almost certainly correct that the *Iliad* and *Odyssey* were passed down through an oral tradition of traveling singers long before they were converted to readable texts (*Essay*, chap. 6). Even after writing came to the Greeks, probably from the Phoenicians, Greek remained a much more musical and expressive language than those of the North.[67] But it is no accident that Homer has a special place in Greek culture: "It was when Greece began to abound in books and written poetry that all the charm of Homer's poetry came to be felt by comparison. The other Poets wrote, Homer alone had sung, and these divine songs ceased to be listened to with rapture only when Europe was covered with barbarians who involved themselves with judging what they could not feel" (ibid., 390).

The corruption of Greek—the diminution of its musicality and thus its moral and emotional expressiveness—resulted from a certain kind of improvement. First, the progress of reasoning led to the perfection of grammatical rules and concomitantly to musical rules involving the calcu-

[66] Charles Darwin believed that the half-human progenitors of our race instinctively used music in courtship before they had articulate language, and he saw evidence of this in popular music. "Love is still the commonest theme of our own songs … The sensations and ideas excited in us by music, or by the cadences of impassioned oratory, appear from their vagueness, yet depth, like mental reversions to the emotions and thoughts of a long-past age" (*Descent of Man*, 2:320–21).

[67] "[Melody] is what the Greek language had, and what ours lacks" (*Essay*, chap. 12, *O.C.*, 5:411).

lation of intervals. Gradually, delicacy of inflection was reduced in favor of increased clarity of expression. "Once Greece was filled with Sophists and Philosophers it no longer had either celebrated poets or musicians. In cultivating the art of convincing, that of stirring [an audience] was lost. Plato himself, jealous of Homer and Euripedes, decried the one and could not imitate the other" (ibid., chap. 19, 425).[68] Political subjection to the Romans, and the influence of their less musical language, accelerated the loss of musicality in Greek. Finally, the influx of barbarians from the North, with their harsh and relatively unmusical tongues, destroyed Europe's "sciences, her arts, and the universal instrument of both, namely a harmonious and perfected language" (ibid., chap. 18, 425).[69]

## Language, Music, and Modern Science

As we have seen, Rousseau expected that advances in comparative anatomy and the observations of naturalists would eventually enable scientists to engage in "solid reasonings" about the physical evolution of human beings. That prediction, of course, proved correct. More significantly, the findings of modern science have proved surprisingly consonant with crucial aspects of Rousseau's speculations about the course of human evolution. He does not seem to have expected comparable progress with respect to the origin of languages. Correct again. In recent decades, scientists trained in a wide range of disciplines have sought to explain how languages arose. Their researches have generated a large body of data bearing on the prob-

[68] Rousseau's allusion to Euripides may reflect a report that Plato wrote tragedies early in his life. See Diogenes Laertius, *Lives of Eminent Philosophers* 3.6. The attacks on Homer in the dialogues are well known, but Rousseau was also well aware of the educational use to which music is put in both the *Republic* and the *Laws*. The critique of Homer that Plato puts in the mouth of Socrates is in many ways ironic, and is more subtle than it may first appear to be. See, for example, Timothy W. Burns, "Philosophy and Poetry: A New Look at an Old Quarrel." The same could be said of Rousseau's critique here of Plato.

[69] In the *Emile*, Rousseau tentatively extends his analysis in the following way:

> Minds (*têtes*) are formed by languages, thoughts take on the color of the idioms, reason alone is common, the mind (*l'esprit*) in each language has its particular form; a difference that could well be partly the cause or the effect of national characters, and what appears to confirm this conjecture is that in all the nations of the world the language follows the vicissitudes of *mœurs* and is conserved or altered as they are. (*O.C.*, 4:346, Bloom, 109)

lem, and there is no shortage of elaborate theories and debates. But no definitive answer has emerged.

When one looks into the recent literature, it is striking how many obvious questions have not been answered. Here are some examples:

- When did humans develop compositional systems that can generate expressions of unlimited number and complexity by using a finite group of symbols according to grammatical conventions?
- Did such language arise only once, giving birth to all other human languages, or did it arise independently on multiple occasions?
- Did any now-extinct human species—some of which have been identified from the fossil record—have compositional languages?
- How did our ancestors communicate with one another before they had such languages?
- Was the immediate precursor of compositional language a collection of words that later came to be used according to grammatical conventions, or a collection of sentences, or holistic utterances, that were later resolved into words? Or were both in use?
- Did human language develop suddenly, or only over a prolonged period of time?
- What environmental factors contributed to the origin of human speech, and what role did genetic mutations play?
- Were the dramatically enhanced cognitive abilities of modern humans primarily a cause or an effect of the development of speech?

Rousseau's central claim in the *Essay* begins with the proposition that human communication was originally a form of music, dictated by the passions, appealing to the passions, and aimed primarily at influencing the behavior of other people. As individuals were driven by external forces to develop their intellectual powers in struggles to survive, they were also driven into closer relationships with larger groups of people. Under those circumstances, the instinctively musical forms of communication would gradually have been modified (differently in various environments) by conventions that enhanced their capacity to transmit intellectual content. This enhancement in turn promoted the social accumulation of information in and through language, while simultaneously reducing the musical and emotionally powerful capacity of the evolving new forms of communication. What we call music is rooted in the original musical instinct. It has become separated from our primary means of communication, but it continues to serve its original purpose of expressing and appealing to our passions.[70]

Does this account remain plausible today? Modern scientists have generated a significant body of new knowledge that was unavailable to Rousseau. The data fall into four main categories.

*Comparative linguistics.* When it was founded in 1866, the Société de Linguistique de Paris adopted a standing rule against discussions of the origin of language. In retrospect, this looks like a pretty sensible form of censorship because it channeled the efforts of scholars into the study and comparison of known languages. Linguists now know a great deal about how living languages evolve, and they can make educated guesses about a few features of some extinct languages from which living tongues have descended. This method of backward extrapolation, however, becomes altogether unreliable beyond the past 6000-odd years, which is long after the time that compositional languages must have become fully developed.

*Observations of naturalists.* The past few decades have seen an explosion of observational and experimental studies of intelligence and communication in animals. It has perhaps always been obvious to unprejudiced observers that many animals both think and communicate with one another, often in very effective and complex ways. Recently, however, it has become increasingly undeniable that many animals (and not just primates) think, feel, communicate, and even transmit cultural traditions in ways that were once widely thought to be uniquely human.

*Evolution of species.* Physical evolution has been observed at least since the time that people began manipulating the process through selective breeding of domesticated plants and animals. Darwin's argument for evolution through natural selection, when integrated with the subsequent development of genetic science, led to the modern theory of speciation that

[70] Adam Smith, who was familiar with the *Discourse on Inequality* but not with the *Essay on the Origin of Languages*, offers an account of the development of languages that agrees with Rousseau's in many respects. See "Considerations Concerning the First Formation of Languages." Smith's speculations about the evolution of languages, however, focus almost entirely on what Rousseau regards as the intellectual aspect of speech. Unlike Rousseau, he gives virtually no attention to the role of moral passions. It is therefore striking that Smith contends that ancient languages, especially Greek, were superior in "variety" and "sweetness," and that our tongues are "more and more imperfect, and less proper for many of the purposes of language" (ibid., 224). Rousseau's attention to the relative musicality of different languages, and his richer account of the multiple purposes of language, enables him to offer an account of the beauty and power of ancient Greek that Smith recognized but could not fully explain.

is now accepted in some form by most scientists. According to the modern synthesis, evolution in general and speciation in particular are driven by natural selection acting on variations arising from genetic mutations and genetic recombination. Although many uncertainties remain, there is now little doubt about the proposition that our species is descended from an extinct common ancestor that we share with the great apes, and ultimately from much older life forms.

The fossil record has revealed the existence of a number of extinct species that are more closely related to us than any of the extant primates are. Scientists generally classify these animals as early humans because they shared the distinctive design of upright posture, and one can make a few reasonable inferences from the archeological record about the social lives of some of these human types. But there are major gaps in the record, including a gap of well over half a million years, and possibly much more, between the remains of modern humans and those of any species that is likely to have been a direct ancestor of ours (Klein, *Human Career*, 432–34, 725–26).

In recent years, major improvements in genetic analysis have enabled scientists to supplement the fossil record with additional information about the history of our species and our relationships with other primates, but this new knowledge reveals little about the origin of languages.

*Neuroscience.* The brain is obviously the most important organ of language. Until recently, it was widely believed that a specific part of the brain is responsible for speech, a part that presumably developed through the process of evolution, as eyes and lungs have evolved. Experiments and observations, often involving people with damaged or defective brains, and new kinds of brain scans, appear to have disproved this notion. Many areas of the brain are recruited in the process of using language, including some that are very old in evolutionary terms (Stringer, *Lone Survivors*, 208–09), and the same is true of music. Some areas are used for both, and they appear to use the same neural networks. The brain, moreover, is highly plastic, allowing different areas to perform the same functions. The brain itself is a neural network, but no one knows why the neurons behave as they do.

In *The Singing Neanderthals: The Origins of Music, Language, Mind, and Body*, Steven Mithen reviews the literature in these four disciplines and develops an account of the origin of language that is consistent in all major respects with Rousseau's. Mithen takes sides in some ongoing scholarly debates, and some of his own conclusions are quite speculative.

But much of the evidence he summarizes appears to be non-controversial, and that evidence provides significant new support for the main arguments of the *Essay*. The following discussion, which is based primarily on his book, is supplemented with information from other sources.

*Infant-directed speech.*[71] One of the most powerful signs that our languages evolved from music is all around us: mothers talk to their infant children in a distinctively musical way.[72] Compared with the prosody used in communicating with older children and adults, mothers universally employ a range of pitch that is wider and on average higher; longer vowels and pauses, with exaggerated articulations; shorter phrases; and more repetition. This musical prosody obviously cannot enable an infant to understand the language that is being used. Instead, it is adopted (sometimes subconsciously) because the infant responds to such prosody in ways that it does not respond to "adult" speech. In addition, experiments have shown that babies pay attention to recordings of their mothers' voices for longer periods when the mother is singing than when she is speaking with infant-directed prosody.

There appear to be four main stages through which this form of interaction passes as children develop. At first, the baby's responses are minimal but detectable. Sounds with a gently rising pitch, for example, may elicit an opening of the eyes, while the baby may close its eyes in response to an abruptly rising pitch. With slightly older infants, a low and falling pitch contour will tend to soothe a distressed baby, while a rising pitch will tend to engage its attention. Later, the melodies and rhythms used by the mother will communicate her own feelings and intentions, to which the child responds. Finally, when children begin to understand the meaning of words, mothers use specific patterns of intonation and pauses to assist in the acquisition of language.

Experiments have confirmed that this distinctive prosody is more effective than adult speech for communicating intent to children. Moreover, the same prosodic patterns are used in very different languages. A given child will respond similarly to infant-directed speech spoken in different languages, or even when nonsense words are employed. This strongly suggests that the musical character of a universal infant-directed prosody is not primarily a device for teaching language, but rather an independently

[71] Mithen, *Singing Neanderthals*, chap. 6.

[72] Rousseau was well aware of this phenomenon. See *Emile*, *O.C.*, 4:285, Bloom, 65.

effective and natural mode of communication.[73] That in turn supports Rousseau's claim that music and language were originally the same thing.

Conversely, experiments have shown that very young children have perfect pitch, which is useful to musicians but very rare in adults. Perfect pitch is somewhat more common among accomplished musicians, and extremely common in musical savants (who often have severe linguistic deficits) and in those who suffer from autism. It appears, therefore, that the acquisition of a conventional language (whether it is tonal or atonal) tends to suppress our natural ability to recognize pitch in absolute terms because it fosters a preferential reliance on relative pitch. Once again, these phenomena support Rousseau's analysis, according to which early languages would have become less musical as they became more conventional.

*Animal behavior*.[74] Many animals have natural languages that serve, in varying degrees, the primary functions of human language: communicating information about the world and about their own emotional state and intentions. So far as anyone knows, modern humans are the only animals that use grammatical conventions to combine a finite number of symbols in potentially infinite and infinitely complex ways. This kind of conventional language is a universal feature of every known human society, but our ancestors must have been communicating with one another in some more naturally determined manner before they developed such conventions. Observations of our closest living relatives should provide some clues about the nature of this prelinguistic mode of communication.

Many primates have elaborate systems of vocal communication. Some of them convey information about the world. Vervet monkeys, for example, use different calls that warn one another about specific predator threats, and rhesus monkeys utter various calls that are associated with different kinds and quantities of food. Others, such as geladas and macaques, use melody and rhythm to provide social cues in much the same way that modern humans do. Acoustic analysis has shown a strong similarity

[73] One piece of evidence is especially telling. Chinese is a tonal language, so the use of exaggerated prosody toward children risks linguistic confusion. Chinese mothers do it anyway, intuitively evading and sometimes violating the conventions of their native tongue (Mithen, *Singing Neanderthals*, 73–74). A separate study showed that when speaking to pet cats and dogs, to whom we want to convey our feelings and intentions, people employ a prosody that resembles infant-directed speech, with one important exception. People do not use hyperarticulation of vowels when talking to their pets, which suggests that this one aspect of infant-directed speech is used primarily to assist in the acquisition of language (ibid., 74–75).

[74] Ibid., chap. 8.

between the waveforms used by humans and some monkeys to express specific emotional states, and humans are strikingly adept at interpreting these monkey vocalizations. Gibbon vocalizations sound to us like singing, and some gibbon species engage in extended duets.

All of this suggests that infant-directed speech, and adult speech to a lesser extent, reflects a basic inheritance from our primate forebears. Oddly, this does not appear to be the case with our closest extant relatives, the great apes. These animals have a relatively limited vocal repertoire, which seems to be the result of anatomical features in their throats and mouths that we and many other primates do not share. Many of their facial expressions and gestures, however, are quite similar to those used by humans, and recent research indicates that great apes effectively use intentional gestural language, both with humans in captivity and with one another in the wild.[75] It may just be an accident of evolution that these apes lack the physical equipment needed for a natural language that would sound more like human speech and human singing.[76] Such an accident might also help explain why the ape lineages probably never made the leap from a natural language to the conventional compositional language that is distinctively human.

*The fossil record and genetic analysis.*[77] The fossil record as we have it contains a small and possibly quite unrepresentative sample of the many kinds of organisms that once existed. This may well be true specifically of the human family. But we do know that several hominin species once lived in Africa, Europe, and Asia.[78] Some of them had relatively large brains and were able to produce sophisticated tools, and some lived for a time in proximity to modern humans. Apart from indications that brain size seems to have increased fairly steadily in hominins beginning about

[75] See, for example, Anna Ilona Roberts, et al., "Chimpanzees Modify Intentional Gestures to Coordinate a Search for Hidden Food"; Catherine Hobaiter and Richard W. Byrne, "The Meanings of Chimpanzee Gestures."

[76] See Mithen, *Singing Neanderthals*, chaps. 9–10.

[77] Ibid., chaps. 9, 15–16.

[78] Current usage among scientists classifies humans and great apes as hominids, and reserves the term hominins for modern humans and other descendants of the last common ancestor that we share with the chimpanzees. The extent of our ignorance about our closest extinct relatives is suggested by the recent discovery of a freshwater shell marked with geometrical engravings. These engravings are some 300,000 years older than any that had previously been found, and they were apparently produced by a hominin who lived hundreds of thousands of years before our own species emerged in Africa. See Josephine C. A. Joordens, et al., "*Homo erectus* at Trinil on Java Used Shells for Tool Production and Engraving."

2 million years ago, the fossil record has yet to reveal much about the origin of speech or the social lives of these people. One important exception is the Neanderthals, who probably arrived in Europe from Africa more than 250,000 years ago. Many fossil sites have been found and carefully studied, from which scientists have been able to make inferences about their way of life. They evidently lived in small groups of hunter-gatherers, and they survived climatic changes that made the environment much more harsh than it had been.[79] The Neanderthals became extinct sometime after modern humans arrived, probably around 30,000 years ago.

The Neanderthals probably encountered modern humans arriving from Africa approximately 40,000 years ago, and scientists are now reasonably confident that a significant fraction of people alive today have Neanderthal ancestors.[80] No one knows how much contact the Neanderthals had with our ancestors, or whether our ancestors played a significant role in their extinction.[81] Nor does anyone know how much contact occurred among various other populations of hominins that seem to have coexisted with each other at various times and places. But assuming that Neanderthals did have significant encounters with our ancestors, some tentative inferences can be drawn about the origin of languages.

Neanderthals were somewhat more physically robust than modern humans and had slightly larger brains, but both seem to have been anatomically equipped to produce a wide range of vocalizations (unlike the extant great apes). What the Neanderthals probably did not share with the new arrivals was a culture that included the institution of compositional

[79] In addition to the fossil evidence, preliminary genetic analysis also suggests that Neanderthals lived in small, isolated groups (Sergei Castellano, et al., "Patterns of Coding Variation in the Complete Exomes of Three Neanderthals").

[80] The evidence is based on genetic analysis, and it is possible that other hominins contributed to our gene pool as well. See Svante Pääbo, *Neanderthal Man: In Search of Lost Genomes*; Henry Gee, *The Accidental Species: Misunderstandings of Human Evolution*, 91–92; Dimitra Papagianni and Michael A. Morse, *The Neanderthals Rediscovered: How Modern Science Is Rewriting Their Story*, 170–71.

[81] For an argument that the extinction of the Neanderthals and the success of modern humans was almost entirely a matter of luck, in a kind of lottery created by significant and disruptive climate change, see Finlayson, *Humans Who Went Extinct*. For a competing explanation, which treats our ancestors as an invasive species that outcompeted Neanderthals and several other large predators, see Pat Shipman, *The Invaders: How Humans and Their Dogs Drove Neanderthals to Extinction*. The evidence currently available seems to allow for a variety of scenarios in which chance and some peculiar characteristics of modern humans (both physical and cultural) played greater or lesser roles in the extinction of the Neanderthals.

language. The fossil record suggests that Neanderthal tools remained unchanged for some 250,000 years, and there is little evidence of any sort of symbolic artifacts, economic division of labor, trade relations, or even sites where large numbers of people gathered.[82] It is therefore possible, perhaps even likely, that the only form of communication used by Neanderthals was a musical and non-grammatical language that conveyed emotions and intentions, perhaps along with some onomatopoetic words and imitative gestures.

The precursors of human speech might easily have been similar. Modern humans, therefore, might have been able to decipher a lot of what Neanderthals were saying, just as we can understand a lot of what some monkeys are saying to one another. The modern humans who encountered the Neanderthals, however, probably possessed compositional language. Genetic analysis and the archeological record suggest that a very dramatic cultural shift occurred approximately 50,000 years ago.[83] Population densities increased and humans began spreading from Africa into Europe and Asia, where they eventually replaced Neanderthals as well as other hominins.

A recent statistical study of phonemic inventories (i.e., the number of perceptually distinct units of sound that differentiate words) in various extant languages suggests that such diversity parallels the levels of genetic diversity found in various locations throughout the world. The genetic studies provide strong evidence that our species originated in Africa and spread throughout the globe along identifiable pathways. The new study of phonemic diversity reinforces this evidence. It also suggests that complex language arose prior to the most recent expansion of modern humans out of Africa and that it may have permitted that expansion to occur.[84]

Nobody knows exactly how or why compositional language developed. It is likely, however, that an increased need to communicate with strangers

[82] Some minimal cultural change appears to have occurred after, and possibly because of, the arrival in Europe of modern humans.

[83] This suggestion has not gone unchallenged. Some scientists argue that the most important changes occurred between about 60,000 and 80,000 years ago. Others place the date much earlier, between 100,000 and 250,000 years ago. If the earlier estimates are correct, the expansion of our ancestral population out of Africa about 50,000 years ago might not have been caused primarily by a significant change in behavior that arose at that time. For a short introduction to the debate, see Stringer, *Lone Survivors*, 125–28.

[84] See Quentin D. Atkinson, "Phonemic Diversity Supports a Serial Founder Effect Model of Language Expansion from Africa."

stimulated the invention of new means of doing so. This would have led to more such communications, and thus to further improvements in the means of conducting such dealings. It could have taken a long time for true compositional languages to emerge. But we know that it did happen, and we know that such languages have enabled modern human beings both to live in very large groups and to exploit the resources in every environment on earth. In this sense, compositional language is the most powerful tool ever invented by any animal. It most emphatically distinguishes our kind from any other that now exists, for better and for worse.[85]

The evidence now available is fully consistent with Rousseau's basic claims: that human language was originally a form of music or song; that it only gradually lost that character after environmental conditions and economic incentives induced people to begin living in large groups and to have routine dealings with strangers; and that the enormous intellectual capital that has accumulated through the use of compositional language has led to a diminution of the musicality in prelinguistic oral forms of communication that suited people who lived in very intimate family groups. Rousseau's account is in my view at least as plausible as any of the numerous other theories that have been advanced, though none can be regarded as proven.

## Conclusion

In the last chapter of the *Essay*, Rousseau draws the principal political conclusion that follows from his analysis. Modern European languages and politics both reflect the separation of music from speech:

> In ancient times when persuasion took the place of public force, eloquence was necessary. Of what use would it be today, when public force replaces persuasion? ... I say that every language with which one cannot make oneself understood by the people assembled is a servile language; it is impossible that a people remain free and speak that language. (chap. 20, *O.C.*, 5:428–29)

If such statements may seem to partake of hyperbole, they also reflect a plausible claim that conventional languages originated from a prelinguistic

[85] For all we know, other hominins may have developed such languages and yet gone extinct, perhaps because of environmental changes in the areas where they happened to live.

need or desire to form bonds in relatively small groups. Even today, communal song and music are frequently used to promote a sense of solidarity and common purpose in the military, in churches, and in many other contexts.[86] Spoken languages could have continued serving this function as societies grew larger, but there are natural limits to this progression. In Rousseau's view, modern European politics and modern European languages both indicate that those limits have been passed.

Just as Rousseau did not believe that we can return to the healthy freedom of "the happiest epoch, and the most durable," or that this way of life was without its inherent tensions, neither did he imagine that we can reconstitute languages like Homer's or that they were some kind of social panacea. What he does maintain is that understanding where we came from and how we got here can help us to be guided by nature in dealing with our current situation. The remainder of this book will begin to explore Rousseau's efforts to set forth that guidance.

[86] See, for example, Mithen, *Singing Neanderthals*, chap. 14.

CHAPTER 4

# Greatness of Soul and the Souls of Women: Rousseau's Use of Plato's *Laws* in the *Letter to d'Alembert*

In his first public statement as a political philosopher, Rousseau condemned the public entertainments of his time and railed against a culture of luxury in which "men have sacrificed their taste to the Tyrants of their liberty" (*Discourse on the Sciences and the Arts*, *O.C.*, 3:21). In a footnote to this statement, he offered an intriguing aside:

> I am far from thinking that this ascendancy of women is a harm in itself. It is a gift bestowed upon them by nature for the happiness of the human race: better directed, it might produce as much good as today it does harm. We are not sufficiently aware of what advantages would arise from giving a better education to that half of the human race that governs the other. Men will always be what is pleasing to women: if then you want them to become great and virtuous, teach women what greatness of soul and virtue is. The reflections this subject provokes, and which Plato made in bygone times, greatly deserve to be better developed by a pen worthy of following such a master and of defending a cause so great.

The reflections to which Rousseau refers are found primarily in Plato's *Laws* and are developed by Rousseau himself in his *Letter to d'Alembert on the Theater*. This chapter takes a new look at the education of women in the *Laws* and then shows how Rousseau made use of the dialogue in



N. Lund, *Rousseau's Rejuvenation of Political Philosophy*,
DOI 10.1007/978-3-319-41390-7_4

addressing a specific issue of political reform during his own time.[1] As I will show, the obvious parallels involving the political effects of imitative poetry and drama are not the only signs of Plato's influence on the *Letter to d'Alembert*, and perhaps not the most important. I will also argue that the apparent inconsistency between some of Rousseau's most important recommendations and those found in the *Laws* actually reflects a deeper agreement about the principles on which such reforms should be based.

## Economic Equality and the Education of Women in the *Laws*

Socrates is absent from Plato's longest dialogue, in which an elderly Athenian Stranger visits Crete and initiates a conversation with two even more elderly Dorians, a Knossian named Kleinias and a Spartan named Megillus.[2] The most significant way in which the Stranger differs from Socrates lies in his willingness to promote and guide a political reform that is to take place in deed rather than in speech.

In his political activism, the Stranger looks less like Socrates than like Plato himself, or at least the Plato of the *Seventh Letter*, who sought to help bring about philosophically informed laws in Syracuse. There are obvious differences, perhaps most notably the absence of any prospect that a young tyrant might provide the quickest and best way to implement the Stranger's laws in Crete.[3] But neither Plato's involvement with Syracuse and its tyrant nor the Stranger's involvement with Kleinias resembles anything in the life of Socrates as it is presented in Plato's dialogues.[4]

In his one public account of his life, Socrates says that he has never been a teacher of anyone, after having said that he will be a teacher today

[1] Rousseau was intimately familiar with the *Laws*. For evidence, see J.M. Silverthorne, "Rousseau's Plato."

[2] The Dorians, a Greek tribe or ethnic group, controlled Sparta and Crete as well as a number of other cities during Plato's time. The Athenians belonged to a different tribe, called Ionians. Knossos was one of Crete's principal cities.

[3] Compare *Laws* 709d10–710d5 with *Seventh Letter* 335c3–336c1.

[4] In the *Republic*, Socrates suggests that the quickest and easiest way to establish the best city would entail the expulsion of everyone over the age of ten (540d1–541a7). The Stranger emphasizes the efficacy of a certain kind of tyranny in effecting beneficial political reforms, but he does not recommend that Kleinias adopt anything like the radical measures proposed by Socrates (709e–712a).

at his trial.[5] Taken together, these statements suggest that he has never offered the kind of political instruction that the Athenian Stranger offers.[6] In his commentary on the *Laws*, Aristotle appears to identify the Stranger with Socrates, but he later attributes statements made by the Stranger to Plato (*Politics* 1265a1–9, 1271a41–b1). Perhaps the Stranger could be a Socrates who chose to leave Athens for Crete before he was prosecuted. If Socrates wanted the spectacle of his trial and execution in Athens to promote the survival of philosophy, it is at least conceivable that an opportunity to guide the founding of a city in deed would have looked to him like a more promising means of advancing this goal.

However the relationship between Socrates and the Athenian Stranger should be understood, Rousseau could easily have agreed with Leo Strauss that the *Laws* is Plato's most, and perhaps only, political work.[7] That, in turn, might help explain why this dialogue helped shape Rousseau's reflections on a topic that later became a central concern in his most vigorous and successful literary effort to inject himself into a live political controversy.

After the Stranger entices his interlocutors with an extended and subtly provocative critique of the Dorians' understanding of politics and their own institutions, Kleinias discloses that he is one of ten men charged with drawing up laws for a new city to be established in Crete. These lawgivers are to begin with a presumption in favor of Knossian laws, but are free to adopt others that seem better. Kleinias asks that they continue the conversation by constructing a city in speech, which he might find useful in the city that is going to be established in deed.[8] The Stranger enthusiastically

[5] *Apology of Socrates* 21b1–2; 33a5–6. Shortly after denying that he has been anyone's teacher, he repeats his opinion that it is just to be a teacher at his trial (35b9–c2).

[6] For a provocative analysis of Socrates' presentation of himself in the *Apology*, which suggests to me why Socrates did not, and perhaps would not, undertake a project like the Stranger's, see David Leibowitz, *The Ironic Defense of Socrates: Plato's* Apology.

[7] *The Argument and the Action of Plato's* Laws, 1. This claim is consistent with Socrates' own claim in the *Apology* that he never voluntarily involved himself in political affairs (31d5–e1).

[8] It is not easy to believe that the Stranger just happened to encounter Kleinias on the road up to Mount Ida, and just happened to initiate a very probing and sophisticated conversation about laws and regimes, only to be surprised to learn that Kleinias is about to participate in founding a new city. More likely, the Stranger sought Kleinias out in order to assist him with this project.

agrees to help draft laws for the city he calls Magnesia,[9] and he leads the Dorians through an elaborate analysis that mixes Athenian elements (often with significant modifications), along with some entirely novel proposals, into the laws and institutions with which Kleinias and Megillus are familiar.[10]

Among the many themes that Plato weaves together in the *Laws*, I will focus on two that stand out for their relevance to the *Letter to d'Alembert*: the dangers posed by commercial pursuits and economic inequality, and the opportunities offered by what might be called the liberation of women. These themes are closely connected. Before exploring them, however, we must follow the Stranger's effort to prepare his interlocutors for a modification of their traditionally Dorian views on manliness and virtue.

After advocating a novel practice of joining every law with a persuasive prelude, the Stranger proposes that the first law command every man to marry between the ages of thirty and thirty-five; violators are to suffer an annual fine and exclusion from certain honors (721a–d). The prelude asserts that everyone by nature desires immortality and that it is never blameless [or pious: *hosion*] to deprive oneself voluntarily of the share of immortality that one's children promise—the law punishes this behavior in order to prevent the opinion that remaining single brings "profit and ease" (721b6–d6).

It is less than obvious why this should be the first law or why the prelude would be persuasive.[11] Human beings, like other living things, reproduce

[9] No explanation is given for assigning this name to the city in whose founding Kleinias is to be involved. Perhaps none was needed because the location described by Kleinias corresponded to the site of an abandoned city of that name. See Glenn R. Morrow, *Plato's Cretan City*, 30–31; Diskin Clay, "Plato's Magnesia." In any event, the name is provisional (*Laws* 969a5–6).

[10] For a detailed comparison of the Stranger's proposals with institutions and practices that are known to have existed in the ancient world, see Morrow, *Plato's Cretan City*. Morrow's emphasis on Plato's innovations with respect to what we would call separation of powers, or checks and balances, is particularly valuable. What we often credit to Locke and Montesquieu may owe a lot to Plato's influence on the Romans, or perhaps it was simply forgotten through inattention to Plato. Either way, Plato's originality in offering proposals that we have come to regard almost as self-evident truths should provide an incentive to give serious thought to those elements of the *Laws* that may strike us as self-evidently wrong.

[11] Sparta, at least, seems to have had some such law, but there is no reason to think it was "first" in any sense of the word. See Plutarch, *Life of Lycurgus* 15.1–2. In Book VI, when the Stranger begins to present the laws in their proper order, he begins with religious gatherings, which turn out to provide fitting occasions to prepare young people of both sexes for marriage (771a–772a).

quite successfully by nature and without legal compulsion. Male resistance to marriage ordinarily stems from a reluctance to take on the burdens of supporting a wife and caring for her children, not from simple indifference to the kind of immortality that biological reproduction promises. It is therefore true that bachelorhood can sometimes be a source of "profit and ease," and that punishment would discourage it. But the most obvious rationales for such punishment—to prevent depopulation of the community and to prevent men from fathering children irresponsibly—are not the reasons given in the prelude. Instead, the prelude reads as though the law wants to do men a favor by encouraging them to satisfy a natural desire for immortality.

Accordingly, the Stranger soon points out that such an explanation is not the *logos* of the law, but only a device designed to make men more open to learning (723a–b). What might one who is subject to this law learn? A rational citizen might learn to weigh the value of the fine and loss of honor against the estimated value of the profit and ease of bachelorhood, so that he can decide which is greater. That is what the law standing alone would seem to encourage. Its effectiveness would then depend on the size of the fine and the nature of the dishonors imposed on bachelors, both of which the Stranger leaves unspecified.

The prelude is apparently meant to direct the citizen's thought away from this path, but not toward recognizing that marriage is a duty owed to the city, or to its women and his children. Instead, the prelude encourages the thought that doing what is manifestly good for the city, and for women and children, is good for oneself in a way that is both natural and lofty. Whatever the soundness of this thought may be, the prelude offers no argument to support it. Instead, the prelude offers high-sounding allusions to a qualified or even metaphorical kind of immortality, along with an appeal to moral or religious obligations. One cannot help wondering whether a more reliable support for the law would consist in opinions about the forms of "profit and ease" that are good for oneself, opinions that work against strong selfish desires with which nature equips male human beings. The Stranger gradually introduces a number of laws designed to foster such opinions.

Although the Stranger indicates that his initial statements about the use of preludes need some qualification, and seems inclined to pursue the matter in more depth, Kleinias is anxious to move the discussion along (723c–724a). The Stranger acquiesces, and launches into a very lengthy monologue that consumes almost all of Book V. In the course of gratifying

Kleinias, and perhaps implicitly rebuking him for his impatience, the Stranger offers a singularly concise statement of his goal: "The foundation (*hypothesis*) of our laws was looking toward this: how [the citizens] will be as happy as possible and to the greatest extent friends to one another" (743c5–6).[12] The Stranger never fully articulates a definition of the human virtue required for happiness, and he frequently acknowledges that civic friendship will inevitably be tenuous and incomplete. Near the very end of the dialogue, the Stranger aggressively focuses on the incompleteness or inadequacy of what has been said about virtue and on the need for an institutionalized inquiry about virtue in the new city (960b–968c). At many points in the dialogue, the Stranger assumes that there will need to be punishments for deviations from the law, great and small, which indicates that civic friendship will have some pretty sharp limits. He also indicates that a sufficiently precise inquiry would show a tension between the goals of the laws and the institution of private families (807b3–7).

The Stranger believes he has something useful to teach Kleinias, without seeking to lead him into Socratic philosophy. The *Laws* contains only two express allusions to philosophy. One is a reference near the end of the dialogue to mindless attacks by poets on those who philosophize (967c7–d1). The other is a description of a free physician speaking with a free patient, who uses "discourses (*logoi*) that approach philosophizing" (857d1–2).

At least part of the reason for the Stranger's reticence about philosophy, which contrasts so strikingly with what we find in the Socratic dialogues, may be suggested by a strange little drama that the Stranger stages for the benefit of Kleinias. Just after acknowledging that males and females differ by nature and just before recommending that the sexes receive the same education, the Stranger makes a number of remarks about the unseriousness of human affairs, culminating in the claim that we are by nature for the most part puppets, sharing only in small portions of the truth. When Megillus strongly objects to this belittling of "our human race," the Stranger claims to have spoken in this way only because he had been looking away toward the god. He then offers to proceed on the premise cherished by Megillus, that our race is worthy of a certain serious-

[12] As a means to achieving this double purpose, the Stranger indicates that the lawgiver should aim to make the city (understood as something distinct from the citizens) free, prudent or intelligent, and a friend to itself. See the slightly different formulations at 693b2–5, 701d7–9. On the distinction between the city and the citizens, see Strauss, *Argument and the Action*, 175.

ness (803a1–804c1). At least until Socrates, philosophers notoriously did seem to look away from and down on human affairs. Perhaps the Stranger wants to warn Kleinias about the lawgiver's need to indulge many useful but questionable assumptions, an indulgence that philosophy—including Socratic philosophy—does not permit to the philosopher himself.

The Stranger does, however, offer a very brief description of the best regime, which we can recognize as the city instituted in the *Republic* (739c–e). Kleinias and Megillus would never have heard of Socrates or his city in speech, and should have been expected to regard such a polity as ludicrous.[13] The Stranger anticipates this by explicitly indicating what the *Republic* only implies, namely that one could not deliberately establish such a city in deed. The city being constructed in the *Laws* is characterized as one that is modeled on this most beautiful city, while being adapted to the constraints or necessities of action. The Stranger also indicates that Magnesia will presumably have to depart in some respects even from this second-best city in speech.

One consequence of the Stranger's approach is that he will not attempt to maximize both of his goals—individual happiness and civic friendship—but rather will accept tradeoffs in an effort to maximize the sum of what may in some respects be incommensurable goods.[14] As we will see, he

[13]The Stranger mentions that his interlocutors are unfamiliar even with pre-Socratic philosophers (886c–e). Catherine H. Zuckert argues that the dramatic setting of the *Laws* is pre-Socratic, largely because the interlocutors mention historical events up to the end of the Persian Wars but say nothing at all about the Peloponnesian Wars (*Plato's Philosophers*, 53–54). As Zuckert recognizes, it is at least conceivable that the interlocutors might have avoided this topic in order to facilitate a friendly conversation. She rejects this as implausible, but the obvious allusions to the city of the *Republic* make her own conclusion quite implausible, for there is no reason to think that city had been heard of before Socrates began talking about it. In addition, the *Laws* contains some obscure allusions to historical events that may have taken place well after the death of Socrates. See Mark Munn, "*Erōs* and the *Laws* in Historical Context," 33, 45nn6–7. The *Menexenus*, moreover, has Socrates referring to events that took place after his own death—*a fortiori* the *Laws* could easily be set after Socrates died.

[14]Later, the Stranger introduces Kleinias and Megillus to incommensurable magnitudes (819d–820c). He says that all human beings are by nature in a laughable and shameful ignorance about this, which makes them seem more like pigs than humans, and he claims that after learning about incommensurable magnitudes he became ashamed not only for himself but for all the Greeks (819d1–e1). This bizarre confession and indictment is most directly tied to the ensuing discussion, at 821a–822c, of education about the relation between the heavenly bodies or celestial gods and "the greatest god and the whole cosmos" (821a2). But that discussion may in turn help Kleinias to appreciate the difficulties that must arise when dealing with incommensurable political goals.

suggests that the most practical way to do this is through a modification of existing laws and institutions that already aim at civic friendship and at virtue.

Early in the dialogue, the Stranger elicits from Kleinias a very conventional Dorian understanding of politics. The aim of the Cretan laws, says Kleinias, is war, and it needs to be their aim because defeat brings ruin while the victors take from the vanquished all good things (625c–626b). Kleinias then agrees that a state of war also exists among villages and families and individuals. Finally, the Stranger asks whether an individual is an enemy to himself. At this point, Kleinias fairly gushes over the Stranger's success in showing why it is right to say that all are enemies of all in public, and that in private each is an enemy of himself.

What has so pleased Kleinias, it seems, is that his view of universal warfare among human beings has now been logically joined with an edifying vision of individual self-discipline and self-improvement. This seems to make perfect sense of the achievements for which the Dorians were most famous: military success against other cities and the self-discipline on which their victories rested. But what about the other relationships, among villages and households and individuals? If they are all enemies of one another, why should they treat one another any differently than cities treat each other, making war when victory seems feasible and treating peace as nothing but a truce?

The Stranger calls attention to this difficulty by asking Kleinias to consider a household in which more of the brothers are unjust and fewer are just (627c–628e). What judge would we choose for them? One who destroyed the worse brothers and gave self-rulership to the others? One who made the worthy brothers rule and the others willing to be ruled? Or (apparently as an afterthought) one "third in virtue," who could reconcile them all by giving them laws that would secure their lasting friendship? Kleinias thinks the third is obviously best, and the Stranger immediately points out that the aim of such laws would be peace, not war, contrary to the thesis that Kleinias had embraced shortly before.

The second alternative resembles the one presented in the *Republic*; the one chosen by Kleinias is to guide the construction of Magnesia.[15] As Kleinias should surmise from the contradiction between his understanding of Cretan institutions and his choice of the third alternative, this will

[15] Something like the first alternative is touched on by the Eleatic Stranger in the *Statesman* (293d4–e5).

require some fundamental modifications of those institutions. Two of the most important involve the distribution of property and the education of women.

### *Economics and Women*

Both Dorians had said that a well-governed city must be oriented toward victory in war (626c). Consistent with Kleinias' subsequent conflation of victory in war with victory over oneself, the Stranger interprets him to mean an orientation toward the manly virtue of courage, which is associated with the love of honor and of accumulating honor through wealth (630b–632e).[16] The Stranger strongly praises Crete and Sparta for their orientation toward virtue, while showing his interlocutors why virtue cannot be adequately understood as courage or manliness alone. Aristotle presents the same critique from a more straightforwardly practical perspective, and a brief summary may usefully introduce a discussion of the Stranger's proposed reforms of Dorian institutions.

Aristotle singles out the Spartans for special praise, saying that their lawgiver was one of the few who took care about the upbringing and pursuits of the people, and goes so far as to denigrate the private freedom found in most cities as "Cyclopean" (*Nicomachean Ethics* 1180a24–29; see also 1102a8–11). In his evaluation of the Spartan regime, Aristotle specifically cites with approval the criticism in Plato's *Laws* of an exclusive focus on a part of virtue, namely military virtue. Aristotle adds that this focus prevented the Spartans from knowing how to use their leisure from war or how to practice anything but war—they considered the fruits of victory to be better than the virtue that produces victory (*Politics* 1271a41–b10).

Aristotle also identifies numerous practical defects in the Spartan regime, many of which relate to the arrangement of offices. A more fundamental problem has been persistent difficulties with the helots, but he notes that Crete has a similar system that causes less trouble, apparently because the Cretan cities do not have neighbors with an interest in fomenting slave revolts (1269a34–b12; cf. 1272b16–23, noting that this Cretan advantage did not last forever). Aristotle and Plato both cast serious doubt on the justice of slavery, but not on its necessity. As we will see, the Stranger's proposed innovations concerning women are intimately connected with his economic proposals, and those proposals depend on the use of slaves.

[16] The Greek word for courage, *andreia*, literally means "manliness."

Aristotle distinguishes natural from legal slavery and defines the natural slave as one so limited in his mental capacities that he would probably need to be cared for, rather than being a source of much useful labor (1253b–1255b). Even if we supposed that the class of natural slaves included people with enough reason to make them useful to a master, their reason would still have to be so defective as to make slavery advantageous to them as well as to the natural master (1255a1–3; 1278b33–34). Those enslaved by law were captured in war or descended from those captured in war, a class of people that would seldom if ever include natural slaves who happened to be owned by natural masters. In a prescient comment that obliquely calls into question the justice of virtually all slavery, Aristotle notes that slaves are living tools, which we would not need if we could enable machines to do their work (1253b33–1254a1).

In the *Social Contract*, Rousseau notes that Aristotle said that "men are not naturally equal, but that some of them are born for slavery and others for domination" (bk. 1, chap. 2, *O.C.*, 3:353). Purporting to take Aristotle as a defender of actual institutions, Rousseau says that Aristotle was right as a matter of fact, but that he mistook the effect for the cause: "Slaves lose everything in their chains, even the desire to lose them; they love their servitude as the companions of Ulysses loved their brutishness. So if there are slaves by nature, it is because there have been slaves contrary to nature. Force made the first slaves, their cowardice perpetuated them" (ibid., footnote omitted). Whether or not he really believed that Aristotle himself was confused, Rousseau saw why Aristotle's apparent position is not without an element of truth.

In the *Laws*, the Stranger secures even from Megillus an acknowledgment that slaves may sometimes be superior in virtue to free men (776a–e) and then offers Kleinias advice on using them efficiently and humanely (777b–778a).[17] The Stranger recommends that slaves be drawn from a variety of foreign sources, thereby discouraging the solidarity that naturally

[17] The Stranger also cites Homer for the proposition that slaves are untrustworthy because slavery makes their souls unhealthy (776e–777a). Homer's text makes the plausible suggestion that slavery takes away half one's virtue because slaves must be forced to do what they should, but the Stranger alters the quotation so that it advances the much less plausible claim that slavery takes away half one's intelligence. This calls attention to the fact that Homer ironically puts the assertion in the mouth of a remarkably trustworthy and intelligent slave (*Odyssey* 17.322–23). If, as the Stranger hopes, the *Laws* will be studied in Magnesia (811c–e), or wherever statesmanship is taken seriously, intelligent readers will be able to discover the Stranger's own irony.

arises when a culturally united group of people is held in bondage. He also recommends that masters treat their slaves firmly and fairly, but without familiarity, pointedly noting that slavery may be more corrupting of the masters than of the slaves because it offers so much opportunity to commit injustices that will go unpunished.

Later, the Stranger analogizes the recommended treatment of slaves to the way that children should be treated when they have to be disciplined (793e–794a). This calls attention to a certain difficulty with the Stranger's anti-solidarity point. Assuming that the descendants of slaves brought from foreign lands will remain as slaves in Magnesia, the cultural barriers between the slaves can be expected to diminish over time, for the descendants will in a significant sense be children of Magnesia. The new city's novel orientation toward virtue might eventually render politically problematic the practice of enslaving some of the city's children on the basis of their birth and without regard to their natural capacity for virtue.[18]

For the Stranger's purposes, one advantage of Crete over Sparta may have been that the Cretans had less need to employ the kind of brutality for which the Spartan treatment of the helots was notorious. Early in the dialogue, Megillus mentions Sparta's *krypteia*, or "secret police" (633b9–c1), but the parallel institution in Magnesia has a very different function, namely to police the citizens themselves and to educate the police officers in justice.[19]

[18] One can imagine a variety of responses that might be adopted by the Magnesians. They might, for example, sell the children of their slaves and purchase substitutes from other lands, which would follow the model provided by the Stranger's law on metics. Such a practice, however, would encourage slave revolts. The Magnesians might also consider some system of selective emancipation adapted from existing Greek practices, a strategy that Rousseau would later recommend in his *Considerations on the Government of Poland*. See chap. 6, *O.C.*, 3:974. The Stranger leaves such questions unaddressed, perhaps because he sees the tension between the necessity of slavery and its natural injustice as one that the city's founders cannot attempt to resolve at the outset. Subsequent European history—which saw the persistence of slavery well past the time when Christianity threw its injustice into a new light and well after new technologies rendered it unnecessary—suggests that the Stranger's reticence was not without justification. Cf. Tocqueville, *Democracy in America*, vol. 2, pt. 1, chap. 3 (claiming that even the great writers of antiquity were blind to the injustice of slavery, asserting the necessity of Christ's appearance on earth to make it understood that all people are alike and equal, and leaving it to the reader to notice how long slavery persisted after the Christian era began).

[19] See 760b–763c. Leo Strauss assumes that Magnesia's rural police (*agronomoi*, or *kryptoi* as the Stranger calls them at 763b7) would help the citizens to recover runaway slaves (*Argument and the Action*, 89). This may be true, but such assignments would not have anything like the central importance that controlling the helots had for the *krypteia* in Sparta.

The Stranger's acceptance of the traditional institution of slavery appears to be a concession to necessity. Once he determines that his goals require that the citizens have leisure without the inequality that would inevitably accompany large economic surpluses, it follows that they must be restricted to agricultural occupations and that they must be freed from personally occupying themselves with agricultural work. Given the technology of the time, only slavery offered a way out of this dilemma. For his part, Rousseau believes that the abolition of slavery made possible by new technologies was accompanied by more insidious forms of servitude:

> There are some unhappy situations in which one can preserve one's liberty only at the expense of another's, and the Citizen can be perfectly free only if the slave is perfectly enslaved. That was the situation of Sparta. As for you, modern peoples, you have no slaves, but you are slaves; you pay for their liberty with your own. (*S.C.*, chap. 15, *O.C.*, 3:431)

Aristotle's most extended critique of the most fundamental Spartan institutions links greed with the failure to attend to the virtue of women. Sparta's slackness with regard to women, according to the *Politics*, harms both the plan of the regime and the happiness of the city (1269b12–14). "The lawgiver [i.e., Lycurgus], who wanted the whole city to be steadfast, was conspicuous in this concerning the men, but was negligent toward the women; they live intemperately in regard to every kind of intemperance and luxuriously" (1269b19–23). Women, who could inherit and own property (1270a23–25), made wealth a thing of honor by their influence over men (1269b23–34), and this was aggravated by defective land laws that allowed some citizens to become very rich while others fell into poverty (1270a11–18). The result was that the population declined (1270a25–34), and the dissolute women were worse than useless, even when the city itself was threatened by an invasion (1269b34–39).

Why did Lycurgus make this mistake? Not because he failed to recognize a problem, it seems. The men for whom he legislated had already been prepared for the tough discipline of his laws by extended military campaigns against a series of enemies. Lycurgus apparently tried to subject the women to legal discipline as well, but he gave up when they resisted (1270a4–8).

It is not hard to imagine why the women would have resisted, and resisted strongly. In a military culture, men do the fighting, and men get the honor. What would there be for Spartan women to do except to enjoy the goods that their men win in battle, not only against other cities but in the endless war against the helots? Imposing harsh discipline on women would hardly help them play this role, and they would hardly have found such discipline attractive. Spartan women, we should note, were not passive consumers of booty won by their men. Aristotle indicates that they became demanding consumers (1269b23–34), and were thus an important driving force behind the Spartan error of giving more honor to the fruits of virtue than to virtue itself (1271b6–10).

The Athenian Stranger sets out to solve the same interrelated problems of undisciplined women and economic greed that Aristotle saw in Sparta. The economic solution has two main elements. First, the arable land of the city will be divided into plots of equal productive potential, and every family will have one and only one of these plots (along with the equipment needed to put it to use). Citizens will support themselves through farming, an economic activity that can be performed largely by slaves, and one that has a natural limit on the wealth it can produce. The citizens will be forbidden to work as artisans or to pursue commercial activities. These occupations—which generally reward the practitioner in proportion to his talent and effort, and which have almost no limit either on the attention they can demand or on the material rewards they can bring—will be performed solely by metics or other aliens.[20] Second, the allotments of real estate will be inalienable, and no household will be permitted to acquire a total sum of wealth exceeding five times the value of that allotment.

The advantages of this scheme in promoting friendship among the citizens are obvious. By preventing anyone from falling into abject poverty, it guards against the disturbances that a population of pauper citizens so often generates. By preventing anyone from amassing huge amounts of wealth, it discourages the insolence to which the very rich are always prone. And it does so without appealing to dreams of political communism, a fantasy that Aristotle skillfully and concisely punctured long before it fired the modern imagination (*Politics* 1263b15–29).[21]

[20] Citizens will not even be permitted to use their own slaves for these purposes (846d). The Stranger also proposes a number of other laws designed to keep this economic system stable, including a ban on the private ownership of precious metals, a refusal to make contracts among citizens legally enforceable, and a limit on the time that metics can remain in the city. See, for example, 741e–742c; 850b–c.

[21] Non-political communism is a somewhat different matter. See, for example, Chapter 2; *Laws* 678e–680e (and note that at 680a9 the Stranger says that even life before there were cities was already in some way a polity).

No less important, this scheme serves the other purpose of the Stranger's laws. Material goods are useful to the individual only insofar as they benefit his body and soul (743d–e). As we can see if we think about it, some such goods are obviously necessary and beneficial, but pursuing material wealth beyond this point will simply divert one's time and attention away from the ends for which wealth is useful to oneself. This proposition is not hard to accept in the abstract, but it is extremely difficult to follow in practice. It is less than obvious what activities will best foster the well-being of one's soul, what amount of wealth is needed for the pursuit of those activities, which of these activities require the renunciation of pleasures that wealth can buy, and how much wealth one should accumulate as a hedge against future contingencies. In addition, the habit of pursuing wealth is apt to generate a taste for that pursuit, and thus forgetfulness about the properly instrumental nature of material goods.

Establishing a fixed limit on the amount of wealth that a family can accumulate will effectively force the citizens to turn their ambition in a different direction. But that will only create new and possibly worse problems if they are left in a position like that of the Spartan women: provided with leisure by their use of slave labor, but left without guidance in the prudent use of that leisure (806e–807a). An important step in the Stranger's remedy for this problem comes in his proposals for the education of women.

### *The Education of Women*

Consistent with his overall rhetorical strategy, the Stranger begins by praising the unique Dorian practice of common meals, which he supposes must have arisen from accident or necessity during war, and then been found to be more generally beneficial (780b2–d1). With some hesitation, he suggests that Kleinias' new city might be able to do what would not be tolerated anywhere else, namely establish common meals for women as well. Like Aristotle, the Stranger regards the Dorians' failure to discipline their women as a serious mistake. His diagnosis of the problem, however, is considerably more elaborate.

In what sounds at first like a concession to the manly prejudices of his interlocutors, he says, "[T]he race of us humans that is by nature rather more secretive and wily on account of its weakness, the female, being in disorder, was incorrectly neglected by the lawgiver's yielding to it … [W]hat relates to the women, overlooked and left in disorder, is not only half [of the lawgiving task], as it might seem; by so much as our female nature is inferior to that of the male with respect to virtue, it contributes to [the lawgiving task] being more than doubled" (781a2–b4).[22] It is a fact, however, not a prejudice, that women are by nature inferior to men *in the kind of bodily strength required for the exercise of military virtue.*[23] In a military culture, or more generally a culture that celebrates manliness, women would have little choice but to pursue their own welfare through indirect means. Being "secretive and wily" is a natural and reasonable response to the subordination imposed on the physically weaker half of the population, for much the same reason that being secretive and wily is a reasonable way for a slave to cope with the circumstances in which he finds himself.[24]

The Stranger sets out to correct, or at least ameliorate, this defect in the Dorian regime. In some ways, his proposals correct the Dorian view of virtue, and in some ways, they correct nature's disparate treatment of the sexes. The first major step is a reconsideration of marriage. As the Stranger emphasizes, sexual desire produces the most fiery madness (782e6–783a3), a form of mental illness that marriage is meant to treat. But marriage cannot do this very well unless the spouses are physically attracted to each other. Accordingly, he proposes that young people of both sexes appear nearly naked during public dances, "viewing and being viewed," thus helping to avoid mistaken nuptial choices (771e–772a). As we will see, a version of these dances assumes an important place in Rousseau's *Letter to d'Alembert.*

[22] My translation of this difficult passage has been influenced by Tormod Eide, "Including the Women in Plato's *Laws*: A Note on Book 6, 781a–b."

[23] Catherine McKeen believes that Plato regards women as "morally inferior" to men, and that his "clear implication" in this passage is that "women are inferior in virtue as a matter of nature, and not simply as a matter of bad training or teaching" ("Why Women Must Guard and Rule in Plato's *Kallipolis*," 541, 544n2). I believe that McKeen has conflated the impression that Kleinias and Megillus might easily have gotten with what Plato must have thought. For a careful reading of the text, which comes closer to my interpretation, see T.J. Saunders, "Plato on Women in the *Laws*," 592–93.

[24] These are also qualities that enable women to assist men who may not realize they need assistance. Plato, moreover, is himself a secretive and wily writer. Among countless examples, compare the Stranger's proof of the existence of the gods, which assumes that the cosmos came into being, with his much earlier statement that "every man (*anēr*) needs to well understand this much, that the coming into being of human beings either had absolutely no beginning and will never have an end, but always was and surely will be, or that some immensely long time would have elapsed since its beginning" (893b–899b; 781e7–782a2). In their own very different way, the very manly men of the Spartan *krypteia* were also secretive and wily. See, for example, Thucydides 4.80; Plutarch, *Life of Lycurgus* 28.1–4.

The Stranger's institution of "mating dances" is supplemented with exhortations of a different kind: men are to be encouraged to lean in favor of a wife who comes from a family that is economically below his own, and from a family whose natural dispositions seem to complement rather than match his own (773a–c).[25] Unlike the first proposal, the focus of this one is on channeling the citizen's thoughts toward what is good for the city rather than toward what seems most pleasant to oneself. As can easily be seen, this set of proposals resembles the treatment of economic activities. In both cases, citizens are not asked to defy nature by adhering to a strict egalitarian or communistic principle, but are encouraged to temper their self-indulgence out of respect for the common interest.

A similar pattern is followed in the regulation of marital relationships. Childbearing and the rearing of children is to be treated as a public duty (which is not what we would have expected from the prelude to the "first law"), and female officers will be appointed to supervise parents by visiting their homes for inspections and exhortations—these inspectors, moreover, will prosecute recalcitrant parents for raising their children poorly (784a–d).[26] This defiance of parents' natural jealousy about the upbringing of their own children in their own homes is combined with a remarkable concession to natural human selfishness. Married couples are to procreate for no longer than ten years, which will provide leisure from the most onerous duties of parenthood during an extended period of life. Women will be the principal beneficiaries of this law.

The Stranger carries this policy even further. Adultery during these childbearing years, or with a married person who is in the years of childbearing, will incur legal penalties. For those beyond this age, however, there will be no legal penalties for adultery. Those who behave temperately should enjoy a good reputation, and as long as most people live in a measured way, the law should be silent (784e–785a). It is not clear whether the Stranger means that temperance and measured behavior refers to marital fidelity, or to adultery that is infrequent or discreet. What is clear is that the law will be much more tolerant of self-indulgent behavior in these

[25] Rousseau offers somewhat similar advice in the *Emile* (*O.C.*, 4:765–68, Bloom, 407–09). Socrates takes a very different approach when he suggests that the guardians of his city in speech be bred according to scientific eugenics principles, like livestock (*Republic* 458c6–461b7).

[26] Dorian institutions obviously would have prepared the Knossians to accept public supervision of child rearing.

circumstances than of self-indulgent behavior that interferes with the production and rearing of legitimate children.

This discussion ends with a comment that a woman will be eligible for public offices at the age of forty, approximately a decade after she would have had her last child, and a man at the age of thirty, approximately a decade after he becomes an adult (785b). The Stranger recognizes that nature imposes a distinct role for women in human life, but he seeks to limit the onerous effects of that burden on their lives. More provocatively, he adds that men will be eligible for military service between the ages of twenty and sixty, and women from the end of their childbearing until the age of fifty.

The provocation is given a more elaborate form in the educational proposals that follow. Public education, conducted by metics under the supervision of public officials, will be compulsory (804d–e; 813e). Girls are to be given the same musical (or, as we might say, liberal) education as boys, with due allowance for the natural differences between the sexes. Thus, for example, the Stranger recommends that music that is magnificent and inclined toward manliness should be called masculine, and what leans toward the orderly and temperate should be designated as more feminine in law and speech (802d8–e11). Much more surprisingly, the Stranger proposes that girls be given the same military training as boys.[27] This is shocking when one considers the extreme physical demands that were placed on soldiers in the ancient world. One might at least have expected the Stranger to exempt women from hoplite training, especially since Kleinias had mentioned early in the dialogue that the uneven terrain in Crete made hoplites less useful than in some other parts of Greece (625d).[28] But no. Boys and girls will get the same gymnastic and military training, and women will be expected to serve in combat if they are needed (813d–814b).[29]

[27] In a somewhat ambiguous passage, the Stranger seems to allow girls to opt out of the preliminary training in military exercises (794c8–d2). He subsequently withdraws this suggestion (804d6–805d2).

[28] Notwithstanding what Kleinias had said, the Stranger praises hoplite training because it develops steadfastness in a way that other modes of combat do not (706b7–c7). Later, he pointedly makes the possession of heavy arms a condition of voting for certain offices (753b4–7).

[29] The Stranger had prepared this suggestion with a discussion of the relation between the right and left limbs of the human body: nature makes one side somewhat stronger, but we decide whether to cultivate that natural difference or compensate for it through training. In our time, a basketball player practices free throws with his strong arm only, but competitive pressures require him to become as ambidextrous as possible in making layups. The Stranger advocates a literal training in the ambidextrous use of weapons, and invites Kleinias to see the analogy in the city's training of women (794d–795e).

The Stranger insists that women are capable of this, and he cites as evidence the Sarmatian and Amazon warriors (804d–806c). He also develops a practical argument, according to which circumstances could arise in which the male warriors would be unable to protect the city (because of their insufficient numbers or because they are fighting elsewhere). By massively increasing the number of potential combat troops, the Stranger provides for such an eventuality; perhaps more important, he increases the deterrent effect that the city's military resources can be expected to have on would-be invaders. One could easily make similarly practical arguments about the advantages of making women eligible for public offices, a proposal that the Stranger offers almost in passing, presumably because it is less shocking and in any event almost a logically necessary consequence of requiring military service of women.

These arguments are not implausible, but I think that the Stranger's larger aim is to curtail the contempt for women that naturally arises in men when they take on the role of protector for which their greater physical strength in fact suits them well. There is a simple and logical argument that men will almost always find congenial: We the stronger provide and protect, and you the weaker should therefore serve and be ruled.[30] This argument looks all the more plausible when women respond, as they almost must respond, by becoming secretive and wily—the superiority of men is then confirmed in their own minds by the effect that their claim to superiority has on women. The Stranger means to break this chain of logic, for the benefit of both sexes.[31]

Given the natural differences between the sexes, in physical strength and in their reproductive roles, it is true that very few women could ever be expected to excel in military virtue. It is also true, however, that few men can truly excel in it either. Apart from the physical differences among males, moreover, military heroism does not confer a proportion-

[30] In the *Republic*, Adeimantus articulates a version of this argument when he objects to requiring the warriors in the emerging just city to be ill-paid servants of the weaker citizens (419a1–420a8). Aristotle provides a different kind of illustration when he alludes to a madman who receives sound counsel from a woman he took as booty in war—counsel that would have saved him from destruction—and rebukes her with the comment that "silence brings order [or adornment: *kosmos*] to a woman" (*Politics* 1260a30, quoting Sophocles, *Ajax* 293).

[31] Even before Kleinias had revealed that he was to participate in founding a city, the Stranger hinted at his goal by listing seven disparate claims to rule without mentioning the claim of men to rule women (689e–690d).

ately greater claim to rule.[32] That would be especially true in a city, like Magnesia, that is meant to shun wars of conquest. By including women as a part of the city's military force, even if as an auxiliary part, the Stranger's law will make it harder for men to argue or believe that women have less claim to rule than men. Even generals are not required to be heroes (although they certainly should not be cowards), and political rulers need not be distinguished military figures. The military education of women, and their availability for combat, thus qualifies them to participate in the city's public life and political offices, and I believe even in the highest offices.

The text of the *Laws* is quite obscure about which offices are to be open to women. A few are reserved for them: women will be priestesses (presumably for service to female deities, in accord with Greek custom), inspectors of married couples and young children, and supervisors of women at their segregated common meals (759a–e, 783e–784a, 794a–c, 806e). With respect to most of the highest offices, the Stranger does not say that women are forbidden to serve. Although we are often left with the impression that males will fill these offices, this is largely because of a Greek linguistic convention according to which the masculine gender is used when referring to people whose sex is not necessarily specified. The impression we are left with is not required by the text.

I have found three especially important offices for which there is a clear textual indication that they will be filled only by males: the superintendent of education, the auditors, and the nocturnal council (765d4–7, 946a1, 946b7, 969b8). The Stranger's statement that the superintendent of education should be a father with legitimate children might simply reflect the fact that he says this before he has broached his proposals for the education of women, which means that his interlocutors are not yet prepared to consider the possibility of women holding high offices. Later, however, he does use the term *anēr* (male human being) when describing the auditors and the nocturnal council. Even these references, however, should be read

[32] Even in the *Iliad*, the extraordinary personal prowess of an Achilles, an Ajax, or a Diomedes was primarily a source of glory, rather than of a claim to rule, as we can see most strikingly in the relationship between Achilles and Agamemnon. By the time Plato wrote, the desire for glory in warfare had been channeled into behavior that was less individually spectacular than much of what we see in the *Iliad*, and the Greek phalanx provided even less scope for claims to rulership based on individual feats of valor. For the persistent influence of the *Iliad* on Greek warfare, however, see J.E. Lendon, *Soldiers and Ghosts: A History of Battle in Classical Antiquity*.

in light of a speech in which the guardians of the laws are told that they will need to fill in the sketch provided by the *Laws* (770b4–771a4). In the course of this speech, the Stranger refers to a good man (*anēr*), having the virtue of soul of a human being (*anthropos*), *whether his nature be male or female* (770d1–5, emphasis added). With this exceedingly strange formulation in mind, one can easily imagine that women should be allowed to assume any office for which they show themselves qualified.

It may well be that a variety of factors—such as the unequal burden placed by nature on women in reproduction, certain tastes or dispositions that may naturally be more common among women than among men, and the auxiliary role they are to play in the military establishment—will conspire to limit the numbers of women in high office. The Stranger certainly does not propose anything like the modern practice of affirmative-action quotas and preferences, but the text of the *Laws* at least permits the inference that women should have an equal opportunity to participate in the city's most influential public offices. The formulation at 770d1–5 leads me to believe that this inference is not only permitted but encouraged.

A competing alternative to my interpretation has been presented by Michael S. Kochin.[33] On the basis of a careful analysis of the text, Kochin contends that women are excluded from the highest offices and that this exclusion reflects a fundamental defect in the Magnesian regime. That defect, in his view, arises from the Stranger's related decisions to preserve the institution of patriarchal families and to rely on the rule of law rather than the rule of wisdom or intellect. These decisions, in turn, go to the root of why the city of the *Laws* is second-best compared with that of the *Republic.*

Plato's text will bear Kochin's interpretation. I believe that our disagreement turns ultimately on whether the Stranger believes that his laws can—if not immediately then eventually—be modified or interpreted so as to admit women into the highest offices, and especially to the nocturnal council. A confident answer to that question would depend on understanding how far the nocturnal council can go in discovering the unity of human virtue, and how far the law can go in recognizing that unity without abolishing private families. The Stranger leaves us to wonder what those limits are, and I am not persuaded, as Kochin appears to be, that women can never be admitted to the nocturnal council. Thus, in only one respect do I disagree with his statement that "[s]ince the laws of the

[33] *Gender and Rhetoric in Plato's Political Thought.*

*Laws* fail to promulgate properly the unity of human excellence in a single individual, they contain within themselves a permanent tension" (*Gender and Rhetoric*, 126). The tension might not prove to be permanent, or at least not permanently so severe, if the nocturnal council comes to recognize that the sought-for unity of human virtue demands that women be allowed to join in its pursuit. However unlikely that recognition may be, the *Laws* does not seem to me to imply that it is inherently impossible.

In Magnesia, the natural distinctions between men and women are to be less politically significant than the differences among people in their intellectual achievements (e.g., 818a). At one point, for example, the Stranger seems to suggest that military training for women, and perhaps education more generally, will help them avoid an unthinking reliance on religion as a response to serious problems (814a–b). One might suppose that giving the sexes a substantially common education, and substantially common obligations and opportunities to participate in public life, should pretty much be adequate for curing the very serious defect that the Stranger and Aristotle both point out in the Dorian regimes. This thought seems to be confirmed by the Stranger's failure to demand strict equality of the sexes within the family, let alone to abolish the family as Socrates does in the *Republic*. Only men will inherit real property, and it appears that they will assume the traditional role as head of household (e.g., 923c–924a).[34]

The Stranger, however, is not satisfied to leave things here, and he returns yet again to the obstreperous problem of sex and sexual inequality. Early in Book I, he had annoyed the Spartan Megillus by mentioning his city's unsavory reputation for pederasty and for the looseness of its women (636a–637c). Now, having completed the discussion of the edu-

[34] It should be stressed that Magnesian women will have considerably greater rights and privileges in family life than Athenian women did. See T.J. Saunders, "Plato on Women in the *Laws*," 598–602. Arlene Saxonhouse stresses that the *Laws* (unlike the *Republic*) proposes a model that "takes men and women as they are, as they arrive from various communities around Greece" (*Women in the History of Political Thought*, 57). More dubiously, she concludes that "in Plato's vision, [women can never] fit comfortably into the world of political activity" (ibid., 62). Susan Moller Okin, whose interest in Plato is manifestly subordinate to her own commitment to promoting the thoroughly equal treatment of women, appears to believe that Plato's general attitude to and beliefs about women, "which reflect much of the highly misogynic Greek tradition," prevented him from carrying out "his professed intentions in the *Laws* to emancipate women and make full use of the talents that he was now convinced they had" (*Women in Western Political Thought*, 10, 27, 50). Both of these commentators seem to me to have been far less successful than Plato in transcending the climate of opinion in which they lived.

cation of the Magnesian citizens, he describes their situation in a way that can remind us of Aristotle's Spartan women: released from hard labor, forbidden to engage in commercial pursuits, and preoccupied throughout their lives with sacrifices, festivals, and choruses (835d–e). What would stop natural erotic desire from filling the leisured vacuum, upending families, and disordering public life? Pederasty may serve to divert men from fathering illegitimate children, but the Stranger declares that on this issue he must completely reject the practices of Crete and Sparta, which have been found to be such excellent starting points in many other ways (836b–c).

After presenting a very puzzling analysis that approves only of what we would call "platonic" loves among men, the Stranger secures the ready agreement of Megillus, which indicates that the Spartan has stopped defending his city's sexual practices (836d–837a).[35] But how will the Dorian men of Magnesia be persuaded to forsake the pleasures of pederasty? The Stranger expects tremendous resistance, which he describes in comically colorful terms (839b).[36] At the same time, he holds out the hope of discouraging all non-procreative sex, not just homosexuality but also fornication and adultery, and apparently even onanism (838e). The Stranger also mentions abortions and infanticides (838e7–8), a reminder that the desire to escape the expense and trouble of raising children, that is, a desire for "profit and ease" (721d4), provides a significant incentive for choosing extramarital sexual outlets. The "platonic pederasty" that the Stranger had seemed to approve would of course also allow such an escape, but it would presumably be rare for such chaste relationships to be chosen as a complete substitute for physically gratifying forms of intercourse.

The Stranger argues that the taboo on incest shows that such self-denial is feasible since people everywhere have learned to regard the very thought of incestuous acts with horror (838a–e). Because people have proved that they can tolerate a prohibition against having sex with a few close relatives, they should apparently be able to tolerate a prohibition on having sex at all, outside of a monogamous marriage. Apart from the transparently

[35] The Stranger obviously could have presented a less puzzling argument, as Xenophon's Socrates does for the benefit of Lycon (*Symposium* 8; 9.1). But he chose not to do so, and Megillus' immediate acquiescence shows how much progress the Stranger has made in leading him away from allegiance to all things Dorian.

[36] This may help to explain why Kleinias cannot be expected to decide just yet whether the Stranger's proposal is a useful one. See 837e, 842a.

defective logic underlying this supposition,[37] the analogy to incest doesn't fit very well with the Stranger's claim that homosexuality (let alone non-procreative sex more generally) is wrong because it is unnatural. Even the most casual observations of the animal world indicate that the sexual drive has procreation as its natural purpose, but such observations also suggest that the incest taboo (which takes different forms in different cultures) must have a different or additional purpose.

I think the Stranger's effort to extend the incest taboo to male homosexuality has little to do with what is natural and much to do with his goal of elevating women politically. Much of the appeal of homosexuality in Dorian culture must have arisen from the opinion that men, being by nature superior to women, are worthier objects of love. That would help explain Megillus' quick agreement with the Stranger's argument—an argument that is in fact quite puzzling—for the superiority of "platonic pederasty" (837c–d). It would also explain why the Stranger makes a point of noting that the homosexual act happens to involve one of the partners in "imitating the female" (836e1–2).[38] And it would explain why the most specific benefit that the Stranger expects to be gained by his reform of Dorian practices is that it will make "husbands friendly [or dear] to their own wives" (839b1).[39] Precisely because the sexual drive itself is so strong, a taboo against homosexual relations would do little to promote "platonic" friendships among men, and perhaps do a lot to promote conjugal friendships between men and women.[40]

[37] The Stranger also notes that some athletes remain celibate during training, overlooking both the temporary nature of this self-restraint and the fact that serious athletic training resembles nothing so much as the excessive and illiberal physical labor from which Magnesian citizens will be released. The Stranger himself notes that such physical labor "most of all extinguishes wantonness" (835d8–e1).

[38] In one sense, of course, this observation may reinforce the Stranger's claim that such acts are unnatural. More vividly, however, it reminds one that there is a certain illusion involved in supposing that pederasty transcends whatever sordid qualities one might associate with opposite-sex intercourse.

[39] The adjective *philos*, meaning "friendly," has both an active and passive sense. The Stranger exploits the ambiguity to suggest that his reform will lead to mutual affection between husbands and wives, which is something that the marital contract alone cannot accomplish.

[40] For a subtle and erudite exploration of the role of homoeroticism in Greek political thought, see Paul W. Ludwig, *Eros & Politics: Desire and Community in Greek Political Theory*. Ludwig's brief discussion of women in the *Laws*, ibid., 306n116, has a different focus than I offer, but I do not believe the two are at odds.

Consistent with his earlier willingness to tolerate a certain amount of adultery after the procreative period of life has ended, the Stranger concludes this discussion by offering a choice between two laws, or two versions of one law. The first alternative, which goes farther than he had gone before, demands perfect marital fidelity (841d). The second alternative seems to permit adultery, at least with slaves and concubines, so long as such activities are successfully concealed. What the two alternatives have in common is a strict prohibition against male homosexual relations. By saying that these two alternatives might be called one law, the Stranger suggests that this prohibition is the crucial one. What makes it crucial cannot be the non-procreative character of homosexual activity, a feature it has in common with many kinds of heterosexual relations and certainly with onanism, which is now not mentioned at all. Rather, the strict ban on homosexuality looks like an element in the Stranger's larger project of taming the contempt for women that contributes to the Dorian glorification of pederasty and helps to justify it.

### *Alternatives to the Equality of Women*

The Stranger's extremely radical proposals about the role of women in the city had no basis in the practices of any known culture (805d–806c). The Dorians take manly virtue seriously but have not thought enough about the virtue of women. Left to amuse themselves in private life, Dorian women are "liberated" for self-indulgence, and their ineradicable influence over men weakens the virtue of the men by helping to infect them with the love of wealth. At an opposite extreme are the Thracian barbarians who treat women as slaves to be used for manual labor. The Athenians take a third approach, depriving women of education and excluding them from public life, but assigning them to manage the home (805e2–7).[41]

The Stranger frequently emphasizes the practical benefits for the city, especially but not only with respect to war, of pushing women out of the home and into public life. He leaves little doubt, however, that his underlying goal involves the happiness of individual citizens of both sexes, under-

[41] The funeral oration of Pericles offers a particularly vivid expression of the Athenian attitude toward women's natural role. Pericles reluctantly addresses the widows of the fallen, whose loud public display of grief is a central element of such funerals. Without so much as pretending to offer them any consolation, he curtly tells them that a good reputation will be theirs if they are neither praised nor blamed among the men (Thucydides 2.45.2).

stood as something inseparable from the pursuit or practice of human virtue.[42] The Stranger's critique of manly virtue and his implicit rejection of the Athenians' notion of feminine virtue require a novel understanding of human virtue that can justify his novel proposals about the way to pursue that goal.

The Stranger does not purport to provide this new understanding to his Dorian interlocutors. The dialogue ends with the suggestion that the city will have to search for human virtue, and thus for the happiness of the citizens, under the leadership of the nocturnal council.[43] We might see the education of women in the Stranger's city as a means of removing one of the most powerful obstacles to that search, namely the strong male propensity to confuse manly virtue with human virtue. We, in our turn, might be moved to conduct such a search for ourselves.

Rousseau, as I will show, used the *Laws* in a different way. Kleinias repeatedly indicates that he expects to choose what he finds useful among the Stranger's proposals after he has seen them all explained. Rousseau takes up this suggestion for himself and adapts the Stranger's radical teaching about the education of women to serve a highly conservative political goal.

## Preserving Women from Miseducation: The *Letter to d'Alembert*

When Rousseau first mentioned that Plato was the master he would wish to follow in promoting an appropriate education for women, he could hardly have foreseen the occasion that would provoke him to take up his pen in defense of that cause. The *Discourse on the Sciences and the Arts*,

[42] See, for example, 790a8–b6; 828d5–829a8; 840c5–6; 858d6–9; 870b6–c1.

[43] The nocturnal council was first introduced as a body charged with helping misguided religious heretics to reform (908a–909a). In Book XII, it is described in more detail, and assigned to debrief selected citizens who have traveled for the purpose of studying other cities (951a–952e). At the end of the dialogue, this council is assigned to undertake a quest for the knowledge that will be needed for the preservation of the city (960b–968e). It is not clear that all three functions will be performed by exactly the same people. See, for example, Harvey Flaumenhaft, "The Silence of the Spartan: City, Soul, and Study of the Stars in the Epilogue to Plato's Last and Longest Dialogue," 74–75. More important, the Stranger emphatically denies that the preliminary conversation now coming to its end has disclosed what these guardians of the city will need to know about virtue, or its relation to "the beautiful and the good," and he denies that the education they will need can be described in advance (965c–966a; 968d–e).

in which he made this comment,[44] together with the ensuing *Discourse on Inequality*, soon established his position as a major philosophic voice in the French Enlightenment. That voice, of course, was one of rebellion against important elements of the Enlightenment project itself, and against Rousseau's own circle of philosophic friends.

A public break with these friends came in his response to Jean-Baptiste le Rond d'Alembert's article on Geneva in the *Encyclopedia*.[45] The article itself was highly favorable to the city of Rousseau's birth. It described a prosperous, democratic polity populated with industrious and well-educated citizens, largely free of conflicts between the civil and religious authorities, and open to scientific enlightenment.[46] D'Alembert singled out the Genevan clergy for special praise, suggesting that they had largely jettisoned both political ambition and what he considered the superstitious elements of Christianity.[47] All in all, d'Alembert intimated, an admirable

[44] *O.C.*, 3:21n (quoted in context at the beginning of this chapter).

[45] As we frequently find with Rousseau, his public discourse and his personal life become entangled in the *Letter to d'Alembert.* For a brief treatment of the factual background, see Maurice Cranston, *The Noble Savage: Jean-Jacques Rousseau 1754–1762*, 128–37. The subtleties and difficulties presented by Rousseau's use of personal elements in his writings, here and elsewhere, raise a myriad of interesting questions that I will generally not address.

[46] "Geneva," in *Lettre de M. d'Alembert à M. J.-J. Rousseau sur l'article "Genève" tiré du septième volume de l'Encylopédie Avec quelques autre pièces qui y sont relatives* [hereafter cited as "*Geneva Collection*"], 1–40. An English translation of d'Alembert's "Geneva" is available in Allen Bloom's translation of the *Letter to d'Alembert.*

[47] D'Alembert praised the "many" Genevan clergy who reject the divinity of Jesus, the existence of Hell, and all things called mysteries. In his somewhat intricate response to this allegation of theism, Rousseau argues that d'Alembert is either speculating that the pastors are heretics or betraying their confidences (*d'Alembert*, *O.C.*, 5:9–14, Bloom ed., 9–15). In response to Rousseau's criticism, d'Alembert denied that he had betrayed any confidences, and maintained that his claims were based on public statements by Genevan pastors ("Letter to Rousseau," in *Geneva Collection*, 150–56). Whether or not d'Alembert's speculations or inferences were supported by the public record, the Genevan clergy repudiated the claims he had made about their beliefs ("Declaration of the Pastors of Geneva," in ibid., 41–60).

The most striking feature of Rousseau's criticism of d'Alembert lies in what is missing. Rousseau does not criticize the beliefs attributed to the clergy by d'Alembert, nor does he defend the clergy against the charge of having adopted them. Nowhere does Rousseau imply that he disbelieves what d'Alembert said or that he thinks that such heresies and hypocrisies on the part of the pastors would be pernicious. Several years afterward, when the *Emile* was condemned in Geneva, Rousseau indicated that he did not give much credit to the pastors' repudiation of d'Alembert's claims (*Mountain*, lett. 2, *O.C.*, 3:717–18).

Later in the *Letter to d'Alembert*, Rousseau mentions that he has abandoned his own previous opinion that virtue can do without the support of religion, leaving the reader to wonder

small model of what other European nations could aspire to become if the priests and the princes could ever be dislodged from their pernicious grip on power.

Rousseau—who had himself contributed articles to the *Encyclopedia* and long been friendly with d'Alembert and Diderot—found amidst all this praise a mortal threat to the happy institutions that the article described. In what an ordinary reader might have seen as a peripheral and casual comment, d'Alembert suggested that Geneva could become an even more agreeable place if a theater were established there. In his view, the major obstacle was the Genevans' fear that a company of dissolute actors would corrupt the youth, but he thought this could be avoided by strict regulation of their behavior. A good theater would refine the atmosphere of the city, improve the tastes of the citizens, and promote the cultivation of civilizing literature: "Geneva would combine the sagacity of Lacedaemon with the refinement of Athens" (*d'Alembert*, *O.C.*, 5:4, Bloom, 4, quoting d'Alembert's "Geneva").

Rousseau was horrified. In a lengthy open letter to d'Alembert, he attacked this proposal from virtually every angle. The actors would indeed have a corrupting effect, he thought, and one that regulations would be powerless to prevent. But this was only one of a series of objections, which ranged from the narrowly economic to the profoundly moral and political. Rousseau marshals so many different arguments, and so well, that one wonders how a public-spirited Genevan could have failed to find at least one of them dispositive. The *Letter* is an extraordinary piece of political advocacy, and it was apparently an effective one (see Cranston, *Noble Savage*, 137, 148).

The occasion for the *Letter* was dramatically different from the context in which Plato wrote. Plato's philosophic fiction takes a form that is utterly different from Rousseau's polemical contribution to a live political debate. Magnesia, moreover, is to be populated with insular Dorians, while Geneva is a modern commercial city in the center of an increasingly cosmopolitan civilization. Greek polytheism, which seems to have lacked what we would call a coherent theology,[48] strongly contrasts with

about the reasons for both his previous and current views (*O.C.*, 5:89n, Bloom, 97n). In later publications, he had much more to say about all this. See, for example, *Emile*, *O.C.*, 4:632–35n, Bloom, 312–14n; *Mountain*.

[48] For an overview of Greek religion that emphasizes the disconnect between its practice and the poets' stories about the gods, see Jon D. Mikalson, *Ancient Greek Religion*.

eighteenth-century Calvinism, the product of a rich heritage of theological disputes that often had complicated political ramifications.

All these differences were bound to affect how Rousseau used what he had seen in Plato, but there is one more that I think has special significance. Kleinias is to participate in the establishment of a new city with new laws, which gives the Athenian Stranger an opportunity to propose radical reforms informed by an understanding of the impossibly beautiful city of the *Republic*. Even if it is too much to hope that Magnesia will be more than a third-best city (see *Laws* 739e2–5), Kleinias' project justifies a most serious and wide-ranging investigation of the possibilities and limitations of political reform.[49]

Rousseau is faced with an almost diametrically opposite situation. However Geneva arrived at its present condition, Rousseau believes that its current institutions promote both individual happiness and civic friendship to a degree remarkable in the modern world. Rousseau is under no illusion that "we will see Sparta reborn in the bosom of commerce and the love of gain" (*d'Alembert*, *O.C.*, 5:61, Bloom, 67), and his goal is to defend what Geneva has achieved. Whether detached reflection would regard this as a third-best city or a fourth- or fourteenth-best, it is this Geneva with which Rousseau is concerned. His goal is conservation, not radical reform.

In light of these differences, it is striking how many echoes of Plato one finds in the *Letter to d'Alembert*. The most obvious, of course, is the detailed analysis of the moral and political effects of the theater. Rousseau includes a lengthy quotation, in Latin, from Book III of the *Republic*, where Socrates closes his city to poets who offer imitations of anything except the rather austere models set down as fitting earlier in the dialogue (ibid., 109n, Bloom, 120n). More generally, Rousseau's analysis of the corrupting effects that dramatic spectacles can have on those who view them, and the need to combat such effects through legal regulation, manifestly owes a great deal to Plato. Although the *Letter* leaves aside many issues raised in the *Republic* and the *Laws*, the influence of those dialogues is easily visible.

*On Theatrical Imitation*, which Rousseau wrote while he was working on the *Letter to d'Alembert*, shows how deeply Rousseau engaged with the

[49] Among many indications that the Athenian Stranger means to convey an understanding of political reform that has applications beyond the immediate task facing Kleinias, see 736c–737b.

*Republic* as well as the *Laws*. At the head of the piece, Rousseau placed a notice purporting to inform us that he did little more than convert Plato's writing from a dialogue form to a coherent discourse, and that Rousseau had inadvertently released it for publication before deciding what, if anything, to do with it (*O.C.*, 5:1195). There are enough echoes from the *Republic* to make the first assertion superficially plausible, and the second assertion would be hard to disprove.

The notice also mentions that Rousseau had been unable to fit this writing "conveniently" into the *Letter to d'Alembert*, and that assertion is manifestly credible in a way that calls the other two into question. *Theatrical Imitation* is written in the first person (except for four footnotes in Rousseau's own voice), and it thus constitutes an inexact imitation of Plato's inexact imitations of Socratic conversations. If for no other reason than this use of the first person, the essay could not have fit conveniently in the *Letter*. But Rousseau's use of the first person also creates uncertainty as to whether, or to what extent, his paraphrases of speeches from Plato should be attributed to Socrates, or to Plato, or to Rousseau himself. In this way, the rhetoric of *Theatrical Imitation* imitates Plato's refusal to indicate whether, or to what extent, the imitations of Socrates in his own theatrical dialogues are speeches of Plato. Put this together with the irony of attacking imitations in an essay that is an imitation of an imitation, and you find yourself on notice against taking everything in *Theatrical Imitation* at face value.[50]

The thesis of *Theatrical Imitation* is that dramatic authors are "corrupters of the people, or of anyone who, allowing himself to be diverted by their images, is capable neither of considering them under their true point of view, nor of giving these fables the corrective they need" (ibid., 1196). As this formulation intimates, two somewhat different correctives turn out to be required.

The opening strand of argument in *Theatrical Imitation* seems to treat each thing in the sensible world, including human artifacts, as an imperfect image of models or original ideas that exist "in the understanding of the Builder, in nature, or at the very least in its Author together with all

[50] The notice also ironically characterizes the piece as a mere "bagatelle" (*O.C.*, 5:1195). In *Rousseau Judge of Jean-Jacques*: *Dialogues*, a character named "Rousseau" offers a list of six works about which he says, "I doubt that any philosopher ever meditated more profoundly, more usefully perhaps" (Second dialogue, *O.C.*, 1:791). The last item in the list is *Theatrical Imitation*.

the possible ideas of which he is the source" (ibid., 1197). Because painters and poets imitate sensible things, their works are imperfect images of imperfect images, and are thus in the order of being "always one degree farther from the truth than one thinks" (ibid.). God is assumed to be the author of the idea that a builder or craftsman imitates in the work he produces (ibid.).[51] *Theatrical Imitation*'s example of an imitation of an idea is a human artifact, namely a palace.[52] This is instantly puzzling. If anything in the world looks intelligible without the assumption of a divine mind and eternal ideas, it would seem to be the things that human beings make.

The puzzle is deepened a little later when *Theatrical Imitation* argues that the builder or craftsman does not have a true understanding of the thing he makes (ibid., 1203). It is Hector the charioteer, not the saddler, who knows what reins should be. More generally, "[i]f the utility, the goodness, the beauty, of an instrument, of an animal, of an action relates to the use drawn from it, if it belongs only to the one who puts them to work to provide the model and to judge whether this model is faithfully executed," neither the craftsman nor his imitator (such as a painter or poet) can properly judge the qualities of the artifact (ibid.). It is easy enough to agree that the utility, and perhaps the goodness, of an instrument is best judged by its user. But the "model" then turns out to involve specifications of which the user may have no clear idea before a craftsman produces an artifact that does or does not perform in a satisfactory manner. An animal, moreover, is not produced by a human craftsman, and it is difficult to conceive why God the author of all the ideas should be confounded with charioteers and other users of animals. And who exactly is the user who puts a human *action* to work?

These puzzles arise from a conflation of two different objections to painting and poetry, one of which is intellectual and the other moral. One objection is that paintings and poems create illusions about the world, and thus interfere with the search for truth. In the case of paintings, this is manifestly false in an important sense. As *Theatrical Imitation* acknowledges when it seeks to avoid "false analogies," our senses constantly deceive us about the physical world, and we can at least to some extent correct these misleading impressions by reasoning with the aid of "[t]he suspension of the mind, [and] the art of measuring, of weighing, of counting" (ibid.,

[51] Plato's Socrates is more tentative or equivocal in attributing the authorship of ideas to a god (*Republic* 597b).

[52] In the *Republic*, Socrates uses household furniture for examples.

1204–05). Paintings deliberately play upon the susceptibility of the senses to illusions, as with the art of perspective. But the viewer knows that the painting is only an image, and an artful one at that, so viewing the painting does nothing to enhance or aggravate the mistakes about the physical world to which our senses make us prone. Viewing a painting will not make one more likely to believe that the moon is larger when it is close to the horizon than when it is higher in the sky.

Poetry is different. A sufficiently talented poet might persuade a credulous audience that the moon does shrink as it ascends in the sky, perhaps with a story so charming as to deter the suspension of belief that must occur while one tests one's sense impressions by taking measurements. More obviously, poets (and sometimes painters, too) present us with pictures of the world and models of human action that "imitate what appears beautiful to the multitude, without caring whether it is so in fact" (ibid., 1204). This affects us adversely for two somewhat different reasons. First, we may think that a successful poet like Homer "must possess the science of all the [moral and political] things he treats" (ibid., 1200). Could any intelligent reader leave Homer without at least suspecting as much? Second, poets cause us to yield with a sort of pleasure to passions that embarrass and harm us when they overcome us in our own lives, thus making it harder to control them (ibid., 1208–10).

*Theatrical Imitation* suggests two different "correctives." One is quite straightforward. Banish poetry from our lives unless and until the friends of the poets can persuade us of its usefulness (ibid., 1210–11). The other corrective, offered only obliquely, is philosophy. This second suggestion comes in a passage where *Theatrical Imitation* responds to an objection that "the philosopher himself does not know all the arts about which he speaks, and that he often extends his ideas as far as the Poet extends his images" (ibid., 1204). The response offered is that the philosopher does not present himself as knowing the truth and "*even instructs us through his mistakes*" (ibid., emphasis added). Not a bad description of Socrates as he is presented in Plato, but neither the objection nor the response occurs in any of the passages from Plato paraphrased in *Theatrical Imitation*. It also leaves the usefulness of philosophy in considerable obscurity, and it leaves us to wonder how we are to be instructed by *Theatrical Imitation*, whose author seems to have deliberately adopted a more dogmatic rhetoric than Socrates employs in the passages paraphrased by Rousseau.

One clue to Rousseau's intention is provided by a particularly glaring mistake near the end of *Theatrical Imitation*. Not once but twice, he substitutes the name Glaucus for Glaucon in his paraphrase of the discussion that opens Book X of the *Republic*. Glaucus is a mythical god of the sea, whose once human form became unrecognizable through the action of ocean waves and an encrustation of shells, seaweed, and rocks. Socrates likens Glaucus to the human soul "as we see it now" (611b–d).[53] He offers this image after his argument for the immortality of the soul that immediately follows his attack on the poets, and shortly before he presents his own poetic myth of Er. The statue of Glaucus (an imitation of an imaginary being) is used in the *Discourse on Inequality* as an image of the human soul encrusted with an accumulation of effects from social life (*O.C.*, 3:122). Rousseau's mistaken substitution of the name Glaucus for Glaucon thus instructs us, upon reflection, about the need for something that is absent from *Theatrical Imitation*: philosophic poetry.

One of the ways that *Theatrical Imitation* distorts the *Republic* is by starting at the beginning of Book X and paraphrasing part of Book III later in the piece. This reversal of Plato's order calls attention to important differences between the contexts in which Socrates criticizes poetry in Books III and X. Book III's attack on poetry primarily involves Adeimantus as a founder and educator of imaginary men in an imaginary city in speech. There is no claim that he and Glaucon should themselves stay away from poetry, or that they are "not capable of considering [such fables] under their true point of view" (*O.C.*, 5:1196).

When Socrates returns to the topic of imitative poetry in Book X, he has already taken Glaucon and the others on a most fantastic imaginary journey out of the cave and instructed them, so to speak, about the order of being through images involving the divided line and the idea of the good. This is the necessary background (wholly absent from *Theatrical Imitation*) that allows Socrates to invoke the so-called doctrine of ideas when speaking with Glaucon at the beginning of Book X, where it seems less instantly puzzling than it does at the beginning of *Theatrical Imitation*.

This intervening journey has also shifted the emphasis from Glaucon and Adeimantus as educators of imaginary citizens to their own education. Or, to put it another way, the conversation has shifted from the requirements of a just city to those of a just soul. *Theatrical Imitation*, like the discussion of imitation in Book X of the *Republic*, points toward

[53] Ficino's Latin translation of the *Republic*, on which Rousseau relied, correctly distinguishes the name of Plato's brother and the name of the mythical figure.

questions about the role of poetic imitation in private or individual education.[54]

The *Letter to d'Alembert* attacks imitative poetry in a less thorough, perhaps less subtle, and certainly more political manner than *Theatrical Imitation*.[55] In these respects, the *Letter* is related to *Theatrical Imitation* as the *Laws* is related to the *Republic*.[56] Some of the Athenian Stranger's statements about poetry resemble some of Socrates' statements in the *Republic*.[57] Unlike Socrates, however, the Stranger introduces comic imitations into Magnesia, where they will serve the purpose of discouraging ridiculous and shameful behavior (816d–817a).[58] So-called serious or tragic poetry, for its part, will be permitted in Magnesia only if and only to the extent that it conveys exactly the same teachings that the laws of the city do (817a–d). Those teachings are to be conveyed primarily through the preludes to the laws, and by the *Laws* itself, neither of which contains the kind of philosophic poetry found in the *Republic*'s myth of Er. Accordingly, the Stranger wants to tell the tragic poets that the polity or political regime of the *Laws* is itself "the truest tragedy," or "the imitation of the most beautiful and best life" (817b2–5).

As we will see, the *Letter to d'Alembert* adopts a somewhat similar approach. Rousseau treats the lowest form of shameful comedy as tolerable for Geneva, and preferable to the high comedy of Paris. He also

[54]This may help to explain why Rousseau's initial (and supposedly inadvertent) release of *Theatrical Imitation* occurred when he sent the manuscript to his publisher along with the plates for *The New Heloise*. See *O.C.*, 5:1831 (editor's note). That novel, and the kind of private education it depicts, supplies an appropriate complement to *Theatrical Imitation* in a way that the *Letter to d'Alembert* does not. The only quotation from Plato in the *Letter to d'Alembert* is from Book III of the *Republic* (*O.C.*, 5:109n, Bloom, 120n*). This is fitting because both skip lightly over the human response to mortality. That response is treated in Book X of the *Republic* and in *The New Heloise*.

[55]The *Letter* focuses on the theater, not imitation or even fiction in general, and it acknowledges that its "correctives" are finally applicable only to a city like Geneva.

[56]*Theatrical Imitation* itself points toward the *Laws*, though very indirectly. In a footnote, Rousseau interprets Plato as drawing a sharp distinction between a poet's success in becoming popular and a poet's success in teaching useful things. Rousseau then says that Tyrtaeus might be offered as an example to refute Plato, but contends that Plato could "extricate himself" by treating Tyrtaeus as an orator rather than a poet (*O.C.*, 5:1202n). Tyrtaeus is never mentioned in the *Republic*, but he is discussed several times in the *Laws*. Whereas the *Republic* replaces traditional poetry with the philosophic poetry of Socrates, the *Laws* replaces traditional poetry with the philosophic oratory of the Stranger and his "preludes."

[57]Cf., for example, *Laws* 801c–d with *Republic* 398a–b.

[58]Comedy is attacked along with tragedy in the *Republic* (606c).

advocates the introduction of a more serious kind of theater consisting of celebrations of what he thinks is the most beautiful and best life available to the Genevans. Just as the Stranger speaks to the tragic poets as both friends and rivals who must prove that they are beneficial to the city (817a4–d8), Rousseau treats d'Alembert (and implicitly tragedians like Voltaire) as rivals with whom and against whom he can reason in behalf of the interests of Geneva. Thus, the *Letter* has a more direct kinship with the *Laws* than with the passages from the *Republic* that are imitated in *Theatrical Imitation*.

The influence of Plato's treatment of dramatic poetry is very striking, but the *Letter to d'Alembert* also contains important echoes of the Athenian Stranger's analysis of the relations between men and women. On its face, the *Letter* seems to offer recommendations about the education of women that are almost the opposite of the Stranger's, for they resemble the Athenian alternative that was mentioned and implicitly rejected in the *Laws* (805e). The Stranger, however, does not explain what, if anything, is inherently wrong with the Athenian model, focusing instead on his rejection of the Dorian practice of leaving the female to live in a self-indulgent and disorderly way "while managing the male" (806c5). The *Laws* does imply that the Stranger would not replace Dorian customs with those of the Athenians. But it leaves open the possibility that if he were advising a legislator who was offered the opportunity to improve on Athenian laws, rather than Knossian laws, his recommendations might differ significantly.

In the *Letter to d'Alembert*, Rousseau takes up the task of giving advice about laws to a people whose existing customs resemble those of Athens more than those of Crete or Sparta. The superficial dissimilarities between the Stranger's recommendations and Rousseau's do not imply that Rousseau rejected Plato's teaching, or misunderstood it. Rather, Rousseau concluded that Genevan women are already receiving an education that is conducive to combining individual happiness and civic harmony in a modern bourgeois republic. Rousseau does not describe that education, in part perhaps because describing it *as an education* might tend to undermine its effectiveness. From what he does say about life in Geneva, I believe we can infer that girls were generally raised to expect that their lives should be centered around their roles as wives, mothers, and caretakers of the household, and to accept this as the natural order of things. The task Rousseau gives himself is to defend that education on the basis of a philosophically informed analysis against the false philosophy of d'Alembert and other Encyclopedists.

Knowing, as the Athenian Stranger does, that sexual passion is an especially dangerous natural source of threats to social harmony and individual happiness (e.g., 782d10–783b1), Rousseau views Geneva's stable, bourgeois family life as a fragile institution. In the circumstances in which Geneva finds itself, the great danger is not that women will be neglected by excessively manly men. Rather, the danger is that men will be unmanned by giving women excessive and inappropriate attention, to the disadvantage of both sexes. This danger is not just theoretical or abstract. It has a face, and that face is found in Paris.

### *Happy Families*

Although Rousseau's Geneva is a commercial town, open to the world and filled with the spirit of industry, it has sumptuary laws designed to counteract the natural effects of the passion for accumulating honor through wealth. Immediately before proposing the establishment of a theater, d'Alembert himself had approved these laws: "There is perhaps no city where there are more happy marriages; Geneva is on this point two hundred years ahead of our *mœurs* [i.e., customs or habits that have some kind of ethical or moral quality or effects]. The regulations against luxury prevent the fear of having many children; thus luxury is not, as in France, one of the great obstacles to population" (d'Alembert's "Geneva," in *Geneva Collection*, 20–21).[59] Even if Rousseau had thought that the dissolute behavior associated with actors and actresses could be controlled through legal regulations, which he did not, the theater would still be a dagger aimed at the heart of the bourgeois family life that d'Alembert had so heartily praised.

The theater that d'Alembert wants Geneva to have will inevitably be that of Paris.[60] In that theater, love is always the central preoccupation, and love is the realm in which the tastes of women rule. Rousseau develops this thought down to its fundamental basis and up through its political ramifications. Like most of the Athenian Stranger's discourse with his

[59] Rousseau never refers to this passage in d'Alembert's article. The *Letter*, however, makes it clear that Rousseau regarded reliance on sumptuary laws alone as dangerously naïve, and that he thought Geneva was lagging behind French *mœurs*, rather than showing where the French were headed (*d'Alembert*, *O.C.*, 5:102, Bloom, 111–12).

[60] Rousseau asks whether plays appropriate for Geneva might be written by Genevan dramatists. While acknowledging the possibility of such a thing in principle, he concludes that it is almost certain not to occur (ibid., 109–11, Bloom, 120–22).

Dorian interlocutors, Rousseau's arguments are bounded and shaped by his practical purpose.[61] They are nonetheless precise, subtle, and powerful.

Except for a passing reference to the ambiguous thesis of man's natural goodness,[62] the radical anthropology of the *Discourse on Inequality* makes no appearance in the *Letter to d'Alembert.* In place of the solitary and speechless animal of the forests, or the happy savages content with rustic huts and the gentle pleasures of independent dealings among themselves, we get a portrait of human nature dominated by the love of the morally beautiful.[63] Instead of random and casual sexual encounters between free and equal men and women, we are now told that men are made to be the sexual aggressors, that feminine shame and modesty are the voice of nature, and that a woman's voluntary submission to a man is nature's way.[64]

Rousseau recognizes that he must respond to the claim—common among the sophisticates of his time and ours—that sexual desire is equally strong in both sexes, that its satisfaction is normal and harmless, and that feminine shame and modesty is a social invention designed for the benefit of men (*d'Alembert, O.C.*, 5:76, Bloom, 83). He offers two counterarguments based on nature. First, sexual shame is a natural safeguard that inclines humans to conceal themselves while coupling in order to reduce their vulnerability to attacks during a time of weakness and distraction, much as nature inclines us to sleep during the night and moves animals to hide themselves when they are sick or injured (ibid., 76–77, Bloom, 83–84). Second, men cannot perform without being aroused, and they

[61] Leo Strauss characterizes the Stranger's arguments up through most of Book XII as "sub-Socratic" (*Argument and the Action*, 182). By "sub-Socratic," Strauss does not mean unphilosophic. See ibid., 129 (calling Book X "the most philosophic, the only philosophic part of the *Laws*"). Whatever Strauss may have in mind, Rousseau's arguments are both non-Socratic and philosophically informed.

[62] "[M]an is born good, I think it and believe that I have proved it (*d'Alembert, O.C.*, 5:22, Bloom, 23). No such proof is offered in the *Letter*, and Rousseau is manifestly alluding to the *Discourse on Inequality.*

[63] Compare *Inequality, O.C.*, 3:159–60, 171, with *d'Alembert, O.C.*, 5:22 & n, Bloom, 23 & n.

[64] Compare *Inequality, O.C.*, 3:158, with *d'Alembert, O.C.*, 5:77–78, Bloom, 84–85. The *Discourse on Inequality*'s discussion of sexual relations in what Rousseau calls "the pure state of nature" treats sexual desire as a peripheral part of natural human experience, much as Socrates does in the *Republic.* Like the *Laws*, the *Letter to d'Alembert* restores this passion to the central place that it must assume in a more complete understanding of politics and human life.

need to encounter a certain reluctance from women in order to avoid the "boring freedom" (*ennuyeuse liberté*) that would frustrate nature's procreative purpose (ibid., 77, Bloom, 84).

Apart from their inconsistency with the *Discourse on Inequality*, these arguments from nature are transparently deficient. Accordingly, Rousseau immediately substitutes a very different argument. In response to the fundamental objection that sexual desire is equally natural and naturally equal in men and women, Rousseau screams: "As if the consequences were the same on both sides! As if all the austere duties of the woman were not derived from this *alone*, that a child ought to have a father!" (ibid., 77–78, Bloom, 85, emphasis added). Having presented this genuinely plausible reason for socially imposed constraints on natural inclinations, he then seems to rest his case on the dogmatic claim that women display shame and modesty because "[n]ature wanted it so, and it would be a crime to stifle her voice" (ibid., 78, Bloom, 85).[65] Rhetorically, nature gets the first and last word, but Rousseau's true argument is that stable families require that nature be overcome or refashioned.

Rousseau confirms that this is his argument in the following pages. He begins with some amusing exaggerations of the physical softness and natural timidity of women, and with a plainly fallacious claim that the modest women of the Swiss mountains must be more natural than the brazen ladies of Paris because they have less education. Then he rather belatedly concedes that examples drawn from the beasts prove nothing because "the holy image of the upright (*l'honnête*) and of the beautiful enters only the heart of man" (ibid., 79, Bloom, 86–87). In an effort to blur the issue, however, he next points out that some animals do in fact have instincts that lead them to behave rather as he contends humans should act (ibid., 79–80, Bloom, 87). The mating behavior of pigeons, which Rousseau lovingly describes, obviously proves no more than the very different behavior of dogs and wolves, which he had just dismissed as an irrelevancy.[66] He now declares again that nature's voice is not dispositive. "If the timidity, the *pudeur*,[67] and the modesty that are proper to

[65] Rousseau reinforces the implication that his real argument is not based on nature's voice by dropping a long and impassioned footnote distinguishing appropriate male boldness from insolence and brutality.

[66] Rousseau had previously provided an elaborate refutation of a similar argument for the naturalness of monogamy offered by Locke (*Inequality*, Note XII, *O.C.*, 3:214–18).

[67] This word refers to sexual bashfulness, and especially the exhibition (real or feigned) of this sentiment.

them are social inventions, it matters to society that women acquire these qualities" (ibid., 80, Bloom, 87).[68]

Much of the *Letter* is devoted to exploring the ways in which the introduction of a theater into Geneva would undermine the family, and to shoring up that fundamental institution by defending social inventions on which it depends.

### *Unhappy Lovers*

The central underlying thesis of the *Letter* is "that there are no good *mœurs* for women outside a withdrawn and domestic life; … that the quiet cares of the family and the household are their portion, that the dignity of their Sex is in their modesty, that shame and *pudeur* are in them inseparable from integrity (*honnêteté*)" (*d'Alembert*, *O.C.*, 5:75–76, Bloom, 82–83). As we have seen, Rousseau can derive this proposition from nature only by blurring the distinction between what is natural and what is useful in political societies. Despite his hyperbolic appeal to "the unanimous voice of the human race" (ibid., 76, Bloom, 83), moreover, Rousseau cannot and does not believe that such *mœurs* are so widely accepted as to have acquired quasi-natural status (like, say, the incest prohibition).[69] Instead, he adopts the assumption that families of the bourgeois type foster the optimal mix of individual happiness and social cohesion.

That assumption is completely reasonable in the context of the *Letter*'s immediate purpose because it is one shared by the Genevan laws and by d'Alembert himself. Accordingly, Rousseau's arguments are devoted to showing how the roles of men and women can best be structured to foster bourgeois family life. The central proposition to which the arguments lead is that these roles must be differentiated, with men assuming a bolder and

[68] Note, however, Rousseau's use of the word "if" at the beginning of the sentence. The *Emile* offers a more complex account of the relation between female *pudeur* and the requirements of social life, which is explicated in Shell, "Nature and the Education of Sophie."

[69] Perhaps the most significant exception for Rousseau is Sparta. "If the [northern] Barbarians of whom I just spoke lived with women, they nevertheless did not live like them; it was the women who had the courage to live like them, just as the Spartan women did. The woman made herself robust, and the man was not enervated" (*d'Alembert*, *O.C.*, 5:94, Bloom, 103). Sparta (especially as it is described by Plutarch) is frequently Rousseau's exemplar of achievable civic excellence, but Rousseau also discreetly alludes in passing to the reputation Spartan women had for sexual promiscuity. See, for example, ibid., 81–82, 122, Bloom, 89, 133.

more publicly active way of life. Rousseau uses his extended attack on the Parisian theater to explore the effects of apparent social equality between the sexes, which he contends is tantamount to actual female dominance, or even tyranny.

Rousseau agrees with d'Alembert that Geneva approaches the ideal polity toward which Enlightenment principles point. Its citizens are industrious and peaceable. The city has no hereditary nobility or massive inequalities of wealth. The clergy are tolerant and respectful of secular authority. And, as d'Alembert had stressed, Genevan families are stable and fecund. But Rousseau emphatically does not believe that these happy features have been caused or in fact promoted by the French *philosophes.* On the contrary, Geneva's happiness is largely the product of chance factors, including its geographic position, its soil and climate, and accidents of history (ibid., 68, Bloom, 74).[70] Those factors have established the *mœurs* that give Geneva its distinctiveness, and those *mœurs* are in considerable tension with the sophistication of Parisian society and of philosophers.

D'Alembert made the characteristic intellectual's error of overestimating the political power of reason, and so of believing that Geneva could "combine the sagacity of Lacedaemon with the refinement of Athens" (ibid., 4, Bloom, 4, quoting d'Alembert's "Geneva"). The *Laws* makes clear just how difficult and perilous such a project would be, even under the most favorable of circumstances. Geneva, moreover, is no Sparta and Paris is no Athens. Geneva is more like Republican Rome and Paris more like the Roman Empire, by which I mean that Parisian society is just what Geneva could easily degenerate into. And a theater, Rousseau argues, would accelerate that degeneration.

Introducing a theater into Geneva would destabilize Genevan family life in multiple ways, but above all by publicly glorifying romantic love. That glorification, whether it comes through the theater or from other sources, is the great threat to Geneva's domestic *mœurs.* Unlike countless moralizers and fretful parents through the ages, Rousseau does not take the easy path of denouncing the kind of public art, mediocre at best, that

[70] One such accident, the political influence of Calvin, is passed over in silence, though Rousseau comments on it elsewhere. See, for example, *S.C.*, bk. 2, chap. 7, *O.C.*, 3:382n; *Mountain*, *O.C.*, 3:715, 726n. At least one reason for the omission of this factor in the *Letter* may be that it raises issues about the relation between Calvin's political and theological thought. Rousseau's rebuke of d'Alembert for describing the theological views of the Genevan clergy suggests that he believed that no good could come of discussing this matter in the *Letter*.

must have filled the theaters of France, as it does the airwaves and cyberspace of modern America. Instead, he sets out to show that even the very best art produced by the geniuses of a great civilization can be at least as dangerous as the vacuous fare that no sapient adult would defend on its merits.

Beginning with tragedy, Rousseau denies that it can perform a useful social function. All public entertainments must please the audience if they are to have any effect at all, and overtly didactic dramas will not give pleasure to anyone who needs its lessons. Generally speaking, therefore, public art can only reinforce existing *mœurs*. Tragedies, in any event, portray gigantic characters who inhabit a distant world. A talented artist can easily make the audience sympathize with a virtuous hero, but such sympathy is a costless emotion, whereas heroism—or even acting on one's sympathies for heroes—would require real effort and self-denial outside the theater. The heroes of the tragedies, moreover, are so alien in so many ways that their depiction cannot even point the audience toward admiration for the more pedestrian virtues that can actually be cultivated in modern societies. At best, then, such performances are morally useless. And when one adds the ease with which playwrights can and do make us sympathize even with execrable heroes, little or nothing is left of the hope that popular tragedies could improve the *mœurs* of any modern people.

If this were all, perhaps such entertainment would not be much more than one of a thousand distractions from more useful pursuits. Unfortunately, Rousseau maintains, tragedies can have one very big and bad effect on their audiences. By portraying love and love affairs in the monumental style of the tragic theater, the artist plays on a very natural and highly flammable passion. In that way, these spectacles induce an emotional experience that can indeed affect the way that ordinary people live their ordinary lives.

Rousseau develops this point with two examples, Racine's *Bérénice* and Voltaire's *Zaïre*. It so happens that the dilemmas posed in these plays somewhat resemble those in two of Shakespeare's dramas, which are more familiar to us and are thus perhaps especially useful illustrations.[71] Furthermore, if Rousseau's critique can fairly be applied to the works of

[71] In *Bérénice*, Titus must choose between marrying the queen of Palestine, with whom he is in love, and remaining the emperor of Rome. *Zaïre* presents the story of a Christian slave with whom the Sultan of Jerusalem falls in love, and whom the Sultan eventually murders because of an imagined infidelity.

a dramatist who may be a greater genius than either of the French playwrights, that would confirm his claim that the best tragedies can have the worst effects. Here is how I think Rousseau would have seen our English analogues to *Bérénice* and *Zaïre*.

Consider *Antony and Cleopatra* first, beginning with its well-known plot. During the factional struggles after the destruction of the Republic, Mark Antony followed the elder Pompey and Julius Caesar to Egypt and the bed of the world's greatest seductress. Unfortunately, Antony encounters repeated conflicts between this liaison and his Roman duties and ambitions. He gets a lucky break when his wife dies, as he had wished she would, but soon finds it politically expedient to marry the sister of one of his political rivals, Octavius Caesar. Unwilling to abandon Cleopatra, Antony attempts to compete in Roman politics while living in Egypt with his paramour. The cool and prudent Octavius, whose sister has been dishonored, lures Antony into a sea battle in which Caesar has the advantage. Compounding his mistake, Antony allows Cleopatra to accompany him at the head of her own fleet. During the battle, Cleopatra loses her nerve and flees, with Antony chasing after her. Faced eventually with the inevitability of Caesar's triumph, Antony commits a clumsy suicide after failing to persuade one of his men to assist him. Cleopatra enters into negotiations with Caesar, hoping to retain her throne at least in name, but learns that Caesar means to display her as a prize in Rome. She kills herself, and Egypt is absorbed into the Roman Empire, of which Octavius is now the unchallenged ruler.

Anyone who has seen or read the play will instantly recognize how misleading this summary is. Thanks to the speeches that Shakespeare gives his characters, we are presented with one of the great love stories in Western literature. Cleopatra is depicted, unforgettably, as a woman who could rival or surpass Rome itself as an object of a great man's preoccupation. When a Roman soldier who has never seen Cleopatra remarks that political necessities will require Antony to leave her, the perceptive Enobarbus declares:

> Never! He will not.
> Age cannot wither her, nor custom stale
> Her infinite variety. Other women cloy
> The appetites they feed, but she makes hungry

Where most she satisfies; for vilest things
Become themselves in her, that the holy priests
Bless her when she is riggish.[72]

Antony, for his part, is transformed by his love for Cleopatra from a Roman larger than life to a spirit larger than the pedestrian world itself. After his death, Cleopatra tells Dolabella how she sees him:

His face was as the heavens, and therein stuck
A sun and moon which kept their course and lighted
The little O, the earth …
His legs bestrid the ocean; his reared arm
Crested the world; his voice was propertied
As all the tuned spheres, and that to friends;
But when he meant to quail and shake the orb,
He was as rattling thunder. For his bounty,
There was no winter in't; an autumn it was
That grew the more by reaping. His delights
Were dolphin-like: they showed his back above
The element they lived in. In his livery
Walked crowns and crownets; realms and islands were
As plates dropped from his pocket. (5.2.78–91)

Cleopatra herself calls this a dream, but it is one so powerful that it induces Dolabella to betray his leader and tell the conquered Cleopatra the truth about Caesar's plans for her. Tellingly, Antony warned Cleopatra to trust none of Caesar's men but Proculeius—and when she tells him what Antony had said, Proculeius lies to her. Her interview with Dolabella comes afterward, and her dream accomplishes what Proculeius' memory of the living Antony could not.

Sustained reflection on the play in all its complex detail might lead well beyond what one might expect either from the plot summary or from Shakespeare's dazzling spectacle of immortal longings, a lass unparalleled, a Roman by a Roman valiantly vanquished, and a world where 'tis paltry to be Caesar, who not being Fortune is but Fortune's knave. But what

[72] 2.2.244–50. (All citations are to act, scene, and lines in the Arden Shakespeare.) When Antony tells Enobarbus that he wishes he had never met the queen, Enobarbus wryly disagrees: "O, Sir, you had then left unseen a wonderful piece of work, which not to have been blest withal would have discredited your travel" (1.2.160–62). Enobarbus surely knows that Antony agrees, and he probably hopes that Antony will come to be satisfied with *having* seen Cleopatra, who is deeply threatening to Antony's self-interest and his own.

effects would this play have on an ordinary audience, and especially its younger members?

Often, no doubt, not much. But what about a sensitive and restless young woman, raised in a small town and aware of the attention she has begun to draw from boys? She will not think of becoming an actual queen, or that amorous adventures will lead to her doom. But Cleopatra can fill her head with grandiose ideas of what to look for in a relationship, and how to seek it. If she's reasonably attractive, there will be no shortage of obliging young men, though probably none who finds that custom cannot stale her infinite variety. Few boys are likely to find the Antony of this play very interesting or admirable, but all will want to enchant a fetching girl, and some will be enchanted. It will not be hard for them to say, and sometimes feel, that "the nobleness of life / Is to do thus, when such a mutual pair / And such a twain can do't" (1.1.37–39).

One play, of course, would hardly ever alter an individual's life, let alone corrupt the *mœurs* of a whole community. But let the extraordinary power of the poetry in *Antony and Cleopatra* come atop a diet of mediocre dramas in which romance is glorified and civic life deprecated, where great heroes have great affairs, where every member of the audience is made to identify for a moment with doomed lovers. All of this may be harmless amusement in the cosmopolitan atmosphere of a great metropolis, and Shakespeare's art is easily redeemed there by the pleasure he provides to all and the subtleties he offers for those who can attend to them. But what exactly would this do for the children of a city like Rousseau's Geneva? It might encourage some to flee to Paris, hoping perhaps to find that one great love, or at least a larger stage on which to make the search. Others might stay, marry, and raise their children, but with a nagging dissatisfaction and a heightened sense of possibilities foregone. Not a promising recipe for a happier city and happier families.

Rousseau would see the very genius of *Antony and Cleopatra* as a contributor to the miseducation of women, and a goad to their misuse of their natural power over men. Antony repeatedly senses, and sometimes recognizes, that he loses his Roman nobility in allowing himself to be ruled by his love for Cleopatra. His inability to give her up in favor of Roman duties and aspirations is in significant part a consequence of the instability in Roman *mœurs* that accompanied the transition from republic to empire.[73] Cleopatra, a non-Roman who does a far better job than Antony at manag-

[73] For a detailed analysis of the relationship between the instability in Rome and the instability in the relationship between Antony and Cleopatra, see Paul A. Cantor, *Shakespeare's Rome: Republic and Empire*.

ing the tensions between her loves and her political needs,[74] is also given more beautiful speeches (both by and about her) and a bigger place in the hearts of the audience. She overshadows Antony, who is attractive primarily because of the way he is attracted to her.[75] It is she who would be a real threat to Genevan *mœurs*.

Perhaps *Antony and Cleopatra* is a little too easy an example to use in support of Rousseau's argument. Might *Othello* be a counterexample? Desdemona is an anti-Cleopatra. She is pure womanly virtue, devoted and completely faithful to her husband. She erects no obstacles to Othello's performing his civic duties, even as she accompanies him to war.[76] So far is she from Cleopatra's sexual voracity that she saw Othello's visage in his mind, falling in love with the man she knew from what he said about how he had lived. Fittingly, Othello is an anti-Antony. Cleopatra's lover is a dissatisfied republican leftover in the new, decadent Rome. Othello is an immigrant, and a self-made man who rose quickly in Venice through his talents, his virtue, and fidelity to his adopted home.

The action of the play arises from Iago's campaign—apparently triggered by professional or sexual jealousy—to destroy this glorious marriage by tricking Othello into a jealous fury over his wife's imagined adultery.[77]

[74] As a monarch ruling in the shadow of Roman hegemony, Cleopatra had effectively employed sexual diplomacy with the elder Pompey and Julius Caesar. When reminded of how she had once talked about this Caesar, she waves it off as the stuff of "My salad days / When I was green in judgment, cold in blood" (1.5.76–77). But her alliance with Antony was not a bad political bet. He was militarily the strongest of the Roman rivals, and it actually took a series of very foolish mistakes on his part to lose out to Octavius. Had she been more schooled in Roman affairs, and more ruthless, Cleopatra might have managed Antony much better than she did. One can wonder whether she was more deficient in ruthlessness or in prudence, and one can wonder whether Antony would have fallen for her so completely if she were less deficient. In any event, until all hope was gone Cleopatra did keep looking for a way to save her crown and her life, and to pass the throne to one of her sons—presumably Julius Caesar's child, not one of Antony's.

[75] If Octavius looks contemptible compared with Antony, it is mainly because he is impervious to Cleopatra's charm. The only characters who appear more contemptible are Lepidus, who ineffectually seeks to foster civic friendship, and the younger Pompey, who anachronistically and inconsistently struggles to maintain the old ideals of Roman virtue. The youth of Geneva would hardly benefit from juxtapositions like these.

[76] Desdemona accompanies Othello as his wife. It is inconceivable that she would actually participate in war, either incompetently like Cleopatra or independently like Fulvia.

[77] As the play opens, Iago tells Roderigo that he hates Othello for giving Cassio an undeserved military promotion that Iago thought should have been his (1.1.7–65). In subsequent soliloquies, which are presumably more candid, Iago attributes his hatred to rumors or suspicions that he has been cuckolded by Othello (1.3.384–88; 2.1.290–93). There are no other indications in the play that Iago deserved the promotion or that his wife had been

Iago's campaign succeeds, and Othello kills Desdemona, who endures her murder with the grace of an angel. When he learns the truth, Othello has no more defense than to call himself "one that lov'd not wisely, but too well" (5.2.345). He pronounces a just verdict on himself and speaks his last words to his wife's corpse: "I kiss'd thee ere I kill'd thee, no way but this, / Killing myself, to die upon a kiss" (5.2.359–60).

Hard to see any pernicious lessons lurking here. As Rousseau notes in his discussion of *Zaïre*, however, no one who sees such a spectacle can come away more disposed toward the moderate love on which happy families are generally founded. One might well think: "Ah! Let me be given [such a woman]; I will well ensure that I do not kill her" (*d'Alembert*, *O.C.*, 5:51, Bloom, 55). But Rousseau believes that the audience most of all wants a woman who can inspire the towering passion that an Othello exhibits.[78]

Where would you find such a woman, and how would you go about securing her love if you did? Othello is an exotic in ways more profound than his place of birth, the color of his skin, or the religion in which he was presumably raised. For her part, Desdemona is truly the rarest "gem of women."[79] What Antony demands—for "the world to weet / We stand

unfaithful (or even that she had been rumored to have been). Because Iago, "for mere suspicion in that kind / Will do, as if for surety" (1.3.387–88), we have to suspect that he himself does not fully understand the sources of his hatred for Othello.

[78] Rousseau dismisses the popular and superficially appealing theory that tragedy provides a healthy catharsis of dangerous passions. Only reason can purge the passions, and reason has no effect in the theater (*d'Alembert*, *O.C.* 5:20, Bloom, 21). It may well be that tragedy leads to pity through fear, but this pity is only a temporary and vain emotion (ibid., 23, Bloom, 24–25). And perhaps most persuasively:

> It is pretended that we are cured of love by the depiction of its weaknesses ... [B]ut I see that the spectators always take the part of the weak lover, and that they are often vexed that he is not more so. I ask: is this a great way to avoid resembling him? (ibid., 48, Bloom, 52)

Rousseau is well aware of Aristotle's *Poetics*, which he quotes with approval in a different context (ibid., 25, Bloom, 27). But Rousseau argues that tragedy had a distinctive function in Greek political life, where it had far different effects than in our culture (ibid., 26n, 31, Bloom, 28n, 33).

[79] *Antony and Cleopatra*, 3.13.113 (Antony describing Octavia). Rousseau explains the threat posed by characters like Desdemona:

> The most charming object in nature, the one most capable of stirring a sensitive heart and turning it to the good, is, I acknowledge, a pleasing and virtuous woman. But where is this celestial object hiding itself? ... If a young man has seen the world only

up peerless"—might more soberly be granted to Othello and Desdemona. But that is not what the audience wants. Instead, we want to believe that this is what love could be for ourselves. And what it could have continued to be in the play if not for the freakish bad luck of Iago's overwrought malevolence and daring shrewdness.[80] A great many women, for their part, will watch the death of Desdemona with a certain sanguine composure: "a sensitive woman sees without terror the transports of passion [on the stage]; for it is a lesser misfortune to perish by the hand of her lover than to be weakly loved" (ibid., 51, Bloom, 55).[81]

Rousseau's general point is that love well depicted overshadows everything that accompanies it, and thereby usurps the place that virtue ought to have. Cleopatra overshadows both Antony, a decayed representative of republican virtue, and Octavius, the emerging embodiment of imperial political virtue. Like Cleopatra, Othello gets the most beautiful poetry, and his passion overshadows Desdemona's moderate and virtuous love. Rather than watching captivating characters with whom we fall in love because of their love for each other, "young people should be taught to be on guard against the illusions of love, to flee the error arising from a blind propensity that always believes that it is based on respect for merit, and to fear that one will sometimes deliver a virtuous heart over to an object that is unworthy of its cares" (ibid., 52, Bloom, 56). Tragedies in their nature simply cannot do that.

> on the Stage, the first means of pursuing virtue which offers itself to him is to seek a mistress who will conduct him there, quite hoping to find at least a Constance or a Cénie. Thus, on faith in an imaginary model, on a modest and touching appearance, on a counterfeit sweetness, *nescius aurae fallacis* [ignorant of the deceptive breeze], the young madman quickly loses himself while thinking that he is becoming wise. (*d'Alembert*, *O.C.*, 5:44, Bloom, 47–48, footnote omitted)

[80] On this, as on many other points, one's view of the play is apt to change as one gets to know it better. For purposes of understanding Rousseau's argument, however, the initial impression (especially on the impressionable) is more important.

[81] Rousseau does not condemn this womanly inclination, which he assigns in the *Emile* to Sophie, the girl formed to suit a man raised according to nature for life in society (*O.C.*, 4:809–10, Bloom, 439). Ironically perhaps, Rousseau's writings were a smash hit among the ladies of Paris. According to one of their own number, they "praise him with enthusiasm, although no Author treats them with less respect … [H]e has mentioned them with contempt, but with an air of passion, and passion excuses everything" (Melissa A. Butler, "Eighteenth-Century Critics of Rousseau's Views on Women," 133, quoting Mme. Comtesse de Genlis). D'Alembert drew the same conclusion: "[M]any sins are forgiven him because he has loved so much" (ibid., quoting d'Alembert's "Jugement sur *Emile*").

Comedy may be able to do it, by ridiculing the madness of love. Unfortunately, comedy debunks virtue just as it does love.[82] Once again taking as his target the best of the genre, Rousseau demonstrates this point in an extended analysis of Molière's *The Misanthrope*.[83] His key point is that Molière placed a virtuous man in a corrupt society, giving the character just enough shortcomings and inconsistencies to render him fatuously unsociable. In that way, Molière "seduces by an appearance of reason" (ibid., 42, Bloom, 45). The audience gets the pleasure of a laugh at virtue's expense, and is confirmed in the easy lesson that it's best to get along by going along, "that to be a gentleman (*honnête-homme*) it suffices not to be a downright scoundrel" (ibid.). The culmination of the playwright's seduction through sophistry comes with the comically virtuous Alceste's foolish love: "To make the misanthrope fall in love was nothing; the stroke of genius was to make him fall in love with a coquette" (ibid., 52, Bloom, 56).

Rousseau is perfectly willing to concede that the theater, including both great art and the mediocre productions that must predominate in any form of popular entertainment, may actually have a variety of beneficial effects in a corrupt culture like that of Paris (ibid., 59, Bloom, 64). He had previously developed this point at somewhat greater length in the "Preface to *Narcisse*" (*O.C.*, 2:971–73). In the *Letter*, Rousseau also suggests in passing one art form suitable for a modern bourgeois society: the novel. In the course of offering relations between English men and women as an illustration of the benefits of sharply differentiating between the roles of the sexes, he approves the English taste for contemplative readings and novels (*d'Alembert*, *O.C.*, 5:75, Bloom, 82). In a curious footnote, he says that English novels are, "like the men, sublime or detestable," and

[82] We can see an example of this in a comic interlude in *Othello*. Roderigo is so taken with Desdemona that he contemplates suicide after learning of her marriage to Othello. When Iago mocks him, Roderigo confesses that he is ashamed of his infatuation, "but it is not in my virtue to amend it." Iago responds: "Virtue? a fig! … But we have reason to cool our raging motions, our carnal stings, our unbitted lusts … [and reason will show the way to cuckold Othello, thus enabling you to] doest thyself a pleasure" (1.3.317–72).

[83] Rousseau appears to believe that his critique of tragedy applies to all tragedy, including ancient plays presented to modern audiences. Although he says that all comedy is "bad and pernicious," his evidence is drawn exclusively from the French theater (*d'Alembert*, *O.C.*, 5:31, Bloom, 34). I have no reason to question Rousseau's claim that even the best French comedies that would be staged in Geneva were all "bad and pernicious," but his broader generalization is questionable. Had Rousseau been familiar with Shakespeare, which I do not believe he was, he might have qualified his denunciation of all comedy.

bestows the most extravagant praise on Richardson's *Clarissa*. The *Letter to d'Alembert* was written and published while Rousseau was completing work on his own novel, *The New Heloise*, which he hoped would be unneeded in Geneva but beneficial elsewhere. In that book, one of his characters says: "Novels are perhaps the last form of education left for a people so corrupted that every other would be useless" (*N.H.*, pt. 2, lett. 21, *O.C.*, 2:277).

Rousseau was certainly aware that novels, like other books, can have corrupting effects, just as the theater can. That problem did not require attention in the *Letter to d'Alembert*, which is immediately concerned with the relatively tractable problem of suppressing public performances, rather than with the more difficult problem of regulating private pursuits. More generally, however, Rousseau may have thought that novels are somewhat less apt to have destructively inflammatory effects, and more apt to serve a genuinely educational purpose, because the consumption of a book requires a greater mental effort than watching a play. That, of course, might also make a genuinely seductive novel more apt to corrupt those about whose corruption one should be most concerned.

Rousseau shows just how serious he is in attacking the greatest art by expressing a preference for the crude and even smutty amusements that are tolerated in Geneva's marketplace. Although he disapproves of them, he says: "If these insipid entertainments lack taste, so much the better; they will become tiresome more quickly; if they are crude they will be less seductive. Vice hardly insinuates itself by shocking decency, but it does so by taking on its likeness; and dirty words are more opposed to refined manners than to good *mœurs*" (*d'Alembert*, *O.C.*, 5:113, Bloom, 124). It would, of course, be even better that Geneva be rid of these low entertainments, and that the citizens "draw our pleasures and our duties from our state and from ourselves" (ibid.).

## *Men Unmanned*

Parisian society shows what Parisian theater will lead to in Geneva: a degenerate form of Athenian refinement *at the expense* of a sagacity somewhat reminiscent of Lacedaemon. Here is life in the salons of Paris, as Rousseau saw it through his Genevan eyes:

> [C]ravenly devoted to the wills of the sex that we ought to protect and not serve, we have learned to despise it in obeying it, to insult it by our ironic

attentions; and every Parisian woman assembles in her apartment a harem of men more feminine than herself, who know how to render to beauty all sorts of tributes, except the tribute of the heart of which it is worthy. But observe how these same men, always constrained in these voluntary prisons, get up, sit down, go ceaselessly back and forth to the fireplace, to the window, pick up and put down a fire screen[84] a hundred times, leaf through books, run their eyes over some paintings, turn and pirouette about the room, while the idol reposes without moving on her couch, active only with her tongue and her eyes. From where does this difference come unless it is the case that nature, which imposes on women this sedentary and homebound life, prescribes for men the exact opposite, and that this restlessness indicates a true need in them? (*d'Alembert*, *O.C.*, 5:93, Bloom, 101–02)

A kind of modern Egypt, full of faux Cleopatras and little imitation Antonys who resemble him only in their professions of admiration for the queen and their underlying dissatisfaction with serving her. Corresponding to the physical atrophy of Parisian men, Rousseau sees a suppression of male intellectual force. "Given over to these puerile habits, to what that is great could we [men] ever raise ourselves? Our talents and our writings smell of our frivolous occupations, agreeable if one wishes, but small and cold like our sentiments; they have as their whole merit that facile turn that one has no great trouble in giving to nothings" (ibid., 94–95, Bloom, 103).[85]

Rousseau is confident that "instead of gaining by these practices, the women lose," for the obeisance paid them is cynically ironic (ibid., 95, Bloom, 104). The men, for their part, actually lose themselves. The

[84] In Rousseau's time, fashionable ladies had a problem dealing with fireplaces, which could melt the makeup on the side of the face that was turned toward the flames. They used handheld screens, often artfully decorated, to protect themselves against such a disaster.

[85] Rousseau appends to this passage a footnote in which he claims that women are in general bereft of artistic genius. He acknowledges that there are exceptions, but he knows of only two: Sappho and one other whom he does not name. In an effort to provide a kind of proof that he is not just manifesting male chauvinism, Rousseau offers this: "I would wager anything in the world that the *Lettres portugaises* were written by a man." Modern scholarship has uncovered strong evidence, though not absolutely conclusive proof, that Rousseau was correct. See, for example, F.C. Green, "Who Was the Author of the *Lettres Portugaises*?"; Charles R. Lefcourt, "Did Guilleragues Write 'The Portuguese Letters'?"; Anna Klobucka, *The Portuguese Nun: Formation of a National Myth*, 11–15. In any event, Rousseau's point is that men who adopt criteria of literary excellence designed to increase the number of women whose work will qualify should be suspected of offering compliments arising more from diffidence than honest admiration.

refined manners of Paris are already being aped in Geneva, and the sight is appalling:

> It is certain that the boys know how to bow better, that they know how to offer their hand more gallantly to Ladies and to say to them an infinity of genialities for which I myself would have them whipped, that they know how to decide, to interrogate, to interrupt adult conversations, to pester everybody without modesty and without discretion … [T]he only thing the women do not exact from these vile slaves is that they consecrate themselves to their service in the Oriental fashion. Except for this, all that distinguishes them from the women is that, nature having refused them women's graces, they substitute ridiculous affectations. On my last trip to Geneva, I already saw several of these young ladies in tight jackets, with white teeth, plump hands, piping voices, and pretty green parasols in their hands, rather maladroitly counterfeiting men. (ibid., 102, Bloom, 111–12)

### *Republican Entertainments*

As one might anticipate from his contemptuous description of mincing Parisian manners, and from his disapproval of the crude entertainments in the Genevan marketplace, Rousseau must look for a healthy and authentically Genevan alternative to the French theater. He finds it in the small clubs of a dozen-odd men who rent quarters where they can eat, drink, and relax in one another's company, and who sometimes walk or hunt together; women have similar groups, which meet at one another's homes. These so-called *cercles*, private versions of the segregated common meals in Magnesia, provide simple and innocent amusements, the kind that fit with republican *mœurs*.[86] Even more important, they provide forums where men can be their masculine selves, without the need to adapt to women's tastes, and women can get some relief from the endless work of bending men to those tastes. "[T]he two sexes should sometimes gather together and should ordinarily live apart … Our *cercles* still preserve among us some image of ancient *mœurs*" (ibid., 92, 96, Bloom, 100, 104–05).[87]

[86] In *The New Heloise*, Rousseau suggests that these institutions had already lost their vitality (pt. 2, lett. 21, *O.C.*, 2:269n). In the *Letter to d'Alembert*, Rousseau may have hoped to promote their reinvigoration by affecting not to have noticed their decay.

[87] Rousseau was well aware that the *cercles* were not comparable to the institutions of public education among the Greek republics, but he defended them as a practicable alternative to the domestic education provided under monarchies, "where all the subjects must remain isolated, and have nothing in common except obedience" (Rousseau to Théodore Tronchin, 26 Sept. 1758, *Corr. Comp.*, 5:242).

The *cercles* were not the object of universal approbation in Geneva.[88] Along with his praise of what they do well, Rousseau defends even their shortcomings. The women's groups are blamed primarily for gossiping that leads to scandal mongering. Rousseau thinks there may be more good than bad in this feminine vice, which almost performs the office of the ancient censors. It is certainly far better than the Parisian alternative, where ladies can hardly endure the company of other women, and prefer instead to gossip with men.

Rousseau acknowledges that the men's *cercles* have more serious disadvantages, such as frequent drunkenness. While conceding that excessive drinking degrades the soul, Rousseau emphasizes that it "makes a man stupid, not evil," that its effects are temporary, and that it is actually a sign of social health when men do not "dread a state of indiscretion in which the heart reveals itself without deliberation" (ibid., 99–100, Bloom, 108–09). In any event, perfect men and perfect cities do not exist, and "[n]ever has a people perished through an excess of wine; all perish through the disorder of women" (ibid., 100, Bloom, 109). As the Athenian Stranger's discussions of wine and women confirm, he and Rousseau agree about this proposition, and Rousseau expressly invokes the *Laws* as support for allowing old men to reanimate their spirits with drink (ibid., 100 & n, Bloom, 109 & n).[89]

Later, toward the end of his long response to d'Alembert, Rousseau comes as close as he ever does in the *Letter* to imitating the Athenian Stranger by offering an affirmative reform (in contradistinction to a defense of existing practices). That reform is modeled on one of the Stranger's own proposals.

After celebrating the Genevans' passion for public festivals and games, which promote civic friendship, and encouraging the establishment of more such events, Rousseau notes that winter in these mountains favors private entertainments. In the one significant innovation that he proposes, Rousseau attacks the scruples and worries that are apparently associated

[88] See, for example, Charles W. Hendel, *Jean-Jacques Rousseau: Moralist*, 2:62.

[89] The discussion of drinking and drunkenness in the *Laws* arises from a dispute between the Stranger and Megillus, beginning at 636a, that involves a comparison between the Athenian vice of drinking and Sparta's reputation for male homosexuality and female promiscuity. The Stranger argues that public drinking could be put to good use in a well ordered city, a claim that he never makes about pederasty or promiscuity. See also 790a8–b6 (arguing that a stable community depends on the correct legal regulation of private households, as does the happiness of both the household and the city).

in Geneva with dancing. At some length, he insists that if you want to promote happy marriages, the worst way to do it is to prevent young men and women from coming together in public. Instead, Rousseau recommends that elaborate balls be conducted for the purpose of assisting young people to find appropriate mates. In terms that closely track the Stranger's reasoning about his "mating dances," Rousseau argues that the institution of such balls would make it likelier that marriages would be founded on mutual personal attraction, that they would be less circumscribed by social rank and contribute less to the formation of political factions based on family connections, and that economic inequality would be tempered and the spirit of the political constitution promoted (ibid., 119–20, Bloom, 131; cf. *Laws* 771e–773e).

By opposing the prudish disapproval of dancing, Rousseau seeks to give nature's most dangerously insistent passion a respectable outlet at just the point in life at which it can determine an individual's fate.[90] The balls, however, are designed with more than this in mind. Rousseau's proposal in one important respect is quite different from the Stranger's, and that difference illustrates how Rousseau adapted the teaching of the *Laws* to the circumstances of Geneva.

Adults of all ages are to attend the new balls, but the old and the married will be spectators, and married women, in particular, will be forbidden to "profane conjugal dignity" by dancing (*d'Alembert*, *O.C.*, 5:118, Bloom, 129). By spotlighting the young people in this way, Rousseau's rules will offer the girls a regulated opportunity to enjoy the pleasure of displaying themselves in much the same manner that corrupt Parisian women want to parade around throughout their lives. Rousseau goes even further and recommends that a Queen of the Ball be elected at the end of the season by the oldest and most honored spectators. The judges are to choose the girl who has behaved "most decently (*honnêtement*), modestly, and pleas-

[90] Rousseau gratuitously anticipates the mocking suggestion that he would even like to revive the Spartan practice of naked dancing by young women. This objection provides him with an opportunity to illustrate the great gulf between Spartan *mœurs* and those of people who are merely "upright (*honnête*)" (*d'Alembert*, *O.C.*, 5:122, Bloom, 134). In this passage, he points out that artful dress is more provocative than absolute nudity and that "I propose for [Genevans] only the Lacedaemonian institutions of which they are not yet incapable" (ibid.). Such praise of Sparta very near the end of the *Letter* may serve to remind us that the Athenian Stranger's reform of Dorian institutions aims at a kind of equality and friendship between men and women that is beyond the reach of Geneva. Perhaps Rousseau wants to leave a hint that he does not regard such relations as inherently unattainable.

ingly to the public" during the preceding year (ibid., 118, Bloom, 130).[91] A public official will bestow the crown, and her parents will be honored for raising her so well. In a particularly clever touch, Rousseau recommends that the girl receive additional honors or emoluments if she marries during the following year.

The girls will inevitably be the focus of these balls, in a way that they would not be in the Magnesian dances. This is what Rousseau wants, and it is not an oversight that there is to be no King of the Ball. In the Geneva that Rousseau seeks to preserve, men will have their whole lives to display themselves publicly, to achieve civic honors, and to enjoy the dignity that comes with the role of head of household. In many ways, women will always rule these men, but they will do so privately and indirectly. Rousseau believes this is desirable, for the sake of everyone's happiness, but he also recognizes that it does entail a real sacrifice by women. Rousseau's proposed balls reflect a recognition that they should be asked to sacrifice no more than reason demands.

## Conclusion

The common ground on which Rousseau and the Athenian Stranger stand emerges from an understanding of the advantages that would arise from giving an appropriate education to "that half of the human race that governs the other."[92] In Magnesia, that requires a more masculine education for women and a moderation of the masculinity of their men. In Geneva, it means defending bourgeois manliness and educating women to seek their happiness primarily in the role of wife and mother. The differences in the prescriptions, which are striking enough, should not be allowed to conceal the underlying agreement about the fundamental requisites of social life.

It is true that the *Laws* points toward the cultivation of a kind of virtue, and happiness, to which the Genevans cannot aspire. But it is also true that the Athenian Stranger does not claim to have identified that virtue, or to have shown in any but the most obscure ways how the Magnesians

[91] Rousseau recognizes without alarm, and almost with approval, that even elderly judges may depart from strict justice in response to the physical beauty of some contestants (ibid., 119, Bloom, 130). Better that, perhaps, than that the city breed a bunch of old bourgeois Octaviuses.

[92] *Discourse on the Sciences and the Arts*, *O.C.*, 3:21n (quoted in context at the beginning of this chapter).

might discover it. The women of Magnesia are certainly to be offered the possibility of cultivating their own happiness by serving their city beyond the confines of their families, though only after they have fulfilled their duties as wives and mothers. Plato leaves us to wonder how well this measure of equality between the sexes would work out before the nocturnal council has succeeded in its task of discovering what human virtue truly is. Rousseau reflected on this question, and concluded that it could not work out well at all in modern Europe. He leaves readers in our time to ask whether we have subsequently discovered the solution to a dilemma that he believed was inescapable.

Rousseau is quite precise and vivid in describing what he regards as sound *mœurs* for Genevan women, and the proper aim of their education. He is less precise and less vivid about men. This is striking when one recalls his early statement: "Men will always be what is pleasing to women: if then you want them to become great and virtuous, teach women what greatness of soul and virtue is."[93] In the *Letter to d'Alembert*, we are largely left to infer that men should be good providers, faithful husbands, and solid citizens who participate responsibly but not obsessively in republican politics. We are apparently also expected to infer that if women are committed strongly enough to their own roles as wives and mothers, they will be able to discipline their men and keep them happy in this role. One can easily imagine that such a life would be seen as one of virtue, but is it so easy to think it would be regarded as "greatness of soul," either by men or by women?

For all his focus on bucking up Genevan men, and keeping the city's women from usurping the place these men should occupy, Rousseau does not forget about male *thumos*, about the desire to be recognized for greatness, or about the dangers of excessive manliness.

In one of the strangest of the many digressions in the *Letter to d'Alembert*, Rousseau discusses the failed efforts of the King of France to outlaw dueling. The occasion, or excuse, for this digression arose from d'Alembert's assumption that the behavior of a company of actors could be regulated by law and thus prevented from corrupting the Genevan youth. Rousseau has any number of reasons for considering this assumption naïve, but his principal objection is that d'Alembert misunderstands the relation between laws and *mœurs*.

[93] Ibid.

"Where is the lowliest legal scholar who cannot draw up a moral code as pure as that of Plato's laws?" (*d'Alembert*, *O.C.*, 5:61, Bloom, 66). To the extent that laws require coercion for their enforcement, their power is extremely limited. The real challenge is to influence public opinion, as the Athenian Stranger emphasizes through his use of preludes and other forms of education, and this is much more difficult than issuing commands and regulations.

Rousseau chooses as an example the tribunal of the Marshals of France, which was established by the King to adjudicate points of honor. The underlying problem is that the conventions of honor, including the duel, are a vestigial residue from a time when martial attitudes and martial skill had been taken for virtue. Whatever useful function such quasi-Dorian traditions may once have served, the conventions are manifestly contrary to reason, for it is absurd to suppose that the justice of one's claims could be a function of one's ability to kill an opponent.[94] In a modern society, moreover, the conventions are subversive of the social order. A man's honor means more to him than the laws of a republic or the commands of a monarch.

So long as men exhibit their share of the amour-propre that the Greeks called *thumos*, honor will have meaning. The challenge in France was to detach the convention or prejudice in favor of duels from the underlying sentiments that had been channeled into this tradition. Rousseau believes that the French effort to replace duels with the resolution of disputes in a legal tribunal was badly designed in many particulars. But he does not think that the case is completely hopeless.

His first key point is that the tribunals should consist only of respected soldiers, representatives of the tradition of virtue with which dueling is associated,[95] and that the only sanctions available to the judges should be honor and disgrace. Second, the tribunal should have the authority to forbid particular duels, to pass judgment on those who engage in unauthorized combats, and to give advance authorization to some duels. Third, the tribunal should be completely independent of the King's will, and he should even be subject to its judgments. Even if the "laws" administered

[94] In the *Laws*, the Stranger rebukes Megillus for thinking that victory in battle necessarily implies anything at all about who deserved to prevail (638a3–b9).

[95] This had in fact been done, and it is one feature of the King's effort that Rousseau approved.

by the tribunal make no real sense, it is important that the judges be seen as applying the code of honor without arbitrary interferences provoked by the interests or whims of the sovereign. Fourth, the tribunal should be given jurisdiction over insulting speeches in general, not just those involving the social classes in which formal duels have been traditional. Nobles and soldiers fight because others talk, and duels will never be abolished without changing the way everyone talks.

Rousseau thinks that it is crucial at the beginning not to condemn every duelist, and even to authorize some duels before they take place. This would have the effect of legitimating the judgments of the tribunal, and of causing those who dueled in secret to be suspected of doing so for disreputable reasons. Eventually, as the tribunal acquired respectability, it could gradually reduce the number of occasions on which duels would be approved until, perhaps, they could be abolished altogether.

Rousseau doubts that even these devices will succeed without the intervention of women, "on whom men's manner of thinking in great part depends" (ibid., 66, Bloom, 72). And even if all his advice were taken, he doubts that the project could succeed in France because it is contrary to the spirit of monarchy: duels may be a sign of the incompleteness of the King's sovereignty, but the establishment of a formal body that answers to any kind of law beyond his will would put a flashing neon sign on that deficiency. Rousseau's proposed improvement on the King's scheme is inherently subversive of the King's authority, and it would take an exceptionally wise monarch to see the advantages of embracing such subversion.

This calls attention to one very important point on which Rousseau and d'Alembert could agree: France will never achieve the kind of happiness seen in Geneva while its regime, or political form, remains unchanged. Rousseau believed he should contribute to defending what republican Geneva had achieved, but without endorsing the Encyclopedists' far more ambitious project of political activism and intellectual imperialism. In the two and a half centuries since Rousseau attacked d'Alembert's proposal, Enlightenment philosophy has made spectacular progress, both in science and technology and in fostering liberal and bourgeois institutions. In recent decades, these developments have produced, or at least accompanied, some very dramatic transformations of the relations between the sexes and the structure of family life. It is, however, surely too soon to declare that Rousseau's reservations about the assumptions and aims of the French *philosophes* were unjustified. It is therefore not too late to take seriously the reasons for his dissent, and for his decision to look to Plato as a guide in promoting a better education for "that half of the human race that governs the other."[96] If more people were to do so, fewer minds would be imprisoned by politically correct pieties enforced by intolerant proponents of sexual license, of doctrinaire feminism, and of redefining marriage and even sexual identity itself.

[96] *Discourse on the Sciences and the Arts*, *O.C.*, 3:21n (quoted in context at the beginning of this chapter).

CHAPTER 5

# Nature and Marriage: *Emile or On Education*

The *Letter to d'Alembert* was written in the midst of Rousseau's work on *The New Heloise*. Like the *Letter*, this epistolary novel aimed to defend bourgeois family life against the moral corruption that Rousseau thought was being actively accelerated by Enlightenment philosophy. The novel, however, is much more ambitious. Rather than making political arguments designed to conserve healthy institutions where they were already established, *The New Heloise* sought to carry out a legislator's most important work: to promote the health of "*mœurs*, of customs, and above all of opinion" (*S.C.*, bk. 2, chap. 12, *O.C.*, 3:394).[1] A tremendous literary success, the book was the best-selling novel of the eighteenth century, and it remained popular for several decades. It transformed Rousseau himself from a celebrated author into the object of a cult (Cranston, *Noble Savage*, 247), and it had a continuing influence on the great novelists of the nineteenth century.

Today, the appeal of *The New Heloise* is not readily apparent. The book is filled with lengthy and repetitious expressions of love, friendship, and self-pity. Embarrassingly overblown, these letters can easily provoke impatience and even derision. Mixed in with all this sentimentality are didactic disquisitions on topics like religion, culture, and education. These can

[1] The word *mœurs* refers to customs or habits that have some kind of ethical or moral quality or effects.



N. Lund, *Rousseau's Rejuvenation of Political Philosophy*,
DOI 10.1007/978-3-319-41390-7_5

make the reader wonder whether he is reading a novel or taking a class from a showy professor of big ideas. Although it is still possible to appreciate *The New Heloise* as a novel and to see how its author so successfully moved the hearts and minds of his readers,[2] Rousseau's next novel is in many ways more accessible today.

Like *The New Heloise*, the *Emile* is a kind of novel or romance. As its full title suggests, the book is part fiction, part treatise. Most of it describes the education given by an imaginary tutor, whom the author calls Jean-Jacques, to an imaginary pupil.[3] Emile's tutor is invested with all the knowledge and insight that Rousseau's own extraordinary mind had at its disposal when he wrote the book around the age of fifty. The tutor, however, is a very young man and one with an exceptionally patient temperament that Rousseau himself did not possess (*O.C.*, 4:264, 265, Bloom, 50, 51; *Confessions*, bk. 6, *O.C.*, 1:267–68). The tutor takes on the project of educating Emile out of friendship for the boy's father and devotes more than two decades of his life to nothing else. The tutor apparently agreed to accept this commission before the child's birth, and he insists on being given all of the father's rights and powers (*O.C.*, 4:267, 765, Bloom, 52–53, 407). We are not told why the father wanted to abdicate his position in favor of this man, but we are told that the tutor considers himself supremely well qualified for the undertaking, and he asks only for the satisfaction of succeeding at it (ibid., 263–69, Bloom, 49–53).

The boy comes from a wealthy family and is assumed to have a healthy body and an ordinary mind (ibid., 266, 537, Bloom, 52, 245). It is crucial that Emile be both healthy and ordinary. It is not crucial that he be born into a wealthy family, but his education will be expensive so it is convenient to assume that his father will be able to finance the project. In describing the education, Rousseau gives elaborate explanations for what the tutor does, and often steps outside the story to address the reader on subjects that are not directly related to Emile's upbringing.

In the first sentence of the Preface, Rousseau tells us that the book "was begun to oblige a good mother who knows how to think" (ibid.,

[2] For an extended analysis, see Nelson Lund, "A Woman's Laws and a Man's: Eros and Thumos in Rousseau's *Julie, or The New Heloise* (1761) and *The Deer Hunter* (1978)."

[3] Rousseau refers to Jean-Jacques as a *gouverneur* rather than a *precepteur* "because he seeks less to instruct than to guide" (*O.C.*, 4:266, Bloom, 52). In order to convey the same point in English, I will refer to him as a tutor.

241, Bloom, 33).[4] If the book was begun for this purpose, its author was overtaken by a much greater ambition. Rousseau regarded the *Emile* as his best book and one that was not aimed primarily at popular audiences.[5] Without abandoning the goal of giving some useful advice to mothers who know how to think, Rousseau ended by producing a work whose philosophic complement, I believe, is the *Discourse on Inequality*. In that book, which Rousseau considered an especially daring work,[6] he asked the question "What is man?" and began to answer with a depiction of natural or nascent humanity in all its primitive and innocent nakedness. The *Emile* reopens the question raised in the *Discourse* by imagining how one might educate an ordinary man according to nature in the midst of civilization.

It does not take long for Rousseau to let us know how far his ambition extends. In the second paragraph of the Preface, he says, "My subject was still quite fresh after Locke's book, and I greatly fear that it will be so after mine" (ibid., 241, Bloom, 33). His subject is "the art of forming men," which has been forgotten (ibid.). Perhaps this art can never be entirely recovered, but Rousseau also suggests that Locke's *Some Thoughts Concerning Education* is fundamentally misguided. So where did Locke go wrong?

A few pages later, we seem to be told. After a brief discussion of the difference between natural and civilized man, Rousseau describes what you get if you try to have both: "[H]e will never be either man or citizen; he will be good neither for himself nor for others. This will be one of these

[4] The mother in whose behalf he began the project was said "to have philosophy and to know the human heart" (*Mountain*, lett. 5, *O.C.*, 3:783). She is identified and described in the *Confessions* (bk. 8, *O.C.*, 1:358–60; bk. 9, 409–10). The *Emile* contains a great deal of advice that might profitably be adapted in practice by parents who know how to think, but such parents would easily recognize that the book does not give them a method in the sense of a recipe. I will have little to say about using Rousseau's advice in raising a living child today, but I doubt that the book can be fully appreciated without making the effort to see how this could be done.

[5] See, for example, *Confessions*, bk. 11, *O.C.*, 1:566, 568, 573; *Dialogues*, first dialogue, *O.C.*, 1:687 ("Rousseau" is speaking). Rousseau denied that *The New Heloise* is a philosophic novel, calling it instead a depiction of "an association of good people (*un commerce de bonnes gens*)" (Rousseau to Jacob Vernes, 4 July 1758, *Corr. Comp.*, 5:107). By way of contrast, he described the *Emile* as a plan for a new system of education offered for the examination of the wise, not as a method for fathers and mothers (*Mountain*, lett. 5, *O.C.*, 3:783). Similarly, he denied that the *Emile* is a true treatise on education, calling it instead a treatise on the original goodness of man (*Dialogues*, third dialogue, *O.C.*, 1:934, "the Frenchman" is speaking; Rousseau to Philibert Cramer, 13 Oct. 1764, *Corr. Comp.*, 21:248).

[6] See, for example, *Confessions*, bk. 9, *O.C.*, 1:407.

men of our days: a Frenchman, an Englishman, a Bourgeois. This one will be nothing" (ibid., 250, Bloom, 40). Locke's book is aimed at forming a responsible English citizen, and Rousseau asserts that making citizens is no longer possible because polities like Sparta and ancient Rome no longer exist. This is a familiar theme in many of Rousseau's writings, which often evoke Plutarch's world. But here he brings us up short by declaring that the book to read on public education is not Plutarch but Plato's *Republic* (ibid.). The *Emile*, we are left to understand, will be the modern complement to the *Republic*, or a book about private education that will be most unlike Locke's shallow effort to guide the education of an Englishman, a bourgeois, a nothing. Man and citizen will finally be combined, and combined according to nature so far as that is possible.

This chapter will explore Rousseau's effort to articulate an alternative to Locke's *Some Thoughts* that is also a modern complement to Plato's *Republic*. The *Emile* has aims that are both higher and lower than the books Rousseau takes as foils. Emile will be raised more in accord with nature than Locke's young gentleman, which is a higher goal, but he will also be less apt to make a useful contribution to the political and social order in which he finds himself. The educational plan that Rousseau sets out in the *Emile* is also, to put it mildly, far less practicable than the plan sketched in *Some Thoughts*. On the other hand, Rousseau's tutor resembles Locke in educating a child with an ordinary nature, and he thus aims lower than Socrates does in responding to the gifted young adults who challenge him at the beginning of the second book of the *Republic*. But an ordinary child in some ways reveals more about human nature, and is more difficult to elevate. Rousseau's imaginary tutor takes on a more onerous challenge, and in that sense aims higher than Socrates does in the *Republic*. What we see of private education in Plato's dialogue takes place in a single night, while the education of Emile requires more than two decades of unremitting attentiveness.

## Early Education in *Some Thoughts Concerning Education*

Notwithstanding Rousseau's dismissal of Locke at the outset of the *Emile*, his own book contains innumerable points of agreement, and some of his specific criticisms of Locke seem trivial or even unjust. In order to see why Rousseau believes that his own book is seriously opposed to Locke's, one needs to take at least a quick look at Locke's goals and method.

*Some Thoughts* began as a series of letters to a personal friend, offering advice on the rearing of his sons. The friend was a gentleman who must have hoped to see his children become respectable and successful members of his own social class. Locke obviously does not believe that such men are "nothing." On the contrary, he maintains that if the English gentry are "by their education once set right, they will quickly bring all the rest into order."[7] He does not accept the distinction Rousseau makes between public and private education because he sees no conflict between an English gentleman's private happiness and his public usefulness. An education for one is equally an education for the other.

If Locke does not quite imply that all men should in principle be led to the life of an English gentleman, he at least suggests that they are naturally suited to it, and he never suggests that the life of a gentleman need be less happy than that of anyone else. He does acknowledge that children must be educated to take their place in the social class for which they are destined, and that there will inevitably be differences in the educations of a prince, a noble, a gentleman, and a child of the laboring classes (§ 216).[8] These differences, however, presuppose a class structure that could be other than it is.

Locke leaves the reader to ask how properly educated gentlemen "will quickly bring all the rest into order." One possibility, which is consistent with his political writings, is that the nobles will be replaced by gentlemen through political reform, while the laboring classes might eventually be elevated through economic growth and a concomitant spread of education. If we expand the notion of a "gentleman" just a little beyond its technical meaning in the late seventeenth century, the subsequent history of Great Britain and the West proves that such hopes would not have been unrealistic. The nobility are gone in all but name, and the middle class (or what Rousseau calls the bourgeoisie) has in many nations become overwhelmingly dominant in power and numbers.

If something like that outcome is the ultimate goal, what is Locke's method? Always seeking when possible to work with nature rather than against it, Locke aims to make his student sociable, productive, and prudently sober. Nature is preeminently good at forming the body. Accordingly, Locke strongly inveighs against common ways in which chil-

[7] Dedication "To Edward Clarke of *Chipley*, Esquire" (penultimate paragraph).

[8] Somewhat more elaborately, Rousseau offers a similar acknowledgment in the *Emile* (*O.C.*, 4:243, 251–53, Bloom, 35, 41–42).

dren's natural development is frustrated: tight clothing, sumptuous foods and strong drink, too much time indoors, insufficient sleep, unnecessary medical treatments. What nature is above all bad at is forming a sound mind and a virtuous character. The great task of education is to train the child to resist his most natural inclinations, especially the preference for pleasure and the avoidance of pain. But this refers only to immediate pleasures and pains. "I grant that good and evil, *reward* and *punishment*, are the only motives to a rational creature; these are the spurs and reins whereby all mankind are set to work and guided, and therefore they are to be made use of to children too" (§ 54). Similarly, Locke later says that the true principle and measure of virtue is "the knowledge of a man's duty and the satisfaction it is to obey his Maker in following the dictates of that light God has given him *with the hopes of acceptation and reward*" (§ 61, emphasis added; see also § 143, last paragraph).[9]

Education therefore consists primarily in training the mind to discipline itself in hopes of acquiring temporally remote rewards. Children are by nature sufficiently rational to respond to rewards and punishments, but insufficiently rational to appreciate how present pain and deprivation can purchase greater rewards to come. In this, children differ only in degree from most adults, and Locke's entire educational program is directed toward assisting the child's rational inclination to maximize his net welfare over time (§§ 33–34).

*Some Thoughts* sketches the main features of such an educational program, which are generally sensible, frequently shrewd, and sometimes quite unorthodox. Locke's principal tool is the inculcation of wholesome habits, a convenient kind of second nature, especially by instilling shame and a desire for esteem and reputation (§§ 42, 64, 185, 200). The moral qualities that Locke finds most natural in children are the love of freedom and especially of dominion (§ 103). The challenge is to minimize the external restraints on his liberty that a child experiences while he is developing appropriate habits, and to frustrate the desire for dominion by refusing to let it be satisfied.

Locke lays the foundation early in the child's life. The key principle is set forth in a long discussion of the common parental folly of coddling children by tolerating their faults and misbehavior, or even encouraging exhibitions of willfulness that seem harmless or cute in one so weak (§§

[9] Locke makes the same point even more bluntly in *An Essay concerning Human Understanding*, bk. 2, chap. 21, § 61.

34–37). Correlatively, Locke denounces the lazy practice of using corporal punishment on children. The first mistake establishes habits of self-indulgence: "He that is not used to submit his will to the reason of others *when* he is *young*, will scarce hearken or submit to his own reason when he is of an age to make use of it" (§ 36). The second mistake trains a child only to avoid the immediate pain of a beating, through dishonesty if that will do the trick, and in the worst case instills a temper so servile that "he will be all his life a useless thing to himself and others" (§ 51).

What then is the middle alternative? Locke accepts what he thinks is the goal on which all parents agree: "that their children when little should look upon their parents as their lords, their absolute governors, and, as such, stand in awe of them; and that when they come to riper years, they should look on them as their best, as their only sure friends, and, as such love and reverence them" (§ 41). Thus, allow children a great deal of freedom to enjoy themselves in childish activities, and refrain from imposing unnecessary constraints. Give them everything they really need as well as some of what they merely want, but severely refuse every ***demand*** for anything that is not strictly necessary. As the child's own reason and self-discipline gradually develop, this parsimony should be gradually relaxed until the child becomes an adult. Consistent with the goal of instilling awe for the parents, Locke makes one exception to his ban on corporal punishment: if a child exhibits obstinacy, his will must be subdued, and there is no choice but to administer beatings as a last resort (§§ 78–80).

## Rousseau's Alternative to Locke's Early Education

Rousseau is almost perfectly satisfied with Locke's prescriptions about bodily development and even refers the reader to *Some Thoughts* for a treatment of the details (*O.C.*, 4:371, Bloom, 126). He also agrees with many of Locke's specific recommendations relating to the child's moral education. Both writers, for example, insist that children should neither be constrained unnecessarily, nor given anything they do not need in response to childish importunity, nor thoughtlessly subjected to corporal punishment.

Rousseau's proximate goal, however, is radically different. Instead of seeking to put the child in awe of his parents and to subject him to their will, Rousseau tries to postpone as long as possible any conflict at all with the will of any adult. This requires a great deal of ingenuity and assiduity. In his early years, the child must frequently experience resistance to his own will, but as much as possible this resistance should come from things rather than from people. Adults should never submit to the will of the child, but neither should they appear to impose their will on him. Rousseau gives a striking example in the child's very infancy:

> When the child extends his hand without saying anything, he believes he will reach the object because he does not estimate the distance; he is in error; but when he complains and shrieks in extending his hand, he is no longer deceived about the distance; he is commanding the object to approach or you to carry it to him. In the first case carry him to the object slowly and with small steps. In the second, act as though you do not even hear him; the more he shrieks, the less you should listen to him. It is important to accustom him early not to give commands either to men, for he is not their master, or to things, for they do not hear him. (ibid., 287–88, Bloom, 66)[10]

Variations on this technique recur repeatedly during Emile's childhood. One explanation of the theoretical basis for the rules comes in a passage criticizing Locke. "To reason with children was the great maxim of Locke … This is to begin at the end, it is to want to make the instrument out of the completed work. If children understood reason, they would have no need to be raised" (ibid., 317, Bloom, 89). At first, this seems unfair. Locke, after all, is careful to note that "when I talk of *reasoning* I do not intend any other but such as is suited to the child's capacity and apprehension," which means that the child is shown by demeanor no less than by words that the adult is being reasonable (*Some Thoughts*, § 81). Rousseau, however, rejects exactly this approach because "everything that one thinks is obtained from [children] out of reasonable motives is never obtained except from motives of avarice or fear or vanity, which one is always forced to add" (*Emile*, *O.C.*, 4:317, Bloom, 89–90). Instead, the tutor should

[10] Easier said than done, as mothers will easily recognize. Rousseau strongly advocates that mothers not delegate their natural functions to nurses, for a variety of reasons that he presents in some detail. In an early sign of the tensions within his educational project, however, Rousseau tacitly acknowledges that there is a certain advantage to substituting a nurse in place of Emile's mother. Although mothers almost always have the right disposition toward their children—wanting them to be happy, and happy now—they frequently have misguided ideas about how to treat them. Whether the baby is nursed by its mother or a domestic, the caregiver will have to be under the absolute command of the tutor, and a carefully chosen nurse can be expected to be easier to control (*O.C.*, 4:253–279, Bloom, 42–61).

resemble what human law ought to be: benevolent but implacable, in that respect imitating nature itself.[11]

> Never command him anything, whatever in the world it might be, absolutely nothing. Do not even let him imagine that you claim to have any authority over him. Let him know only that he is weak and that you are strong, that through his state and yours he is necessarily at your mercy; let him know it, learn it, sense it; early on let him feel on his haughty head the harsh yoke which nature imposes on man, the heavy yoke of necessity under which every finite being must bend. Let him see this necessity in things, never in the caprice* of men; let the brake that restrains him be force and not authority; do not forbid him to do that from which he should abstain; prevent him from doing it without explanations, without reasonings; what you grant him, grant at his first word, without solicitations, without prayers, above all, without condition. Grant with pleasure, refuse only with repugnance; but let all your refusals be irrevocable, let no importunity shake you, let *no* when pronounced be a wall of bronze, against which the child will exhaust his strength only five or six times attempting to overturn it. (ibid., 320, Bloom, 91)

The footnote signaled by the asterisk in this passage reads as follows: "One should be sure that the child will treat as a caprice every will opposed to his own when he does not appreciate the reason for it. Now a child does not appreciate the reason for anything which clashes with his whims." In this passage, one sees that the tutor's effort to prevent Emile from becoming embroiled in conflicts of will does not necessarily mean that he should be prevented from recognizing that other people have wills, just as he does. What he will experience, rather, is that attempting to satisfy his will by subjecting another person to it is as fruitless as commanding an object to fly through the air and into his hand.

This recommendation has its root in the *Emile*'s theory of happiness, which is more subtle and elaborate than anything found in *Some Thoughts*. We do not experience either absolute happiness, which would require a complete absence of pain, or absolute unhappiness, which would arise from a complete absence of pleasure. For us, whose bodies and souls are always in flux, unhappiness consists in the disproportion between our desires and our faculties, or in the sum of unsatisfied desires to obtain pleasure and to avoid pain. It might seem to follow that human happiness

[11] On the analogy of the tutor to human law, see ibid., 310–12, Bloom, 84–86.

should be sought in minimizing our desires, except for one absolutely crucial fact: if our power exceeded our desires, "a part of our faculties would remain idle, and we would not enjoy all of our being" (ibid., 304, Bloom, 80). In an allusion to the *Discourse on Inequality*, Rousseau maintains that men found their desires and their faculties in close equilibrium in the state of nature, thus approximating what happiness we are capable of, but that nature also put others "as it were in reserve at the bottom of [man's] soul, to be developed when needed" (ibid.). Emile's education aims to approximate the original equilibrium without leaving idle the additional faculties (and thus additional desires) that necessarily develop in civilized men.

Locke and Rousseau are aiming to produce inner dispositions that are fundamentally different, most obviously with respect to their pupils' orientation toward the opinions of other people. Emile will eventually assume an outward resemblance to the man Locke hopes to produce, but that appearance will be misleading (see, e.g., ibid., 665–71, Bloom, 335–39). It order to begin seeing why this is so, let us jump ahead to Emile's first significant discovery of social relations, which is discussed in a series of intricately related passages.

After a lengthy discussion of what Rousseau calls "negative education," which primarily means inhibiting the premature development of moral passions, he notes both the importance of shaping a child's education to that child's particular nature and the impossibility of shielding the child from the spectacle of the passions displayed by the adults among whom he lives (ibid., 323–25, Bloom, 93–95). His first example is anger, an emotion whose effects so strike the senses that they must provoke a child's curiosity.[12] Rousseau recommends that the child be told that he is observing the effects of an illness, which is not untrue. More important, perhaps, this diagnosis gives him a motive to respond to the anger of others with pity and to regard his own anger as a disability. The hard part is to prevent the child from learning how unconventional his new opinion is: "An indiscreet outburst of laughter can spoil the work of six months and do irreparable harm for the whole of life" (ibid., 328, Bloom, 97).

Anger, of course, is a very natural illness, and one to which some people are more prone than others. Rousseau suggests that it has two principal sources. One, virtually universal, is the experience of injustice. The other source is innate violence and ferocity, which is more pronounced in some

[12] This is also the very first passion to which the *Emile* alludes: the book's epigraph is drawn from Seneca's *On Anger* (ibid., 239, Bloom, 31).

children than in others. Earlier in the *Emile*, Rousseau had touched on the first source in an anecdote about a crying infant who was struck by his nurse, not severely but with an obvious offensive intent. When the child fell silent, Rousseau at first thought that he was intimidated and prone to servility, but he soon observed that the boy was suffocating with rage (ibid., 286–87, Bloom, 65–66). Now he draws the crucial inference: "the first sentiment of justice does not come to us from the justice we owe, but from that which is due us," and children should learn their rights before they are taught their duties (ibid., 329, Bloom, 97).

Children with a ferocious nature will have to be introduced to their duties earlier than children with a gentler nature, but the principles of their education will be the same. If a child ever strikes another person seriously, the blow should be "repaid with interest" in a way (presumably without any manifestation of anger) that will repress the desire to repeat the experiment (ibid., 329–30n, Bloom, 97n). This is the only example Rousseau gives of what we would call corporal punishment, and it is almost the opposite of Locke's last-resort cure for obstinacy. To the extent possible during childhood, Rousseau's pupil is meant to find that striking a human being has undesirable consequences—just as he finds a tree branch snapping back in his face when he bends it too far—without perceiving that his will is being subjected to that of another person.

Things will often resist giving Emile what he wants from them, but things do not defend the rights of their owners. His foundational moral lesson will therefore begin with the idea of property. In order to teach this lesson, the tutor stages an elaborate drama (ibid., 329–33, Bloom, 97–100). In a reminder of his previous mention of man's "reserve faculties," Rousseau comments that everyone at every age wants to "create, imitate, produce, give signs of power and activity" (ibid., 330, Bloom, 98). Emile is spending his early childhood in the country, where he sees agriculture being practiced, and will likely express an interest in gardening. Pretending to enjoy working alongside his pupil, the tutor helps him plant some beans, which soon begin to sprout. The boy easily comes to regard the beans as his own, looks forward to consuming them, and almost intuitively adopts Locke's labor theory of property rights. One day, however, Emile is aggrieved to find that his plants have been dug up and destroyed. It turns out that the tutor's secret agent, Robert the gardener, did the deed because Emile had unknowingly destroyed some melons that Robert had planted in that very spot. In a confrontation with Robert, Emile finds out that he has violated another person's rights under the same theory of property that he himself had implicitly adopted. He also learns that all the land in the neighborhood is already taken under that theory, leaving him without a place to plant beans for himself. Accordingly, Emile is induced to become a tenant farmer by agreeing to confine his planting to a designated area and to share the fruits with Robert.

Rousseau stresses that this demonstration is based primarily on actions rather than words and that it leads the child only to ideas that he can clearly comprehend. The lesson, moreover, should stop here, with no further elaboration. We readers are left to notice how limited this lesson is. First, and perhaps most obviously, Emile is encouraged to accept the lesson by some happy accidents that the tutor has arranged: the melons that Emile unknowingly destroyed had been destined for his own enjoyment, and Robert declines to accept the offer of half the future bean harvests (ibid., 331–32, Bloom, 99). Second, Emile is not encouraged to ask how the first person to occupy the land came to have legitimate rights over it. As we know from the *Discourse on Inequality*, this is not the easiest question to answer.[13] Third, Emile is not encouraged to wonder why he should respect the property rights of others when he can violate them with impunity. This is another question to which Rousseau thinks it is difficult to give a satisfactory answer.[14]

Rousseau then gives another example to illustrate how the same technique can be used with an ill-natured child whose impulses lead to deliberately destructive behavior. Once again, the culmination is a mutually beneficial agreement, but the road to that agreement comes through a process that is more Hobbesian than Lockean (ibid., 333–34, Bloom, 100–101). By either route, the child has now entered the moral world. That world is framed by promises based on self-interest, which bring with them the incentive for cheating and lying. Once again, Rousseau departs from Locke by insisting that Emile should not be punished for lying, any more than he has been punished for anything else. Instead, the greatest

[13] See *O.C.*, 3:176–78. In both writings, the establishment of property is the foundation of civilized morality, but here in the *Emile* Rousseau acknowledges more forthrightly that its institution is rooted in the *natural* desire to "create, imitate, produce, give signs of power and activity" (*O.C.*, 4:330, Bloom, 98). Another contrast, less obvious, is that Emile's discovery of the basis for property rights is his introduction to morality. In the *Discourse*, competition had already inflamed a multitude of moral passions before property rights were recognized. By changing the order in which Emile is introduced to moral ideas, the tutor aims to put useful principles on a less tenuous foundation.

[14] See, for example, *Emile*, *O.C.*, 4:522–23, 636–37, Bloom, 235, 314–15.

care should be taken to prevent him from having a motive to lie, and if he does the "punishment" should appear to be only a consequence of the lie itself.

The remainder of Emile's education up to the time of puberty is devoted to retarding the development of social and moral passions, while developing skills and attitudes that will later enable him to conduct himself appropriately in social situations. After acquiring his own Lockean theory of property, Emile's next crucial step involves the passion that Locke thought it most important to cultivate: the desire for esteem and reputation.

At the outset of Book III, Rousseau identifies a short period during late childhood, beginning around the age of twelve or thirteen, that deserves to be treated as a distinct phase of human development. At this time, a boy who has led a vigorous life will have begun to approach adult proportions and strength, but will not yet have the overpowering passions that arise during adolescence. This is the only time of life when one's power can exceed one's desires, and it is therefore especially important now for Emile's energy to be subtly directed by the tutor. This is the moment to arouse "a curiosity natural to man" (ibid., 429, Bloom, 167) by artfully guiding the child toward studies that Emile himself will see as useful. The hallmark of the tutor's technique is akin to the one used to demonstrate the Pythagorean Theorem in Plato's *Meno*: "Render your pupil attentive to the phenomena of nature, soon you will render him curious; but to nourish his curiosity, never hurry to satisfy it. Put the questions within his reach and leave them for him to resolve. Let him know nothing because you told it to him, but because he has comprehended it himself: let him not learn science but discover it" (ibid., 430, Bloom, 168). The tutor had prepared the way for this, and indeed for Emile's later instruction in morality, by using the same technique, *mutatis mutandis*, to instruct him in elementary geometry (ibid., 399–401, 428–29, Bloom, 145–46, 167). The example of discovery in the *Meno*, however, is specious, or at least very easily misinterpreted. Rousseau understands that Socratic education cannot take place unless the student has a real stake in what he learns: "The one who has been taught as his most important lesson to want to know nothing except what is useful, interrogates like Socrates" (ibid., 446, Bloom, 179).

Some of Rousseau's initial illustrations involving the phenomena of nature come from astronomy and geography, where it is easy to give the child a motive for learning, such as finding his way home when lost.

The tutor also ensures that in playing around with various bodies, Emile notices some intriguing effects of static electricity, eventually encounters lodestones, and then learns that this substance can impart its magnetic quality to ordinary iron. One day, the two of them go to a fair, where a magician uses a piece of bread to attract a wax duck floating in a tub of water. At home, Emile figures out that he can perform the same trick by inserting a magnetized needle into a lump of wax and using a piece of iron wrapped in bread to move the object.

Emile, naturally enough, wants to show off his cleverness at the fair, and the tutor acquiesces. When the magician performs his trick again the next day, Emile volunteers to show that he can do it too, and is rewarded with much applause from the crowd. The magician, who is another of the tutor's secret agents, congratulates the boy and offers to round up an even larger crowd for Emile on the following day. Bursting with pride and anticipation, Emile returns to the fair, but this time the little wax duck completely ignores his piece of bread. Worse, the duck dutifully chases the same lure in the hand of the magician. Worse yet, it now turns out that the magician can get the duck to go wherever he wishes, with or without a piece of bread and even in response to oral commands from across the room. The audience erupts in laughter, and Emile is mortified.

That night, Emile and the tutor get a visit from the magician, who sternly reprimands them (especially the tutor) for thoughtlessly interfering with his livelihood. He then explains his second trick, which was to have a child hidden under the table below the tub of water with a strong magnet that he used to guide the duck at the magician's oral commands. The tutor takes Emile back to the fair the next day, where the boy silently watches the magician perform this trick.

The principal purpose of this drama is to give Emile a memorably bad taste of indulging the desire for esteem and reputation. This is exactly the opposite of what Locke recommends. The tutor wants Emile to be focused as much as possible on what is good and useful for himself, and as little as possible on what others think of him. When the time comes, he will be quite capable of pleasing other people, but this will happen primarily because he is himself pleasant and self-possessed, and because he has no reason or desire to offend others. Rousseau is deeply insistent on cultivating what Locke calls good breeding without instilling a passion for living through the eyes of others.

The incident with the "magician-Socrates" (ibid., 440, Bloom, 175) has other effects as well. First, it is a step toward discovering the useful art of constructing a simple magnetic compass. Second, the tutor promises Emile that in the future, he will warn the boy away from making mistakes like the one that led to his humiliation at the fair. As we learn later, humiliating lessons like this one will nevertheless have to occur repeatedly (ibid., 537, Bloom, 245). Rousseau does *not* indicate that the lesson learned from the episode with the beans and Robert the gardener will have to be repeated. On the contrary, Rousseau says that Emile's simple theory of property rights can later be built upon quite easily (ibid., 461, Bloom, 189). This helps to explain why it is much easier to establish political societies than to live happily in them.[15]

## Plato's *Republic* and the Transition to Adulthood

Seventeenth- and eighteenth-century gentlemen customarily capped their formal education with a period of foreign travel during adolescence in the company of their tutors. Locke sees considerable value in such an experience, but strongly objects to its timing. There is much to be learned from observing alien cultures and conversing with serious men who can be found there. But almost all teenagers will primarily be driven to seek pleasure and amusement when away from home, and in any event will not be welcome in the company of "men of worth and parts" (*Some Thoughts*, §§ 214–215). Locke would prefer educational travel to be postponed until this "dangerous and heady age be over," but he concludes that this is a bootless recommendation (§ 215). The boy must come back home by the age of twenty-one because his father is interested in a dowry and his mother must have new babies to play with. "[T]he young gentleman being got within view of matrimony, 'tis time to leave him to his mistress" (ibid.).

Rousseau is not so submissive to custom. Emile, too, will travel with his tutor before he is married, and he will do so during the same dangerous and heady age. But everything else will be different. In place of Locke's resignation, Emile's tutor proceeds with the greatest audacity. In seeking to educate a man who lives according to nature in a modern society, Rousseau's radicalism will rival that of Plato.

[15] Adam Smith makes a similar point by distinguishing justice (narrowly defined), which is sufficient for maintaining societies, from beneficence, which is essential for societies to be flourishing and happy (*Theory of Moral Sentiments*, pt. 2, § 2, chap. 3, ¶¶ 1–4).

Until the age of puberty, pride and vanity need not grip the soul unless the child has experienced the kind of miseducation that Emile's tutor has prevented through such devices as the drama with the magician-Socrates. Finally, however, nature intervenes. "We are born, so to speak, twice: once in order to exist and once in order to live; once for our species and once for our sex" (*O.C.*, 4:489, Bloom, 211). It is therefore time to change method (ibid., 494, Bloom, 215).

More than half of the *Emile* is devoted to exploring the details of this new method. Its culmination comes when Emile and the tutor travel for two years after his betrothal to Sophie, who is the young woman the tutor has selected and arranged for Emile to meet at just the right time. During this journey, Emile receives the political education that will enable him to avoid finding his natural eroticism channeled into the kind of vanity and pride that so often leads to worldly ambition. In order to set the stage for considering some of the critical elements in Emile's education for adulthood, let us return to Rousseau's brief initial comments on Plato's *Republic.*

Rousseau suggested near the beginning of the *Emile* that his book would describe a private or domestic education that would complement Plato's unparalleled analysis of public education (ibid., 249–51, Bloom, 40–41). This passage begins by distinguishing the man, who exists for himself, from the citizen, who lives for others. Rousseau illustrates what he means by a citizen with several examples drawn from Sparta and ancient Rome. No illustration of the man who exists for himself is provided here, but the natural man of the *Discourse on Inequality* is the obvious referent. Rousseau then goes on:

> From these objects [viz., the man and the citizen], necessarily opposed, come two contrary forms of instruction (*institution*); the one public and common, the other individual and domestic.
>
> Do you want to get an idea of public education? Read the *Republic* of Plato. This is by no means a political work, as those who judge books only by their titles think. It is the most beautiful treatise on education that has ever been produced.
>
> When one wants to refer to the land of chimeras, one cites what Plato instituted (*l'institution de Platon*). If Lycurgus had put his own down only in writing, I would have found it much more chimerical. Plato only purified the heart of man; Lycurgus denatured it.
>
> Public instruction (*L'institution publique*) no longer exists, and no longer can exist; because where there is no longer a fatherland one can no

> longer have citizens. These two words, fatherland and citizen, ought to be removed from modern languages. (ibid., 250, Bloom, 40)

This comparison of Sparta and the *Republic*'s city in speech is outlandish on its face. But perhaps it will start to look less preposterous if we focus on Rousseau's use of the words "chimeras" and "chimerical." The chimera is a mythological being composed from parts of three different beasts. Although made up from familiar animals, the composite is so patently unnatural that an adult would have to be most credulous to believe it could exist. Contrast this with a unicorn. It looks no more strange or unnatural than many animals that we commonly see in the world. One might be surprised to see one, but not because one would suppose that no such thing could possibly exist. What Rousseau is stressing in this passage is the artificial jamming together of alien species or natures.[16] Though he does not deny that both Sparta and Plato's city appear chimerical, he claims that what Lycurgus accomplished in fact is more unnatural than what Plato carried out only in speech.

Rousseau's two illustrations of Spartan patriotism are carefully chosen to show what was unnatural about their hearts. After offering to serve in a political office and being rejected, a man rejoiced that Sparta had so many other worthier men. A woman asked a messenger for news of a battle. Told that her five sons had all been killed, she was indignant that her question had not been answered. Informed that Sparta prevailed in the battle, she ran to the temple to thank the gods (ibid., 249, Bloom, 40).

So thoroughly to repress male ambition and female maternal care by substituting love of one's political community plainly does require a severe denaturing of the human heart through education. But why would one think that the education in the *Republic* requires anything less? Consider the analogues in Plato. Those chosen to rule are without political ambition, and so must be compelled to take on the burdens of office—they are therefore not expected to be filled with joy at having to set aside their preferred occupations. As for women, they do not know who their own children are, so they are prevented from experiencing the kind of maternal love that the Spartan woman had to repress in the anecdote retold by Rousseau. Having gone through pregnancy, the women of the *Republic*

[16] Elsewhere in the *Emile*, Rousseau frequently uses the terms "chimera" and "chimerical" in the looser sense of something that exists only in the imagination. He could still have meant for the reader to reflect on its narrower or more precise sense here in this passage.

obviously will not have been completely prevented from experiencing maternal love. Nevertheless, the process of purifying their hearts of this love, to the extent it can be done, would be a less daunting project than in the case of the Spartan women. At least in these respects, one can intelligibly say that the human heart is purified rather than denatured in the *Republic*.

The conflicts between one's personal interests and one's public obligations are minimized in the city of the *Republic* by a device that requires no denaturing of the heart: by hypothesis, everyone is assigned the work that is properly his own by nature. This may be impracticable in fact but it is consistent with nature almost by definition. Once the hypothesis is assumed, "purifying" the heart requires only an education that forestalls a desire to perform work other than that for which one is naturally suited. True, the hypothesized philosopher is compelled to perform what is for him the unnatural work of ruling. But he does so only for a part of his adult life, and then only through the compulsion of arguments that do not require him to love ruling or the city more than he enjoys the contemplation of eternal beings.

But wait! Does not the abolition of the family render the whole scheme of the *Republic* fundamentally unnatural? That device certainly provides the precondition for minimizing conflicts in the hearts of women between their maternal concerns and the interests of the city. It is also a device for discouraging political ambition in men. Such ambition, after all, frequently expresses itself by giving preferences to one's kin, most prominently in attempts to found a dynasty. In light of Rousseau's comparison of Plato and Lycurgus, it may be surprising to find that he does denounce the *Republic*'s abolition of the family, and on the ground of its unnaturalness. But we do not encounter this denunciation until much later in the *Emile*, and then not for the reasons that we might expect.

When he begins to discuss the education of Sophie, the girl meant for Emile, Rousseau pauses to explain where Plato, "that beautiful genius," went wrong in the *Republic* (*O.C.*, 4:700, Bloom, 362). Not, as so many of Plato's careless readers have believed, because of "that supposed community of women," but rather because of "that civil promiscuity which completely confounds the two sexes in the same employments, in the same labors, and cannot fail to engender the most intolerable abuses" (ibid., 700, Bloom, 362–63). The reference to a "supposed community of women" (*prétendüe communautê de femmes*) makes considerable sense. The rigid, scientific eugenics regime of the *Republic* is the farthest thing imaginable from the free love chaos that the term itself suggests. That regime, moreover, does not thwart nature in any way that fundamentally differs from what happens in conventional families. The people of the *Republic* are tricked by the rulers into breeding only when and with whom they should mate according to the rules of an hypothesized science. In actual societies, people are ordinarily directed by their political rulers to breed only with partners who have been selected by themselves or their parents, often for unnatural reasons such as social advancement and sometimes in defiance of natural inclination. Human beings obviously have a natural sexual attraction to a very wide range of people, and it is no more obviously unnatural for one's breeding partners to be chosen by scientific matching than it is to confine oneself indefinitely to one spouse. Everyone knows that such commitments do not extinguish the natural desire for other partners, but everyone should also know that some controls over that natural desire are a necessary precondition of social life. The eugenics scheme of the *Republic* is thus an extension of practices almost universally adopted. The extension may be impracticable, and it is obviously not simply natural. But neither does it require that people be thoroughly denatured.

It bears noting that Rousseau attacks the *least impracticable* of the three proposals for which Socrates expects to face waves of ridicule. No one has ever seen the kind of community of women proposed in the *Republic*, let alone rule by the kind of philosophers whose existence the dialogue hypothesizes. Plato himself was clearly aware that the civil equality of women was the least chimerical of the three proposals in Book V of the *Republic*. In the second-best city of the *Laws*, the family is not abolished, and the rulers are not assumed to be capable of the intellectual achievements that Socrates ascribes to the philosophers in speech of the *Republic*'s city in speech. But the women of the *Laws* are provided with education and employments that are about as close as possible to those of men in a society that has not abolished the family. Today, moreover, we see in front of our eyes something very much like the equality of women described there.

Rousseau's critique of the civil equality of women is framed at first in terms of nature: "Having excluded individual families from his government and no longer knowing what to do with women, [Plato] saw that he was forced to make men of them" (ibid., 699–700, Bloom, 362). If true, this is a devastating criticism of a city that was supposed to institute justice by assigning to each individual the tasks for which he—or she—is most naturally fitted. And Rousseau soon offers a long disquisition on the natural and complementing differences between the sexes that should give more than a moment's pause to those who believe that justice and happiness can be combined by applying the magical solvent of legalized equality. But his first reason for attacking the civil equality of women focuses on the obstacles that the abolition of the patriarchal family creates for the civil order:

> I am speaking of that subversion of nature's sweetest sentiments, immolated to an artificial sentiment which can only stay alive through them; as if there were no need for a natural hold through which to form conventional ties; as if the love of one's nearest kin were not the principle of the love one owes to the State; as if it were not through the small fatherland that is the family that the heart attaches itself to the great one; as if it were not the good son, the good husband, the good father who makes the good citizen. (ibid., 700, Bloom, 363)

This passage indicates that Rousseau has not entirely set aside an interest in what he earlier called the "public and common education" most beautifully described in the *Republic*. Emile and Sophie are not meant to become the kind of citizens at which the laws of Sparta aimed. But neither are they meant to live outside of political society, like a man in the state of nature. Recall that Rousseau's state of nature includes at least three pre-political stages: solitary life in the pure state of nature, isolated patriarchal family life, and primitive tribal life. The last of these stages is the one he calls "the happiest epoch, and the most durable" (*Inequality*, *O.C.*, 3:171). Emile's life with Sophie in modern Europe is meant to recreate as much as possible of what made that epoch the happiest and most durable. To that end, Rousseau wants the couple to find their happiness in "the small fatherland that is the family" while fulfilling the limited obligations of what we call citizens in the modern world. One can think of their life in that one respect as an image of the life of the philosophers in the *Republic*.

The nature of the public education that Rousseau has in mind can be discerned in the political education that Emile receives. It begins with the study of history, initially through Plutarch, and culminates while he is traveling with the tutor before his marriage to Sophie. The main points of this education parallel the principles of political right set forth in the *Social Contract*, which was published almost simultaneously with the *Emile*. But there are two especially important differences. First, Emile's education takes place in a Socratic fashion. Whereas the *Social Contract* is a treatise, proceeding in a logical fashion with arguments and evidence, Emile is shown a variety of political regimes and encouraged to ask the right questions about their legitimacy. The tutor obviously has his own views, which shape the questions he asks, but Emile is expected to work out the answers for himself.[17] Second, Emile is spared from being asked to think much about the conditions and techniques for founding or governing a healthy political regime.

Why the differences? Broadly speaking, the *Social Contract* has two principal aims. First, to show why no regime meets the strict standard of legitimacy that follows from the premises of modern natural rights theory. In that sense, the *Social Contract* resembles the *Republic*'s demonstration that no actual regime meets the strict standard of justice that follows from the philosophic understanding of natural right. Second, the *Social Contract* supplements modern natural rights theory with considerable discussion of the art of statesmanship, which Rousseau believes is always needed and will be needed more than ever in the wake of political revolutions that he saw coming in Europe.[18]

The *Social Contract* is thus aimed at readers who bring to it an interest in politics, often along with some form of political ambition, and the most important of those readers will encounter the book long after its initial publication. Emile, too, may have the seeds of political ambition in his soul, but his tutor aims to prevent those seeds from germinating, both for his own sake and for that of his fellow citizens (*O.C.*, 4:849, Bloom, 467). In that sense, Emile can be seen as an image of Glaucon, whom Socrates seeks to turn away from politics through the *Republic*'s analogue of what Rousseau calls private or domestic education. Emile will be turned away from politics toward life in "the small fatherland that is the family," which

[17] In his discussion of reading history, Rousseau claims that philosophers conclude that "we are all wicked," whereas a savage, and Emile, would look at us and say, "You are mad" (*O.C.*, 4:535, Bloom, 243). Before he travels, it will also be crucial for Emile to know—and feel—that recognizing the madness of others does not imply that he is himself wise. "The [Socratic] adventure with the magician would be repeated in a thousand ways" (ibid., 537, Bloom, 245).

[18] On the coming revolutions, see ibid., 468–69, Bloom, 194; *Inequality*, *O.C.*, 3:187; *S.C.*, bk. 2, chap. 8, *O.C.*, 3:386; *Poland*, chap. 1, *O.C.*, 3:954. Notwithstanding the reputation he acquired as a promoter of political revolutions, Rousseau insisted from first to last on his respect for the laws and his aversion for revolutions and conspiracies (*Observations on the Answer Made to his* [*First*] *Discourse*, *O.C.*, 3:55–56; *Dialogues*, third dialogue, *O.C.*, 1:935, "the Frenchman" is speaking).

Rousseau regards as the appropriate home for a man (unlike Glaucon) of undistinguished natural abilities. Accordingly, Emile's education focuses on those aspects of the *Social Contract*'s teaching that undermine political idealism by demonstrating how far short of legitimacy every actual polity must fall.[19]

If this political education is a kind of capstone in Rousseau's educational project, it is made possible only by an elaborately constructed underlying edifice. We can begin to see the nature of that edifice by considering Emile's introduction to literature.

## Defoe's *Robinson Crusoe*

Emile's first book, and the only book he will read before he approaches puberty, is Daniel Defoe's *Robinson Crusoe*. This novel is meant to channel the boy's emerging energy and curiosity toward seeking useful knowledge. It bears emphasis that the tutor is deliberately using the story to inflame Emile's imagination. Not only will Emile enjoy the story, as so many other boys have enjoyed it now for centuries, but he will subtly be encouraged to fantasize that he is the stranded and resourceful Robinson. He will want to learn from the protagonist's successes and failures, and seek to imitate his hero. "[D]o not doubt that he is planning to go and set up a similar establishment … [I]n any event, let us hurry to establish him on this island while he still limits his felicity to it; for the day is nearing when, if he still wants to live there, he will no longer want to do so alone, and when Friday, who now hardly touches him, will not for long be enough for him" (ibid., 455–56, Bloom, 185).

*Robinson Crusoe* is in the first place a device for ameliorating a most serious practical problem. Natural innocent selfishness—what Rousseau often calls *amour de soi*—cannot be kept within bounds, as it might have been in the pure state of nature, through actual physical isolation from other people. Rousseau had earlier recognized that his theory of "negative education" would seem to demand exactly this impracticable arrangement, and he refers back to that passage in his discussion of Defoe's novel

[19] Addressing the reader (not Emile) in Book II, Rousseau offers a very short summary of the *Social Contract* which clearly implies that it is virtually impossible to combine the advantages of the civil state with those of the state of nature (*O.C.*, 4:311, Bloom, 85). Later, in Book IV, he makes the same point, again to the reader rather than to Emile (ibid., 524–25 & n, Bloom, 236 & n).

(ibid., 455, 325, Bloom, 184–85, 94–95). But Emile will inevitably have contact with many people, and he will inevitably know a lot about the machinery and practices of modern civilization. By drawing Emile into Robinson's world, the tutor gives the boy a model with which he could actually identify, in a way that no one could ever identify with the solitary natural man of the *Discourse on Inequality*. In this imaginary world, a man who is familiar with many of the basic tools of civilized life is thrown back on his own resources, ingeniously provides himself with a commodious living, and finds himself busy, reasonably content, and without an intolerable craving for human companionship. Emile thus builds "the true 'castle in Spain' of this happy age, when one does not know any other happiness than necessity and liberty" (ibid., 455, Bloom, 185).

One striking feature of Defoe's story is that its hero gives no sign of yearning for female companionship. Since Robinson is an adult, that's a little odd, but it makes the book well suited for a boy whose interest in girls has not yet erupted.[20] Rousseau thinks that Emile will not be much concerned with Friday. That may not be entirely implausible since this new friend arrives fairly late in the story and in a way so alien to Emile's experiences that he might not take much more interest in Friday than he takes in Robinson's pet parrot. More important, perhaps, if the Friday relationship does intrigue Emile, the boy will be following what Rousseau sees as the proper order of friendship before love (ibid., 502–03, Bloom, 220–21).[21] That fictional friendship, moreover, arises on a natural foundation of rational pity and mutual assistance, so Emile's interest in it would not undermine the tutor's educational goals.[22]

There is, however, one very important theme in Defoe's novel that Rousseau completely ignores: Robinson's agonized religious reflections. What in the world will his young pupil make of this? At one point, Rousseau says that Emile will read the book "stripped of all its frivolous and useless stuff (*tout son fatras*), beginning with Robinson's shipwreck near his island and ending with the arrival of the ship which comes to take him from it" (ibid., 455, Bloom, 185). This sentence is a little ambiguous. Is the *fatras* all in the beginning and end of the book? Or does something

[20] Defoe subtly suggests in passing that Robinson had experienced the kind of empty sexual encounters common among sailors at that time. This may explain why he expresses no longing for what he is deprived of during his time on the island.

[21] The proper order for men living in society is not the natural order. After puberty, "from the need for a mistress is soon born the need for a friend" (*O.C.*, 4:494, Bloom, 215).

[22] For a detailed discussion of this foundation, see ibid., 502–17, Bloom, 220–30.

need to be stripped from the tale of Robinson's life on the island? Because the theme of religion is woven throughout the portion of the book dealing with this period of the hero's life, it is hard to suppose that the tutor will somehow excise this material. Rousseau suggests at one point that Emile will reach the age of eighteen without having heard of God (ibid., 549, Bloom, 254). I have trouble believing that this is meant to be literally true, and Rousseau later suggests that Emile will have heard of God without taking an interest in the matter (ibid., 557, Bloom, 259). Maybe Emile himself will effectively strip out the religious *fatras* by giving it little attention, just as he is expected to pay little attention to Friday. But it's a bit fantastic to suppose that Emile will have no questions at all, especially since this is his only book. Will the tutor respond to his questions in the same manner that he does to questions about sex, with bland answers designed not to invite further inquiry? Perhaps. Eventually, however, such treatments of these topics will not suffice. Rousseau believes that the need to deal with both matters in depth will come later, and at about the same time because Emile's interest in them has a common source.

## Rousseau and the Savoyard Vicar

The most famous part of the *Emile* is a long passage that purports to recount the religious views of a priest whom the author encountered as a young man. The passage is often read, out of context, as an expression of Rousseau's own beliefs, but the text makes clear that one should not treat it this way. Rousseau the author tells us that the young Rousseau agreed only to give the Vicar's arguments serious consideration, and the author never says that he later came to accept those arguments (ibid., 606, Bloom, 294). If anything, he suggests that he has not accepted all of them. He reports having told the priest that if he remains as convinced as the Vicar is he will be the Vicar's "proselyte until death" (ibid.). In introducing the story, however, the author of the *Emile* says, "I am not proposing to you the sentiment of another or my own as a rule; I am offering it to you for examination," and he reiterates the point immediately after presenting the Vicar's profession (ibid., 558, 635, Bloom, 260, 313). If this is proselytizing, it would seem to be in the ironic fashion of Socrates. That said, the arguments about the existence and characteristics of God, and about the relation between religion and morality, are so detailed and carefully articulated that we are compelled to conclude that Rousseau intended a serious reader of the *Emile* to take those arguments very seriously.[23] Without taxing my own readers with a detailed analysis, but also without suggesting that they should regard such analysis as optional, I will offer a few remarks meant to help illuminate the role of the Profession in Emile's education.

After an autobiographical sketch, the Vicar begins with the reasoning that led him to believe in a God omnipotent, good, and just,[24] and in an immaterial soul that could survive the destruction of the body. In light of the existence of this God and of this distinction between the body and the soul, he derives a view of the conscience as a sentiment or natural instinct that leads us to admire the morally beautiful. The Vicar acknowledges that his beliefs have not enabled him consistently to follow the dictates of his conscience, but he does maintain that he has been freed both from the torments of religious doubt and from the influence of human opinions that deny what he hears his reason and his conscience saying.

The young Rousseau, the author tells us, "saw a throng of objections" that he could make to this teaching (ibid., 606, Bloom, 294). Rather than articulate these objections, he asked the Vicar for his views on revelation, the scriptures, and religious dogma. The priest responded with a lengthy argument about the unreliability of religious authority and reports of revelations. This argument, which is manifestly valid, does not lead the priest to reject the truth of all religious revelation. He concludes instead that the natural religion described in his initial speech is sufficient for him, and that any other religion that is not radically inconsistent with natural religion should be treated respectfully. He has therefore exchanged his "initial pyrronhism," by which he means radical religious doubt, for what he calls "involuntary skepticism" about all religious tenets that are based on reports of divine revelation (ibid., 627–31, Bloom, 308–311). The Vicar concludes by advising the young Rousseau to return to Geneva and the Protestantism of his fathers, which he goes so far as to describe as the

[23] Elsewhere, Rousseau indicated that he took them very seriously himself, although he consistently indicated that he did not necessarily accept them all. See, for example, *Mountain*, lett. 1, *O.C.*, 3:694; *Reveries*, third walk, *O.C.*, 1:1018.

[24] The Vicar at first describes God merely as "powerful" (*puissante*) or as the "supreme power" (*la puissance suprême*) (*O.C.*, 4:580, 583, Bloom, 276, 278). Later, he refers to God as an omnipotent being ([*c*]*elui qui peut tout*), which perpetually produces and conserves, and is "supremely powerful" (*souverainement puissant*), but he infers that because God can do anything he can will only what is good (*bien*), and therefore must be just (ibid. 588–89, Bloom, 282).

revealed religion "that has the purest morality and is most satisfactory to reason" (ibid., 631, Bloom, 311).

When the *Emile* was published, it was widely known that Rousseau had converted to Catholicism after leaving home during adolescence, and regained his Genevan citizenship when he reconverted to Calvinism many years later. In the *Emile* itself, he introduces the Profession of Faith with a tale about his youthful encounter with the Vicar. This story begins in the third person and then abruptly switches to the first person on the pretense that the author is tired of implying that the story might be about someone else (ibid., 563, Bloom, 264). He claims that his urge to conceal the facts about his conversion arose from shame, but that it is more important to honor the unnamed priest who had helped him. Later, in the *Confessions*, he gives a different version of the story, according to which the Vicar is a kind of amalgam of two priests whom he had in fact encountered during this period of his life (bk. 3, *O.C.*, 1:91–92, 119).[25] So, a philosopher briefly pretends to have a moment of shame, which he then pretends to repent of in order to honor a nameless someone who we later learn did not exactly exist. Could anything serious underlie this elaborate joke?

Rousseau plainly wanted to draw a sharp distinction between the pure fiction of Emile and his tutor "Jean-Jacques" on the one hand, and the semi-fiction of the young Rousseau and the Savoyard Vicar on the other. This distinction reinforces the other textual indications that his own views are not identical with the Vicar's, while simultaneously indicating that he has been profoundly influenced by the views presented in the Profession of Faith. One reason for doing this might have been to dispel the suspicion that the Vicar is merely a literary device intended to prevent the political persecution of the author. As Rousseau obviously knew when he wrote the *Confessions*, and as he might have had some reason to expect when he published the *Emile*, the Profession of Faith did provoke the political authorities against him. In this context, it is worth noting that the Vicar shared his thoughts with no one except the young Rousseau (*O.C.*, 4:629–30, Bloom, 310). He also said, "If your sentiments were more stable, I would hesitate to display mine to you; but in your state you will gain from thinking as I do" (ibid., 607, Bloom, 295). Rousseau drops a footnote at this point: "This, I believe, is what the good vicar could say

[25] Later still, Rousseau said that he developed views "approximately" like those in the Vicar's profession many years *after* his youthful conversion to Catholicism (*Reveries*, third walk, *O.C.*, 1:1018).

to the public at present." I think this means that Rousseau saw Europe heading toward the atheism promoted by modern philosophy's materialism and its war against the established religions, a trend that could best be resisted through the promulgation of natural religion.

This inference is consistent with a long argument in another of the author's footnotes, near the end of the Profession. In that passage Rousseau qualifies, without retracting, his own strong opposition to fanaticism, by which he means intolerance, theological and civil. Fanaticism or intolerance is worse than atheism in its immediate effects, but atheism is more destructive in its ultimate consequences because it undermines what the Vicar calls "conscience." By promoting the kind of tranquility that leaves men indifferent to virtue and laudable actions, irreligious Enlightenment philosophy promises to unleash the narrow selfishness that religion can restrain. The overthrow of Christianity in Europe, hastened no doubt by the corruption of the clergy and their political allies, may reduce religious intolerance and persecution. But it will be replaced by a soft despotism of self-indulgence and secret egoism. This despotism will not cause men to be killed but will "prevent them from being born by destroying the *mœurs* that cause them to multiply" (ibid., 633n, Bloom, 312n). Subsequent history has not fulfilled Rousseau's hope that natural religion or theistic Christianity could help to cure this disease. His diagnosis, however, has not been proven wrong, and neither has the prognosis he offered. The ongoing depopulation of secular societies, which is now visible in Europe and elsewhere, should suffice to establish at least that much. And if Europe is eventually repopulated by fecund Muslim migrants, Rousseau will have proved extremely prescient.[26]

Should we then conclude that the Vicar's natural religion is meant only as a politically salutary teaching? I think not. The first part of the Profession effectively supports what I regard as two irrefutable propositions. First, neither the existence nor the nonexistence of God or gods can be established through natural reason alone. Similarly, the precise relationship between the soul and the body and the fate of the soul after death have not been adequately clarified on the basis of the evidence available to natural reason. The Vicar recognizes both propositions, and I have no reason to think that Rousseau himself disagrees.

The "throng of objections" that occurred to the young Rousseau in the story, which the author of the *Emile* could well have shared, prob-

[26] See, for example, *S.C.*, bk. 2, chap. 8, *O.C.*, 3:386.

ably include some reasons to question the Vicar's decision affirmatively to adopt "something close to the theism or the natural religion that the Christians feign to confound with atheism or irreligion, which is the directly opposite doctrine" (ibid., 606, Bloom, 294, purporting to quote the young Rousseau). The Vicar's version of natural religion culminates in his submission to an "inner sentiment" that urges three principal conclusions: the existence of a God through whom the world has been ordered for the good; the beauty of moral virtue; and an assurance of justice, if not in this life then after death, for those who follow this inner sentiment. Having satisfied himself that he can find no solid grounds for rejecting any of these conclusions, and observing that a craving to reach them arises spontaneously in himself and in most men, the Vicar accepts them without pretending to have the genuine or complete knowledge that would absolutely establish them. Rousseau himself might have had a stronger craving for genuine knowledge, or a greater tolerance for a kind of radical doubt that does not degenerate into careless pyrronhism. In any event, he leaves his readers to reflect on the Vicar's arguments and on the significance of his own decision neither to endorse nor to criticize them.

Rousseau sometimes indicated that he personally found radical religious doubt intolerable, and that he accepted some kind of theism because of the consoling effects it had on him. In his *Letter to Voltaire*, for example, he says that theists and atheists are both vulnerable to insoluble objections, and then goes on:

> I agree with all of this, and nevertheless I believe in God just as strongly as I believe any other truth, because to believe and not to believe are the things that least depend on me, because the state of doubt is a state too violent for my soul, because when my reason wavers, my faith cannot remain for long in suspense, and decides without it; finally because a thousand grounds for having a preference draw me toward the more consoling side and add the weight of hope to the equilibrium of reason. (*O.C.*, 4:1070–71)

The *Letter to Voltaire*, in many ways very similar to the Vicar's profession of faith, differs in at least four significant ways. First, it is primarily an argument of a philosopher to another philosopher, couched as a private communication, about the manner in which philosophers should speak to the public. The *Emile*, however, is an example of a philosopher speaking to the public rather than an argument about how to do it. Second, although the *Letter* calls the basis of the atheist's sentiments "even less precise" than those of the theist (ibid., 1070), it characterizes their conclusions as equally unconvincing. Third, in a passage that he deleted before sending the letter, Rousseau emphasizes how strongly he was affected by an argument about the astonishing effects that can result from a large number of chance occurrences. He calls his disbelief in such effects, "however unphilosophic it may be," a proof of sentiment and he does not object to having it called "prejudice" (ibid., 1071).[27] Fourth, the Vicar reports the details of reflections that apparently led him to embrace his theistic beliefs once and for all, whereas the *Letter* implicitly acknowledges that Rousseau repeatedly returns to a state of doubt. Accordingly, I suspect that Rousseau may have been as incapable of remaining in a state of belief about God as he says he was of remaining in a state of doubt.[28]

## Emile and Religion

Whatever Rousseau may ultimately think of the Vicar's beliefs and resolutions, the tutor expects that he will need to introduce Emile to natural religion, apparently by reasoning with him in a manner akin to the way the Vicar supposedly reasoned with the young Rousseau. This is immediately puzzling because the Vicar made a long speech without entertaining questions, which is quite at odds with the Socratic method that the tutor has insisted on using with Emile. In order to see the significance of the puzzle, it may be helpful to compare the trigger for the Vicar's religious quest with the trigger for his profession to the young Rousseau.

Born into a peasant family, the Vicar became a priest for the sake of worldly advancement, not from religious commitment. After taking his vows, he found celibacy intolerable and apparently had a child with an unmarried girl.[29] Punishment and exile followed, and the Vicar considered himself a victim of his respect for the marital rights of other men more

[27] The Vicar dismisses the possibility that chance could produce living things from inanimate matter (*O.C.*, 4:579, Bloom, 275–76). On the importance that Rousseau himself attached to the power of chance to produce effects that appear to be the result of a design, see Kelly, "Rousseau's Chemical Apprenticeship."

[28] For a later account of Rousseau's vacillations between doubt and belief, see *Reveries*, third walk, *O.C.*, 1:1015–23.

[29] The Vicar is vague about the details of the violation of his vows. The *Confessions* provides the story on which this part of the fictional Vicar's life is based (bk. 3, *O.C.*, 1:119).

than of his incontinence.[30] In any event, the combination of his disgrace, his lack of real religious conviction, and a reflective turn of mind eventually drove him into a gloomy and intolerable state of radical doubt.

The Vicar found the young Rousseau in the same incredulous condition, and from somewhat similar causes. Rousseau, however, was younger, sexually inexperienced, and traumatized by the environment in an almshouse for proselytes that he had entered to save himself from destitution. The trauma he experienced there apparently involved two principal elements: a conflict between Catholic dogmatism and the Calvinism in which he had been raised, and some repulsive homosexual advances to which the governors of the almshouse thought he had overreacted.[31] The corruption and hypocrisy of the Church, together with his own poverty and wounded pride, had made him so bitterly cynical that he was heading toward "the *mœurs* of a vagrant and the morality of an atheist" (*O.C.*, 4:561, Bloom, 263).

Rousseau emphasizes that Emile's introduction to natural religion should be postponed as long as possible, but it is obviously not going to wait until the pupil experiences miseries like those that afflicted the Vicar or the young Rousseau. On the contrary, it appears to be meant as an inoculation against what they suffered. Maybe this is plausible if we assume that Emile is led to natural religion at the right time and that he is fully persuaded by the arguments that support such beliefs. But are these assumptions credible?

Once again using Locke as a foil, Rousseau presents an elaborate rationale for refraining from teaching children religious precepts (ibid., 551–57, Bloom, 255–59).[32] The core of the argument is that children are incapable of conceiving non-material substances and that they therefore necessarily acquire false, anthropomorphic ideas of God, which few will ever be able

[30] It is easy enough to understand why incontinent priests would prefer to risk impregnating a married woman, for the mother would have less incentive than an unmarried girl to identify the child's natural father. Why the Vicar thought it better to risk ruining an unmarried girl is a lot less clear.

[31] The allusions to homosexuality in the *Emile* are rather subtle, but they are made explicit in the second book of the *Confessions* (*O.C.*, 4:558–59, Bloom, 260–61; *O.C.*, 1:60–70).

[32] This argument is later qualified when Rousseau discusses the education of girls, who should be indoctrinated with the essential moral tenets of natural religion (*O.C.*, 4:720–29, 751, Bloom, 377–81, 396–97). This is one of many indications that Rousseau's public teachings are much less concerned with the truth about religious beliefs than with their usefulness.

fully to shed. So far, so good. But what changes during adolescence?[33] Just after the conclusion of the Profession of Faith, Rousseau makes this startling announcement:

> [W]hatever human art can do, one's sensual disposition [*le tempérament*] always precedes reason. Until now we have given all our cares to checking the one and exciting the other, so that the man may always be one, so far as that may be possible. In developing [Emile's] natural disposition, we have diverted his nascent sensibility; we have regulated it by cultivating reason. Intellectual objects moderated the impression of sensible objects. In going back to the principle of things, we have removed him from the empire of the senses; it was simple to rise from the study of nature to the search for its author. (ibid., 636, Bloom, 314)

Two of the more obvious difficulties in this passage are these: What exactly would give Emile the motive to rise from his study of nature to a search for its author? And how exactly can we be sure that his search will lead him to natural religion?

Rousseau implicitly suggests at least a partial answer to the first question. Nature itself arouses in the adolescent boy an inchoate desire to seek a sexual partner. Even without the kind of care that Emile's tutor exercises, this desire can often be deflected toward friendship of a deeper kind than children are capable of. When teenage girls do not accede to whatever clumsy advances the average teenage boy is brave enough to attempt, and often when they do accede, we observe that boys frequently develop intense friendships with other boys. Even if these friends mostly talk about sports, cars, hunting, and indeed girls, they seem to be experiencing a kind of sublimation that takes them a significant step beyond the superficial social relationships of childhood.

This new openness to relatively intense social relationships is likely to be felt with extra force by Emile, whose previous contacts with his fellows have been kept especially superficial through the tutor's assiduous efforts to preserve his pupil's natural egocentrism. Now, at the moment when nature pushes the boy toward closer relationships than he has needed

[33] The crucial preparation for Emile's introduction to natural religion came earlier, when the tutor sought to inculcate rational pity by carefully introducing him into the world of moral relations. The results of that introduction are summarized in a passage that culminates with the claim that Emile knows nothing of philosophy or God at a time when his age mates are already philosophers and theologians (*O.C.*, 4:547–49, Bloom, 252–54).

before, where is he likely to seek it? Where else than in the one human being who has long been his closest companion and greatest benefactor? Rousseau tells us that the tutor will use this new leverage over Emile to the maximum extent possible.

> Far from being an obstacle to education, this fire of adolescence is the means of consummating and completing it; it gives you a hold over a young man's heart, when he ceases to be less [physically] strong than you. His first affections are the reins with which you direct all his movements; he was free, and now I see him enslaved ... Do you see what a new empire you are going to acquire over him? What chains you have put around his heart before he notices them! What will he not feel, when, opening his eyes about himself, he sees what you have done for him; when he can compare himself with other young people of his age and you with other tutors? (ibid., 520–21, Bloom, 233)

Rousseau goes into considerable detail about the best ways to employ these new reins and chains. But he leaves us to infer that the tutor will use them to set Emile on a quest beyond his very elementary and practical studies of nature toward a search for nature's author. How exactly will that be done? We are not told. Nor are we told why it will be "simple" to do so. My best guess is that Rousseau thinks the "fire of adolescence" will itself do much of the work and that this erotic fire was the ultimate source, if not the proximate cause, of both the Vicar's quest for God and the openness to natural religion that the Vicar saw in the young Rousseau.

Assuming that Emile will be pointed toward a search for the author of nature, is there a good reason to believe that the search will lead him to natural religion? Until now, the tutor has taken the greatest care to avoid providing Emile with incentives to believe anything that he cannot understand very clearly and distinctly. The arguments in the Profession of Faith are far more abstract, and indeed obscure, than anything with which Emile has yet been presented. We know, moreover, that the young Rousseau immediately saw "a throng of objections" to those arguments. Since Emile has only average intellectual gifts—unlike the young Rousseau or the Vicar—perhaps we can imagine that he will not so quickly see such objections. Perhaps he won't see them at all. But if that is so, why should we think that Emile will understand the arguments for natural religion well enough to accept them?

Sublimating sexual desire into friendship is one thing, but sublimating it into theological conviction looks like something very different. Emile's study of elementary astronomy and mechanics could easily be enough to incline him toward the belief that our world is governed by intelligible physical laws. His experience of the operation of his own will would certainly prevent him from supposing that the world operates exclusively through mechanical cause and effect. But the Vicar himself acknowledges that the conclusions he reaches about God and the afterlife are only consistent with reason, not established by reason. If Emile understands the arguments for these conclusions well enough to accept them, will he not also have to understand the arguments well enough to see their limitations?

It may be plausible enough for Rousseau to say that it is "simple" for Emile to rise from the study of nature to the search for its author, but it is not so simple to imagine how he will be able to follow that search to the conclusion the tutor wants. Emile's "fire of adolescence" may be fuel for the journey. It may even provide a kind of obscure motive for setting out on the search. But Emile has not been subjected to the suffering and perceived injustice experienced by the Vicar and the young Rousseau. It would therefore seem that the tutor will have to manage the quest with extraordinary dexterity in order to bring Emile to conclusions like those reached by the Vicar and also to leave him content with those conclusions. Rousseau acknowledges the contentment difficulty when he says: "If [Emile] must have another [religion than the kind of natural religion espoused by the Vicar], I no longer have the right to be his guide in that; it is for him alone to *choose* it" (ibid., 636, Bloom, 314, emphasis added). Left unstated is the possibility that Emile may effectively accept or choose natural religion itself out of deference to the tutor rather than out of genuine intellectual conviction.[34]

Even before he sets forth the Profession of Faith, Rousseau suggests why natural reason is radically inadequate for generating either natural religion or any other form of natural morality.

[34] Rousseau introduces the comment about Emile's choosing another religion by saying that "the light of reason alone cannot, in the instruction (*l'institution*) of nature, lead us farther than natural religion" (ibid., 635–36, Bloom, 313). Thus, if Emile chooses another religion—in the sense that he believes it, not in the sense that he professes it for reasons extraneous to his inner convictions—he will not in Rousseau's view have chosen by the light of reason alone. At the same time, this sentence subtly leaves open the possibility that "the light of reason alone" may not be able to bring Emile *even* as far as natural religion.

> If this were the place for it, I would try to show how the first voices of the conscience arise from the first movements of the heart; and how the first notions of good and bad are born from the sentiments of love and hate. I would show that *justice* and *goodness* are not merely abstract words, pure moral beings formed by the understanding; but are genuine affections of the soul enlightened by reason, and are only an ordered progression of our primitive affections; that by reason alone, independent of the conscience, one cannot establish any natural law; and that the whole right of Nature is only a chimera, if it is not founded on a natural need in the human heart. (ibid., 522–23, Bloom, 235, footnote omitted)

Rousseau refuses to defend these claims, on the ground that his business here is not to produce "Treatises on Metaphysics and morality, or courses of study of any kind" (ibid., 523, Bloom, 235). If the *Emile*—a book that includes innumerable little treatises and courses of study—is not the place for such an exposition, it is hard to imagine what would be. The *Discourse on Inequality* had already given an account of the development of moral notions that arise from affections of the soul *unenlightened* by reason. The *Emile*, which depicts the development of nature guided by wisdom, would seem to be *exactly* the place to do what Rousseau announces here that he will refuse to do.[35] It is hard to resist the conclusion that Rousseau believes that his reasons for making these claims cannot be presented to the public in a satisfactory way and that the attempt should therefore not be made.[36]

If Rousseau is cagy about the precise nature of the conscience, he is emphatic about the necessity of nurturing a belief in a lovable God and the promise of justice after death.

> Leave [this belief] behind, and I no longer see anything but injustice, hypocrisy, and lying among men; private interest, which in case of competition necessarily prevails over all things, teaches everyone to adorn vice with the mask of virtue. Let all other men do what is good for me at their expense, let

[35] This connection between the two books is suggested by Rousseau's comment that the *Emile* is a "novel [or romance] of human nature" that should have been the history of the species (ibid., 777, Bloom, 416).

[36] The block quotation above indicates that Rousseau could *try* to show how the conscience first develops, while he would *actually* show that natural law cannot be established by reason alone. The significance of this point is further suggested by the fact that the young Rousseau unsuccessfully tried to interrupt the Vicar when he said that the conscience is to the soul as instinct is to the body (ibid., 595, Bloom, 286–87). See also ibid., 446–47, Bloom, 179.

> everything be related to me alone, let the whole human race die, if need be, in suffering and poverty to spare me a moment of distress or hunger; such is the inner language of every unbeliever who reasons. Yes, I shall maintain it all my life; whoever has said in his heart, there is no God, and speaks otherwise, is nothing but a liar, or a madman. (ibid., 636–37, Bloom, 314–15)[37]

By insisting that it is only through religious belief that Emile finds his "genuine interest in being good," Rousseau goes beyond his previous political argument for the necessity of religion (ibid., 636, 632–35n, Bloom, 314, 312–14n). Emile, unlike the man in the state of nature, apparently requires religious belief in order to be happy as well as good. This requirement appears to be the inevitable consequence for him of the fact that he requires a kind of unnatural virtue in order to live among other men. Rousseau claims that the requirement is in accord with nature because of its contribution to Emile's private happiness.

## Religion and Happiness

Rousseau insists that a minimum of religious sentiment, consistent with what he calls natural religion, is an essential prerequisite for Emile's happiness as a man living according to nature in a modern society. Nonetheless, his religious beliefs will apparently play little direct part in achieving this goal. One occasion on which the tutor appeals to natural religion comes when he introduces Emile to the dangerous subject of sex and its relationship to love (ibid., 648–53, Bloom, 323–26). Rousseau gives few details about this introduction, but it seems that it will be conducted in much the same style that the Vicar used with the young Rousseau, rather than through the Socratic method that the tutor ordinarily employs. It concludes with Emile's promise to follow the tutor's guidance, which contrasts with the young Rousseau's response to the Vicar. The tutor then

[37] Rousseau's emphatic statement that he will always "maintain" what he says here may suggest that he has not fully disclosed his own inner thoughts. He seems to identify the "unbeliever" (*incrédule*) with one who affirmatively denies the existence of God "in his heart." This presumably does not cover certain kinds of agnosticism, including perhaps the thoughts of one whose mind, though not his heart, involuntarily denies the existence of God. Rousseau also lets us know that there may be other roads to virtue than the one pointed out by the Vicar. See, for example, the "profession of faith" of Alexander the Great (ibid., 348–50, Bloom, 110–11).

urges Emile to think it over some more before concluding that he can make the commitment.

After this point, we hear very little about natural religion. Its small direct role in Emile's continuing education inevitably makes us wonder whether religion is always indispensable for happiness.[38] Rousseau is consistently ambiguous about the exact connection between the two. He is, of course, quite clear about the importance of fostering religious beliefs that support the morality needed for life in political society. In the *Emile*, however, it is less clear why religion is needed for the happiness of a man raised according to nature. A similar obscurity can be found elsewhere in Rousseau's writings, as we can see in the following three examples.

### *Letter to Beaumont*

After the *Emile* was condemned by the Parlement of Paris, the Archbishop of that diocese, Christophe de Beaumont, issued a long pastoral letter that is mostly taken up with criticisms of the treatment of religion in the book. The letter accurately notes Rousseau's departures from Catholic doctrine, which might be thought sufficient to justify Beaumont's decision to forbid his flock to read the book. But the letter also contains rhetorically unrestrained personal attacks on Rousseau himself and concludes that his book is a seditious attack on the very foundations of Christianity and Christian morality.

Rousseau's response, which was published as an open letter to the Archbishop, offers detailed responses to Beaumont's criticisms of the *Emile*. He also expresses surprise at Beaumont's belated discovery of the danger in his writings. He specifically notes that the *Discourse on Inequality*, the *Letter to d'Alembert*, and *The New Heloise* had been circulating without objection for years, and he says that his own profession of faith is expressed there with less reserve than in the Savoyard Vicar's (*O.C.*, 4:933). Whatever Rousseau means by referring to his own profession of faith, the *Letter to d'Alembert* is considerably more reserved in its

[38] During the courtship of Emile and Sophie, they jointly pour out their feelings and express their devotion to virtue before the author of nature (ibid., 791–92, Bloom, 426). This may have more to do with Sophie's education than Emile's, for Rousseau maintains that every woman should have the religion of her husband (ibid., 721, Bloom, 377).

treatment of religion than the Savoyard Vicar's profession.[39] The *Discourse on Inequality*, however, does seem quite bold, for it sets religious doctrine aside as something irrelevant, and Rousseau elsewhere calls this a work in which he developed his principles "completely" (*tout à fait*).[40] This suggests that Rousseau may be speaking with a reserve that is tantamount to irony when he says, later in the *Letter to Beaumont*, that "I am Christian, and sincerely Christian, according to the doctrine of the Gospel" (ibid., 960).[41]

In this context, the reader might reasonably expect Rousseau to clear up the relationship between his "profession of faith" in the *Discourse on Inequality* and his claim to be sincerely Christian. He purports to so in a passage that is said to summarize the profession he made in the *Discourse.* Man, he says, is a naturally good being, "loving justice and order," whose only inborn passion is the love of self, a passion that becomes good or bad only through the circumstances in which it develops (ibid., 935–36).

This differs from what he actually said in the *Discourse* because it adds a reference to a natural love of justice and order, and omits any reference to the natural passion of pity or commiseration. The *Letter* then goes farther, saying that man is composed of two substances, which give rise to two forms of self-love. One form is bodily appetite, which serves the well-being of the body, and the other is the love of order, which serves the well-being of the soul. The love of order, developed and agitated along with human enlightenment (*les lumieres de l'homme*), is the conscience, which responds to "moral beauty" (ibid., 936–37).

This account is substantially different from the genealogy of moral sentiments presented in the *Discourse*, and I think it is much less plausible. It is not very difficult to suppose that an inborn passion of pity or commiseration, apparently common to many animals, could be activated by

[39] In the course of defending the *Emile* in Geneva, Rousseau said that the Editor's notes in *The New Heloise* were daring in a way that the Vicar did not approach (*Mountain*, lett. 4, *O.C.*, 3:766n). I have trouble seeing this, though perhaps one could make a case for it based on some of the Editor's comments in the fifth letter of Part V (*O.C.*, 2:589n, 596n**). For a detailed treatment of religion in *The New Heloise*, see Lund, "A Woman's Laws and a Man's."

[40] *Confessions*, bk. 8, *O.C.*, 1:388. See also ibid., bk. 9, 407 (characterizing the *Discourse* as "daring" and even "audacious").

[41] In the *Letters Written from the Mountain*, he defends his claim to be a Christian at great length. The sum and substance of this defense is that he accepts the moral teachings of Jesus in the Gospels, as he understands those teachings.

the imagination and cultivated so as to support the kind of regard for others on which social life depends. Adam Smith does exactly that in *The Theory of Moral Sentiments*, which he wrote after reading the *Discourse on Inequality*. It is much more difficult to see why one would suppose that human beings generally have a natural love of order that responds to moral beauty. In fact, the account of the conscience given here in the *Letter to Beaumont* looks very much like the modern natural law doctrines that Rousseau ridiculed in the *Discourse on Inequality* (*O.C.*, 3:125). Unless Rousseau is speaking ironically in the *Letter to Beaumont*, he must have forgotten what he had published a few years earlier in the *Discourse*.

## *Moral Letters*

Sometime before he wrote the *Emile*, Rousseau composed a series of six letters to the only woman with whom he ever fell in love, Sophie d'Houdetot. She was high born, eighteen years his junior, married with children, and the mistress of one of his friends. Devoted to her own lover, she did not reciprocate Rousseau's passion, but she did respond with a provocatively intense friendship during a time when both her husband and her lover were away on military duty. Rousseau respected her rejection of his amorous advances, and even praised it, but he struggled painfully with the asymmetric nature of their feelings. The so-called *Moral Letters*, written to Sophie toward the end of their involvement with each other, were not put into final form and were never sent.[42]

The draft letters appear on their face to be a response to a request from Sophie for moral guidance, but they are not merely personal correspondence. In the first letter, Rousseau encourages Sophie to consider making them public, and portions of some letters would later appear almost unchanged in the Profession of Faith of the Savoyard Vicar. Because Rousseau retained the drafts, he must have expected that they would eventually be published.

An adequate analysis of the *Moral Letters* would have to give full consideration to the nature of the addressee, to the author's relationship with her, to the circumstances in which they were written, and to the fact that they point only to the first steps in the moral education that Rousseau is

[42] This episode in Rousseau's life was more dramatic and complicated than this brief summary might suggest. For a detailed account, see Cranston, *Noble Savage*, 55–131.

recommending. Even without such an analysis, however, we can find in the letters some illuminating contrasts with the *Letter to Beaumont* and the Vicar's profession in the *Emile*.

Unlike those discussions, the *Moral Letters* say nothing at all in favor of religion and next to nothing about God. Instead, Rousseau offers an exceptionally vigorous critique of the human intellect. He draws a fundamental distinction between reason and the art of reasoning. Reason is the tool that secures the object of human life, namely the felicity of man; it is in other words "the faculty of ordering all the faculties of our soul suitably to the nature of things and to their relations with us" (lett. 2, *O.C.*, 4:1087, 1090). The art of reasoning compares known truths in order to discover new truths, but this art cannot teach us the primitive truths on which others depend. It therefore often becomes an abuse of reason because we substitute opinions, passions, and prejudices for these primitive truths, and are led astray in countless ways.

In elaborating this distinction, Rousseau insists that we can never obtain genuinely certain knowledge of the world in which we live because our only access to this world is through our senses. We know that our senses often deceive us, and we do not know whether we would need other senses to perceive aspects of the world that remain hidden from us.[43] Rousseau agrees with Descartes that the sure starting point is "I think, therefore I exist," but questions the two-substance thesis that he would later profess to Archbishop Beaumont (lett. 3, *O.C.*, 4:1095–96; *Letter to Beaumont*, *O.C.*, 4:936). A century and a half before Einstein and Heisenberg, he predicts that Newton's system will not last (lett. 3, *O.C.*, 4:1096). In the most striking statement of all, Rousseau says: "[W]e do not even know what largeness and smallness are … All of Geometry is founded only on sight and touch and these two senses perhaps need to be rectified by others that we lack; what is most completely demonstrated there for us is thus still suspect and we cannot know whether the *Elements* of Euclid are not a tissue of errors" (ibid., 1094–95). A very remarkable claim made prior to the invention of non-Euclidian geometries, and before physicists began to tell us that the Euclidian-Newtonian world we experience is an even more radical illusion than the one that underlies Ptolemy's *Almagest*. Descartes'

[43] This discussion includes an allusion to Plato's provocative treatment of knowledge as recollection, and Rousseau's marginalia include a reference to the myths about transmigration of souls in the dialogues (lett. 3, *O.C.*, 4:1097; 1794, editor's note d).

*cogito*, as Rousseau understands it, is not only the beginning of knowledge, "it is all we know" (ibid., 1099).[44]

Rather than proceed from radical Cartesian doubt to a search for God, as the Vicar does, Rousseau instead appeals to "that secret inquietude that torments us at the sight of our misery and that becomes indignant about our weaknesses as about an insult to the faculties that elevate us" (lett. 4, *O.C.*, 4:1101). One might suspect that this self-interested inquietude is the source both of the grandiose philosophic systems that Rousseau has just derided and of our desire for a God whose justice will relieve our indignation, if not in this life then after death. Rather than pursue this rather obvious possibility, Rousseau immediately appeals to a different experience, in which some of us are inflamed by the moral beauty and the intellectual order of things in a way that carries us "into the empyrean next to God himself" (ibid.). The reference to the intellectual order of things is a little hard to reconcile with the preceding critique of human reasoning and intellectual ambition. Rousseau implicitly recognizes the problem: "*However that might be*, we at least feel in ourselves a voice that forbids us to despise ourselves; reason crawls but the soul is elevated; if we are small through our enlightenment (*nos lumières*), we are great through our sentiments, and whatever rank ours may be in the system of the universe, a being that is a friend of justice and sensitive to virtues is not abject by its nature" (ibid., emphasis added).

Rousseau seeks to shore up this self-interested moral ambition in two ways. First, he briefly describes his own extraordinary life, and claims that Sophie has led him to happiness by helping him conquer his sexual passion for her. This story could hardly provide Sophie with the moral guidance *she* sought, and Rousseau goes on to derive the conscience from the natural passion of pity, just as we might expect from the author of the *Discourse on Inequality* (lett. 5, *O.C.*, 4:1106–08). Oddly, however, he cites as evidence the passions we experience in the theater, which he treats as cheap substitutes for virtue in the *Letter to d'Alembert*.

[44] This claim about our access to the truth is not inconsistent with Rousseau's many acknowledgments that research in the arts and sciences leads to progressively increased enlightenment. It is, on the contrary, perfectly consistent with the modern understanding of natural science as the process of formulating, testing, and modifying hypotheses. For an extended discussion of the distinction between genuine knowledge and progressive enlightenment, written (more cheerfully) by a sophisticated modern physicist, see Marcelo Gleiser, *The Island of Knowledge: The Limits of Science and the Search for Meaning*.

The reason for appealing to what we feel in the theater becomes evident in the last of the *Moral Letters*. Sophie is a member of the highest social class in France, and people in her very privileged circumstances are especially prone to the empty boredom that so often accompanies a way of life that is easy and frivolous. Rousseau recommends that she begin spending some of her time alone in the country, in order to focus sustained attention on the condition of her own soul. Rather than use this time for philosophic reflections of the kind that occupied the Savoyard Vicar, Sophie is encouraged to begin devoting her energies to mingling with the common people and trying to relieve distressed individuals.

We know from other sources that Sophie d'Houdetot displayed a natural goodness resembling that of Julie d'Etange in *The New Heloise*.[45] Given her wealth and privileges of rank, along with this sweet disposition, she probably had little cause to experience the kind of remorseful conscience that so often afflicts us when we selfishly harm other people. But life in her social circles would also have provided few occasions to display the kind of generosity that enables one to think especially well of oneself. It is this form of self-love that Rousseau urges Sophie to cultivate, and the *Moral Letters* at least suggest that this kind of good conscience can probably be acquired without religion or a belief in God, and without a love of intellectual order.

### *Letter to Franquières*

Seven years after the *Emile* was published, Rousseau replied to a young man who had sent him two letters about his religious and metaphysical doubts. Rousseau asked that his reply be returned without comment, and he apparently intended to publish it in some form.

The rhetoric of this letter is suffused with the spirit of Plato. It opens by saying that the young man has imposed on him a duty, but strongly warns him never to yield to the reasoning of another person. He then goes on to claim that he can only report the results of his own thinking because he has forgotten how he arrived at the opinions he holds.

Much of the letter resembles what Rousseau wrote elsewhere. He attacks the atheistic materialism of the Enlightenment; stresses the limits of human reason; maintains that a belief in God (described at one point as an "active principle" that exists eternally along with inactive matter) is

[45] See Cranston, *Noble Savage*, 55.

exposed to fewer intellectual objections than he can bring against atheism; appeals to the interior voice of nature, or conscience, as a healthy alternative to the excesses of reasoning; and asserts that "[t]o uproot all belief in God from the heart of men is to destroy all virtue there" (*O.C.*, 4:1142).

Rousseau denies that the unenlightened and truly natural man has or needs a belief in God: governed only by his appetites, he follows natural instinct, and his impulses are always right (*droits*) (ibid., 1137). At the other extreme, a true philosopher eventually senses the limits of his understanding and "finds in these limits the notion of his soul and that of the author of his being" (ibid.). Nineteen-twentieths of mankind fall between these extremes. They see God in the world, and though they dress him up in diverse ways, false philosophers can only temporarily persuade them of atheism (ibid., 1138).

Near the end of the letter, Rousseau reminds us of his opening statement about the duty that the young man has imposed on him. After a discussion of death and evil (*le mal*) that seems to allude at one point to Plato's *Phaedo*,[46] he refers to the speech on justice by Glaucon (whose name he purports to have forgotten) at the beginning of the second book of the *Republic*. Rousseau's summary stresses the horrifying picture that Glaucon draws of the just man whom fortune and the injustice of others have made "prey to all the opprobrium for crime while meriting all the rewards of virtue" (ibid., 1144). Rousseau then says that Socrates cried out in alarm, and felt obliged to invoke the gods before responding. He concludes that Socrates would have answered badly for this life without the hope of life after death. In an odd twist, he seems to qualify this last assertion by suggesting that it may be sufficiently consoling to believe that God sees that one has suffered undeserved adversity. Rousseau thus leaves us to wonder whether it might not be sufficiently consoling to believe that our undeserved sufferings, or the virtues we display despite such adversity, will be recognized by other human beings whose respect we crave. One could even wonder whether maintaining one's own self-respect might be sufficiently consoling, at least for some individuals.

As Rousseau must have known, Socrates was not alarmed by Glaucon's speech. On the contrary, he says that he was particularly delighted with Glaucon and Adeimantus (367d6–368a1). Apparently, this was because they were driven to press the argument against justice even though it was

[46] See *O.C.*, 4:1141 ("At the very moment I am writing this I have again experienced how the cessation of an acute pain is an intense and delicious pleasure."); *Phaedo* 60a9–c7.

against their own opinions and contrary to their characters. Nor does Socrates invoke the gods or say anything about life after death. Instead, he says that he is incapable of satisfying the young men's demand for proof that justice leading to misery is preferable to an injustice that reaps the rewards due to justice. He does say that it might not be blameless [or pious: *hosion*] for him not to attempt a defense of justice, but he neither implies that his obligation depends on the gods nor suggests that he can succeed in such a defense (368b4–c2). At this point, he begins to articulate what he calls his "opinion" that they should look for justice starting with that of a city rather than of a man (368c7–d7). Not until Book X does Socrates offer what he calls a myth about life after death.

The duty that Franquières imposed on Rousseau appears to parallel the one that Glaucon and Adeimantus imposed on Socrates. By pointing implicitly to the very long conversation about justice in the city and in the soul that precedes the myth of Er, Rousseau seems to be calling attention to the difficult relationship between justice and what he calls in the *Moral Letters* "the faculty of ordering all the faculties of our soul suitably to the nature of things and to their relations with us" (lett. 2, *O.C.*, 4:1090). That relationship is the dominant theme of the *Republic*, and the appreciation of its difficulty displayed by Glaucon and Adeimantus could be the source of the delight that Socrates took in their challenge to him.

In the immediate sequel, Rousseau gives further evidence of the irony in his altered description of Socrates' response to Glaucon by taking issue with Franquières' preference for Socrates over Jesus.[47] Rejecting the divinity of Jesus, Rousseau treats him solely as a moral reformer who initiated a revolution through the influence that his life and death had on his disciples. Similarly, he claims that Socrates would have been treated only as another Greek sophist were it not for the manner of his death and the descriptions

[47] Adeimantus offers the less radical challenge, so it is not surprising that Rousseau focuses in this letter on Glaucon's or that Socrates seems especially concerned in the *Republic* with the education of Glaucon. Unlike Plato and Adeimantus, Glaucon does not seem to have stood in support of Socrates at his trial. See Plato, *Apology of Socrates* 33e7–34a1. While the presence of Plato in this role indicates that philosophy can become a way of life for some people who are able and willing to entertain the most radical thoughts, Glaucon's absence may indicate the extreme difficulty of inducing a genuine turn to philosophy. This may also help to explain why Rousseau challenges Franquières to reconsider his opinion that Socrates is preferable to Jesus.

of his life found in Plato and Xenophon.[48] By pushing his young correspondent to reconsider his admiration for the paragon of philosophy whom Plato and Xenophon have made so attractive to so many, Rousseau implicitly relies on the distinction in the *Moral Letters* between reason and the art of reasoning, and more openly recalls the treatment of Socrates and Jesus by the Savoyard Vicar (*Emile*, *O.C.*, 4:624–25, Bloom, 307–8). He is no doubt quite serious in urging his correspondent, and us, not to assume that the pursuit of philosophy is an easy substitute for religious belief. He may be equally serious in leaving Franquières, and us, free to compare the "opinion" offered in this letter with the opinions and reasonings that Socrates offers in the *Republic*. That would seem to require us to refrain from assuming that philosophy can never be an alternative to religious belief.[49]

## Love, Politics, and Fénelon's *Telemachus*

The remainder of the *Emile* is devoted largely to directing Emile's natural eros—the sexual urge that lacks a naturally fixed or determined target (*O.C.*, 4:493–94, 502, Bloom, 214, 220)—into human relationships that will be the source of his happiness. That happiness will not depend on the truth of his religious beliefs, for the tutor will not seek to prevent him from choosing among a range of different revealed religions. If Emile remains content with natural religion, and perhaps even if he chooses to

[48] In their writings about Socrates, Plato and Xenophon place different aspects of his life in the foreground, apparently in order to combat different sources of resistance or opposition to philosophy and philosophers. Both of them, however, give special attention to the conduct of Socrates in connection with his trial and death, which supports Rousseau's suggestion that this part of his life was crucial in preventing him from being regarded as just another Greek sophist.

[49] As Rousseau put it at the outset of his reply to Franquières:

> My design in telling you my opinion here on the principal points of your letter is to tell it to you with simplicity, and without seeking to make you adopt it. That would be against my principles and even against my taste. For I am just, and as I do not like for someone to seek to subjugate me, neither do I seek to subjugate anyone … [W]hoever yields to the reasoning of another, something already very rare, yields through prejudice, through authority, through affection, through laziness; rarely, perhaps never, through his own judgment. (*O.C.*, 4:1133–34)

Accordingly, Rousseau frequently forces readers who are most intent on finding the truth to confront distortions that he has deliberately introduced into his portrayals of figures like Socrates and Jesus.

accept a revealed religion, that will reflect the tutor's success in directing the intensity of his sexual eros into human relationships that are fulfilling enough to spare him the kind of crises experienced by the Savoyard Vicar and the young Rousseau.

Emile's happiness is to be found in life with his family, and a full third of the book is devoted to describing and analyzing the tutor's efforts to prepare Emile for marriage. The process, which reflects Rousseau's conviction that "a great deal of art must be employed to prevent social man from being totally artificial" (ibid., 640, Bloom, 317), goes in stages. Owing to Emile's physical growth and the onset of the inner violence of adolescence, the boy can no longer be controlled by force and deception. Accordingly, the tutor first cultivates a simulacrum of adult friendship, which wraps Emile in new chains that still respect the principle of avoiding a conflict of wills. Revealing to Emile all that he has done for him, the tutor provokes enough gratitude to induce a promise of obedience that is motivated by the hope of still greater benefits to come (ibid., 651–53, Bloom, 325–27). The immediate context involves refraining from sexual activity before marriage, but the promise will assume even more importance later in the story.

The tutor seeks to distract Emile from his inner adolescent turmoil through activities such as sport hunting (ibid., 644–45, Bloom, 320–21),[50] but he also engages the boy in open discussions about sex and love. In the course of these talks, Emile conceives a vision of the kind of woman worthy of his heart. As we know, and as Emile may suspect, the tutor has already found a girl who fits this vision. But rather than introduce the intended couple to each other, the tutor takes Emile to Paris in search of his bride. During this time, Emile learns much of what Locke seemed to regard as the completion of a gentleman's education, namely how to get on in the world without becoming intoxicated with its glitter and destructive temptations. Needless to say, no woman in Paris satisfies Emile's criteria.

At length, the pair returns to the country, where a seemingly chance event brings them to the home of Sophie, the young woman chosen by the tutor for Emile. After a charming courtship, which Rousseau describes in

[50] The tutor is ambivalent about this device, which is apt to arouse a hard and sanguinary spirit at odds with the ultimate goals of Emile's education. Much earlier, Rousseau had inserted a digression on the moral advantages of vegetarianism, which we are no doubt meant to recall (*O.C.*, 4:411–14, Bloom, 153–55). But strong medicine is needed to counteract strong convulsions. Hunting is a pastime with which young men can easily become quite obsessed without endangering their health, inflaming their sexual imaginations, or becoming ensnared in corrupting relations with other people.

elaborate detail, the couple want to wed. The tutor, however, now invokes the authority Emile had given him, perhaps not for the first time but certainly in the face of the most determined resistance, and takes Emile away for two years of world travel. Finally they return, and Emile is married to Sophie. In an ironic echo of Locke's remark that "'tis time to leave him to his mistress," which Rousseau had recalled in the first paragraph of Book V, the tutor pronounces that his work is completed, and assigns Sophie to take his place as Emile's tutor.

Sophie has a nature and education that suits her to be Emile's wife. Like Emile, she is without extraordinary natural endowments, but there the similarity stops. She is raised in her family home by parents who are caring, sensible, and conventionally respectable in their educational aims. If *The New Heloise* is meant to explore the depths of female human nature, as I believe it is, Sophie has a pretty deep resemblance to the sober English gentleman whom Locke sought to raise.[51] In his long discussion of Sophie's education, Rousseau insists that a woman must cultivate many dispositions from which Emile has been scrupulously preserved: submissiveness to convention, a strong regard for her reputation, a desire to please, and perhaps above all a readiness to submit her will to that of another.

Sophie would seem to fit comfortably in the Geneva that Rousseau depicted in the *Letter to d'Alembert*. She wants to be a wife and mother, and her greatest challenge is to find an appropriate husband. She hardly seems to need a man who has undergone Emile's unique education, and it is easy to imagine that she could find a suitable mate without great difficulty in that city. She might even have been able to find one in the rural area of France where she grew up, but for a momentous accident that befell her. Having chanced to read Fénelon's *Adventures of Telemachus*, she has contracted a romantic vision of what she will insist on in a husband.[52] We cannot help suspecting that this accident was another of the tutor's sly manipulations. In any event, *Telemachus* prepares Sophie to recognize Emile as someone exceptional and exceptionally desirable. No less important, the tutor uses the novel to help bind Emile and Sophie together.

[51] See Lund, "A Woman's Laws and a Man's"; *Emile*, *O.C.*, 4:758–63, Bloom, 402–06 (contrasting Sophie with a girl naturally subject to more profound passions).

[52] In order to stress the importance (and limitations) of *Telemachus*, Rousseau tells us that it is the only book Sophie has read except for books on the principles of accounting. This is not meant to be the end of her literary education, but it is Emile himself who will lead her farther. See *O.C.*, 4:769–70, Bloom, 410.

Fénelon offers an elaborate new version of Homer's Telemachy. When Telemachus leaves Ithaca in search of Ulysses, he is accompanied by Minerva in the guise of Mentor. During this search, Telemachus undergoes a series of mishaps and adventures, many of which recapitulate the trials of Ulysses himself. Fénelon was a knowledgeable classicist, and the novel attempts to capture something of Homer's style and the atmosphere of the *Odyssey*. *Telemachus*, however, is overtly didactic, and it fits in the "mirror of princes" genre. Fénelon's Telemachus has strong natural endowments and a fundamentally sound nature, but Penelope has raised him to be somewhat haughty and egocentric. He has little experience of the world, and he lacks the skills, knowledge, and inner dispositions that will fit him to assume the throne that he is destined to inherit from his father.

If Fénelon's style imitates Homer, his spirit is much closer to Rousseau's. So much so that if one read *Telemachus* without knowing that it appeared in 1699, one might suspect that it was among the many later novels in which Rousseau's influence is so easily visible. In Fénelon we find many characteristically Rousseauan themes: the denunciation of luxury, the glorification of pastoral life, revulsion at the rampant corruption among civilized men, the obligation of political rulers to serve the good of the people and the extreme difficulty of inducing or even enabling them to do so. By the end of the novel, Telemachus has rejected an opportunity to become the crown prince through marriage in a prosperous kingdom that he and Mentor had saved from disaster. Although he wants to marry the princess, he concludes that he can be worthy of her only if he fulfills his duties to his father and his own country. He leaves to continue his journey back to Ithaca, hoping that he will have many years in which to learn from Ulysses before he succeeds him. Not the least of his qualifications for the crown is the fact that he will take it from duty rather than ambition.

In the *Emile*, Sophie reads Fénelon's novel and becomes the "rival of Eucharis," who is one of Calypso's nymphs (*O.C.*, 4:762, Bloom, 404). Calypso is crazy for Telemachus, as she had been for his father, but Eucharis and Telemachus become infatuated with each other. A great battle of wills and stratagems ensues among Minerva/Mentor, Calypso, and Cupid (who is intent on making everyone as miserable as possible). With great difficulty, Mentor at length manages to persuade Telemachus to leave the island. Calypso, however, is not truly the rival of Eucharis with whom Sophie could identify. As she explains to her exasperated parents, she does not want a prince, and certainly does not confuse Fénelon's fictions with reality. But she sees in Telemachus the kind of man whom she has been raised to admire, and she has decided to settle for nothing less.

Only toward the end of *Telemachus* do we meet the novel's own true rival of Eucharis. She is a mortal named Antiope, the daughter of the king whose reign was preserved through the valor and wise counsel of Telemachus and Mentor. This young woman, whom Rousseau never mentions, is an image of Sophie herself: attractive but not seductive, and a paragon of the feminine virtues of modesty, grace, and humanity. In Fénelon, Telemachus conceives a rational love for Antiope, which does not partake of the madness he had seen in Calpyso and experienced himself with regard to Eucharis (whom he has never been able to forget). The education of Telemachus has now made him a worthy object of the love of someone like Antiope, and his esteem and affection are reciprocated. The novel ends happily, with the expectation that Ulysses will consent to their marriage as Antiope's father already has.

What must affect Sophie so powerfully, I believe, is seeing someone so much like herself in the novel. Since she knows that she herself exists, why should it be impossible for someone like Telemachus also to exist? The odds may not favor her hope of meeting him, but neither will she believe that such "a pleasing and virtuous man is only a chimera" (ibid., 762, Bloom, 405). Thanks to Emile's wily tutor, Sophie does not have long to wait before he appears at her door through a seemingly chance event.

Fénelon does not have the depth or subtlety of Rousseau, let alone of Homer, but his novel does have the great merit of being accessible to readers like Sophie and Emile. For Sophie, it fulfills what we could call a didactic purpose by confirming her sense of her own worthiness and giving her a model of the man who is worthy of her. But that is only the beginning of the tutor's use of the novel.

The stories about Eucharis and Antiope are significant but distinctly secondary subplots in *Telemachus*.[53] Most of the novel deals with Mentor's efforts to prepare the son of Ulysses to rule in Ithaca. That education has three principal elements. First, Telemachus is subjected to years of suffering and misfortune, which Mentor uses to inculcate such moral virtues as steadfastness and respect for the gods. Second, his travels expose him to the sight of a great deal of cruelty and folly, especially the kind produced

[53] This is not to say that the subplots are unimportant or that including them is out of place. One finds similar subplots in the first and greatest mirror of princes, Xenophon's *Cyropaedia*.

by political ambition. Mentor seldom misses an opportunity to impress on his pupil the emptiness and fragility of worldly glory and power, the attractions of the true freedom that has no need of political preeminence, and the unavoidable troubles to which one exposes oneself when playing a part in the political world. Third, Mentor involves Telemachus in a refounding of the city of Antiope's father, which provides a detailed object lesson in the kind of political reform that might be possible if a serious man were to undertake a political career.

Shortly before Emile leaves on his premarital trip to see the world, Sophie begins to identify with Eucharis herself, and fears that Emile will never return to her (ibid., 825, Bloom, 450). In an effort to help the disconsolate girl, the tutor proposes that she and Emile make an exchange of books. Emile will take *Telemachus* with him on his journey, and Sophie will keep Emile's copy of *The Spectator*.

This exchange serves two purposes with respect to Sophie. First, she can hope that Emile will be reminded more than once that she is his Antiope and a prize far more worthy than any seductive Eucharis he may encounter while away. Second, Addison and Steele will reinforce her own solid bourgeois moral training, and serve as a frequent reminder that a Eucharis is the last thing she should aspire to become.[54]

*Telemachus* may serve an even more important purpose in Emile's education. As we have seen, one purpose of the two-year sojourn is to inoculate *Emile* against political ambition. That will be accomplished partly by introducing him to the logic of the *Social Contract*, and partly by letting him see with his own eyes how far the world departs from the principles of political right. *Telemachus* will contribute to this education by giving Emile various models of bad political actors, contemporary versions of which will easily be found during his travels, as well as models of good kings and ministers, which Emile will not encounter (see ibid., 4:849, Bloom, 467). Emile comes to Fénelon without a predisposition to seek glory or political office, so there is little danger that he will imagine that he deserves or should want a throne. And because he was given the book by Sophie, who is no princess, he will have every inclination to focus on all

[54] *The Spectator* itself can be seen as an effort to reinforce the kind of education that Locke recommends in *Some Thoughts*. The facts that Emile himself has a copy of *The Spectator* and that the tutor considers it an appropriate token of his betrothal to Sophie are another of Rousseau's subtle indications that Emile will look a lot like the sober English gentlemen on whom Locke pinned his hopes for social and political reform.

the reasons that Telemachus found for regretting his obligation to assume the political office he expected to inherit.

There is another lesson that *Telemachus* will reinforce. At the end of his travels with the tutor, Emile is convinced that he should live with Sophie as a kind of cosmopolitan, without depending on his father's wealth, without allegiance to any government, and without any compelling need to live in one place or another. The tutor is not displeased with this "extravagant detachment," but notes that it will decrease when Emile has children of his own (ibid., 857, Bloom, 473). It is therefore important for him to understand that one "who does not have a fatherland [like Sparta or Rome] at least has a country." Silly as it would be to think that the spirit of the ancient political world could now be recovered, or to try living as if it did now exist, the natural cosmopolitanism of man in the state of nature is neither possible nor desirable. First, even acknowledging that the true social contract is nowhere truly observed, the "simulacra of laws" have protected him against the horrors of anarchy and private violence (ibid., 859, Bloom, 473). Second, and more important, the established institutions of our times have themselves given us duties and made virtue possible, in part by disclosing their own iniquities (ibid.). For both these reasons, Emile should accept his political duties, just as Fénelon's Telemachus did:

> So do not ask: What difference does it matter to me where I am? It matters to you that you are where you can fulfill all your duties, and one of those duties is an attachment to the place of your birth. Your compatriots protected you as a child, you ought to love them as a man. You ought to live among them, or at least in a place where you can be useful to them to the extent you can be, and where they know where to get you if ever they have need of you … [R]emember that the Romans went from the plow to the Consulate. If the Prince or the State calls you to the service of the fatherland, leave everything to go fulfill the honorable function of Citizen in the post assigned to you. If this function is onerous to you, there is an honest (*honnête*) and sure means to free yourself from it; fulfill it with enough integrity so that it will not be left to you for long. Besides, have little fear of being put on the spot by such a responsibility: as long as there are men of this century, it is not you who will be sought out to serve the State. (ibid., 858–60, Bloom, 473–75)

A happy thought. Emile can live up to the fictional model with whom Sophie fell in love, with little chance that he will actually have to perform the kind of onerous duties that Telemachus accepts as his obligation.

## EROS, ADVERSITY, AND PLATO'S *SYMPOSIUM*

If Emile can reasonably expect to avoid the adversities of political life, other threats to his happiness remain. It is true that he has been habituated from birth to accept necessity, and brought to see emptiness in the ambitions fomented by the opinions of the world. But his ability to continue living in accord with nature has not been seriously tested. Has this training been sufficient? The tutor thinks not, as we can see in the longest speech that he makes to his pupil in the *Emile*.[55] That speech occurs before Emile's travels, and it shows that his political education is not the most important reason for the trip.

Some four months after Emile and Sophie first met, they are very much in love. They have each seen enough of the other's character to be convinced that they should wed, and they are desperate to marry. The tutor, however, decides that Emile must now leave her behind. The speech in which he explains this decision to Emile is framed by two clever devices.

The tutor enters Emile's room with a letter in hand, and asks, "What would you do if you were informed that Sophie is dead?" (ibid., 814, Bloom, 442). Understandably, and irrationally, Emile responds that he would never tolerate the man who brought him the news. After he learns that Sophie is still alive, it is easy enough for him to see that his initial reaction was unjust and unreasonable. That recognition is meant to prepare Emile for even harsher news: he must leave Sophie, which Emile takes to mean a permanent abandonment. Understandably, and not at all irrationally, Emile heatedly interrupts to reject this proposal on the ground that it would violate promises he has implicitly made to her. At the very end of the tutor's ensuing speech, he finally tells Emile that the separation is not to be permanent. But rather than secure Emile's consent to the separation, for which he has given elaborate reasons, the tutor rescues his pupil from the risk that he will look like a cad. Invoking the boy's older and express promise to obey the tutor's direct commands, he says, "Emile, you must leave Sophie: I wish it." (ibid., 824, Bloom, 449). After a brief pause, Emile asks when they will depart.

The tutor gives Emile a variety of reasons for postponing his marriage, including the need to learn how to take his place in a world where he will have legal and political responsibilities. But this is only part of a much greater transformation at which the tutor is aiming. As he points out

[55] There are longer speeches in the book, but they are directed to the reader, not to Emile.

during his speech, Emile's education has made him free and good. But goodness is not virtue, precisely because it is naturally egocentric.

> I have taught you less to give each what belongs to him than to care only for what is yours. I have made you good rather than virtuous: but one who is only good remains so only as long as he takes pleasure in being so, [and] goodness is crushed and perishes under the impact of the human passions; the man who is only good is good only for himself. (ibid., 818, Bloom, 444)

Goodness in this Rousseauan sense is no longer enough, not nearly enough, because Emile is no longer free. He has enslaved himself to Sophie, and living in this state will require two related qualities that Emile lacks. First, and most obviously, Emile must now seek to acquire virtue, which requires a recognition that his natural freedom was an illusion, or at least incomplete and insecure. Until now, "you had only the precarious liberty of a slave to whom nothing has been commanded. Now be actually free; learn to become your own master; command your heart, Emile, and you will be virtuous" (ibid.). Second, natural religion evidently needs a supplement that will enable him to free himself even from Sophie when appropriate. That supplement will involve reason, but it will not consist of mere words and arguments.

Virtue, as the tutor presents it to Emile, consists in acting contrary to one's passions when reason or duty commands it. The examples offered by the tutor are carefully chosen. If Sophie dies before Emile, which is perfectly possible, will he behave with the irrationality that he displayed at the beginning of their conversation? If Sophie were to cease being innocent tomorrow, would he stifle his love for her at once? If Emile were to fall uncontrollably in love with a married woman, would he be able to resist *that* passion?

The time to make a trial of Emile's capacity for virtue is now, not when harsh events or overbearing passions require its exercise. And besides, can Emile even know for sure whether he and Sophie ought to marry? "You want to marry her not because she suits you but because she pleases you; as if love were never mistaken about suitability and as if those who begin by loving each other never end by hating each other. She is virtuous, I know it; but is that enough? Does being upright people (*honnêtes gens*) suffice for suiting each other?" (ibid., 822, Bloom, 447).

Thus, an important purpose of separating Emile and Sophie is the separation itself. Fulfilling his earlier promise of obedience to the tutor is Emile's first significant exercise of virtue, and keeping the promise for two long years will serve to test that virtue. At the same time, it will test the strength of the love between Emile and Sophie. This reminds us that when the tutor extracted the original promise of obedience from Emile, he also promised that such obedience would contribute to Emile's happiness. There can be no doubt that Emile's acquiescence in the tutor's present command is affected by, and perhaps crucially dependent on, his faith in the tutor's wisdom and benevolence. Even now, he is not to be tested with a real conflict between virtue and happiness, and he is not given much reason to conclude that he should choose virtue if such a conflict were ever to arise.

Taken as a whole, the tutor's speech is meant to leave Emile with an expectation that no serious conflict will arise between his happiness and the demands of virtue. This is the same impression the tutor later gives Emile when he tells him that he can easily escape the political duties that he must be ready to accept. But will it be so easy for Emile to combine virtue and happiness if his marriage to Sophie goes haywire?

Certainly not, and the tutor offers Emile only one way to deal with that possibility.

> *Attach your heart only to the beauty that does not perish* ... Then you will find in the possession of fragile goods a voluptuous pleasure that nothing will be able to disrupt; you will possess them without their possessing you; and you will feel that man, from whom everything escapes, enjoys only what he knows how to lose ... How many others experience horror because they think that in departing life they cease to be; instructed about its nothingness, you will believe it begins. Death is the end of the wicked man's life and the beginning of that of the just man. (ibid., 820, Bloom, 446, emphasis added)

It is not clear to me what Emile would make of the last two sentences in this quotation. It might mean no more than what the Savoyard Vicar meant when he concluded that the soul must survive the body long enough for divine justice to correct whatever injustices occur during our lives. But it is more easily read to mean that a just man will set out on his true life after death, even if he has experienced little or no net injustice in this life. That sounds like a promise of eternal life, or at least more than a rectification of injustice. Such a promise would seem to be available only from revealed religion or from the kind of wishful thinking that Emile's whole education has been meant to discourage. Perhaps the tutor believes that once Emile has fallen in love with a flesh and blood woman, it would be folly to think that he can any longer get by without a considerable amount of wishful thinking.

In the course of the speech just before his marriage, Emile claims that he can defy death, which he regards as a law of nature, because it will never prevent him from having lived (ibid., 857, Bloom, 472). In a long speech directed to the reader much earlier in the book, Rousseau had imagined a cheerful man cast into despair by a letter bringing bad news, much as Emile had been stricken when he thought a letter had brought news of Sophie's death (ibid., 307–08, Bloom, 83). In the earlier passage, Rousseau had suggested that if the letter to the cheerful man had not reached him, it would not be easy to say whether his apparent happiness would be more of an illusion than the unhappiness he experienced upon actually receiving it. In the same passage, Rousseau declared that resignation to death is a law that nature teaches men and beasts alike, and that once we lose this natural resignation, reason teaches us the same law. Significantly, however, he adds that "this artificial resignation (*resignation factice*) is never as full and complete as the first" (ibid., 307, Bloom, 82). Even if we suppose that Emile will not allow the fear of his own death to prevent him from living, he is not now in a position to appreciate how fragile his reasoned resignation is. Rousseau leaves the reader to notice that the artificial resignation encouraged by natural religion (which is not mentioned here) is "never as full or complete" as the natural resignation that we have all lost.

Emile will express similar sentiments about worldly goods and our short life when he returns from his travels. Such sentiments are easy enough to adopt at the age of twenty-two, and after suffering no more real adversity than a temporary separation from a beloved with whom one expects to find lifelong happiness. On that occasion, the tutor will warn him that he will moderate his views when he has children. But here, in the long speech *before* the trip, the tutor implies that Emile should adopt these views, not just as general maxims but with respect to Sophie herself: "*Attach your heart only to the beauty that does not perish.*"

Is there any reason to suppose that Emile could actually live by this advice? Not yet. Indeed, Emile's immediate response is fear—fear that the tutor is about to deprive him forever of Sophie. The tutor wants him to experience that fear, and then to experience a two-year deprivation. As we've seen, however, he does not plan to subject him to the much greater adversity of a permanent separation from Sophie. A few moments later,

Emile is relieved of *that* terrible prospect. But what if he ever has to face it, or something else that he finds equally horrific?

Earlier in the *Emile*, Rousseau had made a passing reference to Plato's *Symposium* (ibid., 677, Bloom, 344), which is inevitably brought to mind by the reference here to "the beauty that does not perish." The earlier remark occurred in the course of a lengthy disquisition on what Rousseau calls "taste." As we recall, the serious part of Emile's bookish education began with the study of human passions in history, especially as described in Plutarch. The tutor then took his pupil to Paris in search of a wife. During this excursion, Emile was introduced to poetry and the theater in order to assist his study of men by reflecting, indeed "philosophizing," on the central preoccupation of Parisian society, namely "what delights or offends the human heart" (ibid., 671, Bloom, 340).

The principal purpose of this part of Emile's education was to cultivate his taste for a girl like Sophie, whom he had not yet met. But Rousseau's description of the education begins with a somewhat startling and emphatic general definition of taste: "[T]aste is only the faculty of judging what pleases or displeases the greatest number. Leave that behind and you no longer know what taste is" (ibid.). In his explication of this dictum, Rousseau emphasizes that the sound exercise of this faculty is much more difficult than one would expect from its definition. Briefly stated, the difficulties arise because taste is simultaneously natural and variable among individuals and cultures, and because natural taste is easy to corrupt. Developing Emile's taste is thus a kind of homunculus of his education as a whole, which aims at allowing him to live according to nature in society, to the extent that it is possible to do so.[56]

As with Emile's study of history, Rousseau expects that his tastes in poetry will run to the ancients. In this case, it is because "being first, the ancients are closer to nature and their genius is more their own" (ibid., 676, Bloom, 343). More radically, Rousseau then declares without qualification that "there is no true progress of reason in the human species because … all minds start from the same point, and the time employed for knowing what others have thought being wasted for learning to think for oneself, more enlightenment is acquired and less vigor of mind" (ibid.). As this comment suggests, Emile's introduction to poetry and drama is

[56]The structure of good taste resembles that of the general will in the *Social Contract*, which will be discussed in the following chapter.

meant both to give him examples of what good taste finds beautiful and to encourage him to think about what makes those examples beautiful.

Rousseau is confident that Emile will do this: "Picture on one side my Emile and on the other a college rogue reading the fourth book of the *Aeneid* or Tibullus or Plato's *Symposium*; what a difference! How the heart of the one is stirred by what does not even affect the other" (ibid., 672, Bloom, 344). It is easy enough to imagine why a "college rogue" would not be affected. Forced to read such literature—and worse yet, perhaps forced to read it in a dead language that they have been forced to study—most students understandably find such assignments deadly boring. And if they have already been corrupted by the crudeness that almost always flourishes in environments dominated by adolescent males, any effect on their minds is apt to run in the direction of a resolute determination to keep their hearts unaffected.

Emile is not forced to read any of this, and he will have studied ancient languages only if he chose to do so. But what exactly will Emile's adolescent heart be stirred by in these books? It is not hard to imagine the appeal of Tibullus, whose elegies rather resemble some of the more tasteful love songs of our own age. Nor is it difficult to imagine why the fourth book of the *Aeneid* would affect him. He is already familiar with ancient history, full of stories about conflicts between the impulses of the heart and the demands of political duty or ambition. Virgil's presentation of Dido's story is exceptionally powerful in arousing the reader's sympathies for a woman unlucky in love—in different ways with both Sychaeus and Aeneas—without obscuring the complexities created by the political affairs into which she entered.

But Plato's *Symposium*? It is not so easy to see what would "stir the heart" of Emile in this drama, even apart from the obstacles created by its pervasive homoerotic themes. Except for the dark comedy of Aristophanes, the urbane speeches that precede that of Socrates mostly resemble a sophisticated version of the showy chatter that Emile is probably now encountering in the drawing rooms of Paris. For his part, Socrates systematically rebuts the portrayals of eros in the previous speeches, and in a way calculated to stir the mind a lot more than the heart. Emile might be moved by the drunken confession of Alcibiades, but he presumably knows enough history to stop short of being moved too much or too far.

I suspect that most people who first read the *Symposium* during adolescence, or have talked seriously about it with teenaged students who have not been damaged by an excess of casual sex, will expect Emile to be moved initially and most strongly by the speech of Aristophanes. That speech depicts eros as a longing to unite with the one other person in this world who can make us complete. This depiction is so true to youthful experience that the grotesque story in which Aristophanes wraps his supposed praise of eros can actually heighten the movements of a sensitive reader's heart. Emile has not been corrupted with opinions or experiences that would leave him cold or laughing when he reads this speech. But what will he make of the alternative account of eros offered in the speech of Socrates?

Emile will probably focus on what Socrates is supposed to have learned from Diotima, as many readers do. Unlike Aristophanes, who conjures with the youthful desire to complete our needy selves by finding our one true mate, Diotima evokes the dissatisfaction that lovers of the beautiful always experience, in one way or another, with every beautiful thing. She stresses that the eros triggered by a beautiful human body points beyond to the beauty in many bodies, and then beyond that to the beauty in a variety of noncorporeal phenomena. Emile reads the *Symposium* while surrounded by the ladies of Paris and is thus amply exposed to the variety of womanly beauty. Finding the beloved he desires nowhere among them, he might hope to climb Diotima's ladder of eros. The promise that Diotima dangles at the end of the ascent she describes—glimpses of the beauty that does not perish—would have to be as mysterious to Emile as to anyone, but the intermediate steps might draw his interest quite intensely.

Rousseau repeatedly suggests both that true love is obviously founded on illusion and that it sees what cannot otherwise be seen (ibid., 494, 656, 743, 798, Bloom, 214, 329, 391, 430). Both claims could be true if the beauty that the lover sees in the beloved is an image of the beauty that does not perish. Or perhaps Rousseau means that true love enables one to see something in oneself that would otherwise have remained hidden. In either case, Rousseau's position would not necessarily be at odds with Diotima's claim that "eros, in sum, is the whole desire for the good things and for being happy—the greatest and altogether beguiling eros [or the greatest and beguiling eros in everyone]" (205d1–3). Although Emile's most durable approximation of the equilibrium in which truly natural men found themselves will be sought in a marriage, he comes closest to supreme happiness during the period between falling in love and entering into wedlock (*O.C.*, 4:782, Bloom, 419).[57]

For Emile, I think, the most significantly enduring elements of Diotima's teaching would likely be that what eros seeks can be found in many places—including bodies, souls, activities and human accomplishments—and especially that eros also seeks to engender what is beautiful. When Emile eventually encounters Sophie herself, I believe that the tutor does not want him only to feel that he has found his Aristophantic other half, which would lead to inevitable disappointment. Instead, Emile should hope that he and Sophie can together live to engender what is beautiful.[58] This does not merely mean the birth of children, which Diotima belittles (209c2–e4). Nor does it mean the glorious deeds of a successful political career, or indeed the life of philosophy. Rather, what the tutor hopes Emile will achieve is a simulacrum of the self-possession without complacency that characterizes Socrates, a man who continues to engender something beautiful through those who have learned from him.[59] That is an ambition that Emile could take away from the *Symposium*, whatever its limitations may be as an interpretation of the dialogue. And it is an ambition that the tutor believes Emile can safely and satisfactorily pursue within the confines of bourgeois family life.

When the tutor advises Emile, as he is about to order him to leave Sophie, to "attach your heart only to the beauty that does not perish," he is reminding him that the present urgency of his desire to marry is an obstacle to finding what he could have learned from Diotima to seek. Two years later, Emile is in a better position to live by this advice. At the end

[57] During this period, the tutor goes so far as to tell Emile: "You have enjoyed more through hope than you ever will in reality … Except for the sole Being existing by itself, there is nothing beautiful but what is not" (*O.C.*, 4:821, Bloom, 447). This calls attention to another effect of Emile's two-year separation from Sophie: it prolongs the period of his most intense happiness.

[58] This is not to say that the tutor fails to take account of the Aristophantic desire that so many people experience. The trip to Paris exposes Emile to many women who would neither satisfy that desire nor be a suitable companion in life. The tutor never takes Emile to a place, perhaps like the Geneva of the *Letter to d'Alembert*, where he might encounter a fair number of girls with whom he could make a suitable match. Sophie is not only Emile's first love, but she is apparently the only suitable match he has ever encountered.

[59] Rousseau himself hoped to have effects not altogether dissimilar to the effects Socrates has had through Plato and Xenophon. In the first paragraph of the Preface to the *Emile*, he says "though my ideas may be bad, if I cause good ones to be born to others, I will not have completely wasted my time" (*O.C.*, 4:241, Bloom, 33).

of the novel, one can imagine him living out the tutor's dream, which is now also Emile's. Sophie is pregnant, and Emile has seen the world in a way that should allow him to limit his ambitions to the sphere of his family. He has the skills to administer his inherited wealth after the fashion of Wolmar in *The New Heloise*,[60] or to make a living with his own hands if necessary. Sophie does not have a bookish education, and Emile is prepared to engender what is beautiful as he continues to explore the world of literature with her. And far from being complacent with all he has and all he hopes to find in his marriage, Emile expects to continue receiving from his beloved tutor the guidance he will need as a father.

The happiness of a natural man living in society appears to be a reasonable prospect for Emile. Even granting that enough bad fortune of certain kinds can overwhelm anyone, his imaginary education looks like a deeper explication than Seneca's of the dictum that Rousseau placed on the title page of the book: "We are sick with evils that can be cured; and nature itself, having brought us forth sound, helps us if we wish to be improved." Unlike Locke's bourgeois gentleman, Emile has inner dispositions and resources of the kind that Stoic philosophy sought to cultivate through the force of reason. As an adult, he may act and appear much like the man that Locke hoped to form. But his happiness will be much less dependent on luck, on worldly success, and above all on the opinions of other people.

Still, Emile has never faced real adversities of the kind that are commonplace in human life. At the end of the book, Rousseau leaves us to wonder just how robust Emile's stoicism truly is.

## Adversity Without Eros: *The Solitaries*

As it happens, Rousseau left us some additional food for thought on this question. *Emile and Sophie, or The Solitaries* is a fragment of an unfinished sequel to the *Emile*. Like *The New Heloise*, it is epistolary in form. What we have consists of two long letters from Emile to his tutor, the second of which breaks off in mid-sentence. Although Rousseau did not complete the novel, he produced several drafts of the fragment and was apparently pleased with it.[61] One cannot interpret it as one would a finished work, but it will bear careful consideration.

[60] See Lund, "A Woman's Laws and a Man's."

[61] See *O.C.*, 4:clxvii–clxviii (editor's introduction to *Emile*); *Confessions*, bk. 2, *O.C.*, 1:56–57; Cranston, *Noble Savage*, 192.

The first letter describes the collapse of Emile's marriage to Sophie. After a period of living contentedly in the country and having two children, Sophie is thrown into despair by the death in close succession of her parents and her daughter. Emile decides to take her and their son to Paris, away from the things that remind her of her losses. This proves to be a grave error. Emile gradually succumbs to many of the distractions abundantly provided by life in such a city, and begins to neglect his wife. Sophie in turn loses the support for her domestic virtue that had previously been provided by the simplicity of the countryside and by Emile's focus on what Rousseau calls "the small fatherland that is the family" (*Emile*, *O.C.*, 4:700, Bloom, 363).

Eventually, Sophie grows cold toward Emile. When he begins making efforts to regain her affection, she resists and he becomes ever more determined to succeed. Finally, she tells him that she is pregnant with another man's child. This revelation throws Emile into an extraordinary state of consternation. After a time of intense inner turmoil and elaborate reflection, Emile decides against taking revenge on his wife. Instead, he determines to leave and become the kind of independent cosmopolitan without ambition that he had believed he could be when he returned from traveling with his tutor. The tutor had told him then that this was not an option for a father, but Emile now feels free to adopt such a life. And he can think of no better alternative.

The second letter begins to recount his adventures. Briefly stated, he is captured on the high seas by Barbary pirates and sold into slavery after displaying cold physical courage in the face of death. He easily bears the indignities of slavery, and lightens the burdens by making himself useful to those who claim the fruits of his labor. At length, an overseer begins to impose such excessive burdens of work that Emile realizes that he and his fellows will soon die of exhaustion. In the face of this untenable situation, he organizes a work stoppage. This leads to an investigation by the owner, who recognizes the foolishness of ruining slaves. Emile himself is put in the overseer's place, and news of the successful rebellion spreads. As a result, Emile is presented as a gift to the Dey of Algiers, who is described as a wise and honorable ruler. At this point, the fragment ends, but it is easy to predict the next turn. Emile will presumably have the political career that the tutor had promised he could avoid in Europe by the simple expedient of being worthy of political office.

One could read *The Solitaries* as a dark revelation that the happy prospect at the end of the *Emile* was nothing but an illusion. That would be wrong. But the sequel does focus our attention on the fragility of the happiness that the tutor's education prepared Emile to enjoy. Why did it all fall apart? There were two main causes. First, the tutor had apparently retired as the advisor that Emile himself had recognized he needed (though he emphasized his need for advice as a father, not as a husband). If the tutor had remained at hand, he likely would have found a way to dissuade Emile from taking Sophie to Paris. Second, and no less important, Sophie was unable to weather the onslaught of deaths that provoked the despair that in turn led Emile to make his great mistake.

So far as Emile's first letter reveals, his initial error was entirely intellectual. Having easily resisted the false attractions of Paris when he went there looking for a Sophie, he apparently thought he could do the same now that he had her. Emile is a product of art, and *The Solitaries* shows that such an artifact cannot fully embody the wisdom that formed him. Emile's education required putting him in circumstances where his nature could grow in the right direction, and he remained more dependent than he knew on remaining in circumstances that fostered his happiness.[62] Emile's motive for taking Sophie to Paris was only to distract her from grief, not to indulge the vain ambitions against which his tutor had prepared him so well. But good intentions were not enough to prevent disaster.

Even more than Emile, Sophie's virtue and happiness depended on remaining in the right circumstances. In her case, however, it was not so much Paris as Emile that ruined her. It is clear from Emile's first letter that he had been faithful to her, so it was not eros that led him to neglect her. Rather, it was just the frivolous trivialities that are inescapable concomitants of "what is called business (*affaires*)" in big cities (*Solitaries*, *O.C.*, 4:885). While they were still living in the country, Emile had been unable to help Sophie deal with her grief. His first letter does not indicate why, or even that he gave any thought to why. Emile's education had spared him the chronic inner neediness that afflicts almost all civilized people, as the tutor intended. For all his big-hearted sympathy for other people, which the tutor had carefully cultivated, the kind of grief that afflicts Sophie now is completely alien to him. Perhaps for this reason, he was not well prepared to help Sophie through her grief or to appreciate how desperately she needed him to be there always for her. Once Sophie went with Emile

[62] Rousseau intended to develop this point more fully in the completed version of *The Solitaries* (*Confessions*, bk. 2, *O.C.*, 1:56–57).

to Paris, only to find him drifting away, *her* eros took its most natural course.

This outcome was not inevitable. The succession of deaths that so afflicted Sophie was the result of chance. Once that happened, Emile might not have gotten it into his head to go to Paris, and more time at home might have allowed Sophie to adjust. But the outcome does suggest one limit on an education aimed at forming a natural man living in society. Such "a savage made to inhabit towns" (*Emile*, *O.C.*, 4:484, Bloom, 205) may be unable fully to sense how deeply others want him to participate in their joys and sorrows. He is therefore always at serious risk of mishandling human relationships, especially with those he loves most of all. Some extraordinarily independent individuals might be able to manage such risks, as the Socrates of Plato and Xenophon seems to do. But that is not Emile.

After leaving Sophie, Emile does a perfectly creditable job of living by the stoic maxims to which he had been led by his tutor. He never calls himself happy, and he does not see his vagabond existence as an improvement on the life he had with Sophie. But it does appear to him as an alternative that in some important ways is more in accord with nature. He is now more free because he sees himself as enslaved to nothing except necessity. Purged of the wishful thinking that may have been a critical element of his love for Sophie, Emile is now elevated or reduced to enjoying that particular kind of freedom.

## A Quasi-Epicurean Approach to Happiness

An alternative road to a somewhat different kind of cosmopolitan freedom is sketched in a lengthy digression addressed to the reader of the *Emile*. After mentioning Plato's *Symposium* near the end of Book IV, Rousseau says: "My principle object in teaching [Emile] to feel and love the beautiful of all kinds is to fix his affections and tastes there, to prevent his natural appetites from being altered, and to prevent him from one day seeking in his riches the means for being happy, which he ought to find closer to himself" (ibid., 677, Bloom, 34). His immediate point is that even in matters of sensuality, the circumstances in which we find or put ourselves decisively affect what we love. Emile, however, is the product of unique circumstances that none of us can have experienced. Accordingly, Rousseau offers to show the reader a different way to see what he is telling us.

He begins by imagining that he himself has done what is required to become rich, which would have made him callous, contemptuous of the poor, and self-indulgent in using his wealth to serve his pleasures. If this is not universally true of those who have inherited or acquired enough money to live extravagantly without the need to work, neither is it a plainly inapt generalization. In our time, it has become fashionable for the very rich to profess a desire to use their wealth for the relief of the poor or the salvation of the world. Still, one sees countless exposés about inconsistencies between such professions and the way that such people often lead their personal lives.

Having become rich, and having developed such a character, Rousseau maintains that reason would still enable him to resist chasing after social status. His argument has a strong core of common sense based on observations that anyone can make. Even in our time, when social boundaries are far more permeable than in Rousseau's, parvenus frequently fail to achieve the social elevation they seek. Instead, they are apt to make themselves the object of disdain and sardonic jokes, equally among those in the circles to which they aspire and those in the class from which they tell themselves they have risen.

What then to do instead? Reason suggests the whole-hearted pursuit of pleasure. But this pursuit, prudently stripped of attempts to make others admire one's wealth and standing, has significant natural limits. Rousseau gives a series of examples, which culminates in the conclusion "that such agreeable occupations [*tels amusemens*] are within the reach of all men and that one does not need to be rich to taste them" (ibid., 691, Bloom, 354).

As one reads through the examples, one is struck by the absence of any reference to a parent's ambitions for his offspring. That, in turn, calls attention to a certain lacuna in Rousseau's critique of social climbing. If parvenus have little hope of joining a higher social class themselves, they can reasonably expect to buy their children an education that will give *them* the requisite entrée. Rousseau silently passes over this possibility, saying instead that someone in his imagined position would reasonably cultivate pleasantly superficial relationships with other people. His life might include a mistress, but only as a concession to nagging sexual need (ibid., 685, Bloom, 350). What he would definitely want are friends with whom to share the pleasures of food and games, agreeable relations with the plain folk of the neighborhood, and the freedom to travel in pursuit of pleasures unavailable at home. The one allusion to marriage in this digression refers to the pleasure he would take in sharing the joys of the common people by attending country weddings.

One might call this a quasi-Epicurean alternative to the quasi-Stoicism to which Emile has been led. Rousseau presents it only as a device for helping his corrupt readers to better understand the mistake at the heart of the infatuation with acquiring wealth and esteem (ibid., 678, Bloom, 344). But coming as it does just after Rousseau's allusion to the *Symposium*, and just before he presents his account of Sophie and the complementarity of the sexes, this digression may encourage some readers to wonder again at Diotima's disparaging comment about seeking to engender what is beautiful through biological reproduction. Whatever such readers may conclude about the naturalness of the family, or about the nature of family life's contribution to the happiness of those who choose to marry, this quasi-Epicurean alternative should compel the reader to recall the somewhat insecure natural foundations of the family suggested by the *Discourse on Inequality*.

The section on "Sophie or the Woman" at the beginning of Book V of the *Emile* presents an elaborate analysis of the ways in which nature points women toward a kind of marriage in which her share in rulership is largely indirect. Throughout this discussion, as in the entire account of Emile's education, Rousseau remains attentive to the tensions between natural inclinations and the demands of life in society. At one point, for example, he distinguishes between trying to form a natural man and forming the woman who *suits* this man (ibid., 700, Bloom, 363). The discussion may also foreshadow the limits of family life as a source of happiness that are later suggested in *The Solitaries*.

Rousseau never completed his sequel to the *Emile*, and was apparently not sure how it should end. Rather than finish the book, he became engrossed in explaining and defending his own life and works. Unlike Emile's, this story is not about a man with an ordinary nature. Perhaps for that very reason, the *Emile* and *The Solitaries* might serve as useful introductions to Rousseau's later autobiographical writings. He did not, however, abandon his work as a political philosopher. To follow that continuing thread, we turn next to Rousseau's principles of political right and then to his most ambitious effort to apply those principles to a concrete political problem.

CHAPTER 6

# Political Legitimacy, Direct Democracy, and American Politics

American political thought tends to be Lockean in principle and, at its best, Montesquieuian in practice. We can easily see the difference by comparing the Declaration of Independence, based as it is on assertions of universal, timeless, and potentially revolutionary principles, with *The Federalist*, which is devoted to explaining how such principles should be adapted to meet the concrete challenges confronting those who took upon themselves the task of framing our new government.

Contemporary debates about direct democracy generally reflect this same division. Those who focus on democratic principles—especially those involving the consent of the governed and the sovereignty of the people—are naturally predisposed in favor of direct democracy. Those more impressed with the wisdom of our federal Constitution—which banished direct democracy from our national mechanisms of governance—are generally much more skeptical about this approach to politics.

In this chapter, I propose to look for a fresh perspective by exploring Rousseau's views on direct democracy. This may look a little odd, or worse. Rousseau has always had a bad name in American political and legal thought. This is due in part to America's friend, Edmund Burke, who famously accused Rousseau of inspiring some of what was worst



N. Lund, *Rousseau's Rejuvenation of Political Philosophy*,
DOI 10.1007/978-3-319-41390-7_6

in the French Revolution.[1] Beyond that, Rousseau's rhetoric is at once intemperate, paradoxical, and pessimistic, all qualities that run against the grain of the American spirit.[2] It should not be much of a surprise that Rousseau has never even been mentioned in a majority opinion of the U.S. Supreme Court. He is not considered a respectable character.

This is just why Rousseau may help us think more clearly about our own political arrangements. He was the first major philosopher to reject key elements of our political heritage after thoroughly confronting the thought of Locke and other Enlightenment figures. For that reason, Rousseau can help us improve our understanding of what we often take for granted through habit and familiarity. Another reason for turning to Rousseau is his kinship with certain dissident or subdominant strains in American thought—beginning with the Anti-Federalists and extending to our contemporary communitarians and civic republicans. To the extent that he is a more profound thinker than other skeptics about the adequacy of our founding principles, Rousseau may help us avoid the mistake of too easily dismissing their doubts.

But is the topic of direct democracy in America worth approaching with the heavy artillery of Rousseau's political philosophy? We regularly employ this form of decision making in small groups, such as university faculties and homeowners associations. But we never use it as the regular form of government in large polities, where doing so would be manifestly impracticable. True, the use of direct democracy as an occasional instrument of government is both pervasive and quite traditional in this country.

[1] Edmund Burke, "Letter to a Member of the National Assembly" (1791), *Works*, 3:304–11. James Madison called Rousseau's discussion of a plan for perpetual peace "as preposterous as it was impotent" ("Universal Peace," 31 Jan. 1792, *Papers of James Madison* (Congressional Series), 14:206–09). Madison was apparently unaware that this was not Rousseau's plan at all, but that of the Abbé de Saint Pierre. What's more, Rousseau's own judgment about the plan (which Madison must not have read) is quite consistent with Madison's. See *Emile*, *O.C.*, 4:848n, Bloom, 467n; *Abstract of the Plan for Perpetual Peace by Monsieur l'Abbé de Saint Pierre*, *O.C.*, 3:563–89; *Judgment on the Plan for Perpetual Peace*, *O.C.*, 3:591–600. See also *Federalist 43* (Madison) (wishing, but apparently not hoping, that a confederation like that proposed for the United States "could be established for the universal peace of mankind").

[2] During the founding period, John Adams railed against Rousseau in terms similar to those used by Burke, and no prominent political figure—even Jefferson—defended him. Rousseau's works were available in America, and *The New Heloise* was popular. Rousseau's political influence, however, was nil. See Paul Merrill Spurlin, *Rousseau in America: 1760-1809.*

Practical necessity, however, has assured that these devices can operate only at the margins of our political life. Federalism, moreover, already provides a practical mechanism for making decisions about the appropriate mix of representative and direct democracy, without much recourse to theory.

Nevertheless, there are at least two related practical reasons for thinking seriously about the value of direct democracy. First, the internet may soon make it technically feasible for direct democracy to operate as a much more regular form of governance in large polities than it ever has before. Second, the Constitution's Guarantee Clause can be interpreted to outlaw direct democracy, and instead to require the use of representative institutions by the states.[3] Although the Supreme Court long ago declined to impose this requirement,[4] the underlying doctrine has subsequently been modified in ways that could open the door to a reconsideration of the precedents.[5] And even if the textual and historical arguments for regarding direct democracy in the states as unconstitutional were to prove very weak,[6] the Supreme Court is entirely capable of ignoring such weaknesses, and injecting its own theories of democracy directly into the Constitution. I will return to this phenomenon later in the chapter.

## Political Legitimacy

What makes a government legitimate, or worthy of commanding obedience? Most of us would readily answer that the consent of the governed is the basis of legitimacy, though we might have doubts or disagreements about what constitutes genuine consent. But what if one asks the prior question: why should consent be the test of legitimacy? It turns out not to be so easy to give a satisfactory response.

[3] Article IV provides: "The United States shall guarantee to Every State in this Union a Republican Form of Government." For claims that this clause forbids direct democracy, see Marci A. Hamilton, "The People: The Least Accountable Branch," 8; Douglas H. Hsiao, "Invisible Cities: The Constitutional Status of Direct Democracy in a Democratic Republic," 1272.

[4] Pacific States Tel. Co. v. Oregon, 223 U.S. 118 (1912) (dismissing a challenge to a state's adoption of initiative and referendum devices on the ground that its constitutionality under the Guarantee Clause is a political question confided by the Constitution to Congress).

[5] See Baker v. Carr, 369 U.S. 186, 218 (1962); New York v. United States, 505 U.S. 144, 183–85 (1992).

[6] See, for example, Robert G. Natelson, "A Republic, Not a Democracy? Initiative, Referendum, and the Constitution's Guarantee Clause."

### *Natural Rights*

Rousseau was the first great philosophic critic of modern liberalism, which was itself founded on a rejection of classical political philosophy. Perhaps the greatest division in ancient times arose between those who took seriously the search for the naturally right political order that would foster what is naturally best for human beings and those who regarded political life as fundamentally unnatural or merely conventional. Modern liberal thought began to demolish this distinction by attributing to all men certain natural rights that they possess apart from any political order, and then taking as the task of political philosophy the discovery of those conventions that will best protect those natural rights. Our Declaration of Independence sums up the liberal postulates:

> We hold these truths to be self-evident, that all men are created equal, that they are endowed by their Creator with certain unalienable Rights, that among these are Life, Liberty and the pursuit of Happiness. That to secure these rights, Governments are instituted among Men, deriving their just powers from the consent of the governed, That whenever any Form of Government becomes destructive of these ends, it is the Right of the People to alter or to abolish it, and to institute new Government, laying its foundation on such principles and organizing its powers in such form, as to them shall seem most likely to effect their Safety and Happiness.

This is all so familiar and so publicly respectable that even on the rare occasions when we try to think seriously about the foundations of our polity, Americans tend to regard these as self-evident truths indeed. But are they?

Self-evident truths certainly do exist: all human beings are animals, for example. But how obvious is it really that every human being "inherently" has a right to life, liberty, and the pursuit of happiness? Our most obviously inherent qualities are the ones we share with other animals, and few of us believe that other animals have such inherent rights. Think for a moment about the films that most of us have seen of life among the animals of the Serengeti plain. When a pride of lions attacks a wildebeest, nobody objects that the lions have violated the victim's right to life and liberty. And when a pack of hyenas comes along and drives the lions from their kill, no one would seriously maintain that the lions have a right to the property they acquired by mixing their labor with the wildebeest's flesh.

The reason we do not say that beasts have rights that are good against other beasts is the same reason that we do not think any of them has a right to be safe from lightning strikes. Similarly, we do not think that human beings have a right to be spared by a hungry lion, or by a lightning bolt. In ordinary usage, a right implies a correlative obligation to respect that right, and thus at least the possibility of that obligation's being enforced. It makes no sense to impute obligations to beasts or to thunderstorms. The rights that we actually see enforced—especially but not only legal rights—arise from human institutions. And, of course, countless cultures other than our own have existed for long periods without our notions of inherent rights and natural equality. None of this disproves the claims in the Declaration of Independence, but it surely suggests that their truth is a long way from being self-evident.

Shortly before he died, Thomas Jefferson commented: "The general spread of the light of science has already laid open to every view the palpable truth, that the mass of mankind has not been born with saddles on their backs, nor a favored few booted and spurred, ready to ride them legitimately, by the grace of God."[7] This surely is a palpable truth, but it is equally true and palpable that horses are not born with saddles on their backs or people with boots and spurs. But perhaps rights could be inherent without necessarily being natural, if they were given to us by God. We find this suggestion in the Declaration of Independence—which holds that we are self-evidently endowed by our Creator with unalienable rights—but that approach cannot resolve the difficulty. The language used in the Declaration could be another way of saying that such rights are natural, as the document suggests with its allusion to "the Laws of Nature and of Nature's God." In that case, the reference to the Creator adds nothing except an additional undefended assertion to the claim that the existence of natural rights is self-evident. Or perhaps the reference to Nature's God amounts to a claim that the existence of a God who endows us with unalienable rights is self-evident. This is manifestly false, as one can easily recognize by considering the difficulty that many people have in maintaining their belief in God even when they strongly desire to keep their faith. Under either interpretation, I think we are forced to deny that the existence of natural or inherent rights and correlative duties is self-evident, no matter how strongly we may desire it to be true.

[7] Jefferson to Roger C. Weightman, 24 June 1826, *The Portable Thomas Jefferson*, 585.

## *Hobbes*

If the natural rights doctrine proclaimed in the Declaration is not self-evident, we have to ask whether such a truth can be established by evidence and argument. A political manifesto like the Declaration of Independence is plainly not the place for such a demonstration, and the Declaration itself says only that its signatories *hold*—that is, assert—that its claims are self-evident. For two reasons, I begin with Thomas Hobbes. First, he was an early and usefully forthright opponent of the classical approach to which our liberalism offers an alternative. Second, Rousseau takes Hobbes as a particularly important exponent of the principles to which he himself wishes to offer an alternative. Here is what Hobbes says:

> The RIGHT OF NATURE, which Writers commonly call *Jus Naturale*, is the Liberty each man hath, to use his own power, as he will himselfe, for the preservation of his own Nature; that is to say, of his own Life; and consequently, of doing any thing, which in his own Judgement, and Reason, hee shall conceive to be the aptest means thereunto.
>
> By LIBERTY, is understood, according to the proper signification of the word, the absence of externall Impediments; which Impediments may oft take away part of a mans power to do what hee would; but cannot hinder him from using the power left him, according as his judgement, and reason shall dictate to him. (*Leviathan*, chap. 14, 99)

These statements, of course, do not constitute either argument or evidence. They are definitions. The definition of natural right, moreover, is at variance with normal usage—in which a right of one person implies a correlative obligation on the part of others to respect that right—and thus seems to include a tacit claim that normal usage is based on some kind of misunderstanding. Under Hobbes' definition, the natural right of human beings becomes difficult to distinguish from the natural liberty of other animals, who seem to be as free as we are to act for the preservation of their own lives except to the extent that they are constrained by external impediments.[8]

[8] Although the quotation above contains a reference to judgment and reason, qualities that may (or may not) be peculiar to human beings, that reference occurs only in a statement that is said to be a *consequence* (and maybe not the only consequence) of the definition of the right of nature. Hobbes later emphasizes that liberty, which he identifies here with natural right, means the same thing whether it is applied to rational, irrational, or inanimate beings (*Leviathan*, chap. 21, 161).

This leads to a two-fold puzzle. Hobbes does not say that brutes have natural rights, but it is not clear why they would not if such rights are nothing more than a particular example of "the absence of external Impediments." On the other hand, if natural rights belong peculiarly to human beings, why does Hobbes seem to declare that there is only one natural right, namely that of self-preservation? Why would he not recognize additional natural rights as well, including those specified in the Declaration of Independence, as well as the right to do things that are often inconsistent with self-preservation, such as chasing after glory and defending the sacred honor that is pledged at the end of the Declaration?

Hobbes was undoubtedly aware of these questions. With respect to the second, for example, he indicates elsewhere that the human good extends beyond mere life, which suggests that natural right should also cover more than mere self-preservation.[9] With respect to the first question, Hobbes indirectly suggests the possibility that beasts may indeed have natural rights: "But from this reason, that in all free gifts and compacts, there is an acceptance of the conveyance of right required, it follows that no man can compact with him who doth not declare his acceptance. And therefore we cannot compact with beasts, neither can we give or take from them any manner of right, by reason of their want of speech and understanding."[10] If other animals simply lack natural rights, Hobbes could simply have said so, and explained why, rather than declaring that our inability to exchange rights with them arises from their lack of speech and understanding. But if natural rights are such that even animals might have them, what do they add to a true understanding of political obligation? Maybe very little.

> But it was the least benefit for men [in the state of nature] thus to have a common right to all things. For the effects of this right are the same, almost, as if there had been no right at all. For although any man might say of every thing, *this is mine*, yet could he not enjoy it, by reason of his neighbour, who having equal right and equal power, would pretend the same thing to be his. (*De Cive*, bk. 1, ¶ 11, italics in original)

Why does Hobbes say that the effects are "almost" the same, rather than simply the same? We are not told and are thus left to wonder whether his assertions about the natural right to do anything and everything for one's

[9] See, for example, ibid., chap. 13, 98 ("such things as are necessary to commodious living"); ibid., chap. 17, 128 ("a more contented life").

[10] Hobbes, *De Cive*, bk. 2, ¶ 12.

own preservation are more than a kind of play on words. The following passage reinforces that suspicion:

> For every man is desirous of what is good for him, and shuns what is evil, but chiefly the chiefest of natural evils, which is death; and this he doth by a certain impulsion of nature, no less than that whereby a stone moves downward. It is therefore neither absurd nor reprehensible, neither against the dictates of true reason, for a man to use all his endeavours to preserve and defend his body and the members thereof from death and sorrows. But that which is not contrary to right reason, that all men account to be done justly, and with right. Neither by the word *right* is anything else signified, than that liberty which every man hath to make use of his natural faculties according to right reason. Therefore the first foundation of natural right is this, that *every man as much as in him lies endeavour to protect his life and members.* (ibid., bk. 1, ¶ 7, italics in original)

I suppose one can say that a stone has a "right" to move downward in the sense that it is at liberty to do so in the absence of external impediments. Such downward movements are obviously neither absurd nor reprehensible, nor contrary to the dictates of true reason. But nobody would say that the stone moved downward "justly, and with right." Assuming, plausibly enough, that the human desire to avoid death is as natural as the downward motion of a stone, or as natural as the desire of lions to kill wildebeest, it is only by invoking "true reason" or "right reason" that Hobbes can draw the conclusion that using all our endeavors to avoid death is done justly, and with right.

Rather than actually present an argument connecting the "impulsion of nature" with justice and right, however, Hobbes claims that the connection he asserts is universally acknowledged. But it is not true that the unrestrained pursuit of self-preservation is something that "all men account to be done justly, and with right." Many people have denied this, and some have sacrificed their lives for what they thought was a just cause. Indeed, some people even deny that justice can be defined by human reason rather than by God's will. In any event, the allusion here to what all men think sits uneasily with Hobbes' statement elsewhere that "injustice against men presupposeth human laws, such as in the state of nature there are none" (ibid., bk. 1, ¶ 10, 116n‡).[11]

[11] See also *Leviathan*, chap. 13, 100 ("The Desires, and other Passions of man, are in themselves no Sin. No more are the Actions, that proceed from those Passions, till they know a Law that forbids them: which till Lawes be made they cannot know: nor can any Law be made, till they have agreed upon the Person that shall make it.").

In light of this last statement, and of the strangeness of the definition of natural right with which Hobbes begins, it should not be surprising that he also offers a separate argument. This argument rests on claims about the utility of certain human institutions rather than, or at least rather more than, on his forceful but puzzling and equivocal claims about natural right or justice.

This alternative argument may be summarized very briefly as follows. Unrestrained human passions—including the natural desire to avoid that worst of natural evils, death—will lead to a horrible war of all against all until people agree to improve their prospects for self-preservation by mutually relinquishing a great portion of their original natural liberty. Operating in the service of the passion for self-preservation, reason tells us that we can enhance our prospects for self-preservation by seeking peace. Thus, it is in everyone's self-interest:

> *That a man be willing, when others are so too, as farre-forth, as for Peace, and defence of himselfe he shall think it necessary, to lay down this right to all things; and be contented with so much liberty against other men, as he would allow other men against himselfe.* (*Leviathan*, chap. 14, 100, italics in original)

The resulting social contract, whose terms are supposed to be exactly specified by the need to escape from the state of nature, is a unanimous agreement to choose by majority vote a sovereign (which may consist of one or more people) that will have an incentive to keep the peace by virtue of possessing complete authority to rule the entire group (ibid., chaps. 17–18). Alternatively, an agreement to submit to a conqueror who offers to rule you rather than kill you can equally serve one's interest in peace and self-preservation (ibid., chap. 20).

This analysis enables Hobbes to promote the doctrine that consent to any existing political order under which we happen to live is dictated by everyone's self-interest: submission to a standing authority that has an interest in keeping the peace is unambiguously preferable to the state of nature into which we would otherwise fall. And therefore every existing political order is just, in the sense that everyone has either consented to that order or is so outside it that the parties to the social contract have themselves not consented to recognize any duties toward him.[12]

[12] See ibid., chap. 18, 135 ("[B]ecause the major part hath by consenting voices declared a Soveraigne; he that dissented must now consent with the rest; that is, be contented to avow all the actions he shall do, or else justly be destroyed by the rest."). See also ibid., 141 (last paragraph of the chapter), where Hobbes explains why he thinks it is always advantageous to submit to an existing sovereign.

This argument is inconsistent with ordinary notions of natural right, in which one person's right implies a natural and correlative duty in someone else. Hobbes confirms this by defining natural law in a way that renders it subordinate to a right of nature that is bereft of any element of duty or obligation:

> A LAW OF NATURE, (*Lex Naturalis,*) is a Precept, or generall Rule, found out by Reason, by which a man is forbidden to do, that, which is destructive of his life, or taketh away the means of preserving the same; and to omit, that, by which he thinketh it may be best preserved. For though they that speak of this subject, use to confound *Jus*, and *Lex*, *Right* and *Law*; yet they ought to be distinguished; because RIGHT, consisteth in liberty to do, or to forbeare; Whereas LAW, determineth, and bindeth to one of them: so that Law, and Right, differ as much, as Obligation, and Liberty; which in one and the same matter are inconsistent. (ibid., chap. 14, 99)

Does this not render Hobbes' introduction of obligation into the law of nature a kind of play on words?[13] Hobbes confirms at the end of his presentation of the laws of nature that his terminology is indeed misleading: "These dictates of Reason [i.e., the laws of nature], men use to call by the name of Lawes; but improperly: for they are but Conclusions, or Theoremes concerning what conduceth to the conservation and defence of themselves; wheras Law, properly is the word of him, that by right hath command over others" (ibid., chap. 15, 122–23).

Although Hobbes retains the moral connotations of natural right and natural law, human conventions turn out to be the sole basis of justice, right, and law. Thus, for example, Hobbes offers a lengthy discussion of nineteen "laws of nature," one of which is "justice" (ibid., chap. 15). Justice, however, is defined as keeping one's promises, and Hobbes specifically notes that absent a covenant that one has made, "every man has a right to every thing" and nothing can be unjust (ibid., 110). It is true that Hobbes contends that some human conventions are more conducive than others to promoting the natural goal of self-preservation, and thus one might call those conventions "natural" in a certain sense of the word. And it may well be true that these preferred conventions are more likely to be accepted if people come to believe that they are rooted in something with the moral overtones of "natural right." But even if one were to grant the

[13] The passage just quoted follows immediately after the definitions of the right of nature and of liberty quoted above.

utility of such beliefs, that would not establish that any natural obligations can be derived from natural right or natural law.[14] Hobbes therefore does not even purport to establish, by adequate argument or evidence, claims like those in the Declaration of Independence about natural or inherent rights that have correlative obligations.

### *Locke*

John Locke accepts Hobbes' essential claim that the preeminent human desire for self-preservation is so frustrated in the state of nature that it drives us to leave that condition by agreeing to the institution of political rule. Locke, however, emphasizes the role of poverty and the pursuit of wealth, rather than bare mutual hostility and the insatiable desire for power, as triggers for this change.[15] He then draws significantly different implications about what kind of political institutions are most useful.

We are all familiar with his principal conclusions, which are briefly summarized in the Declaration of Independence. Legitimate government depends on the consent of the governed, who must be supposed to consent to be ruled only by settled laws (not the arbitrary whims of the governor), and who always retain the right to change the form of government. Like the Declaration, Locke's presentation strongly suggests both that these political conclusions are useful and that they are also just because they are derived from the natural or inherent rights of human beings. But how does Locke establish this second claim, which is different from the claim that the principles he advances are useful?

One of his statements contrasts sharply with what we find in Hobbes:

> The *State of Nature* has a Law of Nature to govern it, which obliges every one: and Reason, which is that Law, teaches all Mankind, who will

[14] Hobbes himself recognizes this. "And the same [voluntary signs of agreement] are the BONDS, by which men are bound, and obliged: Bonds, that have their strength, not from their own Nature, (for nothing is more easily broken than a mans word,) but from Feare of some evill consequence upon the rupture" (*Leviathan*, chap. 14, 101).

[15] Compare, for example, Hobbes, *De Cive*, bk. 1, ¶ 12 (referring to "this natural proclivity of men, to hurt each other, which they derive from their passions"); Hobbes, *Leviathan*, Chap. 11, 75 ("I put for a general inclination of all mankind, a perpetuall and restlesse desire of Power after power, that ceaseth onely in Death.") with Locke, *Second Treatise* ¶ 32 (referring to the "penury" of the state of nature); ¶ 123 (contending that the motive for the institution of political society is "the mutual *Preservation* of [men's] Lives, Liberties, and Estates, which I call by the general Name, *Property*").

> but consult it, that being all equal and independent, no one ought to harm another in his Life, Health, Liberty, or Possessions. For Men being all the Workmanship of one Omnipotent, and infinitely wise Maker; All the Servants of one Sovereign Master, sent into the World by his order and about his business, they are his Property, whose Workmanship they are, made to last during his, not one anothers Pleasure. And being furnished with like Faculties, sharing all in one Community of Nature, there cannot be supposed any such *Subordination* among us, that may Authorize us to destroy another, as if we were made for one anothers uses, as the inferior ranks of Creatures are for ours. (*Second Treatise*, ¶ 6)

Soothing as this statement is, it is not self-evident,[16] or even generally acknowledged: "[F]or though the Law of Nature be plain and intelligible to all rational Creatures; yet Men being biassed by their Interest, as well as ignorant for want of study of it, are not apt to allow of it as a Law binding to them in the application of it to their particular Cases" (ibid., ¶ 124). How exactly can we be sure that we are not accepting Locke's comforting assertions about the law of nature because we are "biassed by [our] interest"?

Later, in introducing his extended argument for the labor theory of property, Locke makes a statement that is different from his earlier claim that we are all the property of our Maker:

> Though the Earth, and all inferior Creatures be common to all Men, yet every Man has a *Property* in his own *Person*. This no Body has any Right to but himself. The *Labour* of his Body, and the *Work* of his Hands, we may say, are properly his. (ibid., ¶ 27)[17]

This is almost as soothing, and perhaps even more flattering, than his earlier assertion that the will of our Maker obliges others to respect our claims to life and to the means of self-preservation. One could hardly deny that everyone has a strong interest in *claiming* for himself an inherent, or natural, or God-given right to life, liberty, and wealth. That was what Burke suggested when he said that "[t]he little catechism of the Rights of Men is

[16] Nor does Locke base it on divine revelation. See, for example, *Second Treatise*, ¶ 136 ("the Law of Nature being unwritten, and so no where to be found but in the minds of Men").

[17] Compare *Leviathan*, chap. 14, 99 (in the state of nature, "every man has a Right to every thing; even to one anothers body").

soon learned; and the inferences are in the passions."[18] However natural it may be to want or claim such rights, wanting and claiming are not enough to establish that we do have such rights by nature. Like Hobbes, Locke has not established what the Declaration of Independence says is self-evident. Like the Declaration, his *Second Treatise* just asserts it.

## Rousseau on Direct Democracy and Political Legitimacy

Locke's principles underlie the political order into which we Americans are born. Rousseau indignantly rejected the liberal political vision to which we are heirs, believing that it could lead only to cynical interest-group politics in which the rich would always outfox the poor, to societies dominated by money-grubbing hypocrites and courtiers, and ultimately to a culture that would produce the kind of degraded and hollow souls that Tocqueville and Nietzsche foresaw. Rousseau confidently pointed to an alternative that was not based on theory, but rather on recorded fact: the great souls and patriotic political vigor of classical civilization, especially Sparta and the Roman Republic.

If Rousseau were merely nostalgic for Plutarch's world, he might easily be dismissed. But he did not think that political societies like these should or even could be reconstructed in modern times. Even those who do not share his attraction to ancient political institutions need to consider his arguments. He accepted the fundamental premises of Hobbes and Locke—the centrality of self-preservation and self-interest as the basis for politics and the denial of man's inherently political nature—but contended that a genuine understanding of the human soul leads to substantially different political conclusions.

### *Discourse on Inequality*

Rousseau believed that his distinctive political insight, to which he consistently adhered, is "that man is naturally good, and that it is through [our] institutions alone that men become wicked" (*Letters to Malesherbes*, lett. 2, *O.C.*, 1:1136). This deceptively simple formulation is the foundation of all that he wrote about politics. For our purposes here, it may be useful

[18] "Thoughts on French Affairs" (1791), *Works*, 4:28.

to begin by returning to Rousseau's most openly philosophic work, the *Discourse on Inequality.*

Near the beginning, Rousseau summarizes his principal argument as follows:

> The Philosophers who have examined the foundations of society have all felt the necessity of going back as far as the state of Nature, but none of them has arrived there. Some have not hesitated to suppose in Man in that state the notion of the Just and the Unjust, without troubling themselves to show that he must have had this notion, or even that it would have been useful to him: Others have spoken of the Natural Right that each has to keep what belongs to him, without explaining what they mean by belong; Others, giving the stronger authority over the weaker from the first, had Government arise immediately, without dreaming of the time that must have gone by before the sense of the words of authority and of government could have existed among Men: All of them of them finally, incessantly speaking of need, of avidity, of oppression, of desires, and of pride, transported to the state of Nature ideas they had acquired in society; They spoke of Savage Man and depicted Civil man. (*Inequality*, *O.C.*, 3:132)

A little later, Rousseau praises Hobbes by name, saying that he "saw very clearly the defect of all modern definitions of Natural right" (ibid., 153). By this, he means that Hobbes did not make the common mistake of those who work out elaborate systems of socially useful moral and political obligation, and then attribute those obligations to nature (ibid., 124–25).[19] But whereas he thinks that Hobbes was right to say that human passions rather than natural obligation must be at the root of all human justice, Rousseau claims that he went astray by attributing to human nature passions that arise entirely in and through society (ibid., 153).

[19] In the *Emile*, Rousseau includes a passage that echoes Socrates' description of the true or healthy city in Book II of the *Republic* (*O.C.*, 4:466–67, Bloom, 192–93). This passage concludes that the mutually beneficial division of labor is "the *apparent* principle of all our institutions" (emphasis added), and refers the reader to the *Discourse on Inequality* for an exposition of the consequences. Shortly thereafter, in a seemingly offhand comment, Rousseau indicates the extent of his agreement with Hobbes: "Since among all the aversions that Nature has given us, the strongest is that of dying, it follows that everything is permitted by her to one who has no other possible means of living." By implicitly linking his own analysis both to Plato and to Hobbes, Rousseau suggests why he can accept the most fundamental political principle of modern liberalism without abandoning what he saw as the philosophic spirit of Plato.

Rousseau devotes much of the *Discourse* to establishing which passions are natural, in the sense that human beings must have had them in the prepolitical state of nature. He means this inquiry to be as scientific as possible, and accordingly consulted all the literature available to him about primitive peoples and the great apes. In the genuine spirit of science, Rousseau read these reports skeptically and expected that corrections to many of them would become necessary in the future. More dramatically, he leaves open the possibility of *physical* evolution, a question that he expects might be settled by future scientific advances (ibid., 122–23). He even suggests that the relationship between humans and some of the great apes might be investigated through attempts at cross-breeding (ibid., Note XII, 211). When Rousseau distinguishes the physical or natural from the moral, and philosophy or science from soothing political sermons, he is not kidding around (see, e.g., ibid., 131–32). In this respect, he outdoes Hobbes in his provocative amoralism.

Freely acknowledging that precise scientific certainty about the original condition of man is not and may never be available (ibid., 123), Rousseau concludes that natural man must have been essentially indistinguishable from other animals. The principal reason for drawing this conclusion is that languages are not natural but invented, and it is the acquisition of language that makes possible all of the most significant differences between us and the beasts. The argument can be summarized as follows.

First, because language is acquired rather than natural, there must have been a time when human beings lived without language. And because all human societies (apart perhaps from the most primitive kind of families) are inseparable from language and impossible without it, our kind is naturally and profoundly non-political. That does not imply a Hobbesian war of all against all because we are physically designed so as to permit an isolated existence in the mild and fecund environment from which the human race must have emerged. There is no reason to assume that humans originally had any passions except those required for such an existence: the desire for food, drink, and other necessities of self-preservation, along with an inclination for sexual intercourse and a capacity for pity exemplified in the mammalian maternal instinct.

Second, while human beings obviously must have had the natural *potential* to acquire language and all the other distinctively human characteristics that we observe, this potential would have been unleashed only as a result of natural accidents (such as earthquakes and droughts) that pushed humans into environments where the isolated existence of the first ages was not practicable (ibid., 168–69). Once that happened, a train of events was set in motion that would lead eventually to something like the Hobbesian war of all against all, and thus to the necessity of founding civil societies (ibid., 174–78).

This is what Rousseau means when he claims that man is naturally good: our ancestors originally enjoyed the psychic simplicity of a nearly solitary animal because they had no needs or passions beyond those required of such an animal. And they became malicious solely because they entered into relations of interdependence with other people, relations of which they are obviously capable but for which they are not specifically designed by nature. The narrowness of "natural goodness" as Rousseau understands it deserves the utmost emphasis.

One consequence that Rousseau draws from this analysis is that nature does not divide man against himself by giving him duties that are odds with his inclinations. The natural moral law as it is ordinarily understood therefore becomes a kind of contradiction in terms: "All we can very clearly see on the subject of [natural] Law is that not only for it to be law the will of the one it obligates must be able to submit to it knowingly; But also that for it to be natural it must speak immediately through the voice of Nature" (ibid., 125).[20] Accordingly, Rousseau takes the issue in the *Discourse* to be: "To mark in the progress of things, the moment when Right succeeding Violence, Nature was *subjected* to Law" (ibid., 132, emphasis added).

Consistent with this contrast between violence and nature on one hand and right and law on the other, Rousseau sometimes uses the language of natural right in the Hobbesian sense of liberty to pursue self-preservation without self-restraint. But rather than accept the logic by which Hobbes purports to found political obligation on natural right, Rousseau emphasizes the difficulty in reconciling natural selfishness with political obligation. Thus, for example, he says that "moral inequality, authorized by positive right alone, is contrary to Natural Right whenever it is not in exactly the same proportion with Physical inequality" (ibid., 193–94).

This difficulty is most conspicuous in Rousseau's description of the moment when right and law replaced nature and violence. Like Locke,

[20] At the very end of the book, Rousseau qualifies or clarifies this formulation: "[I]t is manifestly against the Law of Nature, in whatever manner one defines it, that a child command an old man, that an imbecile lead a wise man, and that a handful of people be glutted with superfluities while the famished multitude lacks necessities" (*Inequality*, *O.C.*, 3:194).

Rousseau treats the cultivation and division of land as the critical development that must have led to the need to establish political institutions (ibid., 173). And he seems at first to accept Locke's labor theory of property: "It is labor alone which, giving the Cultivator the right to the produce of the land he has worked, consequently also gives him a right to the land, at least until the harvest, and so from year to year, and which making a continuous possession, is easily transformed into property" (ibid.). Rousseau, however, recognizes that this kind of right actually conflicts with another kind of right that has a much more obvious claim to be called natural: "A perpetual conflict arose between the right of the stronger and the right of the first occupant, which only ended in fights and murders" (ibid., 176).[21] Rather than paper over this problem, as Locke did,[22] Rousseau concludes that the labor theory of property does not quite hold up to scrutiny:

> Even those whom industry alone had enriched could hardly base their property on better titles [than those based merely on force]. They might well have said: It is I who built this wall; I earned this ground by my labor. Who gave you its dimensions, they could be answered; and by virtue of what do you lay claim to being paid at our expense for a labor we did not impose on you? Do you not know that a multitude of your brothers perish, or suffer from need of what you have in excess, and that you required the express and unanimous consent of the Human Race to appropriate for yourself anything from the common subsistence above and beyond your own? (ibid., 176–77)[23]

This passage not only says that robbers have no obligations to other robbers but also that the right of first occupancy depends on the impossible condition of the express and unanimous consent of mankind. Nor does Rousseau say that the industrious first occupant lacks a valid answer only to those who are themselves perishing or suffering from need of what he has in excess. A well-fed robber, no less than a starving one, could say that

[21] See also *Poland*, chap. 12, *O.C.*, 3:1013 ("The most inviolable law of nature is the law of the stronger. There is no legislation, no constitution that can provide an exemption from this law.").

[22] See *Second Treatise*, ¶ 32 (asserting that God commanded man to improve the world by cultivating the earth).

[23] See also *S.C.*, bk. 1, chap. 9, *O.C.*, 3:365–66 (denying that the right of first occupancy is a true right).

he neither imposed any labor on the first occupant nor agreed to refrain from taking whatever he found on the land in question.[24]

This passage brings out most clearly what Rousseau considered the latent implications of the non-political nature that he believes Hobbes and Locke correctly attributed to human beings. The most natural "right" is the right of the stronger, and "the first rules of justice" only *follow* from the institution of property.[25] Nature lacks a moral component, and the projection of our notions of right or justice back into the state of nature is anachronistic. Nor would the original social contract have been a reasonable agreement among reasonable people.[26] Whatever the usefulness of political society—and Rousseau acknowledges that by the time governments were instituted, there must really have been no better alternative—it was not founded on principles of natural right or natural justice.[27] The origin of society and laws "fixed forever the Law of property and of inequality, [and] from an adroit usurpation created an irrevocable right" (ibid., 178).[28]

[24] Plato points indirectly to the same problem. The city in speech that Socrates constructs requires a particular high-born (*gennaion*) lie: that the very land on which the citizens live is their mother and nurturer, which gives them both the right and obligation to defend it against attacks (*Republic* 414b–e). Most translators render *gennaion* as "noble," which obscures the playful sense in which Socrates alludes to the lie's pretentiousness about the birth of the citizens.

[25] See *Inequality*, *O.C.*, 3:173–74. See also ibid., 178 (after the spread of political society, "the Law of Nature no longer had a place except between different Societies where, under the name of Right of nations, it was tempered by a few tacit conventions in order to render commerce possible"); *S.C.*, bk. 1, chap. 9, *O.C.*, 3:365 ("[P]ublic possession is in fact stronger and more irrevocable [than private possession], without being more legitimate, at least with respect to foreigners.").

[26] Hobbes goes so far as to present the acquisition of sovereignty by conquest as a reasonable agreement in which the conqueror offers to spare the lives of the conquered in return for submission to his rule, and the conquered reasonably agree to accept the offer (*Leviathan*, chap. 20, 155). Rousseau makes the obvious rebuttal: there is no good reason for anyone to think that an agreement extracted from him by force imposes binding obligations (*Inequality*, *O.C.*, 3:179).

[27] *Inequality*, *O.C.*, 3:164, 177–78. See also *S.C.*, bk. 1, chap. 1, *O.C.*, 3:351–52 (asserting that the social order is a right that does not come from nature, and that it provides the basis for *all* other rights); ibid., bk. 2, chap. 6, *O.C.*, 3:378 (denying that there are any obligations in the state of nature).

[28] Without using a provocative term like "usurpation," Adam Smith later drew essentially the same conclusion: "Civil government, so far as it instituted for the protection of property, is in reality instituted for the defence of the rich against the poor, or of those who have some property against those who have none at all" (*Wealth of Nations*, bk. 5, chap. 5, pt. 2, ¶ 12).

The conclusions drawn by Rousseau from the liberal premise of man's non-political nature led him to regard two questions as far more challenging than they appear to be in Locke and Hobbes. First, if the original social contract must have been a kind of trick or usurpation, rather than a reasonable agreement among reasonable people, how can we distinguish between legitimate and illegitimate political rule today? Second, if human beings are not naturally fit for political life, can nature provide us with guidance in designing political institutions? Rousseau takes up these questions in the *Social Contract.*

### *Social Contract*

The difficulty of the question of legitimacy is reflected in the famously paradoxical formulation found at the outset of the first chapter of the *Social Contract*:

> Born free, man is everywhere in chains. Someone believes himself the master of others, and does not fail to be more a slave than them. How did this change come about? I do not know. What can render it legitimate? I believe I can resolve this question. (bk. 1, chap. 1, *O.C.*, 3:351)[29]

Thus, whereas the *Discourse on Inequality* looked for the source of our chains, the *Social Contract* is devoted to explaining how they can be made legitimate. The very formulation suggests that this is a problem that cannot be solved in a completely satisfactory manner.

Rousseau's solution to the problem of legitimacy is a social contract, which becomes desirable once it has become impossible to remain in the state of nature, consisting of the following terms:

> *Each of us puts his person and all his power in common under the supreme direction of the general will; and in a body we receive each member as an indivisible part of the whole.* (ibid., chap. 6, 361)

[29] In the *Discourse*, Rousseau emphasizes that the train of events that led the human race out of the original state of nature can only be a matter of conjecture. What he is sure about is only that human beings must originally have been little more than animals, and that they are no longer mere animals (*O.C.*, 3:162–63). The conjectural nature of the human history that he describes in that book does not undermine its argument, and that argument is not inconsistent with this statement from the *Social Contract.* The limited scope of the inquiry undertaken here is signaled not only in this quotation, but also by the full title of the book from which it is drawn.

Rousseau does not say that this contract has ever been expressly entered into anywhere, but he insists that it is tacitly recognized everywhere (ibid.).[30] Notwithstanding the obvious similarities with the social contract doctrines of Hobbes and Locke, this legitimizing contract differs from theirs in several respects. I will begin with just one of the differences.

Every right—or, in more precise terms, every bit of strength and freedom—that the individual relinquishes as an individual is completely retained by the same individual in his capacity as a member of the new body formed by the contract (ibid., 360).[31] Precisely because the alienation is both complete and completely mutual, everyone gains additional strength and freedom, and in a formal sense no party to the contract loses any strength or freedom. The completeness of the alienation is necessary, Rousseau explains, because any reservation of rights (or strength and freedom) would leave room for disputes between the whole and its parts, which in turn would lead to a breakdown in the direction of tyranny or anarchy (ibid., 361).[32]

[30] Both the difficulty and the necessity of this tacit recognition are suggested later, when Rousseau says: "In order for a nascent people to be capable of a taste for sound maxims of politics and of following the fundamental rules of political interest (*la raison d'Etat*), the effect would have to become the cause, the social spirit which is to be the work of the institution would have to preside over the institution itself, and men would have to be prior to laws what they should become through the laws" (*S.C.*, bk. 2, chap. 7, *O.C.*, 3:383). Similarly, as Laurence D. Cooper argues in a different context, the rule of philosophers in Plato's *Republic* would seem to be acceptable only to those who had already been ruled by philosophers (*Eros in Plato, Rousseau, and Nietzsche*, 197).

[31] The *Social Contract* contains a few passages that, read in isolation, might suggest that Rousseau believes there are natural or pre-political rights that imply natural or pre-political obligations (bk. 1, chap. 4, *O.C.*, 3:357; chap. 7, 360; chap. 8, 364; chap. 9, 365; bk. 2, chap. 4, 373; bk. 3, chap. 10, 422–23). I believe this inference is unwarranted, and that Rousseau's actual teaching in the *Social Contract* is quite consistent with the implications that I drew from the *Discourse on Inequality*. First, a close look at the references to natural or pre-political rights in the *Social Contract* shows that Rousseau never says that pre-political rights are accompanied by correlative obligations. Second, Rousseau specifically says that conventions and laws are "necessary to combine rights with duties" (ibid., bk. 2, chap. 6, 378). Third, when Rousseau specifies the content of man's pre-political rights, he uses the Hobbesian formulation which, as we have seen, does not imply correlative duties toward other people. See ibid., bk. 1, chap. 8, 364 (referring to man's "natural liberty and an unlimited right to everything that tempts him and that he can reach"). Thus, Rousseau's apparent appeals to natural right, like the parallel appeals in Hobbes and Locke, are potentially misleading. All three authors, however, carefully enable the reader to avoid being misled.

[32] The power of this argument was also acknowledged by Locke, who declared that no political society can exist if *any* of its members retains *any* power to defy its decisions (*Second Treatise*, ¶ 87).

Unlike the social contracts in Hobbes and Locke, this contract implies very little about the goals and characteristics of the polities legitimated by the contract. Whereas Hobbes and Locke both contend that the aim of all civil society is the peace and safety needed for self-preservation and a comfortable life,[33] and that reason instructs us to give our consent to political institutions that serve this purpose, Rousseau's more indefinite formulation is less tethered to the pressing needs of early societies and thus more open to other goals.

Rousseau does agree that peace and safety, and the material goods that conduce to self-preservation, probably did provide the motivation for the first political societies, and he agrees that these benefits always constitute the irreducible minimum goals of any legitimate polity (ibid., bk. 3, chap. 9, 420–21). Nonetheless, Rousseau's formulation of the social contract has a liberating quality that arises from his decision not to focus as much as Locke and Hobbes do on the moment of transition from the state of nature to civil society: whatever the actual origins of any political society may have been, its current legitimacy has to be measured by the desires of its current members. In a different sense, however, Rousseau suggests that Hobbes and Locke offer a false promise of liberation because they neglected the constraints, imposed by nature and circumstance, that might require a people to pursue goals beyond peace and safety in order to attain even those more basic goods (see, e.g., ibid., bk. 2, chap. 11). In both these senses, the *Discourse on Inequality*'s analysis of the long road out of the state of nature prepares the way for the political analysis in the *Social Contract.*

The strength of Rousseau's formula for the social contract lies in its perfect formalism. How could one not consent to an exchange in which one gives up everything only to get it all back and more besides?[34] The harder question is whether such a tacit contract can have much of anything to do with the real world. The natural place to begin considering that question is the central concept of the general will.

Notwithstanding the air of mystery that infuses many discussions of Rousseau's general will, I do not believe that the concept itself is par-

[33] See, for example, *Leviathan*, chap. 17, 128 (first paragraph); *Second Treatise*, ¶ 134. The disagreements between Hobbes and Locke primarily concern the means that are most apt to lead to this end.

[34] This renders Rousseau's claim for tacit consent to his version of the social contract stronger than the parallel claims in Hobbes and Locke.

ticularly difficult to understand.[35] The general will is just what the name implies: it is a will and it is general. This means nothing more than the desire for the common interest, which is something everyone wants wherever people are genuinely cooperating with one another. We all have personal experience with the general will, and with the difference between it and what Rousseau calls the "particular will," which is an individual's desire for what he thinks is in his own best interest (see, e.g., ibid., bk. 1, chap. 7, 363). In order to see why there is nothing mysterious about this, one need only recognize that any individual person can have conflicting wills or desires. We all want what is good for every community that we are a part of, because whatever is good for the community as such is also good for us—and that is true even if we *also* want something else which is not good for the community but which is good for ourselves (see ibid., bk. 4, chap. 1, 438).

Consider a simple illustration based on a family consisting of a father, a mother, and their child. At dinnertime, each of the individuals may have different preferences about what to eat. The mother's perfectly selfish choice might be to go out to a Thai restaurant thirty miles away. The father, who dislikes Thai food and has just returned from the office through horrendous traffic, would prefer to have his wife cook an Italian meal for the family to eat at home. The child's first choice, as always, is the nearby McDonald's.

Since the selfish preferences are all in conflict, this group has a problem that needs to be solved. And we have all seen the problem solved innumerable times. The family might end up deciding to go to McDonald's, with the understanding that they will have Italian food at home tomorrow, and go to the Thai restaurant on Saturday. Or they might decide to have a pizza delivered in, which is acceptable to everyone even though it is not anyone's first choice. Such solutions are driven by a simple fact: each member of the family wants the whole group to have a pleasant meal together. That desire, framed at that level of generality, is a general will.

Of course, the general will may not prevail. The child, for example, might decide that he wants McDonald's more than he wants everyone to have a pleasant meal. So he might refuse to agree to anything else, and try to get his own way through the usual techniques, such as whining and cajoling. This selfish behavior does not mean the general will has

[35] For a detailed textual analysis, to which I am indebted, see Arthur M. Melzer, *The Natural Goodness of Man: On the System of Rousseau's Thought*, 160–69.

ceased to exist. The child probably does want everyone to have a pleasant meal, and he might honestly say so if he were asked. It's just that he wants McDonald's *more* than he wants to achieve the common interest through a mutually satisfactory resolution of the family members' conflicting desires.

Why don't all the members of this family behave like the selfish child, and try hard to satisfy their own first choices every time? The answer has two parts. First, they sometimes (indeed frequently) overcome or suppress their selfish desires in favor of the common interest. Second, they can do that because the common interest is also in each of their individual interests. And that is ultimately because the two adults think they are better off maintaining their cooperative arrangement rather than going their separate ways. If that ceased to be true, the family would dissolve, as of course families sometimes do.

Another possibility is that one member of the family could acquire sufficient power to consistently impose his individual preferences on the others. This could happen, for example, if the mother was economically dependent on the father, and his affection for her was relatively weak. In that case, we might observe something analogous to a despotic government, where people are subjected to a particular will other than their own, rather than to the general will.[36]

One last point is important for understanding Rousseau. The general will has to be understood as aiming at something that the members of an association actually want, which is not necessarily what is best for them. If the people in my hypothetical illustration really knew what was best for themselves, they might have made a completely different choice, such as a vegetarian casserole with yogurt for dessert. Rousseau emphatically does not claim that legitimate rule is the rule of wisdom.[37] At the same time, Rousseau recognizes the need for political leadership that will induce people to want what is good for them: legitimacy is not a sufficient criterion,

[36] The child obviously is subject to the despotic government of the adults, but their particular wills are ordinarily tempered fairly strongly by natural affection.

[37] See *S.C.*, bk. 2, chap. 12, *O.C.*, 3:394 ("[I]n any case, a people is always the master of changing its laws, even the best ones; for if it pleases it to harm itself, who has the right to prevent it from doing so?"); bk. 1, chap. 7, 362 (denying that even the social contract itself can be obligatory on the people as a body); bk. 3, chap. 18, 436 (same).

and perhaps not even the most important criterion, for evaluating political institutions.[38]

If the concept of the general will is easy to understand from our ordinary experience, it is also not very difficult to understand why one might regard the general will as the unique basis for political legitimacy. Once one concludes that human beings are naturally non-political, convention or agreement is the only possible basis other than force or fraud for any enduring political association. And without some common interest, there could be no solid basis for an agreement to enter or remain in a durable association.[39]

What is much more difficult to see is how political societies could actually operate under what Rousseau calls "the supreme direction of the general will." The key to understanding Rousseau's position begins with recognizing that he considers it impossible for any polity to be always or exclusively under the direction of the general will. For that reason, this standard of legitimacy may look like the spurious mirror image of the spurious standard in Hobbes. Whereas Hobbes drains legitimacy of its

[38] See, for example, ibid., bk. 3, chap. 5, 407, where Rousseau acknowledges the force of the view that the wise should rule for the benefit of the ruled, but then immediately qualifies his endorsement:

> In a word, the best and most natural order is to have the wisest govern the multitude, when one is sure that they will govern for its benefit and not for their own; one must not vainly multiply devices, nor do with twenty thousand men what a hundred well chosen men can do even better. But it must be noted that here the corporate interest [of the governors] begins to guide the public force less by the rule of the general will, and that another inevitable decline elevates (*enlève*) a part of the executive power above the laws.

In two somewhat different contexts, Rousseau refers to Plato's *Statesman* in support of the proposition that a human being truly qualified to rule must be very rare (ibid, bk. 2, chap. 7, 381; bk. 3, chap. 7, 412). Drawing this inference from the text of the dialogue is perfectly plausible. Rousseau's own related conclusions are also perfectly plausible: someone qualified to be a founding lawgiver must be even more rare, and seeking to approximate the rule of wisdom through the institution of monarchy involves self-deception. Rousseau may also mean for the reader to draw other inferences from the fact that he twice alludes to the *Statesman*. One possibility is that he ultimately shares the Eleatic Stranger's implicit depreciation of the significance of political legitimacy, or the consent of the governed. As we will see below, Rousseau frequently indicates that even tolerably wise rulers are not and should not be passive agents of the general will.

[39] See ibid, bk. 2, chap. 1, 368 ("if the opposition of particular interests made the establishment of societies necessary, it is the agreement of these same interests that has made it possible").

normal meaning by claiming to show that no actual ruler is illegitimate, Rousseau's standard is one that cannot be met by any actual ruler.

Some societies, however, are guided by the general will more often, or more consistently, or on more important matters than other societies. Legitimacy then becomes a matter of more and less, rather than yes or no. This understanding of legitimacy is hard to avoid if one is truly intent on "taking men as they are, and laws as they can be" (*S.C.*, bk. 1, exordium, *O.C.*, 3:351). It also leads Rousseau to challenge some of our liberal assumptions about the meaning of political liberty.

Above all, he takes much more seriously than liberal thought usually does the inherent and unceasing conflict between the common interests that we share and the naturally selfish interests we all have, and the extreme difficulty of reconciling them through an objective or natural concept of justice.[40] He therefore rejects the notion that political life should concern itself only with aggregating the private preferences of the citizenry, or channeling our naturally selfish desires into pathways that will produce ever greater wealth and material comfort for everyone. The liberal trust in the beneficent effects of unleashed human selfishness, whether in markets or in pluralist politics, is something that Rousseau regarded as a prescription that would ultimately aggravate the disease.

### *Rousseau's Pessimism about Liberalism*

One can and should ask whether subsequent history has shown that Rousseau was wrong to regard the liberal faith as misguided. We Americans have especially strong reasons for doing so, and it is true that Rousseau had nothing to say about the future prospects of England's colonies in the New World.

At the end of an impressive effort to demonstrate the systematic coherence of Rousseau's political philosophy, Arthur M. Melzer finds that philosophy "false" (*Natural Goodness*, 283). He offers two related reasons

[40] See, for example, ibid., bk. 2, chap. 6, 378 ("All justice comes from God, he alone is its source; but if we knew how to receive it from so high, we would need neither government nor laws. Without doubt there is a universal justice emanating from reason alone; but in order for this justice to be accepted among us, it has to be reciprocal. Considering things in human terms, the laws of justice are vain among men for lack of natural sanctions; they merely bring benefits to the wicked and harm to the just when the one observes them with everyone without anyone observing them with him."); *Poland*, chap. 12, *O.C.*, 3:1013.

for this conclusion: it has been empirically disproven, and Rousseau was wrong to believe that man is naturally asocial.

Melzer makes three empirical claims. First, he criticizes Rousseau's statement that: "All other things being equal, the government under which … the citizens populate and multiply the most is infallibly the best" (*Natural Goodness*, 288, quoting *S.C.*, bk. 3, chap. 9). Melzer maintains that Rousseau "is confident that his principles of political right will pass this empirical test," and that Rousseau was wrong because eighteenth-century Europe was more populous under monarchical rule (which Rousseau disfavored) than it was under the ancient republics (which he favored) (ibid., 288–89).[41] This critique is based, I believe, on a misunderstanding of Rousseau's text.

Rousseau's principles do not imply that republican government is always preferable to a monarchy. In the very chapter that Melzer criticizes, Rousseau begins by saying that an absolute answer to the question of the best government is impossible because "it has as many good solutions as there are possible combinations in the absolute and relative positions of peoples" (*S.C.*, bk. 3, chap. 9, *O.C.*, 3:419).[42] Nor is Rousseau presenting an "empirical test" that his principles of political right must pass. Increasing population is a sign (*un signe*) of good government, not a "test" of Rousseau's principles. He expressly says, moreover, that it only applies when all other things are equal, which they seldom are. Accordingly, he notes that the people enjoyed relative prosperity under corrupt governments in ancient Greece, medieval Florence, and seventeenth-century France (ibid., bk. 3, chap. 9, 420n).[43] Governments that exploit and oppress the people are among the most significant causes of depopulation, but there are many other possible causes.

[41] He adds that France was undergoing something of a population boom at the time Rousseau was writing (*Natural Goodness*, 289).

[42] It is true that Rousseau believes that monarchical government is inherently inferior to republican government (*S.C.*, bk. 3, chap. 6, *O.C.*, 3:410). But that does not mean that he thinks republican government is always possible: "People are always disputing about the best form of Government, without recognizing that each of them is the best in certain cases, and the worst in others" (ibid., chap. 3, 403).

[43] Elsewhere, he acknowledges that special factors allowed the population to increase even under the extreme despotism of China (*Mountain*, lett. 8, *O.C.*, 3:843n). The various exceptions that Rousseau mentions involve periods during which would-be tyrants were distracted from oppressing the people because they were fighting among themselves.

Rousseau's principal point in this passage is to distinguish the wealth or brilliance of a nation, which is not a reliable sign of good government, from the prosperity of the people.[44] Taking population trends as a generally reliable sign of genuine prosperity makes perfectly good sense.[45] When people are so poor that they fear for their ability to support their children, they are apt to raise fewer offspring. Conversely, when people are so obsessed with acquiring and consuming wealth that they do not expect the benefits of having numerous children to outweigh the burdens, they can be expected to reduce the size of their families.[46] In any event, Rousseau has independent and defensible reasons for regarding extreme poverty and extreme acquisitiveness as primarily the effects of unhealthy political institutions. Exceptions to the population metric, some of which Rousseau himself expressly acknowledged and explained, cannot prove those reasons false.

Melzer's second empirical claim is that the modern phenomenon of nationalism refutes Rousseau's belief that "people will only obey where they obey only themselves—the general will" (*Natural Goodness*, 289). I have not been able to find this claim anywhere in Rousseau. Melzer also contends that Rousseau stated "systematically and unequivocally that human beings, naturally asocial, can be transformed into genuine patriots only in the context of a small, face-to-face, egalitarian, non-commercial, highly intrusive, democratically ruled city-state" (ibid., 290). This is an

[44] In the *Social Contract*, according to Melzer, "self-preservation is the fundamental end of the state and the goal from which the terms of legitimacy are deduced" (*Natural Goodness*, 288). In the passage Melzer refers to, however, Rousseau says that the end or goal of the political association is "the preservation *and the prosperity* of its members" (*S.C.*, bk. 3, chap. 9, *O.C.*, 419–20, emphasis added).

[45] Some years after the *Social Contract* was published, Adam Smith reached the same conclusion: "The most decisive mark of the prosperity of any country is the increase of the number of its inhabitants" (*Wealth of Nations*, bk. 1, chap. 8, ¶ 23). Smith's analysis is more detailed and economically sophisticated than Rousseau's, but he agrees with Rousseau's central political point: a wealthier society is not a better society if the wealth is concentrated in a few hands. "No society can surely be flourishing and happy, of which the far greater part of the members are poor and miserable" (ibid., ¶ 36).

[46] One important benefit of having children has traditionally been the expectation that adults will support their aged parents. This benefit has been much reduced in modern welfare states. Obvious advantages arise from making government the default caregiver of the old and disabled, but it can hardly be denied that it reduces the incentive to have children. And it remains to be seen whether entitlement systems of the modern type can be maintained indefinitely without leading to a kind of demographic suicide. For further discussion, see the analysis of Plato's *Laws* and the *Letter to d'Alembert* in Chapter 4.

overstatement that fails to take account, for example, of *Considerations on the Government of Poland*. Notwithstanding modern nationalism, moreover, we now seem closer than ever to observing what Rousseau thought he saw developing: "Today there are no longer Frenchmen, Germans, Spaniards, even Englishmen, whatever is said; there are only Europeans" (*Poland*, chap. 3, *O.C.*, 3:960). "European patriotism" is a phenomenon that has yet to be observed.

Melzer's third empirical claim is based on what he calls "[t]he most massive, most revealing, and also the most damning prediction that Rousseau is led to make on the basis of his principles, [namely] his whole pessimistic assessment of the future of Europe" (*Natural Goodness*, 290). Melzer agrees that Rousseau was right to see an advanced state of corruption in the Europe of his time. What damns Rousseau's philosophy, in his view, is that Rousseau did not foresee "the extraordinary renewal and self-regeneration of the West, and eventually [] the spread of this regeneration around the globe" (ibid.). Rousseau certainly made predictions about the future of Europe that did not come true as quickly as he expected, and I think this is Melzer's strongest argument. It is, moreover, one to which any halfway patriotic American must feel especially attracted. But it is not as strong as it may seem.

In the first place, Rousseau's principles of political right are not the basis for his predictions. But even if we treat the *Social Contract* as a work of positive political science, which in some respects it is, mistaken forecasts by its author would not necessarily condemn the principles of political *right* that it seeks to establish. At some point, of course, massively mistaken predictions certainly would call the underlying analysis into serious doubt. The question for us, then, is whether Rousseau's mistaken predictions were of a kind that proves the falsity of his principles.

Melzer's claim about the regeneration of the West and its spread around the globe must have seemed especially plausible when his book was published, just after the collapse of the Soviet Union. That was when one of Melzer's fellow political theorists announced the end of history, by which he meant the Hegelian "end point of mankind's ideological evolution and the universalization of Western liberal democracy as the final form of human government."[47] At the time, serious people thought this

[47] Francis Fukuyama, "The End of History?," 4. Fukuyama expanded his argument in *The End of History and the Last Man*.

was an illusion,[48] and it has become more dubious, to say the least, in succeeding years.

This is not to deny that Rousseau failed to foresee some important developments, not the least of which is the United States itself. Nor will I predict that our own future will necessarily be one only of advancing corruption and decline. It is, however, premature to say that Rousseau's philosophy has been disproven by little more than two centuries of what Melzer calls "liberal, welfare-capitalist, representative, mass democracy" (*Natural Goodness*, 290). Sparta and the Roman Republic lasted far longer before they were undone by the corruption to which Rousseau thought every political body must eventually succumb. Perhaps our form of governance is immune to the mortal degeneration that Rousseau considered inescapable. Once welfare-capitalist mass democracies have proved more durable than Rome and Sparta, it will be safer to draw this conclusion than it is today.

Having concluded that Rousseau "takes a far too narrow and skeptical view of what is possible in politics," Melzer finds the cause of this mistake in Rousseau's belief that man is not naturally social (ibid., 291). For reasons set out in Chapters 2 and 3 of this book, I do not believe that natural sociality, in any stronger sense than Rousseau himself recognized, has been established by verifiable evidence. Melzer's empirical critique therefore rests precariously on the inconclusive historical evidence summarized above.

Melzer supplements his empirical argument with appeals to authority, declaring that "most premodern as well as contemporary theorists have [acknowledged] that man has within him at least the potential for genuine sentiments of cooperation, deference, emulation, and obedience which are not reducible to motives of selfish exchange or identification" (ibid.). Rousseau, however, affirmatively and emphatically agrees that man has the potential for such sentiments, which were vividly displayed in ancient Rome and Sparta. Melzer, moreover, is compelled for obvious reasons to omit the early modern theorists from the authorities to whom he is appealing. If Rousseau mistakenly concluded that man is naturally asocial, a far worse mistake was made by those thinkers who did not recognize the potential source of social virtues in what Rousseau called natural pity. But the principles of those early modern theorists underlie the same liberal

[48] See, for example, Samuel P. Huntington, "The Clash of Civilizations?"; Samuel P. Huntington, *The Clash of Civilizations and the Remaking of World Order*.

democracies whose successes supposedly refute Rousseau. I cannot see how one can have it both ways.[49]

As for the premodern thinkers to whom Melzer refers, none was a proponent of "liberal, welfare-capitalist, representative, mass democracy." Melzer assumes throughout his book that all of these premodern thinkers fundamentally disagree with Rousseau. One goal of my book is to reopen that question, at least with respect to Plato and perhaps with respect to Aristotle as well.

### *Rousseau's Alternative to Liberalism*

The most important element of Rousseau's proposed alternative to our liberalism involves the need for active political measures aimed at inducing citizens to subordinate their selfish interests to the common interest. We all know, from experience in our families, that it is perfectly possible for such mutually beneficial self-suppression to occur. But whereas families are held together in part by natural ties of affection, this is not true of political associations.[50] Rousseau denies that arguments based on self-interest, like the arguments we find in Hobbes and Locke, are sufficient to produce any real community. In order to prevent what he thought would inevitably become a complex and ultimately self-defeating system of mutual exploitation, Rousseau concluded that it is necessary to create *unnatural* ties of affection among citizens through a thoroughly politicized system of education. That is what Sparta did preeminently well, and Rousseau contends that it is not altogether impossible even in some modern bourgeois societies.[51]

[49] Throughout his book, Melzer focuses heavily on Rousseau's agreements and disagreements with Hobbes. He gives no attention to Adam Smith, who may present the most serious of all modern challenges to Rousseau's political philosophy. An adequate analysis of that challenge would have to take full account of the many important points of agreement, as well as the disagreements, between Smith and Rousseau.

[50] For elaborations of this point, see *S.C.*, bk. 1, chap. 2, *O.C.*, 3:352; *Economy*, *O.C.*, 3:241–44. Joel Schwartz points out that Rousseau's understanding of female human nature, according to which it is even more difficult for women than for men to generalize their wills beyond their own family, points toward the advisability of limiting their direct role in public affairs (*The Sexual Politics of Jean-Jacques Rousseau*, 41–44). In his writings on political legitimacy, however, Rousseau refrains from drawing this conclusion because it is not implied by the principles of political right.

[51] See, for example, *Economy*, *O.C.*, 3:260–62; *Poland*, chap. 4.

We children of liberalism tend to be scandalized by such proposals, whether we meet them in Rousseau or Plato, but perhaps for the wrong reasons. According to Rousseau, the self-discipline that is required for healthy political life must overwhelmingly be the product of an education that arises from a shared social consensus, not from the kind of coercive reeducation projects that we observed in the totalitarian regimes of the last century. It is true that a highly politicized form of public education can be used as an instrument of oppression (in violation of the general will), or as an instrument that makes possible the most ferocious and selfish behavior toward outsiders (often in accord with the general will). But it is not as clear as we sometimes think that such phenomena are necessarily concomitants of a highly politicized civic life. Nor is the absence of the kind of educational institutions favored by Rousseau a guarantee against internal oppression or outward aggression. Ancient Athens, for example, could be no less aggressive toward its neighbors than Sparta was. Athens, moreover, "was not in fact a democracy, but a very tyrannical aristocracy, governed by intellectuals (*savans*) and orators" (*Economy*, *O.C.*, 3:246). And countless despotic regimes have been quite content to oppress their subjects without making any effort to educate them at all.

The consensus underlying the kind of civic education recommended by Rousseau cannot be formed by political or governmental actions alone. The real spring of genuine social cohesion, where it exists, is not in institutional mechanisms, but rather in the influence of those who shape public opinion, either at a founding moment or in the course of a people's history (see, e.g., *S.C.*, bk. 2, chap. 12, *O.C.*, 3:394). In the most practically important respects, it is not the tacit social contract itself that produces political liberty, but the leadership of those who mold a people so as to make it capable of fulfilling that implied contract. A Moses, a Lycurgus, or a Calvin, not a crowd of would-be bourgeois desperate to escape the state of nature, is the indispensable element in establishing the social contract (see, e.g., ibid., chap. 7; *Economy*, *O.C.*, 3:251–52).

Rousseau's focus on the importance of shared political sentiments as a prerequisite for political self-government also leads him to revive another commonplace of ancient political thought, namely skepticism about the possibility of maintaining free or republican institutions in large polities. This skepticism did not lead Rousseau to the conclusion that large republics were strictly and necessarily impossible, and he believed that federalism might provide a way to combine the advantages of small republics with those of a large state (see, e.g., *S.C.*, bk. 3, chap. 15, *O.C*, 3:431n*). This aspect of Rousseau's thought, along with his attention to cultivating public virtue, produces a real kinship between him and our Anti-Federalists.

To the extent one believes that the Anti-Federalist position was not completely defeated by the adoption of our federal Constitution and by the changes that occurred after the Civil War, Rousseau's political analysis may still have relevance for Americans today. What makes this particularly true is Rousseau's discussion of the fundamental difference between what he calls the "sovereign" and what he calls the "government."

Perhaps surprisingly, given what I have already said about the perpetual conflict between the general will and particular wills, Rousseau concluded that the greatest obstacle to the effective political expression of the general will is competition from *other general wills*, or in terminology more familiar to us, the problem of faction.[52]

In the *Social Contract*, Rousseau defines sovereignty as the exercise of the general will, and the product of an exercise of the general will as a "law" in the strict sense of that term.[53] For the will to be general, it must be general not only in its source—reflecting something that everybody without exception wants—but also in its object:

> [W]hen the whole people enacts statutes for the whole people it considers only itself, and if a relation is then formed, it is a relation between the entire object from one point of view and the entire object from another point of view, without any division of the whole … [S]ince the law joins the universality of the will and that of the object, what any man, whoever he may be, orders on his own authority is not a law; what even the Sovereign orders regarding a particular object is not a law either, but a decree, nor is it an act of sovereignty but of magistracy. (ibid., bk. 2, chap. 6, 379)

One consequence of this analysis is that no society can actually be governed by the sovereign. Legislative authority, or the power to make law in the strict sense, belongs and can only belong to the people as a whole. The power to carry out these laws, which Rousseau calls the executive power,

[52] For the enduring significance of this problem, one need only refer to *Federalist 10* and the academic literature of our own time in the field of public choice. It is worth noting that Rousseau had already articulated Madison's key insight: "if there are partial societies, their number must be multiplied, and inequality among them prevented, as was done by Solon, Numa, Servius" (*S.C.*, bk. 2, chap. 3, *O.C.*, 3:372). As his allusion to ancient Romans indicates, Rousseau would expect us to think for ourselves about the best way to go about multiplying factions in various circumstances, as Madison certainly did.

[53] See ibid., bk. 2, chap. 1, 368 (sovereignty); chap. 6, 379 (law).

necessarily has particular objects and therefore cannot constitute an exercise of sovereignty. Accordingly, there must be what Rousseau calls "government," a body of people whose function is to act as the intermediary between the people in their sovereign capacity and the people in their individual capacities (see ibid., bk. 3, chap. 1, 396). Even if the members of the sovereign and the government were precisely identical (what we might call pure democracy), they would still be performing different functions.

The distinction between the sovereign and the government may be the most important in the *Social Contract*, for it illuminates what Rousseau regarded as the most enduring and intractable practical problem of political organization. That problem can be articulated in the following way. Pure democracy, which in theory might seem capable of carrying out the social contract most perfectly, in fact cannot do so because the people's constant and repeated attention to particular objects will inevitably stimulate the activity of their particular wills, and thereby result in the corruption of the sovereign. Thus, even aside from the practical difficulties that must arise in any but the very smallest communities, pure democracy is an inherently self-destructive form of self-governance. "If there were a people of Gods, it would govern itself Democratically. A Government so perfect is not suited to men."[54]

That means that the sovereign must delegate the business of government to a smaller portion of the citizenry. But once that is done, this smaller body will necessarily generate a general will of its own, corresponding to the common interests of the members of the government, which will act as a particular will in relation to the sovereign. Because the concentration of wills increases their relative force, governments will always tend to undermine the sovereign:

> In a perfect legislation, the particular or individual will [of the magistrates, or officers of the government] should be null, the Government's own corporate will very subordinate, and consequently the general or sovereign will should always be dominant and the sole rule of all the others.
>
> According to the natural order, on the contrary, these different wills become more active to the extent they become more concentrated. Thus the general will is always the weakest, the corporate will has the second rank, and the particular will the first of all: so that in the Government each member is first himself, and then a Magistrate, and then a citizen. A grada-

[54] Ibid., bk. 3, chap. 4, 406.

> tion directly opposed to what the social order demands. (ibid., bk. 3, chap. 2, 401)[55]

A number of consequences follow from this analysis, some of which are quite compatible with our liberal presuppositions and traditions, and some of which are not. Perhaps most obviously, the inherently usurpative tendencies of all governments point toward the need for devices like the separation and balancing of powers, and periodic elections.[56] Rousseau endorses the use of such devices, without claiming that any of them are matters of principle or more than matters of expedience. This puts him in substantial agreement with *The Federalist* on what may seem to be a surprising range of issues.

In another respect, however, Rousseau departs dramatically from our tradition:

> It does not suffice for the people assembled to have once settled the constitution of the State by giving its sanction to a body of laws: it does not suffice for it to have established a perpetual Government or to have provided once and for all for the election of magistrates. Besides extraordinary assemblies that unforeseen circumstances might demand, there must be fixed and periodic assemblies that nothing can abolish or prorogue, so that on the designated day the people is legitimately convoked by law, without need of any other formal convocation. (ibid., bk. 3, chap. 13, 426)

Rousseau devotes several chapters of the *Social Contract* to exploring this proposition and defending it against obvious objections about its

[55] See also ibid., bk. 3, chap. 10, 421:

> As the particular will incessantly acts against the general will, so the Government makes a constant effort against the Sovereignty. The greater this effort grows, the more the constitution is debased, and since there is no other corporate will here to balance the will of the Prince [i.e., the governors or magistrates] by resisting it, sooner or later the Prince must succeed in oppressing the Sovereign and breaking the Social treaty. This is the inherent and inevitable vice which relentlessly tends to enfeeble the body politic from its birth, just as old age and death destroy a man's body.

[56] See, for example, ibid., bk. 3, chap. 5, 406–07 (periodic elections); chap. 7, 413–14 (separation of powers). See also *Poland*, chap. 7, *O.C.*, 3:975–78; chap. 8, 993–94. Rousseau also advocates some of the same devices that we use to promote stability, such as supermajority voting rules for especially important decisions (*S.C.*, bk. 4, chap. 2, *O.C.*, 3:441).

practicality.[57] The theme of this extended treatment essentially boils down to the strong claim that political legitimacy, or what we might call political liberty, has a real price, particularly in terms of what might be called private or personal liberty. In what looks like a direct slap at us, Rousseau writes:

> Any law that the People has not ratified in person is null; it is not a law. The English people thinks it is free; it is greatly deceived, it is free only during the election of members of Parliament; as soon as they are elected, it is a slave, it is nothing. In the short moments of its liberty, the use it makes of it shows that it well deserves to lose it. (ibid., bk. 3, chap. 15, 430)

This denunciation of our representative form of government is matched by a contemptuous dismissal of our reasons for adopting that form:

> It is the tumult of commerce and the arts, it is the avid interest in gain, it is softness and love of comforts that exchange personal services for money. One gives up a part of one's profit in order to increase it at one's leisure. Give money, and soon you will have chains. This word *finance* is a slave's word; it is unknown in the City. In a truly free State the citizens do everything with their hands and nothing with money: Far from paying to be exempted from their duties, they would pay to fulfill them themselves. I am very far from the commonly held ideas; I believe that corvées are less contrary to liberty than taxes. (ibid., 429)

From these and other passages, it is easy to conclude that Rousseau would regard the United States as much more like the Roman Empire than the Roman Republic, and that his political science has little more to teach us about how to conduct our affairs than his description of the state of nature does. Just as Rousseau clearly believes that the human race could not return to the state of nature, he also believes that the corruption and decline of free societies are inevitable. Thus, it might seem, we might as well enjoy our bread and circuses, leaving Rousseau's lessons—if they have any truth in them—to be learned by those who live in circumstances happy enough to permit their implementation.

[57] See *S.C.*, bk. 2, chaps. 1–2; bk. 3, chaps. 12–15; bk. 3, chap. 18. In *Rousseau and Representation*, Richard Fralin identifies a number of seemingly inconsistent statements and inadequate arguments on this topic in Rousseau's various writings. In the end, he concludes that Rousseau's views changed over time and that Rousseau never escaped from the grip of a fundamental ambivalence about the value of direct citizen participation in the political process. For reasons that I will sketch out below, I disagree with these conclusions.

I think this conclusion would be a mistake. It is true that Rousseau, like Montesquieu and many earlier thinkers, believes that political liberty is impossible in many circumstances.[58] But I think it is equally true that Rousseau believed that *perfectly* legitimate political institutions are *always* impossible. The root of the problem lies in the unnaturalness of political society, which requires that a conventional or legal equality replace the natural inequalities of physical and mental power among people, and which requires the cultivation of unnatural affections for one's fellow citizens. The impossibility of a final or complete victory in this war against nature is reflected in Rousseau's rejection of the possibility of pure democracy. *All* institutional arrangements are necessarily compromises that have to be evaluated in practical terms: Do they increase or decrease the likelihood that political outcomes will reflect the general will? That means that there can be few, if any, absolute affirmative requirements about institutional arrangements,[59] although there can of course be many institutions

[58] See, for example, *S.C.*, bk. 3, chap. 8, *O.C.*, 3:414 (citing Montesquieu for the proposition that "[l]iberty not being the fruit of all Climates, it is not within the reach of all peoples"). In a lengthy polemic about Genevan politics written after the *Social Contract* was condemned by the authorities in his native city, Rousseau warned against efforts to model institutions for modern bourgeois societies directly on those adopted by ancient peoples (*Mountain*, lett. 9, *O.C.*, 3:880–82). But he did not conclude that freedom has now become impossible. Instead he argued that institutional mechanisms must be adapted to the changed situation:

> Not being idle as the ancient Peoples were, you [Genevans, who are always occupied with private and commercial interests] cannot ceaselessly occupy yourselves with the Government as they did: but by the very fact that you can less constantly keep watch over it, it should be instituted in such a way that it might be easier for you to see its intrigues and provide against abuses. Every public care that your interest demands should be made so much easier for you to fulfill since it is a care that costs you and that you do not make willingly. For to wish to unburden yourselves of them completely is to wish to cease being free. (ibid., 881)

[59] It is sometimes said that Rousseau objects to representative legislatures on the purely theoretical ground that will by its nature cannot be represented. See, for example, Fralin, *Rousseau and Representation*, 81–82. The very passage in which Rousseau makes an argument against the possibility of the general will's being alienated, however, goes on to add: "This is not to say that the commands of the chiefs may not be taken for general wills, as long as the sovereign is free to oppose them and does not do so" (*S.C.*, bk. 2, chap. 1, *O.C.*, 3:369–58). It is certainly true that will, unlike power, cannot be alienated, or represented in one technical sense of the term. But so long as representatives are understood as agents of the sovereign rather than as possessors of sovereignty itself, this theoretical objection to representative legislatures disappears. Although Rousseau does say that agents of the sovereign

whose gross illegitimacy is manifest. Notwithstanding Rousseau's statement, quoted above, that the English are slaves, he elsewhere says that they "are closer to liberty than all the others," referring apparently to other large European nations (ibid., bk. 1, chap. 6, 361–62n).

Right in the middle of his extended discussion of the need for direct enactment of all laws by the assembled people, Rousseau reminds us rather dramatically that perfect legitimacy is impossible. Sparta—which Rousseau throughout his writings treats as the freest people that ever existed—was able to maintain itself only through the use of slavery, an institution that Rousseau argues is always and everywhere illegitimate.[60] Thus, Rousseau believes that he can, without being inconsistent, offer the highest praise for a polity that included, and indeed was founded on, a fundamentally illegitimate institution.

One might belittle the significance of Rousseau's remarks condemning slavery on the ground that slaves (like foreigners and domestic animals) are outside the polity and therefore cannot affect the legitimacy of the relations among those who have contracted to form the polity. Whatever the force of this objection may be, Rousseau gives other indications in the *Social Contract* that his insistence on what we would call direct democracy is deliberately overstated. In the course of his discussion of Roman institutions, whose details he pointedly commends to the attention of a

"cannot conclude anything definitively," he later makes it clear that the real theoretical touchstone of legitimacy is consistency with the general will, not such formalities as in-person ratification (ibid., bk. 3, chap. 15, 429–30; bk. 4, chap. 2, 440–41).

[60] For example, *S.C.*, bk. 1, chap. 4; bk. 3, chap. 15; see also *Discourse on the Sciences and the Arts*, *O.C.*, 3:24n** (suggesting, with Montaigne, that the educational regimen of Lycurgus was "in truth monstrous in its perfection"). Rousseau's precise argument against the legitimacy of slavery is that it would have to be based on an absurd agreement in which one party gives up everything and receives nothing in return. It is therefore a kind of mirror image of what Rousseau presents as the genuine social contract. In both cases, Rousseau's argument is highly formalistic, with only an ambiguous connection to political practice. The argument applies, moreover, only to slavery in the narrowest sense of the term. It does not rule out indentured servitude, for example, or even forms of slavery for life that offer economic opportunities and some protections rooted in law or custom. Cf., for example, Morris Silver, "Contractual Slavery in the Roman Economy." Rousseau's deeper argument against slavery extends to a much wider range of relationships of dependency. The conclusion of that argument is stated most concisely in the *Emile*: "Not having any morality, dependence on things does not impair liberty and does not engender vices. Being disordered, dependence on men engenders them all, and by it master and slave are mutually depraved" (*O.C.*, 4:311, Bloom, 85, footnote referring to the *Social Contract* omitted).

"judicious reader,"[61] Rousseau describes without disapproval an extreme form of malapportionment (supposedly adopted by Servius under a military pretext) that effectively gave a hugely disproportionate share of legislative power to the wealthiest elements in the society and effectively deprived the urban poor of any power at all (ibid., bk. 4, chap. 4, 47–48).

Rousseau's tacit approval of a trick designed to concentrate political power in the more stable elements of society, while maintaining a kind of formal equality that gave every citizen the vote, is a striking indication that we should not take at face value his statement that genuine laws can only be enacted by the assembled people. If we go back to Rousseau's conception of the social contract itself, its crucial feature is that legitimate political rule consists of rule "under the supreme direction of the general will." Rousseau's later claim that the only legitimate laws are those adopted by the people in person is not a necessary consequence of the terms of the social contract, for the general will *could* guide a representative assembly or even a single representative like a monarch.[62] A representative body might not be likely to adopt measures dictated by the general will as often or as consistently as an assembly of the people, but it is not inherently precluded from doing so. And, as Rousseau acknowledges, even the assembled people are perfectly capable of *failing* to express the general will (ibid., bk. 4, chap. 1, 438).

This last point leads to another reason for not treating popular assemblies as the *sine qua non* of legitimate laws. Rousseau is fond of saying that the people can never be corrupted, but can easily be deceived.[63] One obvious implication of this is that the government can, and can be expected to, make efforts to deceive the people into adopting or going along with measures that are good for the government and bad for the community. Hence, Rousseau's emphasis on the usefulness of convening the people

[61] *S.C.*, bk. 4, chap. 3, *O.C.*, 3:443. The only other place where Rousseau makes such a remark is when he introduces his technical discussion of the relation between the sovereign and the government (ibid., bk. 3, chap. 1, 395). Rousseau generally treats Sparta as a model when discussing the molding of genuine citizens, and Rome as a model when discussing institutions of governance.

[62] Rousseau expressly acknowledges this point in the *Discourse on Political Economy* (*O.C.*, 3:250–51).

[63] For example, *S.C.*, bk. 2, chap. 3, *O.C.*, 3:371; bk. 2, chap. 6, 380; *Poland*, chap. 7, *O.C.*, 3:978. These statements presuppose that the people really are a people, not just a collection of individuals who happen to be subject to a common ruler.

regularly for what amount to votes of confidence or no-confidence in the government (ibid., bk. 3, chap. 18, 435–36).[64] A less obvious implication, however, is that the government will also have the ability to deceive the people and manipulate them into adopting measures that are *good* for the community, but which would likely not be adopted except for this manipulative behavior.

The most dramatic examples of this phenomenon occur when a people receives its formative laws from one of those rare founding legislators like Lycurgus, who obtain consent by falsely claiming that the laws they are promulgating were actually dictated by the gods (ibid., bk. 2, chap. 7, 383–84). But the same kind of thing can happen later, in more routine circumstances, as when governments design tax systems that are meant to prevent excessive economic inequality from arising.[65] This example is particularly revealing because it calls attention to an important feature of Rousseau's discussion of sovereignty and government, namely that he never draws a really clear distinction between those matters that must be governed by law (and thus supposedly require direct action by the assembled people) and those matters that may and should be handled by regulations adopted by the government.

At the extremes, it is clear that some matters fall into one category or the other. The basic constitutive decisions of the society, such as whether to adopt an aristocratic or monarchic form of government, would require

[64] Elsewhere, Rousseau provides a more general theoretical statement that explains why periodic popular assemblies can be important, though not absolutely indispensable:

> The Legislative power consists in two inseparable things: to make the Laws and to maintain them; that is to say, to have supervision over the executive power. There is no State in the world in which the Sovereign does not have this supervision. Without that, all connection, all subordination between these two powers being missing, the latter would not depend on the other; execution would have no necessary relation to the Laws; the *Law* would only be a word, and this word would signify nothing. (*Mountain*, lett. 7, *O.C.*, 3:826)

[65] "It is, therefore, one of the most important tasks of *government* to prevent extreme inequality of fortunes, not by taking treasures away from those who possess them, but by taking away from everyone the means of accumulating them, nor by building poorhouses, but by guaranteeing the citizens against becoming poor" (*Economy*, *O.C.*, 3:258, emphasis added). See also ibid., 277–78, where Rousseau argues that luxury taxes do not require the consent of the sovereign because they are really voluntary contributions to the public fisc by people who choose to acquire things that they do not need. This sophism has a kinship with Lycurgus' much bigger lie about the divine origin of the laws he promulgated.

action by the sovereign, though even here substantive consistency with the general will, rather than the formality of a popular assembly, is more important. At the other extreme, Rousseau tells us that decisions directed at particular individuals, such as the condemnation of a criminal, can only be taken by the government (ibid., bk. 2, chap. 5, 377). But in many cases it will not be clear which category a certain matter belongs in, as for example when a tax system employs general rules that will have foreseeable effects on particular people.[66]

Perhaps even more strikingly, Rousseau advocates the adoption of laws that provide the government with authority to convene assemblies of the people and to set the agenda for such assemblies, and that forbid the people from convening without authorization from the government. He purports to make an exception for the regularly scheduled assemblies, but he qualifies this exception by praising the Roman practice of holding assemblies only when the auguries were favorable, which enabled "the Senate [to hold] in check a proud and restless people and when necessary [to temper] the ardor of seditious Tribunes" (ibid., bk. 4, chap. 4, 449). In other words, the Roman Senate tricked the people about the appropriate occasions for assemblies, using the same technique that Lycurgus adopted in persuading the Spartans to adopt his laws. And rightly so, according to Rousseau.[67]

The appropriate conclusion to draw, I think, is that Rousseau's principles require that what we would call direct democracy—namely, the adoption of general laws by the entire people—always has to be recognized as a desirable possibility, and that real efforts ought to be made to put it into actual practice as a check on the usurpative nature of all governments. Contrary to some exaggerated statements in the *Social Contract*, however, I do not think that Rousseau's principles require us to conclude that what we call representative government—where elected conventions or legislatures are delegated the authority to adopt general laws or even to adopt or modify the constitution—necessarily violates the principles of political right or legitimacy. Popular assemblies are desirable as a prudential check

[66] Another example involves the creation of classes of citizens. Rousseau declares that the law can set the qualifications for membership in a particular class, but cannot nominate particular individuals for membership (*S.C.*, bk. 2, chap. 6, *O.C.*, 3:379). Whoever sets the qualifications will likely have a very good sense of which individuals will meet those qualifications.

[67] Elsewhere, Rousseau says that "the greatest talent of chiefs is in disguising their power in order to render it less odious" (*Economy*, *O.C.*, 3:250).

on governments, not as a strict demand of principle. Conversely, checks on popular assemblies are desirable in order to guard against demagogues who would mislead the citizenry into making decisions that are contrary to the general will and the common good. Representative legislatures may in some or many circumstances provide the best alternative that can practicably be adopted, but they are not a "solution" to the problem of legitimacy. The more a people relies on such shortcuts to self-governance, the more likely it becomes that its claims to be self-governing will become illusory.

## *Considerations on the Government of Poland*

This interpretation—according to which the *Social Contract*'s statements about direct democracy should be understood as a warning against unnecessary or excessive reliance on representative institutions—is supported by Rousseau's later analysis in *Considerations on the Government of Poland*. This work was prepared in response to a request in 1770 from a group of Polish politicians who sought Rousseau's advice about political reform during a moment of crisis in Polish affairs.[68] It provides his only detailed effort to apply his political theory to a large, modern state.[69]

In addition to being militarily impotent against her neighbors, Poland's political system was seriously dysfunctional, most notably because of an ancient and notorious institution (the *liberum veto*) that required unanimous votes in the national Diet. One might have expected that the first task of any reformer would be to secure the nation from foreign invasions and to introduce majority rule in order to make it possible for such important things actually to get done. Rousseau, however, did not think these were Poland's most serious problems. Instead, he identified Poland's sheer geographic size as the most severe obstacle to any salutary political reform (*Poland*, chap. 5).

Although Rousseau repeatedly indicates that the *Government of Poland* is meant to be an application of the principles set out in the *Social*

[68] The manuscript was intended as a private communication to the Poles on whose behalf it was solicited. Some years later, it was put into circulation by one or more of its recipients. Rousseau, however, considered this inappropriate, and he never approved its publication.

[69] Rousseau's work had no effect on events, for Poland was partitioned by her neighbors shortly before or after he submitted his manuscript. See Maurice Cranston, *The Solitary Self: Jean-Jacques Rousseau in Exile and Adversity*, 177.

*Contract*,[70] he casually refers to the national Diet—a representative legislature—as the lawgiver or the sovereign authority (ibid., chap. 7, *O.C.*, 3:975, 981). What is more, he expressly acknowledges that "[o]ne of the greatest inconveniences of large States, the one which more than any other makes it most difficult to preserve liberty in them, is that the legislative power cannot show itself there, and can act only by delegation" (ibid., 978). Because Rousseau did not throw up his hands and declare Poland incapable of legitimate government, his principles must be more flexible than they looked when he mocked the English in the *Social Contract*. This conclusion is confirmed by the *Government of Poland*'s more precise criticism of England: the real problem with Parliament, Rousseau now tells us, is that the terms of the legislators are too long, *not* that Parliament is a representative institution (ibid., 975).[71]

The reform that Rousseau proposes for Poland, stated in the most general terms, is the separation of powers, including the kind of separation that we call federalism. His proposals differ from our arrangements because he began with Polish institutions rather than with those that existed in the United States when our federal Constitution was adopted.[72] But Rousseau's scheme is no less complex and sophisticated.[73]

Rousseau's proposals are aimed at strengthening both national and local institutions, and then at enabling each to control the other. At the national level, his main aim is to promote patriotism through a highly politicized system of public education. The key element is to create incentives for politically ambitious adults to spend a significant part of their careers as ordinary schoolteachers.[74] Not the least important effect of this

[70] See *Poland*, chap. 7, *O.C.*, 3:977, 978, 981, 987, 988; chap. 15, 1036.

[71] Rousseau makes this same point in the *Letters Written from the Mountain*, where he also calls England "a model of the just balance of the respective powers" (lett. 9, *O.C.*, 3:874, 877).

[72] A cardinal principle of Rousseau's approach to practical politics is to take full account of existing institutions and circumstances, and to aim at small changes that are apt to produce large effects. See, for example, *Poland*, chap. 1, *O.C.*, 3:953, 955–56; chap. 7, 985; *S.C.*, bk. 3, chap. 18, *O.C.*, 3:435; *N.H.*, pt. 4, lett. 10, *O.C.*, 2:455.

[73] Ultimately, Rousseau wanted to see Poland move toward a system of federalism that bears a striking resemblance to the one that was established in our Constitution. See *Poland*, chap. 5, *O.C.*, 3:971.

[74] This proposal may have much to recommend it in nations that are very different from Poland, including our own. One might think of it as an effort to institutionalize the propagation of what Lincoln called "the *political religion* of the nation" ("The Perpetuation of Our Political Institutions: Address Before the Young Men's Lyceum of Springfield, Illinois," 27

project would be to diminish the dangers arising from Poland's military weakness: "You may not be able to keep [your neighbors] from swallowing you, but make it so they cannot digest you" (ibid., chap. 3, 959–60).[75]

Somewhat more surprisingly, given the *Social Contract*'s emphasis on restraining the inherently usurpative nature of governments, Rousseau recommends that the national executive power be strengthened by concentrating it in fewer hands (ibid., 976–78).[76] Rousseau recognizes, of course, that this will aggravate the natural tendency of the executive to oppress the sovereign, and therefore insists in the end that the real key must lie in strengthening the operation of the sovereignty. But how can this be done, given Rousseau's acknowledgment that a large country like Poland must necessarily employ a representative legislature?

Rousseau's principal suggestion for addressing this problem is to strengthen an existing but underappreciated Polish institution. The so-called Dietines were local assemblies that chose the members of the national Diet, and these Dietines were small enough that all citizens—at that time only the nobility—could participate personally in their deliberations. Rousseau proposes that the Dietines not only elect representatives to the national legislature but also issue instructions to those representatives and then require the representatives to be held accountable for any departure from the instructions. Significantly, Rousseau insists that laws adopted by the Diet as a result of its members disobeying their instructions must be treated as legitimate and scrupulously enforced. The mechanism of accountability must be for the Dietines either to punish, even with death, those representatives who disobey their instructions or to ratify their departure from the instructions (ibid., 979–81).

Jan. 1838). Were we to adopt Rousseau's suggestion, we might get better schoolteachers and better politicians.

[75] Rousseau goes on to explain: "The virtue of [Poland's] Citizens, their patriotic zeal, the distinctive form that national institutions can give their souls, this is the only rampart that will always stand ready to defend her, and that no army could subdue. If you make it so that a Pole can never become a Russian, I assure you that Russia will never subjugate Poland" (*Poland*, chap. 3, *O.C.*, 3:960). Later, Rousseau supplements this recommendation with more specific suggestions about national defense, the most important of which is reliance on a system of local militia rather than a professional, national army (ibid., chap. 12, 1013–14). This recommendation parallels the American preference for militia forces over standing armies at the time of our founding, especially among the Anti-Federalists.

[76] Somewhat inconspicuously, the *Social Contract* also acknowledges that there are circumstances in which the government or executive should be strengthened. See, for example, bk. 3, chap. 1, *O.C.*, 3:396–98; bk. 3, chap. 7, 413–14.

Rousseau provides a number of more detailed suggestions about executive-legislative relations,[77] about the abolition or modification of the *liberum veto*,[78] and numerous other matters. But for our purposes here, the most important point is that his suggestions about the reform of Poland's political institutions are much more practical and flexible than one would expect from some of the *Social Contract*'s more sweeping statements about sovereignty, law in the strict sense, and legitimacy.[79] His most radical proposal to the Poles has little to do with the formalities of legitimacy: he advocates that the Polish nobility begin, very gradually and incrementally, to *expand* the sovereign by granting citizenship to the bourgeois classes and that they aim ultimately even to free the serfs (ibid., chap. 13, 1024–29).

This expansion of the citizenry would necessarily *aggravate* many of the most serious problems that Poland faced in devising political institutions that could reliably reflect the general will. It is almost the last thing one might expect to see advocated by the philosopher who airily proclaimed in the *Social Contract* that "[t]he abuse of large States should not be raised as an objection to someone who wants only small ones" (*S.C.*, bk. 3, chap. 13, *O.C.*, 3:427). It therefore confirms, in yet another way, that Rousseau subordinates the choice of institutional forms to the overriding principle that politics accomplishes the most that it can accomplish when it raises people above their private interests. In thus rejecting the teachings of Hobbes and Locke, Rousseau draws inspiration not only from Plutarch's

[77] American readers may be especially interested to note that Rousseau proposes that the executive and legislative functions be mixed in a way that is strikingly similar to the way they are mixed in our Constitution (*Poland*, chap. 8, *O.C.*, 3:993–94). If Rousseau drew his understanding of the principle of the separation of powers from Montesquieu, he did so intelligently rather than with the simple-mindedness of those who were refuted in *Federalist 47*.

[78] Rousseau suggests three different alternatives for dealing with this problem: (1) abolish the *liberum veto*; (2) restrict its use to the most fundamental elements of the constitution, which by "the natural right of societies" must have been adopted by unanimous consent and which might therefore be thought to be alterable only by unanimous consent; or (3) preserve the *liberum veto* but require that anyone who uses it be put on trial six months later, with only two possible verdicts: death or a reward and public honors for life (*Poland*, chap. 9, *O.C.*, 3:994–97). Rousseau appears to prefer the first option: "The only way to eliminate this fatal abuse is to destroy its cause entirely" (ibid., 995). The fact that he did not insist on the second option is one of many examples of his refusal to allow procedural arguments about legitimacy to become the decisive means of evaluating political institutions.

[79] For example, *S.C.*, bk. 1, chap. 8, *O.C.*, 3:362–63; bk. 2, chap. 6, 379; bk. 3, chap. 15, 429–30.

world but from the most jarringly hard-headed of all modern political philosophers. In the *Social Contract* itself, Rousseau proclaims that "[o]ne should pay less attention to apparent repose, and the tranquility of the chiefs, than to the well-being of entire nations and above all of the most numerous estates" (ibid., chap. 9, 420n). Rousseau goes on to invoke Machiavelli as he concludes: "A little agitation gives spirit to souls, and what makes the species truly prosper is less peace than liberty" (ibid.).

The *Social Contract* repeatedly treats Machiavelli as a friend of Rousseau's own principles.[80] In a footnote added after the initial publication of the *Social Contract*, Rousseau explains his admiring characterization of the *Prince*: Machiavelli was forced by his attachment to the House of Medici to disguise his love of freedom by choosing an execrable hero and by sometimes contradicting the genuine maxims found in the *Discourses* and the *History of Florence* (*O.C.*, 3:1480, editor's note). Only superficial or corrupt readers, he indicates, could fail to see that the *Prince* is meant as a warning to peoples about the true nature of politicians.[81]

[80] See ibid., bk. 2, chap. 3, 372n (quoting *History of Florence*); bk. 2, chap. 7, 384n (quoting *Discourses on Livy*); bk. 3, chap. 6, 409 (calling the *Prince* "the book of republicans"); bk. 3, chap. 9, 420n (paraphrasing a passage from *History of Florence*); see also *Economy*, *O.C.*, 3:247 (referring to "the satires of Machiavelli").

[81] Leo Strauss maintains that Rousseau's own interpretation is "insufficient" (*Thoughts on Machiavelli*, 26). He argues instead that the superficial view of Machiavelli as "a teacher of evil" is ultimately more consistent with the deepest reading of his works. See, for example, ibid., 9–14. Rousseau would then also seem to be a teacher of evil, for he shares the Machiavellian view that "moral virtue, wished for by society and required by it, is dependent on society and therefore subject to the primary needs of society" (ibid., 294). Without pretending to match Strauss' understanding of Machiavelli, I can suggest that Rousseau might have considered the following assertion by Strauss "insufficient," and perhaps unduly superficial: "The classics understood the moral-political phenomena in the light of man's highest virtue or perfection, the life of the philosopher or the contemplative life" (ibid., 295). I am confident, however, that Rousseau would have agreed with the concluding sentences of Strauss' book: "It would seem that the notion of the beneficence of nature or of the primacy of the Good must be restored by being rethought through a return to the fundamental experiences from which it is derived. For while 'philosophy must beware of wishing to be edifying,' it is of necessity edifying" (ibid., 299). Or, to put my point a little differently, if Strauss is right that Rousseau's interpretation of Machiavelli is "insufficient," it may still be usefully edifying. Rousseau, moreover, also knew what Strauss himself undoubtedly recognized: rethinking the notion of the beneficence of nature or of the primacy of the Good requires a lot more than allusions to the life of the philosopher or the contemplative life.

## Rousseau and the Supreme Court's *Term Limits* Decision

Extreme caution is always required in any effort to draw "lessons" from a philosopher like Rousseau, who emphasized the foolishness of trying to apply pat formulas to politics.[82] Two related themes in his work, however, are particularly relevant to the American experience. First, his stress on the incessant tendencies of governments to develop interests of their own contrary to those of the citizenry. The most dangerous faction of all is the government itself. Second, his attention to the need for political leaders to take affirmative steps to cultivate the public sentiments that are required for self-government.

An illustration of the contemporary relevance of these themes can be found in a Supreme Court decision that deals with direct democracy. I must stress at the outset that I do not believe that recourse to Rousseau or any other philosopher is needed in order to evaluate the *legal* validity of the Court's decision. And I do not mean to suggest that the principal utility of Rousseau's political thought lies in the light that it might throw on something so trivial as a decision of the U.S. Supreme Court. With Rousseau's help, however, this case may be used to clarify some of what is at stake in contemporary debates about direct democracy.

In 1992, the people of Arkansas adopted an amendment to their state constitution that had been put on the ballot through a citizen initiative procedure. That amendment provided that any person who had been thrice elected to the federal House of Representatives or twice elected to the Senate would no longer be eligible to have his or her name on the ballot for that office. In *U.S. Term Limits, Inc. v. Thornton*, 514 U.S. 779 (1995), the Supreme Court held by a vote of 5–4 that this provision of the Arkansas constitution violated the Qualification Clauses of the federal Constitution, which the majority interpreted to create not only the minimum but also the exclusive qualifications for election to Congress.[83]

The majority opinion, written by Justice John Paul Stevens, and the dissenting opinion, by Justice Clarence Thomas, are lengthy and complex.

[82] See, for example, *S.C.*, bk. 2, chap. 11, *O.C.*, 3:392–93; bk. 3, chap. 18, 435.
[83] The Constitution provides:

> No Person shall be a Representative who shall not have attained to the Age of twenty five Years, and been seven Years a Citizen of the United States, and who shall not, when elected, be an Inhabitant of that State in which he shall be chosen.

Much of the debate between them revolved around the proper inferences to be drawn from the text and structure of the Constitution, its legislative history, and early practice. None of these standard sources provided an absolutely and conclusively compelling answer to the precise issue in the case. Boiled down to the simplest possible terms, Thomas takes the position that because the Constitution is silent on the issue of state-imposed term limits, "it raises no bar to action by the States or the people" (514 U.S. at 845). Stevens, on the other hand, concludes that the imposition of any term limits "would be inconsistent with the Framers' vision of a uniform National Legislature representing the people of the United States" (ibid., 783).

Thomas' legal arguments, from historical sources and especially from the text and structure of the Constitution, seem to me overwhelmingly more powerful than those offered by Stevens, primarily because I agree with Thomas that the only constitutional constraints on the states are those that the Constitution imposes expressly or by clear implication. But rather than rehearse the legal arguments here, I want to focus on several aspects of Stevens' opinion that seem particularly troubling when considered in light of Rousseau's analysis of political institutions.

First, and apparently in tacit recognition that his textual and legislative-history arguments are inconclusive, Stevens takes as the centerpiece of his argument the proposition that it is a "fundamental principle of our representative democracy ... 'that the people should choose whom they please to govern them.'"[84] This language is taken from *Powell v. McCormack*, 395 U.S. 486 (1969), and the internal quotation is taken from a statement by Alexander Hamilton at the New York ratifying convention. As a statement of "democratic principles," Stevens' application of this slogan to the term limits issue is nothing short of fatuous. As Thomas points out, the people of Arkansas simply "chose to be governed" by people who had

> No Person shall be a Senator who shall not have attained to the Age of thirty Years, and been nine Years a Citizen of the United States, and who shall not, when elected, be an Inhabitant of that State for which he shall be chosen.

[84] Stevens repeats this quotation, or parts of it, at least six times. 514 U.S. at 783, 793, 795 (twice), 796 n12 (without quotation marks), 819. Stevens clearly regards this as his principal argument. Other than the Qualification Clauses themselves, for example, it is the only authority cited in the introductory summary at the beginning of the majority opinion. Similarly, Stevens says that the text and structure of the Constitution and the relevant historical materials about its meaning are less important than the "basic principles of our democratic system" (ibid., 806).

not served more than a specified length of time in Congress.[85] There is no "democratic principle" that requires the people to express their choices only at elections rather than in their constitution, or at least no principle for which Stevens provides any argument. The inanity of his position is particularly dramatic because the Qualification Clauses—the provisions of the Constitution that he thinks the people of Arkansas violated—*are themselves in violation* of the very same rule that Stevens claims is a "fundamental principle of our representative democracy." Those Clauses forbid the people to choose to be governed by twenty-four-year-olds, or by recently naturalized citizens, or by those who do not inhabit the state they represent.

One might without much trouble find other examples of appallingly simple-minded expressions of democratic theory in the Court's precedents, especially during the era in which *Powell v. McCormack* was decided. But the Stevens opinion is especially egregious because the *Powell* Court's use of the Hamilton quotation made perfectly good sense in that case, which dealt with the authority of one house of Congress to exclude a member who satisfied the Qualification Clauses and had been elected by the people of his district. A democratic theorist who cannot see a meaningful difference between *Congress* taking away the people's right to "choose whom they please" to send to Congress and the people making their *own* choice not to be governed by certain classes of people is someone who really ought not to engage in such theorizing.

A related aspect of the Stevens' opinion, which is also troubling if one looks at it with Rousseau's analysis in mind, is the Court's refusal to give any consideration to the fact that the Arkansas constitutional provision had been approved directly by the voters, rather than indirectly through the state legislature. The reason Stevens gives for paying no attention to this fact is the standard rule of law according to which state legislation that violates the federal Constitution is equally invalid no matter what its process of adoption was. I have no dispute with this rule of law, but Stevens' use of it here assumes the conclusion that the Qualification Clauses impose exclusive rather than minimum qualifications. As Thomas points out, one could somewhat more plausibly conclude that state legislatures

[85] Technically, the Arkansas provision only kept these long-term incumbents off the ballot, while allowing them to be reelected as write-in candidates. For purposes of my discussion, this distinction is unimportant, and for convenience I will treat the Arkansas provision as though it imposed strict term limits.

are forbidden to impose term limits, not because of the Qualifications Clause but rather because the Constitution confers the choice of federal representatives on "the people" rather than on their state legislatures. But this conclusion would allow, indeed would even point toward, the further conclusion that term limits adopted directly by the people themselves are perfectly constitutional.

Apart from this legal argument, although related to it, is the failure of Stevens to recognize the possibility that democratic theory, properly understood, should have suggested a rule of interpretation under which the federal Constitution should not be held to constrain the operation of direct democracy unless it clearly so specifies. This rule of interpretation would, of course, be perfectly consistent with the general rule that state legislation that violates the federal Constitution is equally invalid no matter what its process of adoption was. Apparently because of his hostility to direct democracy, Stevens draws every possible inference, no matter how weak or strained or equivocal, in favor of finding a ban on the Arkansas term limits lurking beneath the actual words of the Constitution and of those who created it. The fundamental democratic principle that the people are sovereign, if one took it seriously, would suggest just the opposite approach.

Rousseau's analysis of democratic principles offers a powerful theoretical reason for an especially strong presumption in favor of upholding laws directly adopted by the citizenry. The natural course of political evolution is strongly in the direction of reducing the role of the citizenry in legislation, and the natural end point of that evolution is the abolition of citizen participation. Precisely because there are innumerable efficiencies and conveniences that promote this trend, the spirit of statesmanship should be to resist it. In our predominantly representative system, this suggests that we should adopt a stronger presumption that direct acts of the people are constitutionally valid than that acts of their representatives are valid. By straining so hard to find arguments for invalidating the directly expressed will of the people of Arkansas, the *Term Limits* majority contributed unnecessarily, and even perversely, to the enervation of popular sovereignty.

What makes the *Term Limits* decision especially shocking from a Rousseauan point of view is that the particular measure that the Court invalidated was one designed to counter the deepest vice in even the most legitimate political institutions: the tendency of governments to develop a will of their own, which is general with respect to its members and particular with respect to the sovereign people. The term limits movement was consciously and deliberately aiming to address exactly this problem. Congress had piled a multitude of incumbent-protection devices one on top of another for many years. This finally became so notorious that a genuine nationwide grassroots movement arose, devoted to countering the perceived development of a self-perpetuating congressional oligarchy. The imposition of term limits was a perfectly sensible device for reducing or partially counteracting the tendencies in government toward this vice, and there were good reasons for any rational citizen to heavily discount the hand-wringing objections from members of Congress and their interest-group courtiers.[86]

The plainest form of self-interest made it virtually inconceivable that Congress would impose term limits on its own members, even if the Constitution would have permitted it to do so.[87] And state legislatures would likely have been reluctant to adopt term limits, even if there were no constitutional questions about their authority to do so.[88] It was thus only through the direct action of the people that term limits could be used to curb Congress' self-interested promotion of incumbent-protection devices, and it would be hard to think of a goal more appropriate for direct action by the people. In this nigh-perfect case for the operation of direct democracy, the Supreme Court chose to reach out to stifle the people's action. By relying primarily on what Stevens claimed was a fundamental principle of democratic theory—the people's right to choose—the Court pushed the perversity of the *Term Limits* decision to an excruciating extreme.

*Term Limits* is an exceptionally vivid example of judicial disregard for what Rousseau regarded as core principles of political right. The Court snuffed out one of the more promising and easily defended devices through which the people have recently sought to reduce the inherent tendencies of government to pursue its own common interests, or its particular general will, at the expense of the common interests of the nation.

[86] On the rationality of the movement for term limits, see Einer Elhauge, et al., "How Term Limits Enhance the Expression of Democratic Preferences." Rousseau advocated the adoption of term limits in Poland (*Poland*, chap. 7, *O.C.*, 3:979).

[87] Under *Powell*, which I believe was correctly decided, the Constitution would not permit this.

[88] At the time of the *Term Limits* decision, twenty-one of the twenty-two states with some type of term limit provision had adopted them through a direct vote of the people.

For all we know, the term limits device might not, in fact, have resulted in a significant improvement in governmental behavior. Nor does the *Term Limits* decision necessarily imply that every attempt by the people to participate directly in its own governance will meet with the same hostility from the Supreme Court. Unfortunately, the misuse of democratic theory by the Court in this case suggests at least the possibility that a majority of the Justices have or may be susceptible to a deep hostility toward institutions of direct democracy. If that is so, the Court might eventually work its way toward eliminating these institutions from our political life.

The most direct path to that goal would run through the Guarantee Clause, whose language is much more ambiguous than that of the Qualifications Clauses.[89] It is not impossible to imagine an opinion of the Court that would bootstrap the *Term Limits* analysis in much the same way that *Term Limits* bootstrapped *Powell v. McCormack*. Recall that *Powell* invoked Alexander Hamilton's statement, "that the people should choose whom they please to govern them," in order to bolster its entirely plausible conclusion that the Constitution does not permit *Congress* to make up its own criteria for who is eligible to govern the people. *Term Limits* took the Hamilton quote out of its context in *Powell*, and misread it to mean that *the people* are forbidden to adopt laws establishing criteria for who is eligible to govern them.

Once one accepts that misreading, why not also interpret Hamilton's statement to mean that because the people should choose whom they please to govern them, they may not choose to govern themselves? Apply that interpretation of what *Term Limits* called a "fundamental principle of our representative democracy" to the textually ambiguous Guarantee Clause, and the Court could easily draw the following conclusion: a republican form of government is exclusively a representative form of government. All forms of direct democracy in the states would then be considered unconstitutional, and we would have taken a significant new step toward what Rousseau would regard as the death of the body politic.[90]

In *Arizona State Legislature v. Arizona Independent Redistricting Comm'n*, 135 S. Ct. 2652 (2015), the Supreme Court upheld a state

[89] Article IV provides: "The United States shall guarantee to every State in this Union a Republican Form of Government."

[90] "The law of yesterday does not obligate today, but tacit consent is presumed from silence, and the Sovereign is presumed to constantly confirm the laws which it does not abrogate, *when it can do so*" (*S.C.*, bk. 3, chap. 11, *O.C.*, 3:424, emphasis added).

ballot initiative that reassigned the function of drawing congressional districts from the legislature to an unelected independent commission. The Court's opinion includes a paean to the value of direct democracy, and it features the Hamilton quotation that figured so prominently in the *Term Limits* opinion. Unfortunately, the *Arizona* decision is flatly inconsistent with the text of the Constitution,[91] and with the Constitution's historical meaning, as Chief Justice John Roberts shows in his dissenting opinion. Nor is the majority's decision genuinely based on a regard for direct democracy. As Justice Thomas' dissenting opinion emphasizes, the Court in recent years has consistently shown a pronounced lack of respect for ballot initiatives. Furthermore, the Court's sudden apparent exception to this pattern of hostility involved an initiative, "unlike those that the Court has previously treated so dismissively, [that] was unusually *democracy-reducing*" (135 S. Ct. at 2698, Thomas, J., dissenting, emphasis added). If this decision is a harbinger of anything, it probably signals an acceleration of the body politic's deterioration.

## Conclusion

The Supreme Court may not be likely to abolish all devices of direct democracy, at least in the short term. The *Social Contract*, however, argues that there is good reason to be especially vigilant about the usurpation of sovereignty through distortions of a fundamental law like our Constitution. And there are signs beyond those found in the *Term Limits* decision that we have good reason to take his warning seriously.

Rousseau draws no fundamental distinction between the functions played by the various parts of what he calls the government. Nor does the concept of the independent judiciary get any special attention in the *Social Contract*. There is, however, one passage in which he describes an institution that resembles our Supreme Court in certain respects.

This institution, which Rousseau calls the "Tribunate," can serve either to protect the sovereign from the government, or to uphold the government against the people, or to maintain an appropriate balance between the government and the people. This special body should have neither legislative nor executive functions, he says, and its power should consist

[91] "The Times, Places and Manner of holding Elections for Senators and Representatives, shall be prescribed in each State by *the Legislature* thereof" (emphasis added).

entirely in defending the fundamental laws by exercising a kind of constitutional veto (*S.C.*, bk. 4, chap. 5).

At least in general terms, this resembles the most significant political role that our Supreme Court has claimed for itself. Notwithstanding the occasional dissent, we have a strong tradition that takes as its starting point the notion that the Court's main political function is to act as a great constitutional umpire charged with keeping each of the more active elements of the political system within its assigned sphere. For that reason, our belief in the vital importance of the independent judiciary seems quite consistent with Rousseau's claim that "[a] wisely tempered Tribunate is the firmest support of a good constitution" (ibid., *O.C.*, 3:454). But Rousseau immediately adds a warning: "but if it has even a little too much strength it overturns everything." Even Rome and Sparta, he says, perished because of usurpations carried out by their versions of this institution (ibid.).

Rousseau offers what he considers a novel device for preventing the abuse of this valuable but dangerous institution. He argues that the Tribunate should not be a permanent body. Instead, it should periodically be suspended for a legally prescribed period of time, after which it should be reconstituted with entirely new members. "This means appears to me free of inconveniences because, as I have said, the Tribunate not being part of the constitution, it can be removed without harming it; and it appears to me efficacious because a newly installed magistrate starts not with the power his predecessor had but with the power that the law gives him" (ibid., 455).

If one were to apply this suggestion to our system, it might mean that the power to render judicial decisions about the meaning of the Constitution should be taken away from the ordinary courts and reposed in a special body that would sit only occasionally and always with a new set of members. To the extent that the *Term Limits* decision is typical of the Court's approach to law and democracy, perhaps such an idea is not quite so outrageous as it may initially appear.

There is, moreover, good reason to think that *Term Limits* is rather typical of the Supreme Court's disrespect for the sovereignty of the people. The Court has frequently been tempted to substitute its own views of morality and political wisdom for those reflected in the Constitution and in laws adopted by the people's elected representatives. In recent decades, the Court has become increasingly inclined to succumb to that temptation, often in the belief that the Justices have some way of intuiting what public opinion does or should or will eventually favor. The *Social Contract* assigns the function of expressing public opinion to what Rousseau calls the Censorship, an institution that has no coercive power (ibid., bk. 4, chap. 7). By combining the enforcement power of the Tribunate with the moral or political function of the Censorship, our Supreme Court has become dangerously powerful.

Rousseau's proposed device for curtailing that power hardly seems out of proportion to the risks it is designed to address. As a practical matter, however, the extreme difficulty of formally amending our Constitution will prevent the adoption of this device. Congressional incumbents could not control the Arkansas referendum process, but they can certainly suppress any effort to enact an Article V amendment.

Perhaps, in the spirit of the *Government of Poland*, it would be better to suggest only a little tinkering with our present arrangements.[92] Unlike Rousseau's Tribunate, our Supreme Court is both a constitutional umpire and an ordinary court of law. Perhaps its members could be given new incentives to behave more like judicial magistrates and less like would-be shepherds of the people or philosopher-kings. That might be done by creating some new obstacles to the operation of the general will of the Court and the particular wills of its members.

Congress has the authority to create such obstacles, which might include jurisdictional rules requiring the Justices to decide a higher proportion of less glamorous cases, requirements that they issue their opinions anonymously, an end to the use of high-powered law clerks who free the judges to think big thoughts instead of studying the law, and a restoration of the Justices' obligation to spend a significant part of the year hearing ordinary cases in the lower courts.[93] To be sure, the adoption of such proposals by Congress may now be unthinkable. By stifling efforts by the people to make Congress more responsive to the general will, the *Term Limits* decision made it less likely that such reforms of our version of the Tribunate will ever be possible.

"If Sparta and Rome perished, what State can hope to endure forever?" (ibid., bk. 3, chap. 11, 424). When our republic finally perishes, there will have been many causes, some of them latent from its birth (ibid.). But the timing of its death will be affected by seemingly trivial decisions that contributed to the corruption of the sovereign. The *Term Limits* decision may turn out to have been one of them.

[92] "To put the law above man is a problem in politics that I compare to that of squaring the circle in geometry" (*Poland*, chap. 1, *O.C.*, 3:955).

[93] For a detailed presentation of these suggestions, see Craig S. Lerner and Nelson Lund, "Judicial Duty and the Supreme Court's Cult of Celebrity."

CHAPTER 7

# Conclusion

Rousseau adopted as his motto a line from Juvenal's *Satires*, translated as "To consecrate one's life to the truth." When he first proclaimed this motto, he said that he wrote to be useful to others without soiling his writings with an eye to his own views or interests (*d'Alembert*, *O.C.*, 5:120n, Bloom, 132n). He referred to the motto repeatedly, and the last allusion to it was followed by a lengthy discussion of lying.[1] I cannot do justice here to the relationship between Rousseau's devotion to the truth and to the welfare of others.[2] Instead, I will briefly address his continuing usefulness to us.

Rousseau is often studied in order to understand the progress of modernity, for elements of his thought appear to foreshadow a great diversity of subsequent developments. The French Revolution. Communism. Fascism. Contemporary communitarianism. Romanticism and its vision of the sensitive artist as a moral preceptor. Montessori schools and related forms of child-centered education. The hippies of the 1960s and the quasi-religious environmentalists of today. The animal rights movement. Depth psychology and our contemporary culture of public confessions. The politics of compassion and political leaders who take on the role of public comforters. Many of these innovations have had extremely pernicious effects.

[1] *Emile*, *O.C.* 4:558, Bloom, 260 (in connection with the Profession of Faith of the Savoyard Vicar); *Mountain*, *O.C.*, 3:683 (epigraph); *Reveries*, fourth walk, *O.C.*, 1:1024.

[2] The best treatment I have seen is Christopher Kelly, *Rousseau as Author: Consecrating One's Life to the Truth.*



N. Lund, *Rousseau's Rejuvenation of Political Philosophy*,
DOI 10.1007/978-3-319-41390-7_7

It is, therefore, tempting to dismiss Rousseau as the mad father of mad fantasies. This is a mistake. The poisonous fruits of Rousseau's supposed influence all rest on distorted extensions of some aspect of his thought. They are, moreover, better seen as the results of inner weaknesses in the Enlightenment project, which Rousseau only diagnosed.

The technological advances and political reforms triggered by the Enlightenment have brought unquestioned material benefits to mankind. Nevertheless, we can see before us countless signs of the corruption that Rousseau saw emerging in eighteenth-century Europe. Atheism has begun to dominate the West. The egoism at the heart of Enlightenment philosophy is reflected in the ongoing collapse or redefinition of the family and in declining birthrates that threaten a kind of social suicide. It is also reflected in a politics suffused with crony capitalism, interest-group feeding frenzies, and a voracious appetite for government entitlements that has proved politically uncontrollable even while it appears financially unsustainable. Rousseau did not propose a political cure for the corruption that he saw in Europe, and he offers no such remedy for the ills of our time. But he does offer an incisive analysis of the underlying causes. Properly understood, that analysis does not invite us to abandon the sober political teachings of John Locke, Adam Smith, or the American founders. But neither does the respect they are owed refute his diagnosis.

While cautious in proposing political reforms, Rousseau was bold in promoting moral reform. He attacked the Enlightenment's false promise of a happiness attainable through the rational and egoistic pursuit of wealth and power. Even within the kind of society promoted by Enlightenment thought, he believed, it was possible for people to find a refuge from the corrupting influence of modern philosophy. The key institution that made this possible was traditional family life. Rousseau used all of his literary skill to defend and ennoble that institution, and thus to reinforce "the small fatherland that is the family" which supports liberal political societies like our own.

For all his desire to be useful to others, Rousseau was no mere sermonizer, or what we might call a cultural critic or public intellectual. "[W]hen I desired to learn, it was in order that I myself might know (*pour savoir moi-même*) and not in order to teach" (*Reveries*, third walk, *O.C.*, 1:1013). His efforts to be useful to the public had a foundation in the most uncompromising personal search for the truth, which led him to acknowledge many truthful elements in Enlightenment philosophy. The wackier intellectual movements that are superficially Rousseauan are not signs of his madness, but rather of intellectual deficiencies in later thinkers. He is not responsible for the inner weaknesses in modern liberal societies, and his exposure of those weaknesses did not cause the dysfunctions and dissatisfactions of our time. Those who aspire to defend and preserve the American republic, as Rousseau sought to serve the Republic of Geneva, need more than pious appeals to the authority of our founders, or to libertarian theories of natural rights. And they certainly need more than proposals for public policies that promise to promote economic growth.

It is an open question whether anyone or anything can prevent an irremediable deterioration of America and the West more generally. It should therefore be especially significant for us that Rousseau did not write only for the public, or for those who want to serve the public. Rousseau also spoke to those who are, like himself, impelled to learn solely in order to know. For them, his analysis of politics and the human soul can help to rejuvenate political philosophy as an entrance to philosophy as a way of life. The skill with which he invites those readers to think for themselves makes Rousseau a useful introduction both to Plato and to philosophy.

# Bibliography

Atkinson, Quentin D. 2011, April 15. Phonemic Diversity Supports a Serial Founder Effect Model of Language Expansion from Africa. *Science* 332: 346–349.

Balling, John D., and John H. Falk. 1982. Development of Visual Preference for Natural Environments. *Environment and Behavior* 14(1): 5–28.

Bartal, Inbal Ben-Ami, Jean Decety, and Peggy Mason. 2011, corrected version 2012, January 27. Empathy and Pro-Social Behavior in Rats. *Science* 334: 1427–1430.

Bekoff, Marc, and Jessica Pierce. 2009. *Wild Justice: The Moral Lives of Animals.* Chicago, IL: University of Chicago Press.

Boas, Franz. 1938. *The Mind of Primitive Man.* New York: Free Press.

Burke, Edmund. 1839. *The Works of Edmund Burke.* Boston, MA: C.C. Little & J. Brown.

Burns, Timothy W. 2013, May. Philosophy and Poetry: A New Look at an Old Quarrel. *American Political Science Review* 109: 326–38.

Butler, Melissa A. 1995. Eighteenth-Century Critics of Rousseau's Views on Women. In *Rousseau and Criticism*, eds. Lorraine Clark and Guy Lafrance. Ottawa: North American Association for the Study of Jean-Jacques Rousseau.

Cantor, Paul A. 1976. *Shakespeare's Rome: Republic and Empire.* Ithaca, NY: Cornell University Press.

Castellano, Sergei, Genís Parra, Federico A. Sánchez-Quinto, Fernando Racimo, Martin Kuhlwilm, Martin Kircher, Susanna Sawyer, et al. 2014, May 6. Patterns of Coding Variation in the Complete Exomes of Three Neanderthals. *Proceedings of the National Academy of Sciences* 111(18): 6666–6671.



N. Lund, *Rousseau's Rejuvenation of Political Philosophy*,
DOI 10.1007/978-3-319-41390-7

Clay, Diskin. 1993. Plato's Magnesia. In *Nomodeiktes: Greek Studies in Honor of Martin Ostwald*, eds. Ralph M. Rosen and Joseph Farrell. Ann Arbor: University of Michigan Press.

Cooper, Laurence D. 2008. *Eros in Plato, Rousseau, and Nietzsche*. University Park: Pennsylvania State University Press.

Cranston, Maurice. 1991. *The Noble Savage: Jean-Jacques Rousseau 1754–1762*. Chicago, IL: University of Chicago Press.

———. 1997. *The Solitary Self: Jean-Jacques Rousseau in Exile and Adversity*. Chicago, IL: University of Chicago Press.

D'Alembert, Jean-Baptiste le Rond. 1759. *Lettre de M. d'Alembert à M. J.-J. Rousseau sur l'article "Genève" tiré du septième volume de l'Encylopédie Avec quelques autre pièces qui y sont relatives*. Amsterdam: Zacharie Chatelain & fils.

Daura-Jorge, F.G., M. Cantor, S.N. Ingram, D. Lusseau, and P.C. Simões Lopes. 2012. The Structure of a Bottlenose Dolphin Society Is Coupled to a Unique Foraging Cooperation with Artisanal Fishermen. *Biology Letters* 8: 702–705.

Darwin, Charles. 1873. *The Descent of Man, and Selection in Relation to Sex*. New York: D. Appleton & Co.

———. 1979. *The Origin of Species by Means of Natural Selection*. New York: Avenel Books.

———. 1996. *The Power of Movement in Plants*. New York: Da Capa Press.

Dennett, Daniel. 1995. *Darwin's Dangerous Idea*. New York: Simon & Schuster.

De Waal, Frans, and Frans Lanting. 1997. *Bonobo: The Forgotten Ape*. Berkeley: University of California Press.

Dunbar, Robin I.M. 2001. Brains on Two Legs: Group Size and the Evolution of Intelligence. In *Tree of Origin: What Primate Behavior Can Tell Us About Human Social Evolution*, ed. Frans B.M. De Waal. Cambridge, MA: Harvard University Press.

Eide, Tormod. 2002, November. Including the Women in Plato's *Laws*: A Note on Book 6, 781a-b. *Symbolae Osloenses* 77(1): 106–109.

Elhauge, Einer, John R. Lott, Jr., and Richard L. Manning. 1997. How Term Limits Enhance the Expression of Democratic Preferences. *Supreme Court Economic Review* 5: 59–80.

Finlayson, Clive. 2014. *The Improbable Primate: How Water Shaped Human Evolution*. Oxford: Oxford University Press.

Flaumenhaft, Harvey. 2010. The Silence of the Spartan: City, Soul, and Study of the Stars in the Epilogue to Plato's Last and Longest Dialogue. In *Apples of Gold in Pictures of Silver: Honoring the Work of Leon R. Kass*, eds. Yuval Levin, Thomas W. Merrill, and Adam Schulman. Lanham, MD: Roman & Littlefield.

Fralin, Richard. 1978. *Rousseau and Representation*. New York: Columbia University Press.

Franklin, Benjamin. 1905. *The Writings of Benjamin Franklin*. Ed. Albert Henry Smyth. New York: Macmillan.
Franklin, James. 1986. Aristotle on Species Variation. *Philosophy* 61(236): 245–252.
Fukuyama, Francis. 1989, Summer. The End of History? *The National Interest* 16: 3–18.
———. 1992. *The End of History and the Last Man*. New York: Free Press.
Galdikas, Biruté M.F. 1995. *Reflections of Eden: My Years with the Orangutans of Borneo*. Boston, MA: Little, Brown & Co.
Gee, Henry. 2013. *The Accidental Species: Misunderstandings of Human Evolution*. Chicago, IL: University of Chicago Press.
Gleiser, Marcelo. 2014. *The Island of Knowledge: The Limits of Science and the Search for Meaning*. New York: Basic Books.
Good, Kenneth. 1996. *Into the Heart: One Man's Pursuit of Love and Knowledge Among the Yanomami*. New York: Longman.
Goodall, Jane. 1990. *Through a Window: My Thirty Years with the Chimpanzees of Gombe*. Boston, MA: Houghton Mifflin.
Gourevitch, Victor. 2013. On Strauss on Rousseau. In *The Challenge of Rousseau*, eds. Eve Grace and Christopher Kelly, 147–167. Cambridge: Cambridge University Press.
———. 1988. Rousseau's Pure State of Nature. *Interpretation: A Journal of Political Philosophy* 16(Fall): 23–59.
Green, F.C. 1926, April. Who Was the Author of the *Lettres Portugaises*? *Modern Language Review* 21(2): 159–167.
Grene, Marjorie. 1963. *A Portrait of Aristotle*. London: Faber & Faber Ltd..
Hamilton, Marci A. 1997. The People: The Least Accountable Branch. *University of Chicago Law School Roundtable* 4: 1–14.
Hendel, Charles W. 1934. *Jean-Jacques Rousseau: Moralist*. Oxford: Oxford University Press.
Henrich, Joseph. 2004. Demography and Cultural Evolution: How Adaptive Cultural Processes Can Produce Maladaptive Losses—The Tasmanian Case. *American Antiquity* 69(2): 197–214.
Hobaiter, Catherine, and Richard W. Byrne. 2014, July 21. The Meanings of Chimpanzee Gestures. *Current Biology* 24(14): 1–5.
Hobbes, Thomas. 1909. *Leviathan*. London: Clarendon Press.
———. 1972. *Man and Citizen*. Ed. Bernard Gert. Garden City, NY: Anchor Books.
Hsiao, Douglas H. 1992. Invisible Cities: The Constitutional Status of Direct Democracy in a Democratic Republic. *Duke Law Journal* 41: 1267–1310.
Huntington, Samuel P. 1993. The Clash of Civilizations? *Foreign Affairs* 72(Summer): 22–49.

——— 1996. *The Clash of Civilizations and the Remaking of World Order.* New York: Simon & Schuster.

Jefferson, Thomas. 1975. *The Portable Thomas Jefferson.* Ed. Merrill D. Peterson. New York: Viking Press,.

Joordens, Josephine C.A., Francesco d'Errico, Frank P. Wesselingh, Stephen Munro, John de Vos, Jakob Wallinga, Christina Ankjærgaard, et al. 2015. *Homo erectus* at Trinil on Java Used Shells for Tool Production and Engraving. *Nature* 518: 228–231. doi:10.1038/nature13962.

Kano, Takayoshi. 1992. *The Last Ape: Pygmy Chimpanzee Behavior and Ecology.* Stanford, CA: Stanford University Press.

Kelly, Christopher. 2003. *Rousseau as Author: Consecrating One's Life to the Truth.* Chicago, IL: University of Chicago Press.

———. 2015. Rousseau's Chemical Apprenticeship. In *Rousseau and the Dilemmas of Modernity*, ed. Mark Hulliung. New Brunswick, NJ: Transaction Publishers.

Klein, Richard G. 2009. *The Human Career: Human Biological and Cultural Origins*, 3rd edn. Chicago, IL: University of Chicago Press.

Klobucka, Anna. 2000. *The Portuguese Nun: Formation of a National Myth.* Lewisburg, PA: Bucknell University Press.

Kochin, Michael S. 2002. *Gender and Rhetoric in Plato's Political Thought.* Cambridge: Cambridge University Press.

Krützen, Michael, Erik P. Willems, and Carel P. van Schaik. 2011, November 8. Culture and Geographic Variation in Orangutan Behavior. *Current Biology* 21: 1–5.

Langford, Dale J., Sara E. Crager, Zarrar Shehzad, Shad B. Smith, Susana G. Sotocinal, Jeremy S. Levenstadt, Mona Lisa Chanda, Daniel J. Levitin, and Jeffrey S. Mogil. 2006, June 30. Social Modulation of Pain as Evidence for Empathy in Mice. *Science* 312: 1967–1970.

Lee, Richard B., and Richard Daly, eds. 1999. *Cambridge Encyclopedia of Hunters and Gatherers.* Cambridge: Cambridge University Press.

Lefcourt, Charles R. 1976, September. Did Guilleragues Write 'The Portuguese Letters'?. *Hispania* 593: 493–497.

Leibowitz, David. 2010. *The Ironic Defense of Socrates: Plato's Apology.* New York: Cambridge University Press.

Lendon, J.E. 2005. *Soldiers and Ghosts: A History of Battle in Classical Antiquity.* New Haven, CT: Yale University Press.

Lennox, James G. 2001. *Aristotle's Philosophy of Biology: Studies in the Origins of Life Sciences.* Cambridge: Cambridge University Press.

Lerner, Craig S., and Nelson Lund. 2010. Judicial Duty and the Supreme Court's Cult of Celebrity. *George Washington Law Review* 78: 1255–1299.

Lévi-Strauss, Claude. "Jean-Jacques Rousseau, Fondateur des Sciences de l'Homme." In *Jean-Jacques Rousseau.* Neuchatel: La Baconnière, 1962.

Lloyd, G.E.R. 1968. *Aristotle: The Growth and Structure of His Thought*. Cambridge: Cambridge University Press.
Locke, John. 1979. *An Essay Concerning Human Understanding*. Ed. Peter H. Nidditch. Oxford: Oxford University Press.
———. 1988. *The Second Treatise of Government: An Essay Concerning the True Original, Extent, and End of Civil Government*. Ed. Peter Laslett. Cambridge: Cambridge University Press.
———. 1996. *Some Thoughts Concerning Education and Of the Conduct of Understanding*. Eds. Ruth W. Grant and Nathan Tarcov. Indianapolis: Hackett.
Lovejoy, Arthur O. 1936. *The Great Chain of Being: A Study of the History of an Idea*. Cambridge: Harvard University Press.
Ludwig, Paul W. 2002. *Eros & Politics: Desire and Community in Greek Political Theory*. Cambridge: Cambridge University Press.
Lund, Nelson. 2016, May. A Woman's Laws and a Man's: Eros and Thumos in Rousseau's *Julie, or The New Heloise* (1761) and *The Deer Hunter* (1978). *Interpretation: A Journal of Political Philosophy* 43(3): 367–436.
Mabey, Richard. 2015. *The Cabaret of Plants: Forty Thousand Years of Plant Life and the Human Imagination*. New York: W.W. Norton.
Madison, James. 1983. *Papers of James Madison* (Congressional Series). Eds. Robert A. Rutland and Thomas A. Mason. Charlottesville: University of Virginia Press.
———. 2009. *Papers of James Madison* (Retirement Series). Eds. David B. Mattern, et al. Charlottesville: University of Virginia Press.
Marshall, Lorna. 1976. *The !Kung of Nyae Nyae*. Cambridge: Harvard University Press.
Marshall, Lorna J. 1999. *Nyae Nyae !Kung: Beliefs and Rites*. Cambridge: Peabody Museum Monographs.
Marshall, Terence. 2013. Epistemology and Political Perception in the Case of Rousseau. In *The Challenge of Rousseau*, eds. Eve Grace and Christopher Kelly. Cambridge: Cambridge University Press.
Masson, Pierre-Maurice. 1913. Questions de Chronologie Rousseauiste. *Annales de la Société Jean-Jacques Rousseau* 9: 37–61.
Masters, Roger D. 1997. Rousseau and the Rediscovery of Human Nature. In *The Legacy of Rousseau*, eds. Clifford Orwin and Nathan Tarcov. Chicago, IL: University of Chicago Press.
Mayr, Ernst. 1982. *The Growth of Biological Thought: Diversity, Evolution, and Inheritance*. Cambridge: Harvard University Press.
McComb, Karen, Graeme Shannona, Katito N. Sayialelb, and Cynthia Moss. Elephants Can Determine Ethnicity, Gender, and Age from Acoustic Cues in Human Voices. *Proceedings of the National Academy of Sciences* (early edition, approved 3 Feb. 2014).
McKeen, Catherine. 2006. Why Women Must Guard and Rule in Plato's *Kallipolis*. *Pacific Philosophical Quarterly* 87: 527–548.

Melzer, Arthur M. 1990. *The Natural Goodness of Man: On the System of Rousseau's Thought*. Chicago, IL: University of Chicago Press.

——— 2014. *Philosophy Between the Lines: The Lost History of Esoteric Writing*. Chicago, IL: University of Chicago Press.

Mikalson, Jon D. 2010. *Ancient Greek Religion*, 2nd edn. West Sussex, UK: Wiley-Blackwell.

Mithen, Steven. 2006. *The Singing Neanderthals: The Origins of Music, Language, Mind, and Body*. Cambridge: Harvard University Press.

Morrow, Glenn R. 1960. *Plato's Cretan City*. Princeton, NJ: Princeton University Press.

Munn, Mark. 2013. *Erōs* and the *Laws* in Historical Context. In *Plato's Laws: Force and Truth in Politics*, eds. Gregory Recco and Eric Sanday. Bloomington: Indiana University Press.

Natelson, Robert G. 2002. A Republic, Not a Democracy? Initiative, Referendum, and the Constitution's Guarantee Clause. *Texas Law Review* 80: 807–857.

Okin, Susan Moller. 1979. *Women in Western Political Thought*. Princeton, NJ: Princeton University Press.

Pääbo, Svante. 2014. *Neanderthal Man: In Search of Lost Genomes*. New York: Basic Books.

Papagianni, Dimitra, and Michael A. Morse. 2013. *The Neanderthals Rediscovered: How Modern Science Is Rewriting Their Story*. New York: Thames & Hudson.

Peters, John F. 1998. *Life Among the Yanomami*. Ontario: Broadview Press.

Pinkerton, John, ed. 1814. *A General Collection of Voyages and Travels*. London: Longman, Hurst, Rees, Orme, and Brown.

Plato. 1980. *The Laws of Plato*. Trans. Thomas L. Pangle. New York: Basic Books.

Richards, Richard A. 2010. *The Species Problem: A Philosophical Analysis*. Cambridge: Cambridge University Press.

Roberts, Anna Ilona, Sarah-Jane Vick, Sam George Bradley Roberts, and Charles R. Menzel. 2014, January 16. Chimpanzees Modify Intentional Gestures to Coordinate a Search for Hidden Food. *Nature Communications*. doi:10.1038/ncomms4088.

Rousseau, Jean-Jacques. 1960. *Politics and the Arts: Letter to M. D'Alembert on the Theatre*. Trans. Allan Bloom. Ithaca, NY: Cornell University Press.

———. 1979. *Emile or On Education*. Trans. Allan Bloom. New York: Basic Books.

———. 1959–1995. *Œuvres Complètes*. 5 vols. Eds. Bernard Gagnebin and Marcel Raymond. Paris: Bibliothèque de la Pléiade.

———. 1997. *Rousseau: The Discourses and Other Early Political Writings*. Ed. Victor Gourevitch. Cambridge: Cambridge University Press.

———. 1997. *Rousseau: The Social Contract and Other Later Political Writings*. Ed. Victor Gourevitch. Cambridge: Cambridge University Press.

———. 1965–1998. *Correspondance Complète*. 52 vols. Ed. R.A. Leigh. Banbury, Oxfordshire: Voltaire Foundation.

———. 2008. *Diskurs über die Ungleichheit/Discours sur l'inégalité*. 6th edn. Ed. Heinrich Meier. Paderborn: Verlag Ferdinand Schöningh.

———. 1990–2009. *The Collected Writings of Rousseau*. 14 vols. Eds. Roger D. Masters and Christopher Kelly. Hanover, NH: University Press of New England.

Russon, Anne E. 2004. *Orangutans: Wizards of the Rainforest*. Buffalo, NY: Firefly Books.

Sato, Nobuya, Ling Tan, Kazushi Tate, and Maya Okada. 2015. Rats Demonstrate Helping Behavior Toward a Soaked Conspecific. *Animal Cognition* 18(5): 1039–1047. doi:10.1007/s10071-015-0872-2.

Saunders, T.J. 1995. Plato on Women in the *Laws*. In *The Greek World*, ed. Anton Powell. London and New York: Routledge.

Saxonhouse, Arlene. 1985. *Women in the History of Political Thought*. New York: Praeger.

Schwartz, Joel. 1984. *The Sexual Politics of Jean-Jacques Rousseau*. Chicago, IL: University of Chicago Press.

Sedley, David. 2007. *Plato's Cratylus*. Corrected version. Cambridge: Cambridge University Press.

Shell, Susan Meld. 2001. *Émile*: Nature and the Education of Sophie. In *The Cambridge Companion to Rousseau*, ed. Patrick Riley. Cambridge: Cambridge University Press.

Shipman, Pat. 2015. *The Invaders: How Humans and Their Dogs Drove Neanderthals to Extinction*. Cambridge, MA: Harvard University Press.

Silver, Morris. 2011. Contractual Slavery in the Roman Economy. *Ancient History Bulletin* 25: 73–132.

Silverthorne, J.M. 1973. Rousseau's Plato. *Studies on Voltaire and the Eighteenth Century* 116: 235–249.

Simões-Lopes, Paulo C., Marta E. Fabián and João O. Menegheti. 1998. Dolphin Interactions with the Mullet Artisanal Fishing on Southern Brazil: A Qualitative and Quantitative Approach. *Revista Brasileira de Zoologia* 15(3): 709–726.

Smith, Adam. 1976. *An Inquiry into the Nature and Causes of the Wealth of Nations*. Oxford: Clarendon Press.

———. 1976. *The Theory of Moral Sentiments*. Oxford: Clarendon Press.

———. 1983. Considerations Concerning the First Formation of Languages. In *Lectures on Rhetoric and Belles Lettres*, ed. J.C. Bryce, 203–226. Oxford: Clarendon Press.

Smith, Brian D., Mya Than Tun, Aung Myo Chit, Han Win, and Thida Moe. 2009. Catch Composition and Conservation Management of a Human-Dolphin Cooperative Cast-Net Fishery in the Ayeyarwady River, Myanmar. *Biological Conservation* 142: 1042–1049.

Sorabji, Richard. 1980. *Necessity Cause, and Blame: Perspectives on Aristotle's Theory*. Ithaca, NY: Cornell University Press.

Spurlin, Paul Merrill. 1969. *Rousseau in America: 1760–1809*. University, AL: University of Alabama Press.

Strauss, Leo. 1953. *Natural Right and History*. Chicago, IL: University of Chicago Press.
———. 1958. *Thoughts on Machiavelli*. Chicago, IL: University of Chicago Press.
———. 1975. *The Argument and the Action of Plato's Laws*. Chicago, IL: University Chicago Press.
Stringer, Chris. 2012. *Lone Survivors: How We Came to Be the Only Humans on Earth*. New York: Henry Holt and Company.
Suddendorf, Thomas. 2013. *The Gap: The Science of What Separates Us from Other Animals*. New York: Basic Books.
Thomas, Downing A. 1995. *Music and the Origins of Language: Theories from the French Enlightenment*. Cambridge: Cambridge University Press.
Thomas, Elizabeth Marshall. 1989. *The Harmless People*, Rev. edn. New York: Vintage Books.
———. 2000. *The Hidden Life of Dogs*. New York: Simon & Schuster.
———. 2000. *The Social Life of Dogs*. New York: Simon & Schuster.
———. 2006. *The Old Way: A Story of the First People*. New York: Farrar Straus Giroux.
———. 2007, March 29. Reply to Melvin Konner. *N.Y. Rev. of Books* 54(5): 50.
———. 2013. *A Million Years with You: A Memoir of Life Observed*. Boston, MA: Houghton Mifflin Harcourt.
Tierney, Patrick. 2001. *Darkness in El Dorado*. New York: W.W. Norton.
Tocqueville, Alexis de. 1951. *Œuvres, Papiers et Correspondances*. Ed. J.P. Mayer. Paris: Gallimard.
Van Schaik, Carel. 2004. *Among Orangutans: Red Apes and the Rise of Human Culture*. Cambridge, MA: Belknap Press.
Van Schaik, Carel P. 2013, April 8. The Costs and Benefits of Flexibility as an Expression of Behavioural Plasticity: A Primate Perspective. *Philosophical Transactions of The Royal Society, Biological Sciences* 368: 20120339. doi:10.1098/rstb.2012.0339.
Velkley, Richard L. 2002. *Being after Rousseau: Philosophy and Culture in Question*. Chicago, IL: University of Chicago Press.
Wells, Spencer. 2003. *The Journey of Man: A Genetic Odyssey*. New York: Random House.
Wilkins, John S. 2009. *Species: A History of the Idea*. Berkeley: University of California Press.
Williams, David Lay. 2007. *Rousseau's Platonic Enlightenment*. University Park: Pennsylvania State University Press.
Wokler, Robert. 1978, Summer. Perfectible Apes in Decadent Cultures: Rousseau's Anthropology Revisited. *Dædalus* 107(3): 107–134.
Zuckert, Catherine H. 2009. *Plato's Philosophers: The Coherence of the Dialogues*. Chicago, IL: University of Chicago Press.

# Index


A
Alexander the Great, 183n37
amour-propre, 13, 27, 55–9, 75, 145
Anti-Federalists, 214, 244, 255n75
Athens, 1, 44, 45, 93, 117, 124, 129, 243

B
bonobos, 54n29
Buffon, 15, 40n3
Burke, Edmund, 2, 213, 214n1
Burns, Timothy W., 79n68
Butler, Melissa A., 136n81

C
Calvin, John, 129n70, 243
Cantor, Paul A., 133n73
Censorship, 266
*cercles*, 140, 140n87, 141
chimpanzees, 17n14, 53, 54, 59n41, 85n78
Clay, Diskin, 94n9
conscience, 173, 175, 182, 182n36, 185–90
Cooper, Laurence D., 232n30
Cranston, Maurice, 116n45, 117, 149, 186n42, 189n45, 207n61, 253n69

D
Darwin, Charles, 17n13, 36n39, 41n4, 61n43, 78n66, 81
dueling, 144, 145

E
*Encyclopedia,* The, 43, 116, 117
Euripedes, 79

F
*Federalist Papers*, 213, 214n1, 244n52, 246, 256n77
Flaumenhaft, Harvey, 115n43
Fossey, Dian, 37n42


Note: Page numbers followed by "n" refers to footnotes.



N. Lund, *Rousseau's Rejuvenation of Political Philosophy*,
DOI 10.1007/978-3-319-41390-7

Fralin, Richard, 247n57, 248n59
Franklin, Benjamin, 14, 15n7
Fukuyama, Francis, 240n47

G
Galdikas, Biruté, 37n42, 52
general will, 231, 233–7, 239, 243–5, 246n55, 248, 248n59, 250, 252, 253, 256, 262, 266
Glaucus, 31, 47n14, 122
Goodall, Jane, 10n2, 37n42
gorillas, 54, 59n41, 74n62
Gourevitch, Victor, 15n9, 28n28

H
Hamilton, Alexander, 259, 263
Hendel, Charles W., 141n88
Homer, 49n16, 78, 79, 79n68, 89, 100n17, 121, 195, 196
Huntington, Samuel P., 241n48

J
Jefferson, Thomas, 214n2, 217
Jesus, 116n47, 185n41, 191, 191n47, 192, 192n49
Juvenal, 267

K
Kelly, Christopher, 16n11, 177n27, 267n2
Klein, Richard G., 17n14, 40n2, 41n4, 54n28, 82
Kochin, Michael S., 110

L
Laertius, Diogenes, 79n68
Leibowitz, David, 93n6
Lerner, Craig S., 266n93
*Lettres portugaises*, 139n85
Lévi-Strauss, Claude, 15n8
*liberum veto*, 253, 256, 256n78
Lincoln, Abraham, 254n74
*logos*, 49n16, 95
Ludwig, Paul W., 113n40
Lycurgus, 10n1, 94n11, 102, 105n24, 164–6, 243, 249n60, 251, 251n65, 252

M
Machiavelli, Niccolò, 257, 257n80, 257n81
Madison, James, 15n7, 214n1, 244n52
magician-Socrates, 162, 164, 169n17
Marshall, Lorna, 16, 22n21
Marshall, Terence, 59n40
Masson, Pierre-Maurice, 62n44
Masters, Roger D., 55–60
McKeen, Catherine, 105n23
Meier, Heinrich, 49n16
Melzer, Arthur M., 44n9, 234n35, 237–42
Mikalson, Jon D., 117n48
Mithen, Steven, 66n48, 82, 84n73, 85n76, 89n86
Molière, 137
Montaigne, Michel de, 249n60
Montesquieu, 2n1, 94n10, 213, 248, 248n58, 256n77
Morrow, Glenn R., 94n9, 94n10
Moses, 44n9, 243
Munn, Mark, 97n13

N
natural law or law of nature, 47, 182, 182n36, 186, 222, 228
natural right or right of nature, 37, 169, 216–31, 232n31, 256n78, 269
Neanderthals, 86–7

Nietzsche, Friedrich, 5, 225
nocturnal council, 109–11, 115, 115n43, 144
Numa, 244n52

**O**

Okin, Susan Moller, 111n34
orangutans, 52–4, 57–8, 59n41, 74n62

**P**

particular will, 234, 235, 235n36, 244, 245, 246n55, 266
perfectibility, 28, 28n28, 48, 54–6, 60, 62
Pericles, 114n41
Pliny, 40n3
Plutarch, 2, 94n11, 105n24, 128n69, 152, 168, 203, 225, 256
pre-Socratic philosophy, 5, 46, 97n13

**R**

Racine, 130
Rousseau
- *Confessions*, 4, 10n3, 73n61, 150, 151nn4–6, 174, 177n29, 178n31, 185n40, 207n61, 209n62
- *Dictionary of Music*, 77n65
- *Discourse on the Sciences and the Arts*, 10n3, 16n11, 91, 115, 143n92, 147n96, 249n60
- *Letters to Malesherbes*, 33n34, 225
- *Letter to Philopolis*, 48n15
- *New Heloise, The*, 123n54, 138, 140n86, 149, 150, 150n2, 151n5, 184, 185n39, 189, 194, 207, 214n2, 254n72
- *Preface to a Second Letter to Bordes*, 10n3
- *Preface to Narcisse*, 137
- *Reveries*, 29n29, 173n23, 174n25, 177n28, 267n1, 268
- Savoyard Vicar, 56n33, 59n40, 172–92, 201, 267n1
- *On Theatrical Imitation*, 118–24

**S**

Saunders, T.J., 105n23, 111n34
Savoyard Vicar, 56n33, 59n40, 172–92, 201, 267n1
Saxonhouse, Arlene, 111n34
Schwartz, Joel, 242n50
Sedley, David, 72n57
Seneca, 158n12, 207
Servius, 244n52, 250
Shakespeare, William, 130–6, 137n82
Shell, Susan Meld, 26n24, 128n68
Silver, Morris, 249n60
Silverthorne, J.M., 92n1
slavery, 9, 50, 50n18, 99, 100, 100n17, 101, 101n18, 102, 208, 249, 249n60
Smith, Adam, 81n70, 163n15, 186, 230n28, 239n45, 242n49, 268
Solon, 244n52
Strauss, Leo, 1–4, 28n28, 45n11, 73n60, 93, 96n12, 101n19, 126n61, 257n81

**T**

Thucydides, 105n24, 114n41
*thumos*, 38, 144, 145
Tocqueville, Alexis de, 2, 5, 15n7, 101n18, 225
Tribunate, 264–6
Tyrtaeus, 123n56

**V**

van Schaik, Carel, 52, 53n26
Velkley, Richard L., 15n9
Voltaire, 124, 130, 176

**W**
Wells, Spencer, 18n15, 18n19
Williams, David Lay, 3–4

**X**
Xenophon, 36, 64n47, 112n35, 192, 192n48, 196n53, 206n59, 210

**Y**
Yanomami, 27

**Z**
Zuckert, Catherine H., 97n13